Decision Sciences for Quality and Productivity Improvement

Indrajit Mukherjee · Raghu Nandan Sengupta ·
Bhaskar Basu · Jitendra Kumar Jha
Editors

Decision Sciences for Quality and Productivity Improvement

Towards Operational and Business Excellence

Springer

Editors
Indrajit Mukherjee
Shailesh J. Mehta School of Management
Indian Institute of Technology Bombay
Mumbai, India

Raghu Nandan Sengupta
Department of Industrial and Management Engineering
Indian Institute of Technology Kanpur
Kanpur, Uttar Pradesh, India

Bhaskar Basu
Xavier Institute of Management
XIM University
Bhubaneswar, Odisha, India

Jitendra Kumar Jha
Department of Industrial and Systems Engineering
Indian Institute of Technology (IIT)
Kharagpur, West Bengal, India

ISBN 978-981-95-7544-2 ISBN 978-981-95-7545-9 (eBook)
https://doi.org/10.1007/978-981-95-7545-9

This Springer imprint is published by the registered company Springer Nature Singapore Pte Ltd.
The registered company address is: 152 Beach Road, #21-01/04 Gateway East, Singapore 189721, Singapore

Foreword

In an era characterised by rapid technological advancements and increasing global competition, the pursuit of quality and productivity improvement remains paramount across manufacturing and service industries. With its foundation in data-driven methodologies and analytical frameworks, decision sciences provide essential tools for organisations striving for excellence by enhancing efficiency and effectiveness, apart from optimising their resources for sustainable growth.

This volume on '*Decision Sciences for Quality and Productivity Improvement*' is a testament to the interdisciplinary nature of decision sciences and their transformative impact across diverse sectors. By integrating insights from management science, operations research, artificial intelligence, cognitive psychology, and statistical modelling, this volume presents diverse perspectives on solving challenging quality and productivity enhancement issues that can lead to operational and business excellence.

The chapters in this volume span a broad spectrum of research, highlighting theoretical advancements, practical implementations, and future scope. The Quality Management section delves into critical topics such as healthcare services, manufacturing quality, service quality improvement through digital technology, conversational chatbots, trends in healthcare quality control, the role of Industry 4.0 in Total Quality Management (TQM), and innovative decision science approaches for environmental management. These studies showcase how emerging technologies and analytical models contribute to operational excellence and quality improvement.

In the Productivity Management section, the focus shifts to predictive analytics, digital training, technology adoption models, and integrated data-driven strategies in supply chain management. Topics such as yield prediction in agriculture, digital learning's impact on institutional productivity, and the application of analytics in operational excellence highlight the evolving role of decision sciences in enhancing efficiency and effectiveness across various operational domains.

A distinctive feature of this volume is its ability to bridge theory with practice. The empirical observations, comparative analyses, and real-world case studies presented throughout the volume offer valuable perspectives for researchers, industry leaders, policymakers, and practitioners. Furthermore, discussions on future research directions provide a foundation for continued innovation and exploration in this ever-evolving field.

This collection of scholarly contributions results from rigorous research and collaborative efforts from experts across disciplines. I appreciate the editors, authors, and reviewers whose dedication and insights have shaped this comprehensive work. I hope this volume will be invaluable for those seeking to leverage decision sciences for quality and productivity improvement, inspiring further research and practical applications.

With great enthusiasm, I invite readers to explore the wealth of knowledge in this volume, confident that it will contribute significantly to advancing decision sciences in diverse organisations.

April 2025

Anand G
Professor, Quantitative Methods
and Operations Management, IIM
Kozhikode

Preface

In today's competitive business environment, the concepts of quality and productivity have evolved significantly, both in depth and breadth. Various techniques and methodologies have been proposed and validated to enhance manufacturing and service processes. In this context, decision science theories—drawn from fields such as management science, economics, operations research, statistical methods, machine learning, data mining, artificial intelligence, behavioural decision-making, and cognitive psychology played a crucial role in improving quality and productivity across organisations.

This theme-based volume explores the potential of decision science theories, presenting novel ideas that contribute to enhancing product quality, service quality, process efficiency, and overall organisational productivity. The chapters in this volume offer insights into emerging approaches, managerial implications, case studies, comparative analyses of existing methods, comprehensive literature reviews, and future research directions on various topics of contemporary interest.

The volume specifically focuses on decision science theory-based approaches to quality and productivity improvement across diverse sectors, including manufacturing, supply chain management, services, healthcare, education, technology, artificial intelligence, digital & information technology, and environmental sustainability. The methodologies and theories discussed are drawn from domains such as operations excellence, process quality optimisation, economics, operations research, predictive analytics, statistical modelling, artificial intelligence, and cognitive psychology. This volume serves as a unique platform for addressing real-world challenges in quality and productivity improvement.

By presenting new concepts, innovative solution methods, diverse research perspectives, industry case studies, comparative analyses, and in-depth literature reviews, the chapters in this volume provide valuable insights for researchers, decision-makers, and practitioners. The discussions on future research avenues will catalyse further advancements in the field. Ultimately, this collection of theme-based contributions highlights the immense potential of decision science theories in driving scientific decision-making to enhance quality and productivity across organisations.

I extend my heartfelt gratitude to all the chapter contributors and co-editors, whose efforts have made this volume possible. Finally, I sincerely thank the learned reviewers for their support in the double-blind peer review process and for providing valuable feedback that has helped improve the quality of the chapters.

Mumbai, India Indrajit Mukherjee

Contents

Editors and Contributors

About the Editors

Indrajit Mukherjee is Professor at Shailesh J. Mehta School of Management, IIT Bombay. He did his Ph.D. from the Department of Industrial Engineering and Management, Indian Institute of Technology, Kharagpur. He did his Master's degree in Quality, Reliability & Operations Research from Indian Statistical Institute, Kolkata, India. He has authored and co-authored several research papers published in refereed and reputed journals. His research contributions are published in the European Journal of Operational Research, Journal of Manufacturing Systems, Quality and Reliability Management, Quality Engineering, Computers & Industrial Engineering. His primary research interest is in multivariate quality control, quality management, applied operations research, and sourcing in the supply chain.

Raghu Nandan Sengupta is Professor, Department of Industrial & Management Engineering, Indian Institute of Technology Kanpur. He obtained his Ph.D. from Indian Institute of Management Calcutta and PDF from Princeton University, USA. His research interests are in areas of Sequential Estimation, Statistical and Mathematical Reliability Theory, Risk Analysis, Optimization Techniques in Finance, Meta Heuristic Techniques, Reliability based Optimisation, Robust Optimisation. His research work has been published in EJOR, QF, CSDA, Communication in Statistics, Journal of Applied Statistics, Metrika, Statistics, Marketing Intelligence and Planning, Journal of Marketing Theory and Practice, Annals of Operations Research. He has also edited two books titled (i) Decision Sciences: Theory and Practice, CRC Press, 2016 and (ii) Studies in Quantitative Decision Making, Springer, 2022

Bhaskar Basu is Professor of Information Systems at Xavier Institute of Management, XIM University, Bhubaneswar. He obtained his Ph.D. from Indian Institute of Technology, Kharagpur (India) and is a University Gold Medallist (Jadavpur University, India). He also has a Post Graduate Diploma in Business Management (equivalent to MBA) from Indian Institute of Management, Calcutta. His research interests are in the areas of Knowledge Management, Artificial Intelligence Applications in Business and Sports Management. His research work has been published in journals like VINE, Journal of Modeling in Management, IJITDM etc. He has also edited a book titled "Organizational Learning-Perspectives and Practices", The ICFAI University Press (2006)

Jitendra Kumar Jha is Professor in the department of Industrial and Systems Engineering at IIT Kharagpur. He obtained his Ph.D. from IIT Kanpur. He has received several scholarships and awards from DRPG IIT Kanpur, BITSAA of North America, SJ Jindal Trust New Delhi, IIT Kharagpur. His main areas of teaching and research include Operations Research, Statistical Decision Modeling, Facility Planning, Supply Chain and Logistics planning, and Inventory Control. He published/presented more than sixty papers in international journals and conferences, and his publications appeared in the reputed journals like Journal of the Operational Research Society, Journal of Manufacturing Systems, Applied Mathematical Modelling, Computers & Industrial Engineering, International Journal of Production Research, and other leading journals of Industrial Engineering. He is serving as an editorial board member of International Journal of Industrial Engineering: Theory, Applications and Practice.

Contributors

Ajoy Kanti Das Department of Mathematics, Tripura University, Agartala, India

Prasun Das SQC & OR Division, Indian Statistical Institute, Kolkata, India

Rakhal Das Department of Mathematics, The ICFAI University Tripura, Mohanpur, India

Suman Das Department of Education (ITEP), NIT Agartala, Jirania, India

Nikita Dhankar Amity Global Business School, Noida, India

Carlos Granados Estudiante de Doctorado en Matemáticas, Magister en Ciencias Matemáticas, Universidad de Antioquia, Medellín, Colombia

Nandini Gupta Department of Environmental Science, Bir Bikram Memorial College, Agartala, India

Shrishti Gupta Department of Mechanical Engineering, Malaviya National Institute of Technology, Jaipur, Rajasthan, India

Iliyan Hristov University of Economics—Varna, Varna, Bulgaria

Rakesh Jain Department of Mechanical Engineering, Malaviya National Institute of Technology, Jaipur, Rajasthan, India

Raashi Jatakia Department of Biomedical Engineering, Vidyalankar Institute of Technology, Mumbai, India

Amandeep Kaur Department of Management Studies, ABV-Indian Institute of Information Technology and Management Gwalior, Gwalior, India

Meshack Bashange Mwesiga Department of Engineering Management Studies, Mzumbe University, Morogoro, Tanzania;
Department of Mechanical and Industrial Engineering, College of Engineering and Technology, University of Dar Es Salaam, Dar Es Salaam, Tanzania

Gajanan Nagare Department of Biomedical Engineering, Vidyalankar Institute of Technology, Mumbai, India

Plamena Nedyalkova University of Economics—Varna, Varna, Bulgaria

Suman Patra Department of Mathematics, Tripura University, Agartala, India

Riddhi Parasnaik Department of Biomedical Engineering, Vidyalankar Institute of Technology, Mumbai, India

Priya Patwa Department of Biomedical Engineering, Vidyalankar Institute of Technology, Mumbai, India

Gyan Prakash Department of Management Studies, ABV-Indian Institute of Information Technology and Management Gwalior, Gwalior, India

Vijay Raj Department of Mechanical Engineering, Malaviya National Institute of Technology, Jaipur, Rajasthan, India

Bharti Ramtiyal Faculty of Management and Commerce Poornima University, Jaipur, India

Srikanta Routroy Department of Mechanical Engineering & Joint Faculty, School of Interdisciplinary Research and Entrepreneurship (SIRE), BITS Pilani, Pilani Campus, Pilani, India

Cherian Samuel Mechanical Engineering Department, IIT (BHU), Varanasi, UP, India

Satyaki Basu Sarbadhikary NUS, Singapore

Anagha Savit Department of Mechanical Engineering, Indian Institute of Technology Bombay, Mumbai, Maharashtra, India

Abhinav Kumar Sharma Operations and Quantitative Techniques Area, Indian Institute of Management Shillong, Shillong, Meghalaya, India

Satyendra Kr. Sharma Department of Management, BITS Pilani, Pilani Campus, Pilani, India

Gunjan Soni Department of Mechanical Engineering, Malaviya National Institute of Technology, Jaipur, Rajasthan, India

Ismail W. R. Taifa Department of Mechanical and Industrial Engineering, College of Engineering and Technology, University of Dar Es Salaam, Dar Es Salaam, Tanzania

Prince Kumar Tiwari Mechanical Engineering Department, IIT (BHU), Varanasi, UP, India

Ved Prabha Toshniwal Department of Mechanical Engineering, Malaviya National Institute of Technology, Jaipur, Rajasthan, India

Gergana Tsoncheva-Petkova University of Economics—Varna, Varna, Bulgaria

Part I
Quality Management

Chapter 1
Conversational Chatbot for Enhancing Healthcare Services

Amandeep Kaur and Gyan Prakash

Abstract In healthcare industry, conversational chatbots have emerged as crucial tool that offers several benefits, including personalized healthcare advice, assisting in early diagnosis, and ensuring timely intervention. In order to provide patient-centric healthcare services, it is necessary to understand and capture both intents and slots accurately during the conversation. In recent years, various researchers have utilized Sequence-to-Sequence (Seq2Seq) learning models with Recurrent Neural Networks (RNNs) for intent classification and slot (entity) extraction during conversation in chatbots. However, these models tend to overlook crucial information within the context of patients' inputs and exhibit limitation to capture the dependencies from long-term complex input sequences. To overcome these limitations, this research work proposes a multi-attention mechanism that allows the learning model to understand and capture different aspects of users' utterances. The study aims to develop an end-to-end conversational chatbot that focuses on intent classification, slot extraction, managing dialogue, and response generation during patient' health-related conversation. The proposed model leverages transformer-based multi-head attention mechanisms to effectively handle the complexities of natural language understanding in healthcare contexts. Our experimental and numerical results corroborate the superior performance of proposed model as compare to baseline techniques. Additionally, the dialogue management and response generation capabilities of chatbot are evaluated through patient-chatbot interactions, confirming its effectiveness in managing dialogues and providing appropriate responses.

Keyword Healthcare chatbot · Healthcare quality improvement · Artificial Intelligence · Patient-centric services

A. Kaur (✉) · G. Prakash
Department of Management Studies, ABV-Indian Institute of Information Technology and Management Gwalior, Gwalior, India
e-mail: adeep5524@gmail.com

I. Mukherjee et al. (eds.), *Decision Sciences for Quality and Productivity Improvement*,
https://doi.org/10.1007/978-981-95-7545-9_1

1.1 Introduction

In recent years, Natural Language Processing (NLP) has been incorporated into healthcare to revolutionize conventional approaches to patient care and service delivery.

In particular, conversational healthcare chatbots have emerged as powerful tool that not enhances patient engagement but also streamline administrative processes, and alleviate the burden on healthcare authorities (Palanica et al., 2019). The inclusion of these chatbots in healthcare settings is a new paradigm in interacting with the healthcare delivery system for both patient-provider encounters and medical information access. Such AI-driven systems, using NLP and advanced Machine Learning (ML) techniques, allows users to facilitate human-like patient-centric interactions, providing personalized support, symptom assessment, medication reminders, and digital consultations (Nadarzynski et al., 2019). By providing on-demand support and information dissemination, the conversational chatbots can enhance healthcare accessibility, improves efficiency and patient satisfaction (Milne-Ives et al., 2020).

The healthcare chatbot market According to the recent survey, the chatbot market is growing exponentially at a Compound Annual Growth Rate (CAGR) of 18.93% and is predicted to grow from $238.93 to $1352.83 million by 2033 (Thomason, 2024). However, the critical nature of healthcare sector encompassing emergency response during outbreaks or natural disasters. One of the primary challenges in healthcare chatbots is to accurately interpret the patient queries. This involves correct intent detection and slot (entity) recognition, which are crucial for providing appropriate responses (Javaid et al., 2023; Patel & Lam, 2023). To address this challenge, researchers have explored several advanced ML techniques (Bi et al., 2020; Sarrouti & Alaoui, 2020) such as Recurrent Neural Networks (RNNs) and their variants in NLP. Mesnil et al. (2014) proposed RNN-based architecture to effectively extract past and future temporal dependencies in the sentence. The bidirectional RNN makes it possible to process inputs in both forward as well as backward direction. These enable the model to receive infinite amount of contextual information (Hakkani-Tur et al., 2023). Further, Gated RNN family members, namely Long Short-Term Memory (LSTM) and Gated Recurrent Unit (GRU) (Rastogi et al., 2018; Wu et al., 2019; Yang & Liu, 2015; Žilka & Jurčíček, 2015) extract the historical dependencies within the input sentence as they deal with long-term dependency in data.

Sequence-to-sequence (Seq2Seq) models, often combined with RNN or LSTM cells presents numerous applications in literature. These models can represent historical data using the hidden states of RNNs. Further, the integration of attention mechanism with RNN improves performance by better handling long-term dependencies (Wen et al., 2016; Zhao et al., 2017). The integration of attention mechanism further provide attention on specific parts of the input sequence during conversation. For instance, some researchers have integrated attention layers with gated RNN models to prioritize pertinent information while ignoring less relevant data. This approach has been particularly useful in developing chatbots for specific contexts, such as to respond the patient's queries during COVID-19. Few research studies combine Bidirectional GRU with Conditional Random Fields (CRF) and attention mechanisms for improve the intent classification and slot extraction. However, these approaches have several limitations. Seq2Seq models may struggle with very long sequences and can be computationally inefficient to process sequential information. Additionally, integration of Bi-GRU models for complex, task-specific chatbots can be challenging, especially when deep contextual understanding is required.

Motivated with the above-mentioned challenges, we propose transformer based multi-head attention mechanism for better understanding of entire context of patient conversation, enabling it to understand and respond contextually. The healthcare conversation involves the discussion related to symptoms, treatment recommendations, and general health advice. Transformers, with multi-head attention module, provides better predictions by highlighting the most significant parts of the input sequence.

Section 1.2 briefly covers literature studies on chatbot, intent classification and slot extraction. Section 1.3 describes the proposed architecture of a healthcare chatbot and Sect. 1.4 describes numerical studies performed with physician clinical notes dataset and compared with baseline approaches, finally conclusion and directions for future avenues are presented in Sect. 1.5.

1.2 Related Work

The integration of conversational chatbots in healthcare services has received significant interest among researchers, practitioners, and industry stakeholders alike. This section provides an overview of existing literature pertaining to the utilization of conversational chatbots within the context of healthcare while considering user-centered perspectives and investigations.

In conversational chatbots, understanding and responding to human conversations in natural language is particularly challenging when multiple intents are involved. The complexity of handling multiple user intentions simultaneously requires sophisticated NLP to accurately interpret and generate appropriate responses. Till 2023, there are number of medical apps are available that offers healthcare services. For instance, *Ada Health*, a user-friendly mobile app for self-assessment and seeking treatment for their medical issues. It is basically built on rule-based AI systems with limited context handling concept for mental health assessment. It matches the symptoms reported by patient to those with other patients of similar demographic profiles to provide statistical probabilities of specific health risks (Jungmann et al., 2019). *Healthily* is a personalized health assistant that tracks symptoms and guides users through self-care (Ciesla, 2024). While it uses AI and NLP to understand user queries, separating intent detection and slot extraction into two distinct processes can potentially reduce accuracy, especially when handling multiple intents or complex queries. *Babylon Health* is another well-known AI-driven mobile healthcare application that offers symptom diagnosis and medical consultations. It uses AI and NLP to assess the symptoms and provide patients with medical advice, but the chatbot still faces some challenges due to its incapability of handling long-range dependencies. It operates more effectively for general medical inquiries but may face limitations with complex or multi-intent queries (Magalhaes Azevedo & Kieffer, 2021). In addition, *Florence* helps users manage healthcare routines by tracking medications and vaccinations. While it aids in healthcare management, it uses simpler AI mechanisms for reminder services rather than offering the detailed, real-time personalization.

In recent years, AI and ML are increasingly transforming the healthcare domain by enhancing personalized and real-time assistance to the patients. These technologies enable chatbots to process vast amount of patient data including their symptoms, treatment plans and medical histories, to provide accurate diagnosis. Badlani et al. (2021) proposed multilingual healthcare chatbot system that supports three languages. Five different ML algorithms were used to analyze for disease prediction (Badlani et al., 2021). Xu et al. (2021) provided an overview of 95 healthcare chatbots developed for various applications such as patient monitoring, symptom diagnosis and treatment to improve workflow proficiency (Xu et al., 2021). Rahman et al. (2019) developed ML-based Bangle healthcare chatbot "Disha" to diagnose potential diseases and explored six supervised learning approaches to improve the efficiency of the chatbot (Rahman et al., 2019). Further, Kurup and Shetty (2022) proposed deep learning and NLP based AI conversational chatbot for preliminary diagnosis based on symptoms. Additionally, Few researchers developed web-based chatbot "Ted" based on deep learning techniques to assist the queries related to mental health (Pandey et al., 2022).

Most of the existing studies focused on joint intent classification and slot extraction for chatbot systems in different domains such as education, airlines, and banking applications. A recent work (Firdaus et al., 2021) proposed deep learning model based chatbot model for intent classification and slot filling. The presented methodology includes BiLSTM and Bi-GRU along with character level embedding for joint extraction of both intent and slot. This achieved an accuracy of 92.67, 48.65 and 79.89% on ATIS, FRAMES and TRAINS datasets respectively. In (Kim et al., 2017), the authors jointly identified the domain, intent and slots in user utterance using word and character embedding. The authors in Cao et al. (2021) developed a multi-turn dialogue system that utilizes key sentence mining for intent classification. Another approach integrates a LSTM for sentiment analysis and intent classification, achieving notable performance improvements (Abedin et al., 2021). Another study proposed a retrieval-based model using the pretext of fine-tuning a pre-trained Bidirectional Encoder Representations from Transformer (BERT) mode with source as well as target-domain data to get further improvement in the performance (Yu et al., 2021). The proposed model was evaluated by checking its performances through Conversational Language Interface for Natural Conversation (CLINC) and Speech and Natural Language Processing Systems (SNIPS) datasets.

Few researchers combined the intent and slot filling as a single unit and proposed chatbot architecture with Ro-BERT model (Benayas et al., 2021). The model implemented feed forward network to connect Named Entity Recognition (NER) with intent classification and then SoftMax function for slot extraction. The authors evaluated the performance using ATIS and SNITS datasets and obtained an accuracy of 92.45 and 91.84% respectively. Recent trends in research includes deep learning algorithms along with attention mechanism for better information extraction. The attention mechanism extracts the correlation between encoded sources along with focusing on specific parts of input text (Bahdanau et al., 2014). The authors introduced a model that enables attention to be directed toward various sections of the input sequence concurrently, greatly improving its capacity to process lengthy sequences effectively. With Transformer architecture based on attention mechanisms (Lastname et al., 2017), removed the need of recurrent or convolutional layers. This led to more efficient training and improved performance on a wide variety of NLP tasks. The integrated framework further improves the performance by concentrating on specific parts of the input sequence. This leads to generate tailored response for dialogue systems. For instance, Emotional Chatting Machine incorporates attention mechanisms to generate responses with appropriate emotions (Zhou et al., 2018).

In spite of the significant developments in chatbot architectures, the application of advanced attention mechanisms, including multi-head attention, remains largely unexplored in healthcare chatbots. The potential benefits of multi-head attention, such as its ability to focus on different aspects of the input simultaneously, have not been fully leveraged in chatbot designs. To bridge this gap, this research presents a novel chatbot architecture that can handle complex, multi-faceted conversations more effectively.

1.3 Proposed Methodology

In this section, we propose transformer-based chatbot architecture for conversational chatbot illustrated in Fig. 1.1. The process starts with the user's input, which is handled by the Natural Language Understanding (NLU) Engine. This engine employs a transformer-based multi-head attention mechanism to identify intents and entities within the user's message. These extracted components are subsequently passed to the Dialogue Management system, which monitors the dialogue state and generates suitable responses based on the conversation history.

If necessary, the Dialogue Management system makes API calls to a backend database or URL request to fetch additional information. The subsequent module of Natural Language Generation (NLG) processes the response in human-understandable language and provide it to the user. The structured approach will ensure that the complex health queries that any user may pose are addressed successfully; provide personalized recommendations, and an engaging conversation is maintained with the user. The details of these components are as follows.

(1) ***User Interface***

The methodology encompasses a meticulous design process focusing on the user interface (UI) typically a mobile app where users issue a query to chatbot. The UI

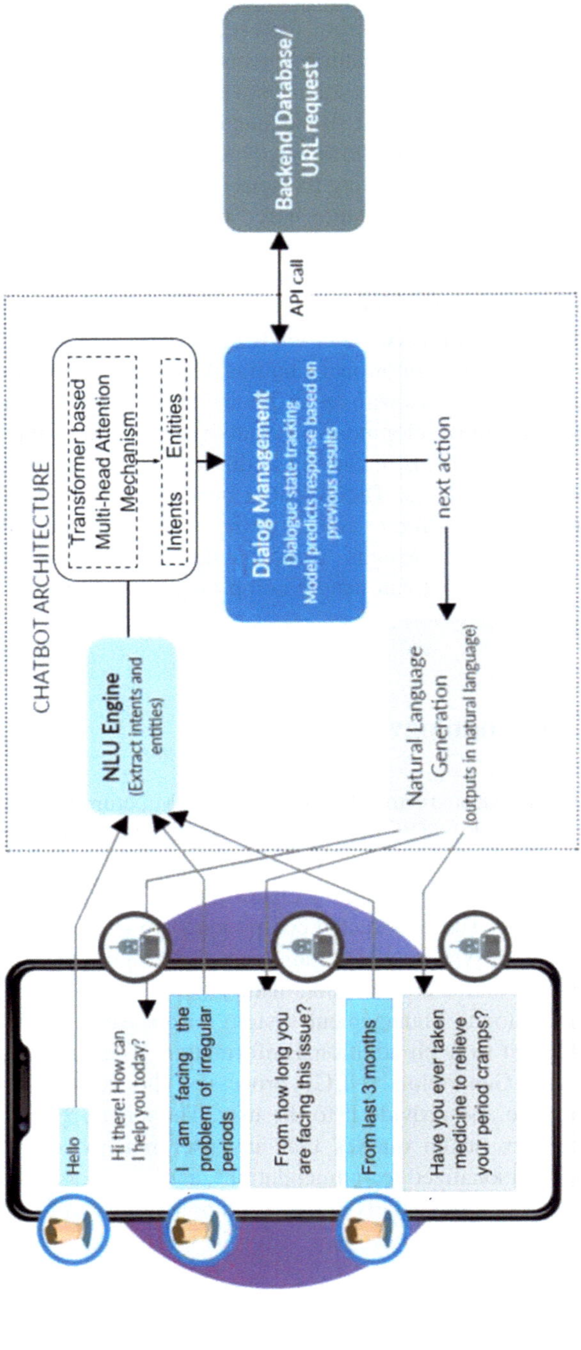

Fig. 1.1 Proposed architecture of healthcare chatbot

design serves as a critical bridge between users and the chatbot system, profoundly influencing the user experience and interaction quality.

(2) ***NLU Engine***

- *Tokenization and Feature Engineering*

Initially, the input is received from the patient as text. The information is extracted from input data using the process of tokenization and feature engineering. Tokenization involves the process of dividing textual input into smaller units called tokens for easier analysis and processing of input data. For instance, the input received form patient is "I have been experiencing cold and fever for three days." Upon receiving this information, the tokenizer tokenizes the input into distinct words or tokens: ["I," "have," "been," "experiencing," "cold," "and," "fever," "for," "three," "days."] This step is crucial for the chatbot to begin understanding the patient's input.

After tokenization, Feature engineering transforms these tokens into machine understandable format to process the input effectively. Using Regex Featurizer, it extracts specific features using regular expressions and with Lexical Syntactic Featurizer, it unifies word-level analysis with grammatical structures. Lexical features Sinvolve cleaning of data and lemmatization whereas syntactic features indicate the roles of each distinct word in order to interpret the relation between words. Additionally, the Count Vector Featurizer creates a numerical representation based on word frequency that helps to identify the occurrence of common symptoms or conditions across multiple patient queries/inputs.

- *Intent and Slot Classification*

Intent classification involves identifying the underlying purpose of patient queries, enabling the chatbot to accurately comprehend user intentions and provide relevant responses. Slot classification, on the other hand, focuses on extracting specific entities or parameters from user input, such as medical symptoms, appointment details, or medication names, to further refine the understanding of user requests. Table 1.1 illustrates few examples of intent and slot label for symptom-based healthcare chatbot.

The first step involves tokenizing the input text stream to segment it into smaller units. After tokenization, features are extracted using both sparse and dense methods. Since machine learning models cannot directly handle text data, it's essential to transform these textual elements into numerical representations. The word embeddings maps the words with conceptual similarity close to each other in a vector space.

- *Word Embedding*

Word embedding models such as GloVe, Word2Vec, and FastText (Dündar et al., 2018) are applied to generate dense vector representations of words based on meaning captured by the context and the usage. Word2Vec comes in two forms: Continuous Bag of Words (CBOW) and Skip-gram. Word2Vec is really efficient for large datasets and effectively captures semantic relationship between words, though

Table 1.1 Examples of intents and slots labels in symptom-based healthcare chatbot

Sentence	Intent	Slot labels
"I have a headache and a slight fever"	Report_Symptoms	B-symptom O O B-symptom
"What can I do to relieve my cough"	Ask Remedies	O O O O O O B-symptom
"Is dizziness a serious symptom"	Symptom Check	O B-symptom O O O
"My child has a sore thorat and feels weak"	Report_Symptoms	O O O B-symptom O O O O
"What medicine should I take for a headache"	Ask Medicine	O O O O O O O B-symptom
"I feel nauseous and have been vomiting"	Report_Symptoms	O O B-symptom O O O

it struggles with out-of-vocabulary words and provides context-independent word vectors. Global Vectors for Word Representation (GloVe) instead aggregates global word-word co-occurrence statistics from a corpus. It constructs a co-occurrence matrix which is factorized to produce word vectors encapsulating statistical information about word occurrences. However, similar to Word2Vec, it also does not perform well on the out-of-vocabulary words and provides context-independent vectors.

FastText extends Word2Vec represents words as bags of character n-grams, where every word could be represented as a combination of its sub-words. This model uses the same architecture as Word2Vec but includes sub-word information, making it better at handling out-of-vocabulary words and capturing morphological features of words. This capability is particularly useful for languages with rich morphology. Despite the additional complexity and slower training time, FastText excels in scenarios where out-of-vocabulary words are common, such as user-generated content or domain-specific texts.

- *Transformer-based architecture*

The architecture, illustrated in Fig. 1.2, is extremely effective for intent classification and slot extraction in healthcare chatbots because it can capture the complex semantic and lexical relationships within the input text. The multi-head attention module in this architecture intends to focus on most relevant parts of the input sequence simultaneously. Basically, the mechanism extends the scaled dot-product attention by using multiple attention heads. The scaled dot-product attention for i-th head is defined as

$$\text{Attention}_i(Q, K, V) = \text{softmax}\left(\frac{QK_i^T}{\sqrt{d_k}}\right)V_i \tag{1.1}$$

where d_k represents the dimensions of the keys. In this mechanism, for each head i, the queries, keys, and values are linearly projected to d_k dimensions, and the attention mechanism is applied independently to each head. The multi-head attention can be expressed as (Ahmed et al., 2023)

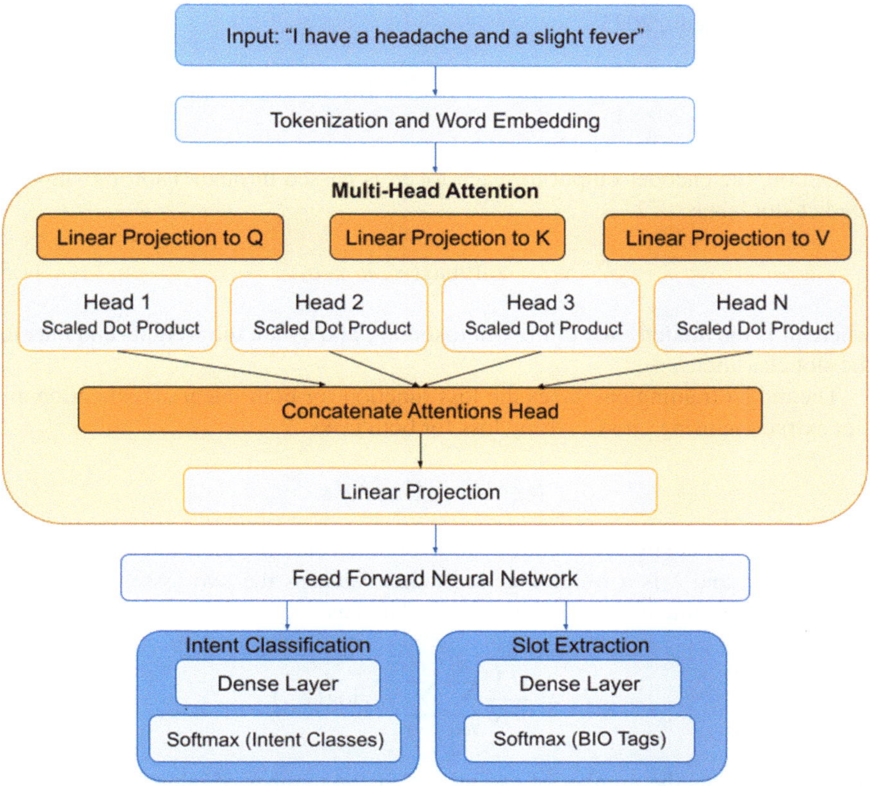

Fig. 1.2 Transformer-based architecture

$$\text{MultiHeadAttention}(Q, K, V) = \text{Concatenation}(\text{head}_1, \text{head}_2, \ldots, \text{head}_h)W^O \tag{1.2}$$

where $\text{head}_i = \text{Attention}\left(QW_i^Q, KW_i^K, VW_i^V\right)$, W^O is the output projection matrix that transforms the concatenated results from all heads into the final output and W_i^Q, W_i^K, W_i^V are learnable weight matrices.

The encoder of the transformer consists of multiple layers of multi-head attention module and feed-forward neural network at every position. Mathematically, it can be expressed as

$$\text{FFNN}(x) = \max(0, xw_1 + b_I)w_2 + b_2 \tag{1.3}$$

where w_1, w_2, b_1 and b_2 are learnable parameters. For joint extraction of intent and slot, the encoder's output is directed into two separate heads of encoder. For intent classification, the encoder output is pooled and passed through a softmax layer (Firdaus et al., 2023)

$$y_I = \text{softmax}(w_I.\text{Pool}(H) + b_I) \tag{1.4}$$

Here, w_I and b_I are the weights and bias for the intent classifier. Similarly, for slot extraction, the encoder output for each token is passed through a softmax layer to predict slot labels

$$y_{s,i} = \text{softmax}(w_S.h_i + b_s) \tag{1.5}$$

where h_i is the hidden state of the i-th token, w_S and b_S are the weights and bias for the slot classifier.

The model training combines the loss function for both intent classification and slot extraction using cross-entropy loss for both tasks

$$L = \lambda L_I + (1 - \lambda) L_S \tag{1.6}$$

where L_I and L_S are the cross-entropy loss for intent classification and slot extraction respectively, and λ is a weighting factor that balances the two losses. The cross-entropy loss for intent classification is calculated as

$$L_I = -\frac{1}{N} \sum_{i=1}^{N} \sum_{c=1}^{C} y_{i,c} \log(\hat{y}_{i,c}) \tag{1.7}$$

where N denotes the number of samples, C is the number of intent classes, $y_{i,c}$ is the true label and $\hat{y}_{i,c}$ is the predicted probability for sample i belonging to class c. Further, the cross-entropy loss for slot extraction is calculated as

$$L_S = -\frac{1}{N} \sum_{i=1}^{N} \frac{1}{T_i} \sum_{t=1}^{T_i} \sum_{k=1}^{K} y_{i,t,k} \log(\hat{y}_{i,t,k}) \tag{1.8}$$

where T_i is the number of tokens in the i-th sample, K is the number of slot classes, $y_{i,t,k}$ and $\hat{y}_{i,t,k}$ are the true and predicted label for the t-th token of i-th sample. The combined loss function ensures simultaneous optimization for both tasks, leading to enhanced performance.

(3) ***Dialogue Management System***

It controls the flow of a conversation and maintains the content and decides appropriate responses based on previous results to deliver response to the user input. Dialogue Management includes contextual understanding tracking, state management, intent handling and dialogue policy to generate most appropriate course of action at each stage of the conversation (Ahmed et al., 2023).

- *Contextual Understanding and Tracking:* This involves maintaining the context of the conversation to understand the patient's query correctly. It keeps track of previous interactions and uses this information to interpret current queries. Contextual understanding confirms that the chatbot can handle multi-turn conversations where the meaning depends on previous exchanges.
- *State Management:* It tracks the present state of the conversation. This includes patient's intent, associated filled slots, the current state of the conversation, and pending actions. Proper state management allows the chatbot to manage complex interactions and provide relevant responses based on the conversation history.
- *Intent Handling:* Intent handling is the process of identifying and managing the patient's intent. The chatbot uses NLU models to identify the patient's need (e.g., getting information about a symptom or asking for medication advice). Based on the identified intent, the chatbot selects the appropriate actions and responses.
- *Dialogue Policy:* It defines the strategies that the chatbot utilizes to decide its next action. It determines the response of chatbot responds to patient's query at each stage during the conversation. The strategy can either be rule-based, ML-based, or hybrid approach that helps the chatbot to generate coherent and contextually appropriate responses.

The dialogue management component involves Rule based approaches, finite state-based approaches, activity-based approaches and frame-based approaches (Brabra et al., 2021).

- *Rule-Based Approaches:* These approaches involve pre-defined rules based on specific domain knowledge to manage the conversation flow. It involves simple and interpretable rule-based systems which is not suitable during complex interactions.
- *Finite-Based Approaches:* These approaches model the conversation as a series of states where each state represents a particular stage in the dialogue, and their transition, triggered by patient inputs. This approach offers a structured way to handle dialogues but can be rigid and difficult to scale for complex conversations.
- *Activity-Based Approaches:* These approaches focus on activities that the user wants to perform. The conversation is driven by user activities, and the chatbot directs the user through the necessary steps to complete them. It provides more flexible strategy than rule-based or finite state-based approaches, allowing for dynamic interaction flows.
- *Frame-Based Approaches:* These approaches use data structures called frames to represent the user's goals and the information needed to achieve them. Each frame consists of slots that the chatbot needs to fill based on the user's input (Jurafsky & Martin, 2020). This approach is effective for information-gathering dialogues and allows the chatbot to handle complex queries by filling in the required slots incrementally.

In the proposed architecture, we use the combination of the above strategies to effectively handle the challenges occurring during dialog management. We use the rule-based strategies for those intents where response has been pre-defined. Further, the finite-state strategy is used for those intents followed by any given pre-defined sequence to achieve that goal. Finally, frame-based strategy is used during complex conversation.

(4) ***Natural Language Generator (Response Generation)***

It is a crucial component responsible for generating appropriate responses to user queries in natural language. The NLG process involves several key stages such as content selection, sentence planning, and grammatical organization. Content selection involves determining what information needs to be conveyed in response to a patient's query. Sentence aggregation involves the grouping of selected content into a coherent set of sentences. This ensures the smooth presentation of the information into human understandable format. The process also involves selecting appropriate referring expressions, such as pronouns and shortened descriptions, to maintain clarity and coherence of the sentence. Further, grammatical organization involves the arrangement the sentence structures that follow the rules of grammar and syntax. The precise specification of grammatical features to produce well-formed sequences of words. Finally, the response generator combines the organized content into a coherent and contextually appropriate response. This stage ensures that the text is generated correctly and maintains a natural conversational flow.

1.4 Numerical Results

1.4.1 Experimental Setting and Dataset

The experiments are conducted using workstation with GPU NVIDIA RTX 3090, 16 GB RAM with windows 10 operating system. For programming code, we use Python 3.7 with necessary libraries. The results are mainly evaluated over clinical notes dataset for healthcare using standard evaluation measures. We evaluate the proposed model on physician clinical notes for healthcare (https://www.shaip.com/healthcare-ai/physician-dictation-audio-data-medical-data-catalog/). The dataset consists of total 11 billion characters within the records and 5.17 million records of transcribed notes with massive number of intents and utterances to train a model. The dataset includes various clinical encounters across 31 specialists with diverse set of intents with the goals such as diagnosing a patient, developing a treatment plan, and document a procedure. Within each intent, specific entities are associates, referred as slots such as symptoms, diagnosis, medications and procedures. Table 1.2 summarizes various hyperparameters consider in the proposed architecture.

The attention heads in this architecture enable the model to focus on different parts of the input sequence simultaneously, capturing complex relationships between words. For this design, eight attention heads are chosen to balance performance and computational efficiency. Additionally, an embedding dimension of 512 helps the

Table 1.2 Hyperparameters used for evaluation of proposed chatbot architecture

Parameter	Value
Number of Attention Heads	8
Input Embedding Dimensions	512
Size of Hidden Layer	2048
Learning Rate	0.0001
Batch Size	64
Dropout Rate	0.1
Epochs	100
Weighting Factor λ	0.5

model learn intricate patterns in the data, which is essential for handling diverse healthcare queries. The hidden layer size is set to 2048, enhancing semantic understanding for accurate responses. The optimizer iteratively updates the weights in the network based on training data. Here, we consider the Adam optimizer with $\varepsilon = 0.00000001$ along with the linear scheduler type. Also, a lower learning rate ensures that the model learns slowly, preventing overshooting optimal minima. Here, we set the learning to 0.0001 to avoid overfitting or underfitting. Moreover, we select the batch size of 64 in order to balance between computational units and model generalization. For model robustness, the dropout rate is set to 0.1. Finally, the proposed model is trained over 100 epochs to ensure sufficient training without overfitting.

1.4.2 Performance Metrics

To order to assess the performance of the proposed conversational healthcare chatbot, the following performance metrics that are considered and defined as follows (Ahmed et al., 2023):

- *Accuracy (Acc):* It measures the fraction of classifications for which the judgments made are correctly computed.

$$\mathrm{Acc} = \frac{\mathrm{TP} + \mathrm{TN}}{\mathrm{TP} + \mathrm{FP} + \mathrm{TN} + \mathrm{FN}} \tag{1.9}$$

where TP and TN represent the number of true positives and true negatives, FP and FN denote the number of false positives and false negative, respectively.

- *Macro-Precision (M-P):* It measures the precision for each class separately and then averaged together. For each class $i \in N$, macro-precision is calculated as

$$M - P = \frac{1}{N} \sum_{i=1}^{N} \frac{\mathrm{TP}_i}{\mathrm{TP}_i + \mathrm{FP}_i} \tag{1.10}$$

where N is the number of classes.

- *Macro-Recall (M-R):* It calculates the recall for each class separately and then averaged together. For each class $i \in N$, macro-recall is calculated as

$$M - P = \frac{1}{N} \sum_{i=1}^{N} \frac{\mathrm{TP}_i}{\mathrm{TP}_i + \mathrm{FN}_i} \tag{1.11}$$

- *Macro F1-Score:* It is the harmonic mean of macro-precision and macro-recall.

1.4.3 Baseline Approaches

- **BiRNN + Attention Layer** (Liu & Lane, 2016): Captures bidirectional context using attention mechanisms to prioritize the most important parts of the input query.
- **BiLSTM + CRF** (Xiang et al., 2016): Combines the capability of BiLSTMs to understand long-term dependencies with the sequence labeling strength of CRF, ensuring coherent and valid label sequences for task involving sequence prediction.
- **CNN + LSTM** (Firdaus et al., 2023): Leverages CNN to detect local features within the data, while LSTM handle the sequential patterns to process contextual information.
- **BERT** (Nuruzzaman & Hussain, 2020): Based on self-attention, BERT captures relationships between words across a sequence, understanding context in both forward as well as backward direction simultaneously.

1.4.4 Performance Comparison with Different Word Embeddings

In the section, we compare the performance of proposed model using different word embedding models. As illustrated in Table 1.3 and Fig. 1.3, with Word2Vec word embedding, for intent classification, the accuracy starts at 48.10% for 20 epochs and steadily improves to 91.85% after 100 epochs. Similarly, for slot extraction, the accuracy begins at 54.28% and reaches 94.34% at 100 epochs. Macro-Precision and Macro-Recall follow a similar trend, showing consistent improvement with more epochs, indicating that Word2Vec effectively capture the semantic meaning of words effectively over time, allowing the chatbot to make better predictions with more training.

The performance with GloVe embeddings shows a robust start with a higher initial accuracy compared to Word2Vec as illustrated in Table 1.3. Intent classification accuracy begins at 46.10% for 20 epochs and rises to 93.85% at 100 epochs. Slot

Table 1.3 Performance comparison of proposed framework with different Word Embeddings

		Intent classification			Slot extraction		
Word embedding	Epochs	Acc (%)	M_p (%)	M_r (%)	Acc (%)	M_p (%)	M_r (%)
Word2vec	20	48.10	49.21	49.23	54.28	54.21	58.93
	40	64.31	62.98	59.43	70.01	70.23	67.25
	60	75.23	75.98	71.25	76.87	75.11	74.68
	80	89.21	87.12	88.23	86.92	89.24	93.46
	100	**91.85**	**88.27**	**91.32**	**94.17**	**93.85**	**91.39**
GLoVe	20	46.28	43.28	49.31	63.31	60.13	63.11
	40	65.43	66.78	64.21	75.12	76.89	73.84
	60	78.27	75.88	70.28	85.27	84.22	85.95
	80	88.35	88.19	88.15	89.98	85.41	88.65
	100	**93.12**	**92.77**	**90.11**	**94.11**	**93.75**	**91.77**
FastText	20	39.11	41.67	40.01	58.25	50.01	57.81
	40	62.66	62.84	63.84	69.97	68.18	66.40
	60	73.25	75.88	67.71	78.19	77.42	75.59
	80	87.23	83.39	85.47	87.11	85.76	86.27
	100	**89.91**	**88.93**	**90.87**	**91.05**	**91.14**	**90.02**

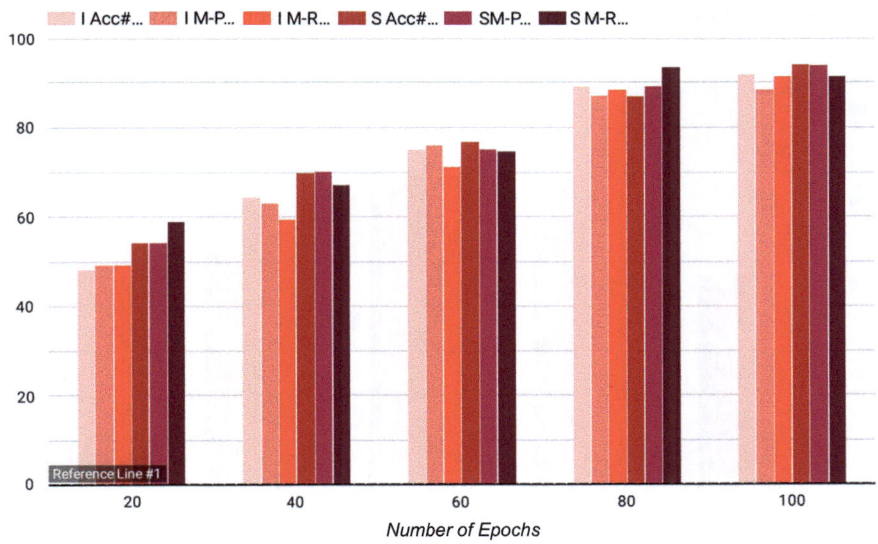

Fig. 1.3 Comparison of macroF1-score and accuracy using Word2vec word embedding layer

extraction accuracy starts at 63.31% and reaches 94.34% at 100 epochs. The Macro-Precision and Macro-Recall metrics also show significant improvement, highlighting the effectiveness of GloVe embedding in capturing semantic understanding of the text from the start and overall better performance.

Using FastText embeddings, the intent classification accuracy starts lower at 39.10% for 20 epochs but shows significant improvement, reaching 89.80% at 100 epochs as depicted from Figs. 1.4 and 1.5. Slot extraction accuracy starts at 58.31% and improves to 91.04% at 100 epochs. Macro-Precision and Macro-Recall show notable growth, indicating that FastText embeddings effectively capture sub-word information, which is particularly useful for understanding misspelled words or variations of the same word, common in user inputs. It has ability to handle out-of-vocabulary words better than the other two embedding models makes it a valuable tool for chatbots dealing with diverse and noisy input data.

The choice of word embeddings impacts the chatbot's ability to learn and generalize from user inputs, with GloVe providing a slight edge in this evaluation. It is also observed that GloVe consistently outperforms the other models, followed by Word2Vec and then FastText. This comparison highlights the superior ability of GloVe model to capture semantic relationships, making it the most effective embedding model for intent classification in this healthcare chatbot context. Figure 1.6 shows the accuracy trends of the proposed architecture with different word embeddings for healthcare dataset using for training and validation purposes. It presents the accuracy of intent classification and slots extraction over 100 epochs.

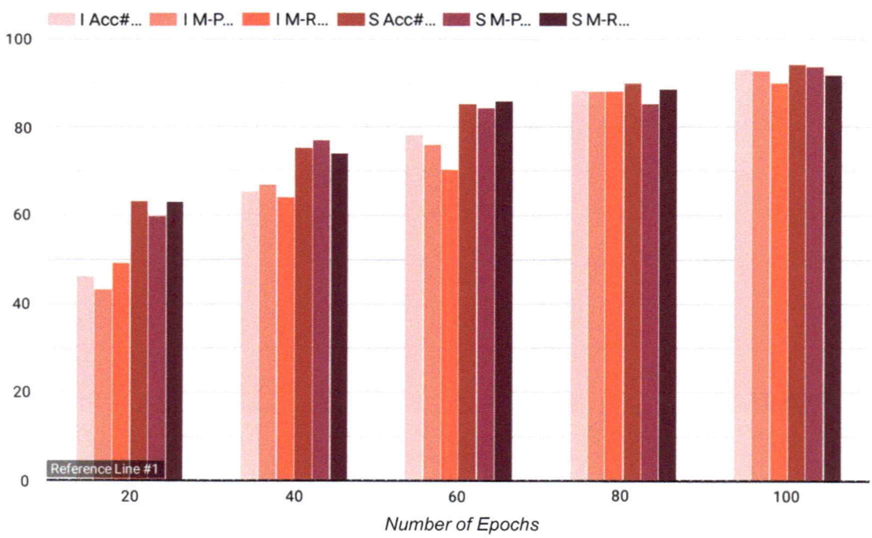

Fig. 1.4 Comparison of macroF1-score and accuracy using GloVe word embedding

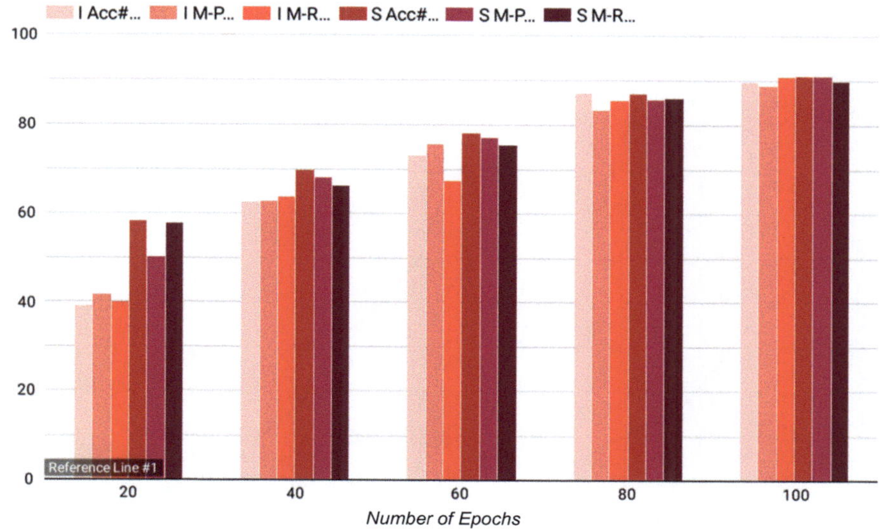

Fig. 1.5 Comparison of macroF1-score and accuracy using FastText word embedding

1.4.5 Performance Comparison with Baseline Approaches

We evaluate the proposed model against baseline approaches to examine the performance of proposed architecture, including BiRNN with an Attention layer, BiLSTM with a CRF layer, CNN with LSTM, BERT as illustrated in Table 1.4. For intent classification, the BiRNN with an Attention layer achieves an accuracy of 78.32% and an F1-score of 81.54%. The BiLSTM with CRF layer improves performance with an accuracy of 88.15% and an F1-score of 90.42%. The CNN with LSTM records 86.21% accuracy and an F1-score of 84.00%, while BERT attains 86.72% accuracy and an F1-score of 92.80%. Among the proposed models, the one using FastText outperforms previous approaches, achieving 89.91% accuracy and an F1-score of 92.20%. With Word2Vec, the proposed model reaches 91.85% accuracy and an F1-score of 91.54%. The GloVe-base model shows the highest performance, with 93.12% accuracy and an F1-score of 92.60%.

For slot extraction, the BiRNN with an Attention layer attains an accuracy of 80.69% and an F1-score of 80.19%. The BiLSTM with CRF layer performs notably better, with 90.06% accuracy and an F1-score of 91.84%. The CNN with LSTM records an accuracy of 88.42% and an F1-score of 86.72%, while BERT achieves 89.67% accuracy and an F1-score of 91.78%. The proposed model with FastText shows improvement with an accuracy of 91.05% and an F1-score of 91.80%. The Word2Vec based model reaches the highest accuracy of 94.17% and an F1-score of 90.39%. Finally, the GloVe-based model achieves an accuracy of 94.11% and the highest F1-score of 93.99%.

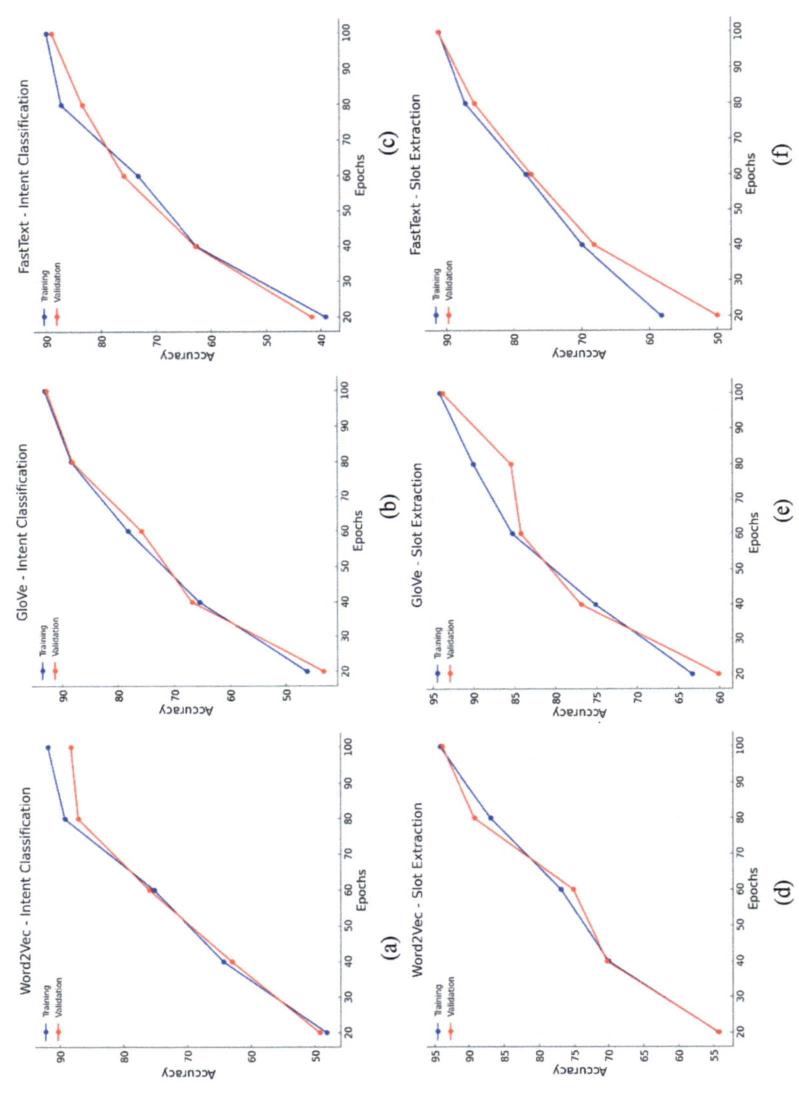

Fig. 1.6 Comparison of training and validation accuracy using different word embeddings

Table 1.4 Performance comparison with baseline approaches

Model	Intent classification		Slot extraction	
	Acc (%)	Macro F1-score (%)	Acc (%)	Macro F1-score (%)
BiRNN + Attention layer	78.32	81.54	80.69	80.19
BiLSTM + CRF	88.15	90.42	90.06	91.84
CNN + LSTM	86.21	84.00	88.42	86.72
BERT	86.72	92.80	89.67	91.78
Proposed + fastText	89.91	92.20	91.05	91.80
Proposed + Word2Vec	91.85	91.54	**94.17**	90.39
Proposed + GloVe	**93.12**	**92.60**	94.11	**93.99**

As illustrated, the proposed model with different word embeddings outperforms the state-of-the-art approaches in both intent classification and slot extraction tasks. Among the proposed models, the one using GloVe embeddings consistently shows the highest accuracy and F1-scores for both tasks, indicating its superior ability to capture semantic relationships in text. FastText and Word2Vec also perform exceptionally well, but GloVe edges them out slightly, especially in slot extraction where it achieves the highest F1-score of 93.99%. The results highlight the effectiveness of using advanced word embeddings with proposed architecture in improving the accuracy and precision of intent classification and slot extraction in a healthcare chatbot context.

1.4.6 Numerical Results

In this section, we showcase interactions with the healthcare chatbot addressing various health issues. The chatbot initiates the conversation by asking the user about their symptoms. Based on the responses, it searches for and asks about additional symptoms related to the primary concern, aiming to provide a more accurate assessment of the condition. Figure 1.7 illustrates an example where the chatbot identifies the issues of dimorphic hemorrhoids and arthritis based on the symptoms provided and offers some recommended measures to follow in these conditions. The ability of chatbot to perform intent classification and slot extraction that allows it to understand and process patient's query accurately. The system's decision-making process involves:

- *Intent Classification:* Identifying the primary concern (e.g., "nausea" as a symptom).
- *Slot Extraction:* Extracting detailed information about related symptoms and the duration of the primary symptom.

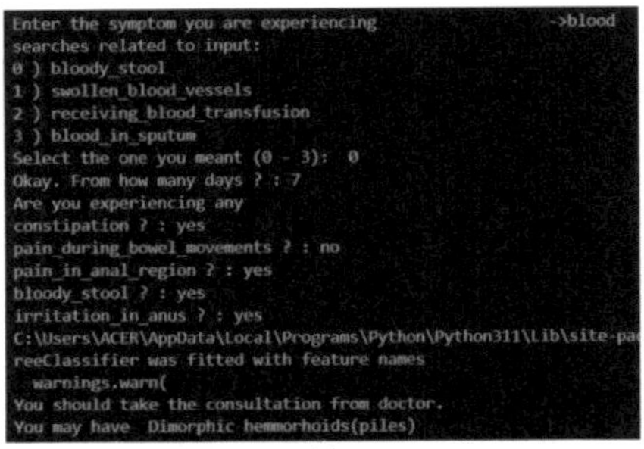

(a)

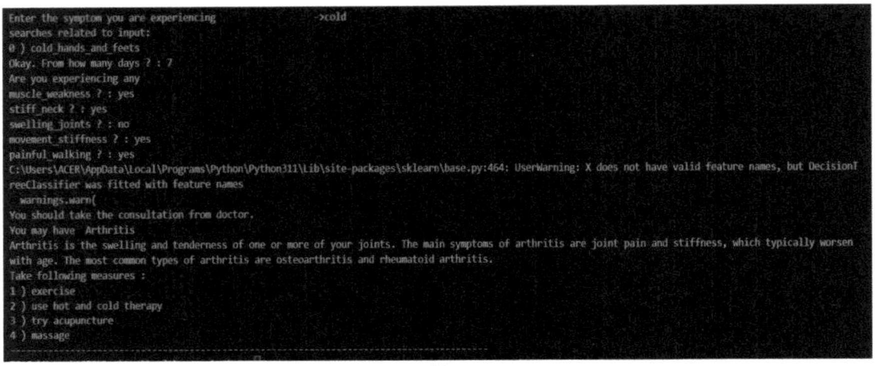

(b)

Fig. 1.7 Example of patient's interaction with healthcare chatbot

- *Response Generation:* Providing a diagnosis suggestion and recommending further consultation with a healthcare professional.

By incorporating these advanced technologies, the healthcare chatbot demonstrates its potential to offer personalized healthcare support, aiding in early diagnosis and timely intervention, ultimately enhancing patient care and health outcomes.

1.4.7 Theoretical Implications

Advancements in AI and ML in healthcare is driving enhancements in patient care and leading to better health outcomes. The development of Transformer-based models for intent classification and slot extraction in healthcare chatbots presents significant progress advancement in chatbot design. It is crucial to correctly identify the patient intent—whether it pertains to symptoms or medication inquiries. The proposed architecture effectively captures long-range dependencies within the input text and historical chat records that enables accurate detection of the patient's intent.

Additionally, accurate extraction of patient's intent further allows the identification of critical patient information, results in more precise diagnostic suggestions.

The research carried out in this study has broader implications for future healthcare sector. It would provide an interface to both patients as well as healthcare authorities to integrate electronic health record (EHR) systems. This could further streamline clinical workflows, and enable patients to access their medical records anytime and anywhere easily while consulting with doctors. The proposed chatbot has ability to handle large datasets that allows personalized healthcare recommendations, leading to more accurate symptom tracking and patient-centric advice. This could improve patients' health by promoting proactive healthcare management. Furthermore, the chatbots significantly improve the healthcare accessibility, particularly in regions with limited healthcare professionals.

1.5 Conclusion and Future Research

In this study, we propose a conversational healthcare chatbot to diagnose medical condition and provide patient-centric health recommendations based on the symptoms provided as input. The proposed model utilizes a transformer-based architecture with multi-head attention for intent classification and entity extraction, to accurately understand the patient's input. Further, the proposed architecture offers dialogue management and response generation to provide home remedies, routine changes, and non-prescription medications for minor ailment based on symptoms. The performance of proposed model is validated using annotated physician clinical notes and compared with baseline schemes. The experimental results corroborate the superior performance of the proposed model. The performance is also validated by incorporating various word embeddings in transformer-based neural network model to improve its accuracy and precision.

In future work, several avenues of this research could be explored to expand its applications in healthcare sector. One possible direction is to integrate EHR that includes multi-modal data such as images and text, which further improve the diagnostic accuracy. Further, the expansion of chatbot's knowledge base to incorporate a wide variety of medical conditions and their treatments. Finally, the proposed work could further integrate teleconsultation facility that helps to expand the 24×7 healthcare services in remote areas to potentially revolutionize access to medical advice and preliminary diagnoses.

References

Abedin, A. F., Mamun, A. I. A., Nowrin, R. J., Chakrabarty, A., Mostakim, M., & Naskar, S. K. (2021). A deep learning approach to integrate human-level understanding in a chatbot. arXiv preprint arXiv:2201.02735

Ahmed, M., Khan, H. U., & Munir, E. U. (2023). Conversational AI: An explication of few-shot learning problem in transformers-based chatbot systems. *IEEE Transactions on Computational Social Systems, 11*(2), 1888–1906.

Badlani, S., Aditya, T., Dave, M., & Chaudhari, S. (2021, May). Multilingual healthcare chatbot using machine learning. In *2021 2nd International Conference for Emerging Technology (INCET)* (pp. 1–6). IEEE.

Bahdanau, D., Cho, K., & Bengio, Y. (2014). Neural machine translation by jointly learning to align and translate. arXiv preprint arXiv:1409.0473

Benayas, A., Hashempour, R., Rumble, D., Jameel, S., & De Amorim, R. C. (2021). Unified transformer multi-task learning for intent classification with entity recognition. *IEEE Access, 9*, 147306–147314.

Bi, M., Zhang, Q., Zuo, M., Xu, Z., & Jin, Q. (2020). Bi-directional LSTM model with symptoms-frequency position attention for question answering system in medical domain. *Neural Processing Letters, 51*, 1185–1199.

Brabra, H., Báez, M., Benatallah, B., Gaaloul, W., Bouguelia, S., & Zamanirad, S. (2021). Dialogue management in conversational systems: A review of approaches, challenges, and opportunities. *IEEE Transactions on Cognitive and Developmental Systems, 14*(3), 783–798.

Cao, B., Ma, K., Liu, Y., Xu, Y., & Zhu, L. (2021). Intention classification in multiturn dialogue systems with key sentences mining. *Computational Intelligence, 37*(2), 758–773.

Ciesla, R. (2024). AI and Chatbots in healthcare. In *The book of Chatbots: From ELIZA to ChatGPT* (pp. 91–107). Springer Nature Switzerland.

Dündar, E. B., Cekiç, T., Deniz, O., & Arslan, S. (2018). A hybrid approach to question-answering for a banking Chatbot on Turkish: Extending keywords with embedding vectors. In *KDIR* (pp. 169–175).

Firdaus, M., Ekbal, A., & Cambria, E. (2023). Multitask learning for multilingual intent detection and slot filling in dialogue systems. *Information Fusion, 91*, 299–315.

Firdaus, M., Golchha, H., Ekbal, A., & Bhattacharyya, P. (2021). A deep multi-task model for dialogue act classification, intent detection and slot filling. *Cognitive Computation, 13*, 626–645.

Hakkani-Tur, D. Z., Celikyilmaz, A., Chen, Y. N., Deng, L., Gao, J., Tur, G., & Wang, Y. Y. (2023). U.S. Patent Application No. 18/457,708.

https://www.shaip.com/healthcare-ai/physician-dictation-audio-data-medical-data-catalog/

Javaid, M., Haleem, A., & Singh, R. P. (2023). ChatGPT for healthcare services: An emerging stage for an innovative perspective. *BenchCouncil Transactions on Benchmarks, Standards and Evaluations, 3*(1), 100105.

Jungmann, S. M., Klan, T., Kuhn, S., & Jungmann, F. (2019). Accuracy of a chatbot (Ada) in the diagnosis of mental disorders: Comparative case study with lay and expert users. *JMIR Formative Research, 3*(4), e13863.

Jurafsky, D., & Martin, J. H. (2020). *Speech and language processing: Chatbots & dialogue systems* (3rd ed.) [Online]. Available: https://web.stanford.edu/~jurafsky/slp3/

Kim, Y. B., Lee, S., & Stratos, K. (2017, December). Onenet: Joint domain, intent, slot prediction for spoken language understanding. In *2017 IEEE Automatic Speech Recognition and Understanding Workshop (ASRU)* (pp. 547–553). IEEE.

Kurup, G., & Shetty, S. D. (2022). AI conversational chatbot for primary healthcare diagnosis using natural language processing and deep learning. In *Computational Intelligence in Pattern Recognition: Proceedings of CIPR 2021* (pp. 259–272). Springer Singapore.

Vaswani et al., (2017). Attention is all you need. *Advances in Neural Information Processing Systems, 30.*

Liu, B., & Lane, I. (2016). *Attention-based recurrent neural network models for joint intent detection and slot filling*. arXiv preprint arXiv:1609.01454

Magalhaes Azevedo, D., & Kieffer, S. (2021). User reception of AI-enabled mHealth Apps: The case of Babylon health.

Mesnil, G., Dauphin, Y., Yao, K., Bengio, Y., Deng, L., Hakkani-Tur, D.,... & Zweig, G. (2014). Using recurrent neural networks for slot filling in spoken language understanding. *IEEE/ACM Transactions on Audio, Speech, and Language Processing, 23*(3), 530–539.

Milne-Ives, M., de Cock, C., Lim, E., Shehadeh, M. H., de Pennington, N., Mole, G.,... & Meinert, E. (2020). The effectiveness of artificial intelligence conversational agents in health care: Systematic review. *Journal of medical Internet research, 22*(10), e20346.

Nadarzynski, T., Miles, O., Cowie, A., & Ridge, D. (2019). Acceptability of artificial intelligence (AI)-led chatbot services in healthcare: A mixed-methods study. *Digital Health, 5*, 2055207619871808.

Nuruzzaman, M., & Hussain, O. K. (2020). IntelliBot: A dialogue-based chatbot for the insurance industry. *Knowledge-Based Systems, 196*, 105810.

Palanica, A., Flaschner, P., Thommandram, A., Li, M., & Fossat, Y. (2019). Physicians' perceptions of chatbots in health care: Cross-sectional web-based survey. *Journal of Medical Internet Research, 21*(4), e12887.

Pandey, S., Sharma, S., & Wazir, S. (2022). Mental healthcare chatbot based on natural language processing and deep learning approaches: Ted the therapist. *International Journal of Information Technology, 14*(7), 3757–3766.

Patel, S. B., & Lam, K. (2023). ChatGPT: The future of discharge summaries? *The Lancet Digital Health, 5*(3), e107–e108.

Rahman, M. M., Amin, R., Liton, M. N. K., & Hossain, N. (2019, December). Disha: An implementation of machine learning based Bangla healthcare chatbot. In *2019 22nd International Conference on Computer and Information Technology (ICCIT)* (pp. 1–6). IEEE.

Rastogi, A., Gupta, R., & Hakkani-Tur, D. (2018). *Multi-task learning for joint language understanding and dialogue state tracking*. arXiv preprint arXiv:1811.05408

Sarrouti, M., & El Alaoui, S. O. (2020). SemBioNLQA: A semantic biomedical question answering system for retrieving exact and ideal answers to natural language questions. *Artificial Intelligence in Medicine, 102*, 101767.

Thomason, J. (2024). Data, digital worlds, and the avatarization of health care. *Global Health Journal, 8*(1), 1–3.

Wen, T. H., Vandyke, D., Mrksic, N., Gasic, M., Rojas-Barahona, L. M., Su, P. H.,... & Young, S. (2016). *A network-based end-to-end trainable task-oriented dialogue system*. arXiv preprint arXiv:1604.04562

Wu, C. S., Madotto, A., Hosseini-Asl, E., Xiong, C., Socher, R., & Fung, P. (2019). *Transferable multi-domain state generator for task-oriented dialogue systems*. arXiv preprint arXiv:1905.08743

Xiang, Y., Zhou, X., Chen, Q., Zheng, Z., Tang, B., Wang, X., & Qin, Y. (2016). Incorporating label dependency for answer quality tagging in community question answering via CNN-LSTM-CRF. In *Proceedings of COLING 2016, the 26th International Conference on Computational Linguistics: Technical Papers* (pp. 1231–1241).

Xu, L., Sanders, L., Li, K., & Chow, J. C. (2021). Chatbot for health care and oncology applications using artificial intelligence and machine learning: Systematic review. *JMIR Cancer, 7*(4), e27850.

Yang, X., & Liu, J. (2015). Dialog state tracking using long short-term memory neural networks. In *INTERSPEECH* (Vol. 2015, pp. 1800–1804).

Yu, D., He, L., Zhang, Y., Du, X., Pasupat, P., & Li, Q. (2021). *Few-shot intent classification and slot filling with retrieved examples*. arXiv preprint arXiv:2104.05763

Zhao, T., Lu, A., Lee, K., & Eskenazi, M. (2017). *Generative encoder-decoder models for task-oriented spoken dialog systems with chatting capability*. arXiv preprint arXiv:1706.08476

Zhou, H., Huang, M., Zhang, T., Zhu, X., & Liu, B. (2018, April). Emotional chatting machine: Emotional conversation generation with internal and external memory. In *Proceedings of the AAAI conference on artificial intelligence* (Vol. 32, No. 1).
Žilka, L., & Jurčíček, F. (2015, September). Lectrack: Incremental dialog state tracking with long short-term memory networks. In *International Conference on Text, Speech, and Dialogue* (pp. 174–182). Springer International Publishing.

Chapter 2
Current and Future Trends in Healthcare Quality Control and Improvement

Riddhi Parasnaik, Raashi Jatakia, Priya Patwa, and Gajanan Nagare

Abstract Healthcare is an important part of human health and provides services that promote, maintain and improve health. Quality improvement aims to provide quality care that is accessible to all, regardless of socioeconomic, cultural, and financial considerations. Rigorous procedures and methods should be established to improve treatment. Artificial intelligence and machine learning are used to improve diagnosis and treatment planning, including telemedicine, remote monitoring, electronic medical records, and research. However, international inequalities in healthcare, patient participation and health literacy, workforce shortages, resource availability and urine technology pose serious problems. With the use of electronic health records (EHR), electronic medical records (EMR), and remote patient care (RPM), decision-making and monitoring site analysis become more efficient and reliable. Big data leverages AI for diagnosis, prognosis, and treatment planning. Cloud-based data security enables innovation in healthcare by re-encrypting and keeping patient data private. AI plays a key role in early detection of terminal illnesses, personalized medical services, and studying patterns in biological diseases. Research on quality healthcare, such as access to surgery, hospital-based care, and data-driven approaches to overcoming inefficiencies, health equity, demonstrate the importance of solving these problems. This study suggests that technology-based AI will continue to improve healthcare by replacing administrative tasks, collaborating in hospitals, and providing preventive treatment.

Keywords Healthcare · Quality improvement · Case studies · Service management · Artificial Intelligence · Quality control

---

R. Parasnaik · R. Jatakia · P. Patwa · G. Nagare (✉)
Department of Biomedical Engineering, Vidyalankar Institute of Technology, Mumbai, India
e-mail: gajanan.nagare@vit.edu.in

R. Parasnaik
e-mail: riddhi.parasnaik@vit.edu.in

R. Jatakia
e-mail: raashi.jatakia@vit.edu.in

P. Patwa
e-mail: priya.patwa@vit.edu.in

I. Mukherjee et al. (eds.), *Decision Sciences for Quality and Productivity Improvement*,
https://doi.org/10.1007/978-981-95-7545-9_2

2.1 Introduction

Healthcare is the cornerstone of public health and includes a variety of services designed to promote, maintain, and improve health. It is committed to providing easy and equal care to all, regardless of socioeconomic status, cultural differences, and financial concerns. Effective healthcare management is an essential part of safe and effective patient care in healthcare systems. It includes methods for monitoring, evaluating, and improving all aspects of healthcare, including clinical outcomes, patient feedback, and quality of work. In this study, we discuss research data on current measures, current trends in quality control, challenges faced by current initiatives, the use of advanced technologies, research data on previous measures, and future changes in the medical industry, detailing the current state of the art.

In a rapidly evolving world and dynamic technology, patients' symptoms, diagnoses, and recovery are different. The methods used by health professionals may not be applicable to every person living in rural areas. Their expertise, combined with new technologies, can lead to changes in healthcare. Health management aims to minimize variation in practice, ensure consistency, and improve resource utilization by establishing rigorous standards, procedures, and processes. Figure 2.1 provides an overview of all the topics and issues covered in this section.

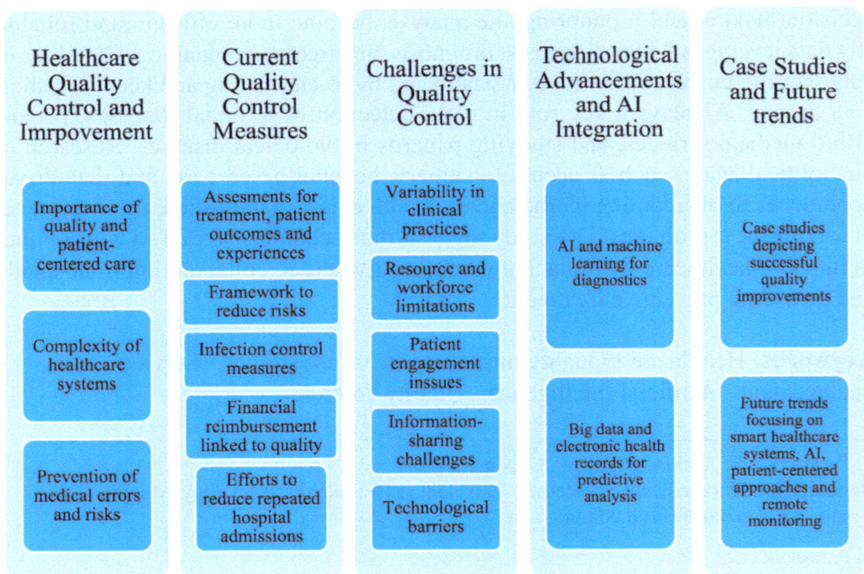

Fig. 2.1 A diagrammatic representation of all the issues presented in this work

2.2 Study of Existing Healthcare Quality Improvement Measures

2.2.1 Clinical Quality Measures

Quality assurance measurement (CQM) is a tool for clinical assessment, evaluation, process and patient outcomes, and diagnosis after drug administration (EHR Incentive Program; Quentin et al., 2019). CQM focuses on patient and family interactions with healthcare providers, patient safety, and well-being during treatment and diagnosis, and public and public health measures that lead to better care at a better price (Quentin et al., 2019). CQM regularly evaluates the quality of services provided to patients to ensure efficient use of resources. CQM integrates with electronic medical records to facilitate data collection and reporting. CQM improves healthcare quality based on national strategic planning.

Emergency services are the backbone of first responders, medical care is essential to ensure patients receive quality care, and outpatient services include emergency services (Pulsiri et al., 2019). Outpatient services include X-rays, blood tests, biopsies, and minor surgeries (Pulsiri et al., 2019). Mobile clinics are used for prevention and primary care. This provides protection from routine checkups, vaccinations, and chronic disease testing. Outpatient care treats minor illnesses such as colds and flu. Manage chronic conditions by ensuring continuity of care (Pulsiri et al., 2019).

The organization works to improve and implement quality care each year. They also work to identify and assess public health issues. The National Health Commission compiled Healthcare Effectiveness Data and Information Set (HEDIS) from the Special Needs Project (SNP) (National Committee for Quality Assurance, 2023). HEDIS measures and produces data to track the success of quality improvement projects, using data from the SNP to identify opportunities for improvement and to compare with other plans prepared by HEDIS. The Centers for Medicare and Medicaid Services (CMS) selects a set of HEDIS measures to ensure equity. The report focuses on measures that need to be maintained for another 5 years (National Committee for Quality Assurance, 2023). These include early care planning, colon cancer screening, geriatric care, use of spirometry for COPD diagnosis, use of beta-blockers after heart attack, and dietary bone health in women, etc.

Value-based purchasing (VBP) programs focus on paying providers based on their performance (Chee et al., 2016). VBP ties compensation to performance on quality measures. It is used by the Centers for Medicare and Medicaid Services to improve quality and efficiency (Chee et al., 2016). These services are evaluated against efficiency and patient care goals to improve the overall patient experience and outcomes, including patient-centered care (Chee et al., 2016). VBP ensures that unnecessary costs are not paid and is designed to reduce the financial costs of care and improve the quality of care. VBP relies heavily on data collection and transparency. The main goal of VBP is to encourage doctors to provide quality care at low costs, thus providing better health outcomes for patients and making health clean and stable (Chee et al., 2016).

2.2.2 *Ensuring Patient Safety Through Standardized Procedures*

Patient safety is one of the most important activities designed to create a culture, processes, procedures, behaviors, technology, and environment that regularly reduces the risk of treatment, reduces the potential for injury, reduces errors, and reduces the impact of errors when they occur. Many patients lose their lives due to misuse and incorrect treatment prevention. The Health and Safety Manager works to improve safety measures and improve monitoring and implementation. There are currently 26 Patient Safety Indicators (PSIs) providing specific safety-related events that occur in hospitals during various surgical procedures (Kontopentalis et al., 2010). The PSIs are designed to reduce mortality, promote patient recovery, reduce the risk of developing further symptoms after diagnosis, prevent patients from falling out of bed and reduce the risk of bad medicines. PSI is a common cause of many diseases and may not include certain genetic or infectious diseases (Kontopentalis et al., 2010). These indicators are divided into various levels, such as the physician's safety index, regional safety index, and other causes of injury (Kontopentalis et al., 2010).

During a normal visit, a patient may become infected. These diseases may not be detected during hospital care but may develop over time. Healthcare infections are divided into different types depending on how the patient is infected: catheter-associated urinary tract infection (CAUTI), central line-associated bloodstream infection (CLABSI), ventilator-associated pneumonia (VAP), and surgical site (SSI) (Taye et al., 2023). Infected individuals may experience upper respiratory tract infections, gastrointestinal tract infections, and organ infections. Soft tissues are easy targets for infection. According to a report by the National Center for Biotechnology Information (NCBI), the statistics differ between genders, with more cases of the disease occurring in women. The data is also divided by age; infants (15.62%) and people aged 14–19 (16.27%) are the most common (Kontopentalis et al., 2010). This classification also depends on the location and characteristics of the respiratory tract, where the human immune system is weak and children are more susceptible to infection and continue to develop resistance to different diseases.

Patients are referred to the hospital for a number of problems/the same condition when they leave the hospital. Readmission costs, lack of follow-up after discharge, Medicare and Medicaid programs, time, demographics, and mental health are significant concerns due to possible causes (Walker, 2023). Patients with cardiovascular conditions such as heart disease, congestive heart failure, pneumonia, chronic obstructive pulmonary disease (COPD), and total hip and knee replacement surgery are expected to be referred to the hospital for pain. Sepsis is a major cause (Walker, 2023). The public has realized that race can create communication problems between patients and physicians. This should be followed by a simple discharge procedure with prior contact with the patient in the hospital and timely follow-up (Walker, 2023).

Patient assessments included questions on various aspects of patient care, scheduling follow-up appointments, managing demanding work schedules, and the quality of care provided by the individual's sense of well-being. Psychometric results from these studies are associated with improved patient care outcomes. These factors include cost-effectiveness, acceptability, and educational impact (Beattie et al., 2015). All of these aspects are examined using different measurement tools, which are fully worded, with all responses to the questionnaire being recognized in a binary format, such as "yes" or "no" (Beattie et al., 2015).

2.3 Current Trends in Healthcare Quality Improvement

Medicine plays an important role in society. Quality of care is very important for healthcare organizations and councils. In recent years, the application of AI in various processes has increased worldwide. Over the past few years, the healthcare sector has undergone significant changes in the integration of automation and other AI applications. The basis for good work in healthcare is to do the right thing, in the right way, for the right person, at the right time, with the best results. It affects the balance between overuse, misuse, and abuse, thus avoiding unnecessary tests, undiagnosed blood pressure, and incorrect medications (Tiwary et al., 2014). The quality of healthcare can be improved by targeting patients at risk for certain conditions and ensuring timely provision of services. Professionals can request, evaluate, adopt and use performance measures to track treatment performance. This approach allows for continuous improvement and monitoring of clinical quality (Quality in Healthcare, 2021).

2.3.1 Patient-Centered Care

Patient-centered care, which places the patient at the center of care, has become increasingly common in recent years. This approach emphasizes the importance of collaboration and communication between patients, families, and providers. The National Academy of Medicine (formerly the Institute of Medicine [IOM]) views patient cardiology as an essential part of good healthcare (Kiel et al., 2022). Patient-centeredness is defined as: Healthcare that establishes a partnership among practitioners, patients, and their families (when appropriate) to ensure that decisions respect patients' wants, needs, and preferences and that patients have the education and support they need to make decisions and participate in their care (Medicine IO, Services B on HC, Delivery C on the NQR on HC, 2001).

2.3.2 Implementation of Evidence-Based Practices

Research and clinical trials have demonstrated the effectiveness of medical procedures referred to as evidence-based practice. Healthcare organizations use evidence-based methods to improve patient safety and clinical outcomes. Evidence-based clinical practice can improve patient, staff, and organizational outcomes, such as reduced hospital readmissions, longer survival, and resource use (Bahtsevani et al., 2004). Evidence-based practice is key to improving care and patient outcomes (Chien, 2019). Certification and regulatory requirements are the foundation for ensuring patient safety and quality care. In order for a healthcare facility to maintain its certification or license, it must meet the requirements. Following these guidelines will help ensure that patients receive effective and efficient care. Hospital accreditation helps improve clinical quality and patient safety by encouraging staff thinking, modeling practice, and the right focus for improvement (Melo, 2016).

2.3.3 Integration of Technology

Healthcare companies are using analytics and data to improve patient safety and quality of care. This includes using predictive analytics, performance dashboards, and electronic health records (EHRs) to identify areas for improvement and track progress over time. Data mining and predictive analytics can improve healthcare by extracting insights from big data in electronic medical records and performance dashboards (Malik et al., 2018). Online patient access to electronic medical records can have a positive impact on patient safety by identifying medication errors and encouraging greater use of preventive services (Mold et al., 2015).

Technology has become critical to patient safety and quality of care. This includes the use of mobile medical applications, telemedicine, and remote patient care. These innovations have the potential to improve patient outcomes, reduce healthcare costs, and increase access to care. Telemedicine consultations have the potential to improve patient health outcomes, reduce healthcare access, and reduce healthcare costs (Flodgren et al., 2015). Mobile interventions, including short messaging services (SMS) and mobile applications, can improve environmental care by improving medication administration, administration, and hospitalization pain and reducing readmissions and emergency department visits (Lu et al., 2018).

2.3.4 Interprofessional Collaboration

The term "collaboration" refers to collaboration between healthcare professionals across specialties, including physicians, nurses, and pharmacists. By improving collaboration and communication between healthcare providers, collaborative care can improve standards of care and protect patients. Collaboration between nursing staff and physicians in different hospitals has not yet been studied, but major challenges include ensuring mutual understanding between professionals and overcoming differences in cultures and processes (Karam et al., 2018).

Doctors are of great importance in ensuring patient safety and quality of care. Employers are investing more in education and training to ensure that healthcare professionals have the resources, skills and knowledge they need to provide quality care. Education and training can improve patient safety and ensure quality care through the use of educational processes and resources, especially when new technologies are used (Borycki, 2015).

2.4 Challenges in Existing Healthcare Quality Control

2.4.1 Variability in Clinical Practice

Multiplicity: Clinical practices vary as per the guidelines given by federations. With the multiplicity of clinical guidelines issued by local medical societies or by recognized international institutions, the practitioner may doubt which guidelines to follow. The problem can be resolved by establishing a standard high-quality clinical guideline (Franco & Arancibia, 2020).

Multimorbidity: A person may be suffering from multiple diseases, but a clinical practitioner focuses on individual complaints. The diagnosis of each complaint would require a different guideline and lead to different complications for the patient (Franco & Arancibia, 2020). These are a few of the challenges faced by the clinical practitioner and persist until they are formulated by the mandatory and worldwide accepted guidelines.

2.4.2 Patient Engagement and Adherence

Patient involvement is the patient's involvement in making careful decisions. Working with patients is stressful because it leads to decisions that vary from person to person. This can create better information sharing and trust and improve communication between patients and doctors (Kadaei, 2023).

- Information Accessibility: Accessing the information, which is comprehensive and accurate is a difficult task. Lack of health information makes an individual withdraw himself from decision-making (Kadaei, 2023).
- Health Literacy: Patients come from different economic backgrounds, ethnicities, and cultural backgrounds. The patients may be aware of their medical conditions but understanding its medical terminologies is difficult (Kadaei, 2023).

- Technological barrier: Access to the latest updates and technology is not available to every individual—people who are technophobes or who do not rely on information available online. People prefer to have direct interaction with the care provider (Kadaei, 2023).
- Communication Challenges: A major challenge in diagnosis is a language barrier, which leads to misunderstanding which results in misdiagnosis, and inappropriate treatment plans (Kadaei, 2023).

There is a shift to ambulatory care; this shift needs to address many issues and take steps to meet the needs of the patient. Infection prevention is extremely important in ambulatory care due to the high risk of infection, and hand hygiene, antibiotics, and personal hygiene management are important (Procloz, 2024). Ambulatory care services must comply with government regulations. Poor communication between staff during referral puts patients at higher risk. Patient data for this individual has not been previously disclosed (Procloz, 2024). Timely referrals, briefings, and electronic medical records are sent to patient care staff.

2.4.3 Resource Constraints and Workforce Shortages

There are geographic differences in healthcare between urban and rural areas, and providers and quality of care also differ in many ways (Ortiz, 2021). Costs and efficiency are higher in large cities than in rural areas. Healthcare is experiencing serious staff shortages. As the population grows, demand increases and workers retire. With a limited workforce, potential resources cannot reach the people who need them. People do not have access to basic medical services, vaccines, drug distribution, etc. Citizens are not aware of these programs due to unemployment. Resources are limited because developing countries tend to have better post-secondary services and doctors are more likely to migrate because of better jobs, higher wages and better living.

2.4.4 Data Silos and Information Sharing and Implementation Challenges

In healthcare, information silos refer to information that is fragmented and separated from various departments, systems, and organizations (Antonacci et al., 2023). If the system fails to collect data, there will be problems in communicating patient information. Physicians cannot access all patient information, which leads to inconsistencies in care (Antonacci et al., 2023). Lack of information sharing leading to tests and procedures can reduce care efforts, which can delay treatment and jeopardize patient safety (Antonacci et al., 2023). Information sharing is a concern because it creates the risk of patients' personal information being leaked and misused. Information sharing also raises legal and regulatory issues (Antonacci et al., 2023). One of the challenges of sharing is the consumer's ability to use electronic medical records efficiently.

The use of medical technology includes telemedicine and electronic medical records. The use of technology increases the forensic effect and limits the diagnosis when the process is stopped (What Are the Challenges of Ambulatory Care, 2022). Many difficulties are experienced due to the lack of access by many people, such as the elderly who do not use technology, and people living in places where there is no internet. The cost of services continues to increase with the introduction of technology, and a large portion of the population in the middle-income group faces difficulties in accessing basic health services. The use of complex technology is resisted by staff because it can increase workload and create problems in ongoing patient care. Without digital health information, safe and reliable information, patients face problems (What Are The Challenges of Ambulatory Care, 2022).

2.5 Implementation of Artificial Intelligence and Machine Learning in Healthcare Quality Control for Decision-Making and Analysis

Artificial Intelligence (AI) refers to the body's ability to perform tasks that require human assistance, such as training, learning, reasoning, and decision-making (Khosravi et al., 2024). It includes many technologies such as deep learning, natural language processing, machine learning, robotics, and image processing. Especially in healthcare, AI can be very useful in making accurate diagnoses and decisions. Doctors' diagnoses vary according to personal opinion. AI allows doctors to collect these details and also create personal information.

2.5.1 Healthcare Database Management System

Healthcare is a growing industry that includes a lot of patient information and medical information. Processing medical information is the main responsibility of doctors to prioritize the following main goals: prevention, diagnosis, prognosis, and treatment. It has been proven that AI can achieve very high accuracy in terms of algorithm reliability and can use clinical data to simulate automated decisions and predictions. The term "big data" is often associated with the healthcare industry, which uses machine learning and deep learning algorithms to store historical patient data. In fact, big data-related analysis can increase computational efficiency by using higher resolution. The problem with big data is its volume. Hence, the traditional software and platforms it runs on are not powerful enough to support the same volume of data (Dash et al., 2019). Electronic Health Record (EHR), Electronic Medical Record (EMR), Interplanetary File System (IPFS), and Remote Patient Monitoring (RPM) are some shared healthcare systems that use big data such as location and location to record the patient's RPM time (Zaabar et al., 2021). Before the advent of computers and their capabilities, medical information was generally available in the form of written or printed documents. The adoption of EHRs and EMRs has enabled the data to be associated with modern healthcare. These systems can process data from a variety of sources, including hospital records, patient records, physical exam results, and devices connected to the Internet of Things (IoT). These systems have become the primary source of information management in most medical companies and hospitals. Businesses are already using human genome data to help doctors make personalized treatment decisions.

Information security in medical systems is important because it contains confidential information that cannot be disclosed to the public. For the timely storage and provision of electronic medical records and big data, but data encryption with cloud data is very important to protect known patient privacy. When users upload patient data to a cloud service provider (CSP), the public key is used to encrypt the data to ensure data security. This information can only be decrypted by doctors or patients. Cloud storage technology continues to use re-encryption technology (Lv, 2016), which allows data to be re-encrypted by converting the ciphertext of the key data into a ciphertext that does not contain information about important matters. Then, the data is decrypted and a security is created for both parties to secure the confidential information (Lv, 2016). In addition, cloud computing (CC) technology has also become a platform for improving medical services and promoting innovation (Darwish et al., 2017).

2.5.2 Implementation of AI Assistance for Diagnosis

Although innovation in the healthcare sector is difficult, AI is rapidly emerging and entering the sector by bringing changes in the care of human pain and external aid (Ahmad et al., 2021). Machine learning (ML) is an AI discipline that works based on training and testing on data. Algorithms include machine learning that uses statistical analysis and data interpretation techniques, making them ideal for diagnosis. Deep learning (DL) is another AI that provides excellent results in image processing and classification. Advances in machine learning algorithms in medicine have replaced clinical tasks that require human expertise. Machine learning models are trained using large datasets and then tested on similar datasets to identify desired features and check the accuracy of the model. Various diseases can be diagnosed using ML and DL algorithms on scanned images and further development of clinical skills can be beneficial (Ahmad et al., 2021). Radio companies are rapidly adopting AI and are already taking advantage of its advantages, increasing the accuracy of detection (Ahmad et al., 2021). Pathology, especially surgical pathology, has also started using this technique very quickly.

The healthcare sector is struggling with operational disruptions during the COVID-19 pandemic and has to rely on intelligence and its distribution, machine learning, and deep learning to complete most of the medical tasks. Machine learning is used on a larger scale to analyze medical images obtained from computed tomography (CT) and X-ray scans. The use of machine learning is mainly aimed at combating this pandemic. Many learning machines, such as decision trees (DTs), random forests (RFs), and support vector machines (SVMs), are based on their ability to learn and use without explicit training (Heidari et al., 2022). RF is often used to solve classification problems in COVID-19 tests. SVM is another technique used when there is widespread transmission due to its ability, accuracy, and efficiency to solve classification problems. Also, convolutional neural networks (CNN), a branch of deep learning, have been used in many applications involving graphics. Preprocessing and segmentation methods also provide treatment and model intelligence with filtered data for precise interpretation.

Machine learning can perform tasks that doctors perform. ML and DL models are now widely used in disease prediction, diagnosis, and even personalized treatment planning. The main algorithms used in machine learning are classification, regression, clustering, and decision-making. The images obtained from the technology are integrated into these models and the data is analyzed step by step. Usually, preprocessing is applied first, followed by feature extraction for better performance and greater accuracy. Deep learning has been used with great success in detecting diseases in images, including the use of CNNs. This model achieves high classification accuracy when using medical images for disease diagnosis and classification (Ghaffar Nia et al., 2023). Clinical oncology is another medical field that seeks the help of machine learning and deep learning algorithms to predict cancer cell proliferation, early diagnosis of malignant tumors, and treatment with precision medicine. The field of clinical oncology has taken a step toward intelligent knowledge to determine the molecular pathogenesis of cancer by understanding the biological processes of cancer cells. It is also exploring the studies of millions of related problems in big data and computational biology to prevent cancer worldwide. The use of AI in medical decision-making will increase the possibility of early detection and diagnosis of diseases through the use of NGS sequencing and high-resolution imaging technology. It will also provide new biomarkers for cancer diagnosis and provide valuable information for developing personalized medicine and treatment strategies using specialized bioinformatics tools (Iqbal et al., 2021).

2.6 Case Studies on Healthcare Quality Control

An important part of the quality improvement process is feedback and reporting. Data analysis is a good way for businesses to analyze and evaluate the quality of their products and services. Ideally, in the healthcare sector, data science plays an important role for doctors and nurses. We have compiled some important studies for you that focus on the steps to be taken in times of crisis and the negative consequences. Table 2.1 also provides a summary of all six studies.

Table 2.1 A brief summary of the 6 case studies presented in this work

Reference	Organization	Domain	Issues faced	Methodology	Future scope
Quigley et al. (2011)	Surgical Specialty Medical Practice	Customer service data for surgical practice	– Challenges in patient access – Resistance from staff toward new training	Plan-Do-Study-Act (PDSA) cycle	Continuous monitoring with scorecards and patient surveys
Ward et al., 2022	A private hospital in Ireland	Healthcare quality and patient safety data	– Staff resistance due to hierarchical culture and "projectitis" – Managing interdepartmental collaboration and alignment with strategic goals	Lean Six Signma (LSS) and a sociotechnical systems CUBE framework	Expanding system-wide data integration to support patient-centered metrics and sustain improvements
Joint Commission International (2020)	Surgical Specialty Medical Practice	Health plan customer service data	– High staff turnover and lack of experienced representatives – Low staff retention and limited career advancement for service reps	Plan-Do-Study-Act (PDSA) cycle	Further improvements in customer experience metrics
Institute for Healthcare Improvement (n.d.)	Miscellaneous	Health Inequality Data	– Inconsistencies in data collection practices – Staff reluctance	Scoping review methodology	Developing patient trust through transparency and utilizing multidisciplinary approaches

(continued)

Table 2.1 (continued)

Reference	Organization	Domain	Issues faced	Methodology	Future scope
Moorthie et al. (2022)	Ochsner Health	SARS-CoV-2 Diagnostic Testing	– Delayed turnaround times due to testing demand – Limited personal protective equipment	Departmental collaboration and cross-training	Emphasis is placed on maintaining high-quality standards, even under resource constraints
Caruso et al. (2020)	Oulu University Hospital and University of Oulu	Healthcare Innovation and Co-creation	– Complexity of healthcare innovation due to fragmented stakeholders – Difficulties in aligning stakeholders' interests	Co-creation	Improving collaboration frameworks, knowledge sharing, and integrating patient input in healthcare innovation systems

2.6.1 Case Study on Improving Customer Service and Access in a Surgical Practice

The authors in Quigley et al. (2011) describe the steps taken by the teaching hospital in 2006 to improve its clientele and access. The hospital is a center specializing in liver diseases and surgery, and includes other specialties such as pancreatic diseases and liver diseases. Initially, the practice manager identified some problems with client service and access, but this problem was revealed when patients expressed concerns to the physician about access to services and monitoring when patients interacted with staff. The hospital and health center decided to follow the 6-step performance improvement cycle in Fig. 2.2. Customer Service Assessment (CAHPS) (Quigley et al., 2011). We have taken steps to improve customer service and access for patients.

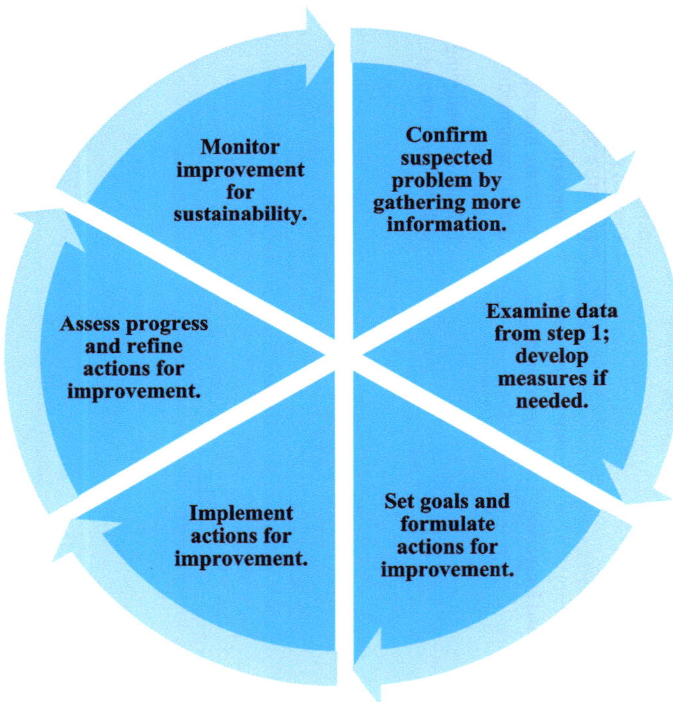

Fig. 2.2 The figure illustrates the six-step strategy applied by the specialty practice to improve customer service and service access to patients

2.6.2 *Case Study on Improving Hospital Inpatient Nursing Care*

In 2014, an organization recognized a significant failure to improve health (Ward et al., 2022). The organization was recently recognized by Joint Commission International (Joint Commission International, 2020) for its outstanding resources. Achieving the certification creates support for its core purpose. The organization's mission is to create patient care in hospitals that is based on compassion, kindness, and respect. They proposed an application of the CUBE model for the analysis of sociotechnical processes, focusing on four elements: culture, work, study, and thought (Ward et al., 2022). All employees and offices are the most important, have dignity and communication, and play an important role. The framework has proven to be one of the most effective measures to improve the quality of care.

2.6.3 *Case Study on Improving Performance for Health Plan Customer Service*

The six-step approach used in Fig. 6.1 was also used by the CAHPS intervention to improve the effectiveness of consumer health plans (Joint Commission International, 2020). The report (Quigley et al., 2007) describes the organization's efforts to create a comprehensive health service to improve patient care. A study conducted by CAHPS in 1995 reported a need for improvement in hospital health programs. The 6 steps shown in Fig. 2.2 were adapted from the Plan-Do-Study-Act (PDSA) cycle (Institute for Healthcare Improvement, n.d.). The staff of the private hospital took care of the improvements made to improve healthcare services and customer service.

2.6.4 *Case Study on a Data-Driven Approach to Rise Above Health Inequity*

A review was conducted in Moorthie et al. (2022) to analyze the approaches taken in the healthcare context to improve the data quality in order to monitor health inequalities. Good data management is important to understand the context of health inequalities in the population. Inequality often varies by health characteristics, geography, race, or disability. The collected documents are grouped by different topics, such as laws, legal procedures, data collection tools and procedures. Before content analysis, all documents were read by at least one author and sent to another reviewer for further analysis. The author (Moorthie et al., 2022) conducted a systematic review to examine this problem, which occurs frequently in the United States.

2.6.5 Case Study on How Ochsner Health Accesses Critical Supplies and Medications During the Pandemic

Ochsner Health, a nonprofit healthcare provider, has launched a diagnostic test for severe acute respiratory syndrome coronavirus 2 (SARS-CoV2), the virus that causes COVID-19 (Caruso et al., 2020). Months before Ochsner Health admitted its first patient on March 9, 2020, department officials began researching the new threat from the coronavirus and made several plans in advance for an Emergency Use Authorization (EUA). The endogenous test was developed with the help of Roche Diagnostics and Abbott Laboratories, two companies that play a key role in effectively and rapidly diagnosing the disease. As a result of all these negative measures, Ochsner is a leader in COVID-19 testing in Louisiana (Caruso et al., 2020).

2.6.6 Case Study on How Collaboration, Leadership and Data Help Improve Patient Care

The development of innovation in healthcare is still a very difficult concept due to the fragmented and complex nature of the work. To achieve this, a joint initiative was created in collaboration with many research partners, hospitals, doctors, and companies (Hyrkäs et al., 2020). This project uses the concept of Open Innovation (OI) to create products and services in collaboration with customers. It also shows the difficulties that arose during the work and had to be solved, such as new challenges, multiple options, lack of planning. However, the general reaction to this idea was positive.

2.7 Future Trends in Healthcare Quality Control and Improvement

One of the main drivers of this change is healthcare management, which allows healthcare companies to deliver medical care with a focus on improving medical benefits and patient safety. To stay ahead in the market and achieve significant improvements in patient outcomes and operational efficiency, organizations need to adopt innovative and effective management practices, including changing patient needs and increasing medical needs. To foster a culture of quality improvement and improve patient care, companies need to adopt the quality control and innovation methods described in this section.

2.7.1 Integration of Technology and Artificial Intelligence

Artificial intelligence such as machine learning, pattern recognition, and deep learning can help solve complex engineering problems, make quick decisions, reduce errors, and improve computer performance (Salehi & Burgueño, 2018). Artificial Intelligence technology, especially in AI and edge computing, can improve the efficiency and effectiveness of personalized medicine by identifying abnormal patterns in physiological data for timely intervention (Shumba et al., 2022). The features of intelligence integration include disease diagnosis and prognosis, treatment recommendations, drug discovery and development, implementation of healthcare services and devices, electronic medical records, intelligent gene sequencing, fraud and billing optimization, telemedicine integration, AI in disaster management, Quality Management laboratories creation. Artificial Intelligence, AI Robots, and AI research in Healthcare.

AI and machine learning in healthcare bring many benefits, but also ethical issues. Data privacy is important because AI and machine learning are trained on large amounts of medical data that must be protected from unauthorized access. If the information used is not evaluated as the target population, bias will occur, resulting in incorrect or unfair treatment for patients. Therefore, it is important to prevent bias in diagnosis or treatment recommendations. Transparency and accountability are important because AI and machine learning systems can be complex and difficult to understand, so it is important to ensure that they are used fairly and honestly. Overcoming these challenges is critical to the healthcare AI ecosystem to ensure patients receive the best outcomes.

AI and machine learning can transform the work of doctors and patient care by assisting them, replacing administrative tasks, and improving clinical knowledge (Aung et al., 2021). Understanding these technologies is important for viewers and other healthcare professionals, as AI and machine learning have the potential to improve patient care, decision-making, and treatment. They can also use Learning Prompt Engineering to create prompts that will help the AI model make differential diagnoses, teach effective learning, and even create interactive patient information. Doctors can be at the forefront of medical development and provide the best treatment to patients through AI and machine learning. As the healthcare industry continues to expand, experts in these technologies will be needed. Artificial intelligence and machine learning are revolutionizing healthcare, providing better patient care, personalized treatment, and access. As technology continues to advance, new innovations and future changes will occur.

Today, devices that use intelligence, the internet, cloud connectivity, and other devices are called smart technologies. Some examples of technology in healthcare are AI-powered inventory management systems that track and monitor inventory and automatically order new supplies when needed, or smart beds that detect patient movement and alert nurses when the patient gets out of bed. Smart and interactive medical systems, such as cloud-based smart medical applications, can enhance patient experience and improve quality of care (Zhang et al., 2017). Some of the key areas of smart healthcare integration include remote monitoring and automated medical services, telemedicine and remote monitoring, connectivity to emergency solutions, and smart hospital management.

2.7.2 Fostering Smart Collaborations

Collaboration and collaboration in specific activities can enhance short-term development of effective collaboration in the absence of cultural support, time, and resources (Hulscher et al., 2013). The Health Promotion Association frequently uses collaborative development to train and develop health professionals. However, the knowledge and skills required to enable these collaborations to develop, or the extent to which these skills are developed, have not yet been investigated. Collaborative performance improvement can improve patient care, particularly by focusing on changing "skills" and thinking skills in management and change (Weggelaar-Jansen & Wijngaarden, 2018). Collaborative patient care increases physical access to health services. Collaboration between hospitals and clinics also increases the availability of medical services.

Preventive collaboration between patients and physicians leads to positive outcomes. However, there are important differences in the impact of shared leadership on access to care. Therefore, the use of leadership strategies such as patient care, hospital collaboration, and preventive care may improve patient access to care (Okpala, 2017). An organizational culture that includes non-hierarchical collaboration, recognition, respect, time, and information gathering may help patients collaborate with their healthcare providers to improve the quality of care (Renedo et al., 2014).

2.7.3 Remote Health Quality Control and Improvement

E-health uses communication and technology (ICT) to better manage patients and their health and improve the overall quality of care. ICT-based tools such as home blood pressure monitoring and smartphone applications can improve blood pressure control by increasing patient participation and adherence to medical prescriptions (Albini et al., 2016). Telemedicine and mHealth are popular electronic medical tools that allow patients and physicians to exchange medical information over the Internet. Electronic health solutions, especially telemedicine, can improve blood pressure control and prevent heart disease by improving patient self-management and encouraging medication adherence (Gray & O'Malley, 2019). E-health services can lower blood pressure and improve blood pressure control in hypertensive patients (Omboni, 2019). Remote blood pressure monitoring (BPT) is the most popular telemedicine application in hypertension, sending blood pressure and medical information to the doctor or hospital from the patient's home or local area.

Multiple randomized controlled trials have shown that data managers providing counseling in the distal and distal care pharmacy can reduce blood pressure and optimize the use of antihypertensive medications in patients using BPT. BPT can also provide educational support, vaccination, reminders, and remote counseling services as mobile health solutions. This will promote patient autonomy and participation in medical decisions, thus improving blood pressure control and increasing medication adherence. In conclusion, e-solutions, especially telemedicine, are important in the management of patients with hypertension and have the potential to improve quality of care, improve blood pressure control, and prevent heart disease.

Future directions for electronic health records (EHRs) for healthcare management and mobility focus on creating integrated, data-driven processes focused on patient values and quality of work. Blockchain-based EHR management systems have the potential to improve privacy protection, access control, and quality storage, thereby improving collaboration in healthcare (Sonkamble et al., 2021). Future electronic medical records can combine AI and machine learning to analyze data in real time to predict outcomes, identify risks, and make good diagnoses to increase accuracy and reduce errors. These systems will also support personalized and precision medicine by integrating genetic, lifestyle, and environmental data to support public health and address healthcare disparities. Patient engagement will be enhanced through patient portal access and mobile monitoring, allowing individuals to manage their health information at home and participate in their care. In healthcare, Blockchain-based decentralized networks can enhance cybersecurity measures to ensure data integrity, availability, and privacy while incorporating patient consent into the enterprise governance of data sharing (Barbaria et al., 2022). NLP has great potential to interpret medical data and extract health-related decisions from medical data by helping to develop diagnostic tools, risk models, and clinical decision-making (Patra et al., 2021). In line with this vision, electronic medical records have become a new system that not only stores information but also actively helps in the delivery of quality healthcare, change management, patient flow, and access to global healthcare.

2.7.4 Big Data in Healthcare

With advanced analytics, integration, and patient-centric approaches, big data in healthcare promises to transform patients, improve operations, and refine future research. Big data analytics will enable medical systems to extract insights from big data, uncovering trends that can be used to identify risk factors, predict patient benefit, and guide individualized treatment. Big data analytics can reduce costs by identifying patients, readmissions, triage, decompensation, adverse events, and effective treatment for diseases that affect many bodies (Bates et al., 2014). By integrating information from multiple sources, including technology, genomic data, and electronic medical records, a better view of patient health can be achieved, as can drinking clean. Big data analytics can reduce costs by identifying high-value patients, readmissions, triage, decompensation, adverse events, and optimal treatment for diseases that affect many bodies (Bates et al., 2014). This supports precision medicine and customized services. Big data in public health management can reveal patterns in large populations, guide strategies and policies to reduce inequalities and improve public health. By combining AI and machine learning, doctors can improve diagnostic accuracy, perform task management, and monitor performance indicators in real time (Ahmed et al., 2020). This reduces human error and increases efficiency. Information security and privacy are important, and the development of blockchain and encryption technology will protect private medical information while building patient trust. Big data will facilitate self-management and enable patients to interact with their own health information through portals and remote monitoring tools, enabling continuous monitoring and study (Kalid et al., 2018). Furthermore, by combining big data with technologies such as natural language processing (NLP), non-objective data (such as medical data) can be sorted to reveal hidden insights without the work of doctors (Patra et al., 2021). Big data in healthcare will ultimately change the rules of the game by providing insightful insights that support efficiency, effectiveness, and quality of care.

2.8 Conclusion

Healthcare management has undergone changes due to technological advances and changing patient expectations. Traditional metrics such as clinical quality indicators (CQMs), patient safety indices (PSIs), and hospital-acquired events (HACs) were used to evaluate medical services and benefits. However, today's care needs a better and more comprehensive approach. Current trends in patient-centered care, use of data and analytics, and evidence-based practices. Integration of technologies such as electronic health records (EHRs), telemedicine, and health information systems are essential to streamline work, improve patient access, and facilitate effective communication.

To address issues in the quality control process, such as changes in clinical practice, patient engagement issues, and limited resources, artificial intelligence (AI) and machine learning (ML) hold promise for improving decision-making and assessment in healthcare. AI's capabilities in areas such as disease detection, resource management during outbreaks, and AI-assisted diagnostics suggest it has the potential to improve quality control processes.

The future model of effective medical management will focus on the deep integration of artificial intelligence, the promotion of intelligent collaboration, and the emergence of smart medicine. Effective telemedicine management and development will also be addressed, especially by relying on telemedicine services. The adoption of these standards is of great importance for healthcare organizations to adapt to changing conditions and provide fair and affordable healthcare for all.

References

Ahmad, Z., Rahim, S., Zubair, M., & Abdul-Ghafar, J. (2021). Artificial intelligence (AI) in medicine, current applications and future role with special emphasis on its potential and promise in pathology: Present and future impact, obstacles including costs and acceptance among pathologists, practical and philosophical considerations. A comprehensive review. *Diagnostic Pathology*, [online] *16*(24). https://doi.org/10.1186/s13000-021-01085-4.

Ahmed, Z., Mohamed, K., Zeeshan, S., & Dong, X. (2020). Artificial intelligence with multi-functional machine learning platform development for better healthcare and precision medicine. *Database: The Journal of Biological Databases and Curation*. https://doi.org/10.1093/database/baaa010

Albini, F., Liu, X., Torlasco, C., Soranna, D., Faini, A., Ciminaghi, R., Celsi, A., Benedetti, M., Zambon, A., di Rienzo, M., & Parati, G. (2016). *An ICT and mobile health integrated approach to optimize patients' education on hypertension and its management by physicians: The Patients Optimal Strategy of Treatment (POST) pilot study*. [online] IEEE Xplore. https://doi.org/10.1109/EMBC.2016.7590753

Antonacci, G., Benevento, E., Bonavitacola, S., Cannavacciuolo, L., Foglia, E., Fusi, G., Garagiola, E., Ponsiglione, C., & Stefanini, A. (2023, October 18). *Healthcare professional and manager perceptions on drivers, benefits and challenges of telemedicine: Results from cross-sectional survey in the Italian NHS*. https://doi.org/10.1186/s12913-023-10100-x

Aung, Y. Y. M., Wong, D. C. S., & Ting, D. S. W. (2021). The promise of artificial intelligence: A review of the opportunities and challenges of artificial intelligence in healthcare. *British Medical Bulletin, 139*(1), 4–15. https://doi.org/10.1093/bmb/ldab016

Bahtsevani, C., Udén, G., & Willman, A. (2004). Outcomes of evidence-based clinical practice guidelines: A systematic review. *International Journal of Technology Assessment in Health Care*, [online] *20*(4), 427–433. https://doi.org/10.1017/s026646230400131x

Barbaria, S., Mont, M., Ghadafi, E., Machraoui, H., & Rahmouni, H. (2022). Leveraging patient information sharing using blockchain-based distributed networks. *IEEE Access, 10*, 106334–106351. https://doi.org/10.1109/ACCESS.2022.3206046

Bates, D., Saria, S., Ohno-Machado, L., Shah, A., & Escobar, G. (2014). Big data in health care: Using analytics to identify and manage high-risk and high-cost patients. *Health Affairs, 33*(7), 1123–1131. https://doi.org/10.1377/hlthaff.2014.0041

Beattie, M., Murphy, D. J., Atherton, I., & Lauder, W. (2015). Instruments to measure patient experience of healthcare quality in hospital: A systematic review. *Systematic Reviews*. https://doi.org/10.1186/s13643-015-0089-0

Borycki, E. (2015). Editorial: Advances in healthcare provider and patient training to improve the quality and safety of patient care. *Knowledge Management & E-Learning: An International Journal, 7*, 348–352. https://doi.org/10.34105/J.KMEL.2015.07.022

Caruso, L. J., Chang, D. D., Hovis, K. B., Linscott, A. J., Goens, E. F., Yang, T., & Occhipinti, E. (2020). Getting ahead of the curve: How Ochsner became a leader in SARS-CoV-2 diagnostic testing. *Ochsner Journal, 20*(2), 139–143. https://doi.org/10.31486/toj.20.0055

Chee, T. T., Ryan, A. M., Wasfy, J. H., & Borden, W. B. (2016). Current state of value-based purchasing programs. *Circulation*, [online] *133*(22), 2197–2205. https://doi.org/10.1161/circulationaha.115.010268.

Chien, L.-Y. (2019). Evidence-based practice and nursing research. *Journal of Nursing Research*, [online], *27*(4). https://doi.org/10.1097/jnr.0000000000000346

Darwish, A., Hassanien, A. E., Elhoseny, M., Sangaiah, A. K., & Muhammad, K. (2017). The impact of the hybrid platform of internet of things and cloud computing on healthcare systems: Opportunities, challenges, and open problems. *Journal of Ambient Intelligence and Humanized Computing, 10*(10), 4151–4166. https://doi.org/10.1007/s12652-017-0659-1

Dash, S., Shakyawar, S. K., Sharma, M., & Kaushik, S. (2019). Big data in healthcare: Management, analysis and future prospects. *Journal of Big Data*, [online] *6*(1), 1–25. https://doi.org/10.1186/s40537-019-0217-0.

EHR Incentive Program. *Centres for Medicare and Medicaid Services* https://www.cms.gov/regulations-and-guidance/legislation/ehrincentiveprograms/downloads/guidetocqms_remediated_2011.pdf

Flodgren, G., Rachas, A., Farmer, A. J., Inzitari, M., & Shepperd, S. (2015). Interactive telemedicine: Effects on professional practice and health care outcomes. *Cochrane Database of Systematic Reviews*, 9. https://doi.org/10.1002/14651858.cd002098.pub2

Franco, J. V. A., Arancibia, M., Meza, N., Madrid, E., & Kopitowski, K. (2020). *Clinical practice guidelines: Concepts, limitations and challenges*. Medwave. https://doi.org/10.5867/medwave.2020.03.7887 http://viejo.medwave.cl/link.cgi/English/Reviews/MethodlogicalNotes/7888.act?ver=sindiseno

Ghaffar Nia, N., Kaplanoglu, E., & Nasab, A. (2023). Evaluation of artificial intelligence techniques in disease diagnosis and prediction. *Discover Artificial Intelligence*, [online] *3*(1). https://doi.org/10.1007/s44163-023-00049-5

Gray, J., & O'Malley, P. (2019). Review: E-health interventions improve blood pressure level and control in hypertension. *Annals of Internal Medicine, 170*(12), JC68. https://doi.org/10.7326/acpj201906180-068

Heidari, A., Jafari Navimipour, N., Unal, M., & Toumaj, S. (2022). Machine learning applications for COVID-19 outbreak management. *Neural Computing and Applications*. https://doi.org/10.1007/s00521-022-07424-w

Hulscher, M. E. J. L., Schouten, L. M. T., Grol, R. P. T. M., & Buchan, H. (2013). Determinants of success of quality improvement collaboratives: What does the literature show? *BMJ Quality & Safety*, [online] *22*(1), 19–31. https://doi.org/10.1136/bmjqs-2011-000651

Hyrkäs, P., Haukipuro, L., Väinämö, S., Iivari, M., Sachinopoulou, A., & Majava, J. (2020). Collaborative innovation in healthcare: A case study of hospitals as innovation platforms. *International Journal of Value Chain Management, 11*(1), 24. https://doi.org/10.1504/ijvcm.2020.10027214

Institute for Healthcare Improvement. (n.d.). *Home*. [online] Institute for Healthcare Improvement. Available at: https://www.ihi.org/

Iqbal, M.J., Javed, Z., Sadia, H., Qureshi, I.A., Irshad, A., Ahmed, R., Malik, K., Raza, S., Abbas, A., Pezzani, R., & Sharifi-Rad, J. (2021). Clinical applications of artificial intelligence and machine learning in cancer diagnosis: Looking into the future. *Cancer Cell International*, [online] *21*(1). https://doi.org/10.1186/s12935-021-01981-1.

Joint Commission International. (2020). *Joint commission international accreditation standards for hospitals: Including standards for academic medical center hospitals*. Oak Brook, Il Joint Commission International.

Kadaei, M. (2023). *Challenges of patient engagement*. [online] Ambula Healthcare. Available at: https://www.ambula.io/challenges-of-patient-engagement/. Accessed 17 December 2023.

Kalid, N., Zaidan, A., Zaidan, B., Salman, O., Hashim, M., & Hussain, M. (2018). Based real time remote health monitoring systems: A review on patients prioritization and related "big data" using body sensors information and communication technology. *Journal of Medical Systems, 42*, 1–30. https://doi.org/10.1007/s10916-017-0883-4

Karam, M., Brault, I., Van Durme, T., & Macq, J. (2018). Comparing interprofessional and interorganizational collaboration in healthcare: A systematic review of the qualitative research. *International Journal of Nursing Studies, 79*(79), 70–83. https://doi.org/10.1016/j.ijnurstu.2017.11.002

Khosravi, M., Zare, Z., Mojtabaeian, S. M., & Izadi, R. (2024). Artificial intelligence and decision-making in healthcare: A thematic analysis of a systematic review of reviews. *Health Services Research and Managerial Epidemiology*, [online] *11*. https://doi.org/10.1177/23333928241234863.

Kiel, J. M., Kim, G. R., & Ball, M. J. (2022). *Healthcare information management systems*. Springer Nature.

Kontopentalis, E., Roland, M., & Ravees, D. (2010). *Patient experience of access to primary care: Identification of predictors in a national patient survey*. https://doi.org/10.1186/1471-2296-11-61

Lu, K., Marino, N. E., Russell, D., Singareddy, A., Zhang, D., Hardi, A., Kaar, S., & Puri, V. (2018). Use of short message service and smartphone applications in the management of surgical patients: A systematic review. *Telemedicine and e-Health, 24*(6), 406–414. https://doi.org/10.1089/tmj.2017.0123

Malik, M. M., Abdallah, S., & Ala'raj, M. (2018). Data mining and predictive analytics applications for the delivery of healthcare services: A systematic literature review. *Annals of Operations Research, 270*(1–2), 287–312. https://doi.org/10.1007/s10479-016-2393-z.

Medicine IO, Services B on HC, Delivery C on the NQR on HC. (2001). *Envisioning the national health care quality report*. National Academies Press.

Melo, S. (2016). The impact of accreditation on healthcare quality improvement: A qualitative case study. *Journal of Health Organization and Management, 30*(8), 1242–1258. https://doi.org/10.1108/JHOM-01-2016-0021

Mold, F., de Lusignan, S., Sheikh, A., Majeed, A., Wyatt, J. C., Quinn, T., Cavill, M., Franco, C., Chauhan, U., Blakey, H., Kataria, N., Arvanitis, T. N., & Ellis, B. (2015). Patients' online access to their electronic health records and linked online services: A systematic review in primary care. *British Journal of General Practice, 65*(632), e141–e151. https://doi.org/10.3399/bjgp15x683941

Moorthie, S., Peacey, V., Evans, S., Phillips, V., Roman-Urrestarazu, A., Brayne, C., & Lafortune, L. (2022). A scoping review of approaches to improving quality of data relating to health inequalities. *International Journal of Environmental Research and Public Health*, [online] *19*(23), p.15874. https://doi.org/10.3390/ijerph192315874.

National Committee for Quality Assurance. (2023). *Final medicare special needs plan HEDIS performance results: Measurements year 2017–2022.* October 6th 2023. https://www.cms.gov/files/document/snp-hedis-2017-2022-report.pdf

Pulsiri, N., Vatananan-Thesenvitz, R., Sirisamutr, T., & Wachiradilok, P. (2019). Save lives: A review of ambulance technologies in pre-hospital emergency medical services. In *2019 Portland International Conference on Management of Engineering and Technology (PICMET).* https://doi.org/10.23919/PICMET.2019.8893973 https://ieeexplore.ieee.org/document/8893973

Okpala, P. (2017). Increasing access to quality healthcare through collaborative leadership. *International Journal of Healthcare Management, 13*(3), 1–7. https://doi.org/10.1080/20479700.2017.1401276

Omboni, S. (2019). Connected health in hypertension management. *Frontiers in Cardiovascular* Medicine, *6*(76). https://doi.org/10.3389/fcvm.2019.00076.

Ortiz, D. (2021). *The advantages and disadvantages of sharing patient information.* [online] Medtrainer. Available at: https://medtrainer.com/blog/the-advantages-and-disadvantages-of-sharing-patient-information/. Accessed 28 September 2022.

Patra, B., Sharma, M., Vekaria, V., Adekkanattu, P., Patterson, O., Glicksberg, B., Lepow, L., Ryu, E., Biernacka, J., Furmanchuk, A., George, T., Hogan, W., Wu, Y., Yang, X., Bian, J., Weissman, M., Wickramaratne, P., Mann, J., Olfson, M., … Pathak, J. (2021). Extracting social determinants of health from electronic health records using natural language processing: A systematic review. *Journal of the American Medical Informatics Association: JAMIA, 28*, 2716–2727. https://doi.org/10.1093/jamia/ocab170

Procloz. (2024). *5 workforce challenges in healthcare and how to avoid them.* [online] procloz. Available at: https://procloz.com/5-workforce-challenges-in-healthcare-and-how-to-avoid-them/#:~:text=Reasons%20for%20the%20workforce%20shortages. Accessed 28 June 2024.

Quality in Healthcare. (2021). [online] www.ncbi.nlm.nih.gov. Agency for Healthcare Research and Quality (US). Available at: https://www.ncbi.nlm.nih.gov/books/NBK578527/.

Quentin, W., Partanen, V.-M., Brownwood, I., & Klazinga, N. (2019). *Measuring healthcare quality.* www.ncbi.nlm.nih.gov. European Observatory on Health Systems and Policies.

Quigley, D., Wiseman, S., & Farley, D. (2007). *Improving performance for health plan customer service: A case study of a successful CAHPS quality improvement intervention.* https://doi.org/10.7249/wr517. https://www.rand.org/pubs/working_papers/WR517.html

Quigley, D., Wiseman, S., & Farley, D. (2011). *Improving customer service and access in a surgical* practice*: A case study of a successful quality improvement intervention.* RAND Corporation. https://doi.org/10.7249/wr848

Renedo, A., Marston, C. A., Spyridonidis, D., & Barlow, J. (2014). Patient and public involvement in healthcare quality improvement: How organizations can help patients and professionals to collaborate. *Public Management Review, 17*(1), 17–34. https://doi.org/10.1080/14719037.2014.881535

Salehi, H., & Burgueño, R. (2018). Emerging artificial intelligence methods in structural engineering. *Engineering Structures, 171*(171), 170–189. https://doi.org/10.1016/j.engstruct.2018.05.084

Shumba, A.-T., Montanaro, T., Sergi, I., Fachechi, L., De Vittorio, M., & Patrono, L. (2022). Leveraging IoT-Aware technologies and AI techniques for real-time critical healthcare applications. *Sensors, 22*(19), 7675. https://doi.org/10.3390/s22197675

Sonkamble, R., Phansalkar, S., Potdar, V., & Bongale, A. (2021). Survey of interoperability in electronic health records management and proposed blockchain based framework: MyBlockEHR. *IEEE Access*, 1–1. https://doi.org/10.1109/ACCESS.2021.3129284

Taye, Z. W., Abebil, Y. A., Akalu, T. Y., Tessema, G. M., & Taye, E. B. (2023). Incidence and determinants of nosocomial infection among hospital admitted adult chronic disease patients in University of Gondar Comprehensive Specialized Hospital, North–West Ethiopia, 2016–2020. *Frontiers in Public Health*, [online] *11*. https://doi.org/10.3389/fpubh.2023.1087407

Tiwary, A. P., Pradhan, B. B., & Bhattacharyya, B. (2014). Study on the influence of micro-EDM process parameters during machining of Ti–6Al–4V superalloy. *The International Journal of Advanced Manufacturing Technology, 76*(1–4), 151–160. https://doi.org/10.1007/s00170-013-5557-x

Walker, B. (2023). *The top 5 causes of hospital readmissions—And how to prevent them—Upfront healthcare.* [online] upfronthealthcare.com. Available at: https://upfronthealthcare.com/resources/cost-reduction/the-top-5-causes-of-hospital-readmissions-and-how-to-prevent-them/.

Ward, M. E., Daly, A., McNamara, M., Garvey, S., & Teeling, S. P. (2022). A case study of a whole system approach to improvement in an acute hospital setting. *International Journal of Environmental Research and Public Health, 19*(3), 1246. https://doi.org/10.3390/ijerph19031246

Weggelaar-Jansen, A. M., & van Wijngaarden, J. (2018). Transferring skills in quality collaboratives focused on improving patient logistics. *BMC Health Services Research, 18*(1). https://doi.org/10.1186/s12913-018-3051-8

What Are the Challenges of Ambulatory Care. (2022, August 19). *SPLNC and Associates, LLC* https://splegalnurse.com/the-challenges-of-ambulatory-care/. Author name is not mentioned

Wuyou, L. (2016). Design and implementation of an encrypted cloud storage system based on OpenStack Swift. In *7th IEEE International Conference on Software Engineering and Service Science (ICSESS).* https://doi.org/10.1109/icsess.2016.7883089.

Zaabar, B., Cheikhrouhou, O., Jamil, F., Ammi, M., & Abid, M. (2021). HealthBlock: A secure blockchain-based healthcare data management system. *Computer Networks*, [online] *200*(1), 108500. https://doi.org/10.1016/j.comnet.2021.108500

Zhang, Y., Chen, M., Leung, V. C. M., & Lai, R. "Xiaorong" (2017). Topical collection on 'smart and interactive healthcare systems'. *Journal of Medical Systems, 41*(8). https://doi.org/10.1007/s10916-017-0766-8.

Chapter 3
The Adaptation of Industry 4.0 for Total Quality Management (TQM): Empirical Observations from the Banking Service Sector

Meshack Bashange Mwesiga and Ismail W. R. Taifa

Abstract Industry 4.0 (I4.0) emerging concepts affect banking services in multiple dimensions. This research assessed service quality and the successful adaptation of I4.0 to enhance the implementation of Total Quality Management (TQM) in Tanzania's banking sector. Such transformation of I4.0 for TQM is sometimes referred to as TQM 4.0. This study used a mixed-method approach whereby qualitative and quantitative data were analysed from 9 banks operating in Tanzania. The qualitative data were collected through semi-structured interviews, whereas the quantitative data were collected through questionnaires, document reviews, and observations from 150 bank staff and 22 bank customers, all from 9 banks. SPSS® 21.0 performed the Exploratory Factor Analysis (EFA). EFA results were subjected to Confirmatory Factor Analysis (CFA) in AMOS version 21.0 to confirm their usefulness by testing their relationship's strength. The findings indicate that the overall readiness level is 3.54 out of 5, demonstrating a medium level of adaptation readiness. Such readiness level signifies that manual interventions augment some degree of I4.0 adaptation in implementing TQM in banks. The confirmed driving factors for the TQM 4.0 adaptation include legislation, political will, strategy, and policy. Ultimately, this study proposed a TQM 4.0 adaptation framework for the banking sector.

Keywords Total Quality Management · Total Quality Management 4.0 · TQM 4.0 · Industry 4.0 · Industry 4.0 technologies · Operational excellence · Banking Sector · TQM 4.0 Framework

---

M. B. Mwesiga
Department of Engineering Management Studies, Mzumbe University, Morogoro, Tanzania

M. B. Mwesiga · I. W. R. Taifa (✉)
Department of Mechanical and Industrial Engineering, College of Engineering and Technology, University of Dar Es Salaam, Dar Es Salaam, Tanzania
e-mail: itaifa@udsm.ac.tz; taifaismail@yahoo.com

I. Mukherjee et al. (eds.), *Decision Sciences for Quality and Productivity Improvement*,
https://doi.org/10.1007/978-981-95-7545-9_3

3.1 Introduction

The astounding advancement of new industrial technologies has changed economies and societies' sustainability, the design of services, and their strategic position in the development process (Pakkala & Spohrer, 2019). In today's globalised world, pursuing high quality products and services necessitates companies taking advantage of new industrial technologies (Baran & Polat, 2022). Most organisations in developed economies have adopted fourth industrial revolution (FIR) technologies to address new global market challenges (Ebiringa, 2018). FIR is linked to Industry 4.0 (I4.0) (Baran & Polat, 2022). Quality management (QM) has proven effective in planning, implementing, managingand boosting firm efficiency, productivity improvement, operational excellence, business excellence, and competitiveness during societal change (Dias et al., 2022). Offering higher quality at lower prices has become a strategic tactic for establishing and preserving a competitive position for many commercial enterprises throughout the universe. Maganga and Taifa (2023a, 2024) revealed that QM practices can be renewed and improved attributable to the FIR.

I4.0 involves the integration of intelligent digital technologies into the operations or processes of various sectors, such as manufacturing, service, transportation, and supply chain. I4.0 was preceded by Industry (I1.0) to Industry (I3.0) as the first to the third industrial revolutions, respectively (Taifa et al., 2020, 2021). Some commonly integrated technologies include the Internet of Things (IoT), Artificial Intelligence (AI), big data analytics (BDA), industrial robotics (IRs), vertical and horizontal systems integration, collaborative robots (Cobots), Cyber-Physical Systems (CPS) and additive manufacturing (3D printing) (AM) (Jakobo & Taifa, 2025). Other technologies are such as virtual reality (VR), cloud computing (CC), smart sensors (SSs), virtual factory (VF), smart factory (SF), computer simulation, machine learning (ML), digital twins (DTs), cybersecurity, augmented reality (AR), drones, automated guided vehicles (AGVs), and blockchain (Maganga & Taifa, 2023a).

In modern times, quality is more frequently seen in a larger context; the most commonly used term is Total Quality Management (TQM), which refers to all internal processes, operations and the involvement of everyone in the organisation in ensuring quality (Al-Shobaki et al., 2010). TQM is a vital management concept for all organisations that desire competitive advantages (Nguyen et al., 2023). TQM is part of the quality revolution (QR) (Broday, 2022), as it originates from quality inspection (QI), quality control (QC), quality assurance (QA) and ultimately the TQM concepts (Maganga & Taifa, 2023a). Due to the emergence of the FIR, I4.0-leveraged technologies have impacted all organisations, including service, transport, supply, and manufacturing globally. In those organisations, researchers have explored the role of I4.0. For example, Nzumile et al., (2024a, 2024b) explored the role of I4.0 in metrology fields, I4.0 in textile (Gökalp et al., 2018), transportation sector (Rojko, 2017), supply sector/field (Cañas et al., 2020), manufacturing sector (Ntamulyango, 2023), among others. For quality-related fields, there are studies including Antony et al. (2022), Viharos et al. (2017), Maganga and Taifa (2023b, 2023c), and Radziwill (2018), among many. However, there are limited studies on the adaptation of I4.0

for enhancing TQM in the banking sector, thus resulting in the term "TQM 4.0". Theoretical underpinnings have reviewed the concepts, principles, and technologies of Quality 4.0 (Q4.0) as they are adapted from I4.0. Likewise, researchers agree that there is no major difference between Q4.0 and TQM 4.0 when discussed from the I4.0 point of view. For example, Nguyen et al. (2023) classified the application of I4.0 for TQM by using TQM 4.0 and Q4.0 interchangeably. Thus, this study defines TQM 4.0 as an "improved approach to QM in which new technologies are integrated with traditional quality methods (QC, QA, and TQM) to widen the QM scope and boost quality activities" (Nguyen et al., 2023). Some key concepts on the relationship between industrial revolutions (IRs), inventions, quality revolution and their goals are presented in Fig. 3.1.

TQM 4.0 is simply QM in the current I4.0 era (Kulenović et al., 2021). I4.0 for QM can enhance customer focus and satisfaction, better competitive position, higher productivity, elimination of defects and waste, low costs, and higher profitability (Saha et al., 2022; Nguyen et al., 2023). I4.0 has been employed in several manufacturing-related businesses and is gaining traction in the service sector, including insurance, hospitality, aviation, health and banking (Jha, 2016).

Over two-thirds of the labour force on the African continent is employed in the services sector as a significant source of income for the populace (Magoti & Mtui, 2020). There is an increasing need for acceptable quality among service providers due to the significance of the service sector in emerging economies. The benefits are not always trivial to achieve, given that, in reality, implementing I4.0 is a complex and challenging process: two-thirds of TQM adoption attempts are unsuccessful (Amaechi & Sylva, 2021). Moreover, the adaptation of I4.0 for QM or TQM is used

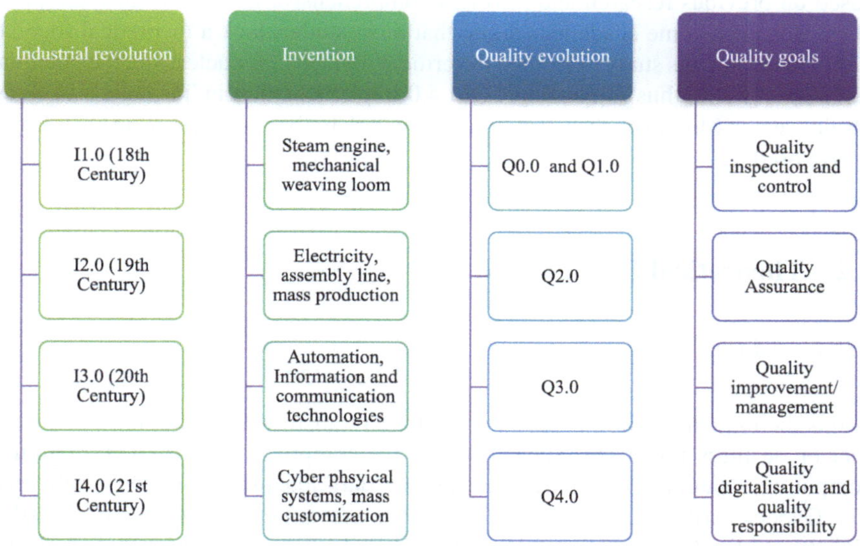

Fig. 3.1 I4.0, quality revolution and their goals. *Source* Created by the authors

in manufacturing and services, but only a few studies have focused on the service sector despite its importance (Kulenović et al., 2021).

According to Maganga and Taifa (2023a), the evolution of quality in Tanzania organisations has lagged behind technological advancements, especially now that the globe is in the I4.0 age. Globalisation's impact on the corporate environment has forced firms to pay more attention to their management strategies (Akhmatova et al., 2022; Magd et al., 2021; Sader et al., 2019). During the FIR, TQM underwent a fundamental transition, expanding beyond the manufacturing industry to encompass service sectors such as the government, healthcare, education, and financial institutions (Baran & Polat, 2022). So, service quality implications are expanding, regardless of the product or service industry. The banking industry operates in a fast-evolving technology environment, where technology is one of the most essential components for achieving long-term growth (Sonono & Ortstad, 2017).

Due to the digital transformation for all organisations, the current banking models may not be sustained for long because customers are shifting towards using digital tools, systems, and models. For example, MoF (2023) mentioned the service sector as the largest contributor to the national economy. However, operational inefficiencies and substandard customer service have consistently been present in Tanzania's service sector (Nyangarika, 2016). Nonetheless, it is widely acknowledged that the banking sector, which often involves significant information technology (IT), requires special attention due to its importance to the overall economy. However, there has been little research on the banking sector (Osei et al., 2023).

Additionally, much research describing Q4.0 or TQM 4.0 is still in the early stages. An inclusive explanation of TQM 4.0, concentrating on TQM 4.0 practices, is hardly explored. It is crucial to determine the most important TQM 4.0 activities based on previous research and having a comprehensive framework of these practices. However, some academics argue that most studies lack a theoretical foundation. Therefore, this study examined the critical variables characterising the potential for adapting I4.0, thus suggesting TQM 4.0 implementation in Tanzania's banking service sector. Moreover, the adaptation framework for banks operating in the country is proposed.

3.2 Theoretical Background

3.2.1 I4.0

I4.0 is the implementation of technology-driven transformation that impacts industrial or business processes. Such technologies comprise AI, ML, AM, cognitive computing, quantum computing, IRs, VF, SF, dark manufacturing, DTs, SSs, IoT, VR, Cybersecurity, BDA, CC, and CPSs, computer simulation (CS) (Rojko, 2017; Gökalp et al., 2018; Cañas et al., 2020; Ntamulyango, 2023; Maganga & Taifa,

2023a), among others. The introduction of water steam power during the first IR facilitated the mechanisation of the production process. The late 1800s saw the second IR, characterised by mass manufacturing, assembly lines, and workforce modernisation made possible by the arrival of electricity (Nhelekwa et al., 2024). The third IR in the twentieth century enabled computers, information technology (IT), and electronics (Maganga & Taifa, 2023c).

According to McKinsey (2019), financial institutions' most popular AI technologies are chatbots and virtual assistants for customer service, robotic process automation for handling repetitive tasks, and machine learning techniques for preventing scams and mitigating risk. Furthermore, AI has effectively detected credit card fraud, which has increased dramatically in recent years due to the growth of e-commerce and online transactions (Nasrallah, 2023). VR is an integrated information technology that combines many technologies such as computer graphics and image processing, sensors, multimedia, Internet, human–computer interaction, and simulation systems (Rana, 2023). According to Yang (2023), one of the main draws of VR technology for financial institutions is its ability to deliver dull content to users in the form of vision and turn it into an immersive experience. This makes it easier for users to comprehend financial products, streamline business processes, and increase institutional performance.

IoT is the network of appliances and other objects with embedded sensors, electronics, software, actuators and connectivity that enable data sharing (Rizvi, 2020). Using IoT-enabled easy computation of the average wait time to suggest the optimal staffing level and number of counters at each branch (Kumar, 2019). Additionally, the number and sophistication of cyber-attacks against financial services businesses are increasing (Lawsky, 2014). Almost all institutions, regardless of size, reported using some or all of the following tools: server-based access control lists, firewalls, intrusion detection systems, antivirus software, spyware and malware detection, intrusion prevention systems, vulnerability scanning tools, encryption for transit data, and encrypted files (Shaaban & Athumani, 2020). "Big data" refers to collecting and analysing enormous volumes of structured and unstructured data (Nzumile, Mahabi et al., 2024a, 2024b). In the banking industry, "big data" refers to using technology and software with sophisticated algorithms and techniques to predict risk and income, obtain deeper insights, and make more educated decisions (Doko & Miskovski, 2019).

3.2.2 Tqm 4.0

TQM is a management tool with principles and philosophy that can be deployed to all organisational processes, operations, and functions to continually raise the bar for customer satisfaction (Ezenyilimba et al., 2019). According to Zainun (2018), the phrase TQM is broken down into two terms: "Quality", which refers to customer compliance or fitness for use (James & Taifa, 2023), and "Total", which refers to all operations in which each individual in a corporation is guided by quality. The implementation of the QM strategy preexisted the product inspection process throughout the First and Second IRs (Hyun Park et al., 2017). Engineering professionals employed Statistical process control (SPC) tools, for example, scatter diagrams, flowcharts, cause-and-effect diagrams, histograms, control charts, Pareto charts, and checklists (Hussein & Taifa, 2024; Kitsovi & Taifa, 2024; Taifa, Makundi et al., 2021a, 2021b). SPCs blossomed during the third IR and served as a foundation for creating numerous more approaches, such as Robust Design and Design of Experiments (DOE) approaches (Deshpande et al., 2021). TQM 4.0 is an upgraded structured method to QM that enlarges QM scope and enhances quality operations by combining novel technology with tried-and-true quality methods (Ali et al., 2022). Fening and Boateng-Okrah (2017) determined the critical success criteria for TQM. These include top management commitment, customer focus, leadership, organisation policy, training and skills, and continuous improvement.

3.2.3 TQM 4.0 Adaptation Frameworks in the Banking Sector

A framework methodically identifies and arranges latent and observable variables to provide a structure that either assesses, creates transition, or implements to influence desired results (Maganga & Taifa, 2023b). The TQM 4.0 adaptation framework is built on TQM 4.0 practices. Establishing a TQM 4.0 framework requires both technological and social elements. The TQM 4.0 technical framework elements use I4.0 technologies such as CPS, AI, ML, autonomous robotics, BDA, CC, and IoT. Social components include qualities of people as well as cultural structure (Nguyen et al., 2023).

Mehdiabadi et al. (2020) documented that I4.0 banking strategies should first be recognised in the existing business setting. A schedule must be established to build the infrastructure and cultivate user interactions. The FIR should be provided with the digital readiness and acceptance program, digital culture, human capital, regulations, technologies and capabilities, and networking in compliance with the global schedule. Pog and Dovleac (2021) documented that many factors are needed when digitalising the banking industry. Such factors include data quality of the framework, customer segments, nature of products and services, nature of the needed operations, and the quality and quantity of the needed data.

Ebiringa (2018) explained key banking services that determine the quality of service, including processing time for loans, new accounts, ATM cards, credit cards, and check encashment; waiting times when the server is down; and queuing time for customers. Other issues include effective interest rates inclusive of all hidden charges and service; statements of accounts and records timeliness and accuracy; efficiency and friendliness; quickness in responding to consumer enquiries, including how quickly the phone is answered, how many rings pass before it is picked up, and how many transfers are necessary until the caller is connected with the appropriate person and lost customer accounts. Table 3.1 summarises the key aspects of TQM 4.0 frameworks developed by authors, and Table 3.2 shows the association between TQM 4.0 practices and the banking sector's performance.

Table 3.1 TQM 4.0 frameworks

Model	Nguyen et al. (2023)	Mehdiabadi et al. (2020)	Pog and Dovleac (2021)
Model focus	TQM 4.0 Framework: Present and Future	Designing a Roadmap for Banking Systems in I4.0	Implementation and impact of I4.0 and Q4.0 in the banking sector
Key aspects	I4.0/Q4.0 technologies	I4.0 technologies and design principles	I4.0 technologies
Model limitations	Absence of practical guidance on how to transition to Q4.0	The model does not provide a clear pathway for firms' adaptation to Banking 4.0	Q4.0 major elements are partially involved in the model

Source Created by the authors

Table 3.2 Relationship between TQM 4.0 and the performance of the banking sector

Source	TQM 4.0 Practices	Effects of TQM 4.0 on the banking sector
Ezenyilimba et al. (2019)	Top management commitment, Customer-focused, customer loyalty and teamwork	TQM has helped in attaining enhanced quality products and eliminating cost
Testa et al. (2023)	Focusing on customers, employee involvement, continuous improvement	TQM practices positively influence the performance of commercial banks
Ali et al. (2019)	Top management communicates, staff involvement, continuous improvement and customer satisfaction	TQM practices gradually improve the efficiency of service, quality of activity, and amount of profit
Ebiringa (2018)	Employee empowerment, continuous improvement and customer focus	TQM influence the sustainability of the banking sector if efforts are made, including proper training and engaging all stakeholders
Magd et al. (2021)	Commitment from the management and leadership; strategic planning; focus on clients and satisfaction	TQM practices have a strong linkage to organisational performance
Philip (2021)	Process management and customer focus, information analysis, strategic management, leadership commitment, people management	Quality measures and TQM practices can influence the performance of service and manufacturing organisations

Source Created by the authors

3.3 Methodology

3.3.1 Research Design and Sampling Design

A mixed-method approach was designed to collect qualitative and quantitative data. Regarding the study's population, the regions with the most active bank branches include Mbeya, Kilimanjaro, Dar es Salaam, Arusha and Mwanza, accounting for fifty-two percent of all active branches in Tanzania (African Economic Research Consortium, 2023). Therefore, this study involved the population of bank branches from Dar es Salaam and Mbeya regions. Customers and employees of 9 commercial banks contained the population of this study. The Dar es Salaam Stock Exchange (DSE) listed the chosen banks.

The study used a stratified sampling approach to get data from bank employees whereby every member of the population has a chance of being chosen. Conversely, this study used quota sampling to obtain data from bank customers, whereby the selected customers shared specific characteristics like age group, demographic location, and frequency of banking service use. According to Kothari (2004), a 10–30% sample is sufficient to reflect a target population. Also, data from the Bank of Tanzania showed that the country had 34 commercial banks by May 2023. Therefore, the study used stratified random sampling to choose 26% of the total population of 34 commercial banks, resulting in a sample size of 9 banks. The population of the study (bank staff and customers) is infinite, so the study applied Cochran's equation of infinite population to establish the required sample size using Eq. (3.1).

$$S_s = \frac{z^2 \times p \times q}{e^2} \tag{3.1}$$

where S_S = the required sample size, p = the estimated proportion of a characteristic existing amongst the bank sector's stakeholders, $q = 1\text{-}p$, Z = selected critical value of the chosen confidence level, and e = the desired level of precision expressed in decimal. Using a 95% confidence level with ± 10% precision; $Z = 1.96$; $e = 0.1$; $p = 0.5$ and $q = 1 - 0.5 = 0.5$

Therefore, the sample size of this study was one hundred and seventy-two bank staff and customers. Table 3.3 illustrates the categories of this study population sample for bank employees and their customers from Dar es Salaam and Mbeya regions.

3.3.2 Data Collection and Analysis

Two methods collected data. The observation method was utilised to observe the physical deployment of I4.0 technologies at various bank branches visited during the study's field survey. A closed-ended questionnaire comprised a series of questions

Table 3.3 Sample size categories in the Mbeya and Dar es Salaam regions

Category of bank staff and customers	Population	Sampling Design	Mbeya		Dar es Salaam	
			Sample size per bank	**Total sample size**	**Sample size per bank**	**Total sample size**
Management staffs	Undefined	Stratified sampling	3	27	3	27
Tellers			3	30	3	30
Technical staffs			2	18	2	18
Customers		Quota sampling	1	11	1	11
Total			9	86	9	86

Source Created by the authors

printed or typed in a specific order on a form or set of forms. The bank employees' questionnaire was divided into the following sections: general demographic and employment information, TQM 4.0 adaptation readiness factors, TQM 4.0 driving forces, applied I4.0 technologies, and staff required digital skills. In contrast, the bank customers' questionnaire was divided into five categories. These included demographics, digital banking service utilisation frequency, perceived service quality offered by the bank and challenges and opportunities for technology adaptation. Questions required a Likert scale response, in which respondents rated their level of agreement with statements on a scale of one to five, with (1) indicating strongly disagree, (2) indicating disagree, (3) indicating neutral, (4) indicating agree, and (5) indicating strongly agree. Collected data were examined using SPSS 21.0. Exploratory Factor Analysis (EFA) was conducted in SPSS 21.0 to determine whether the factors were measuring their respective variables. EFA results were subjected to CFA in AMOS 21.0 to confirm their usefulness by testing their relationship's strength.

3.3.3 Adaptation Framework Development Process

Data from the qualitative study, such as TQM 4.0 awareness, technical adaptation level, driving forces, and setbacks for TQM 4.0 adaptation, were used to construct the framework using the approaches shown in Fig. 3.2. A survey determined the characteristics, components, technology enablers, obstacles, and success factors for developing an adaptation framework.

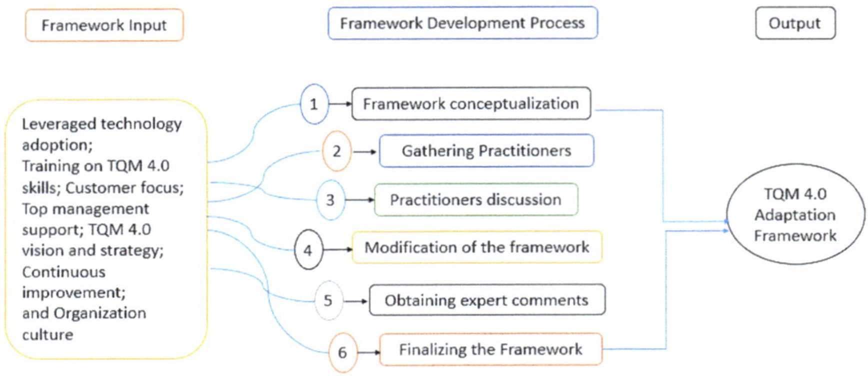

Fig. 3.2 Framework development process. *Source* Created by the authors

Table 3.4 Reliability test results for the collected data

Assessment dimension	No. of items	CA coefficient
TQM 4.0 Adaptation Readiness	14	0.842
TQM 4.0 Driving forces	16	0.773

Source Created by the authors

3.4 Results and Discussion

3.4.1 Validity and Reliability Test

Reliability was conducted in SPSS 21.0 to assess the consistency of data collected. Data reliability was established by determining Cronbach's Alpha (CA) values. When the variables or dimensions have a CA value of at least 0.7, this indicates acceptable internal consistency of the measured data (McNeish et al., 2018). The CA value for the collected data in this study, depicted in Table 3.4, illustrates the reliability test results where all variables meet the minimum values.

3.4.2 Profile of the Respondents

Among the twenty-two customers who responded, 52% were women, and 48% were men. 45.0% of respondents were between the ages of 18 and 25, 26–35 (35.5%), 36–45 (9%), 46–55 (7.5%), and 3% were above 55. Furthermore, 3.5% of all customer respondents had a primary school education, high school (4.5%), an undergraduate degree (55.5%), 23% had a master's degree, and 13.5% had a PhD. Of the 150 bank staff, 44% were women, and 56% were men. Twenty percent were between the ages of 18 and 25, 26–35 (48.5%), 36–45 (19.5%), 46–55 (7.5%), and above 55 (5%).

Table 3.5 MSA results for TQM 4.0 adaptation readiness

KMO and Bartlett's Test		
KMO MSA		0.569
Bartlett's Test of Sphericity	Approx. Chi-Square/df/Sig	1261.364/91/.000

Source Created by the authors

Educational-wise, 61.5% had an undergraduate degree level, a master's degree level (36%), and 3.5% had a PhD.

3.4.3 *TQM 4.0 Adaptation Readiness in Tanzania Banking Sector*

3.4.3.1 Measure of Sampling Adequacy (MSA)

MSA was measured in SPSS 21.0 through the Kaiser-Meyer Olkin (KMO) test. For the suitability of collected data to perform factor analysis, the KMO value must be greater than 0.5 (Fang et al., 2020). The KMO value for the adaptation redness was 0.569, which indicates that the data was suitable for factor analysis (Mange & Taifa, 2026), as illustrated in Table 3.5.

3.4.3.2 Descriptive Analysis for TQM 4.0 Adaptation Readiness

The overall readiness level is 3.54 out of 5, signifying a medium level of readiness. This value means that banks are willing but are required to improve their capabilities to integrate and deploy TQM 4.0 practices in their business and technical practices.

3.4.3.3 EFA for TQM 4.0 Adaptation

EFA was conducted in SPSS 21.0 to assess the adaptation readiness of Tanzania's bank sector. The rotated matrix explains each factor's loading to their respective construct. EFA results extracted 7 variables from data confirming the suggested variables because their loadings were higher than 0.5 (Shrestha, 2021). Table 3.6 shows EFA results for the TQM 4.0 adaptation readiness.

Seven variables extracted from EFA explained 85.5% of total variations in the TQM 4.0 adaptation readiness of Tanzania's banking sector; as a rule of thumb, variables to be extracted from an EFA must have Eigenvalues ≥ 1 (McNeish et al., 2018). Figure 3.3 illustrates the Eigenvalues for the variables associated with the EFA, whereby only seven variables had Eigen values which meet the criterion of one and above.

Table 3.6 EFA results in adaptation readiness

Factors codes	Component						
	1	2	3	4	5	6	7
TA1	0.916						
TA2	0.957						
I1		0.970					
I2		0.943					
VS1			0.916				
VS2			0.934				
AW1				0.862			
AW2				0.839			
GS1					0.848		
GS2					0.893		
AW1						0.778	
AW2						0.931	
TA1							0.814
TA2							0.853

Source Created by the authors

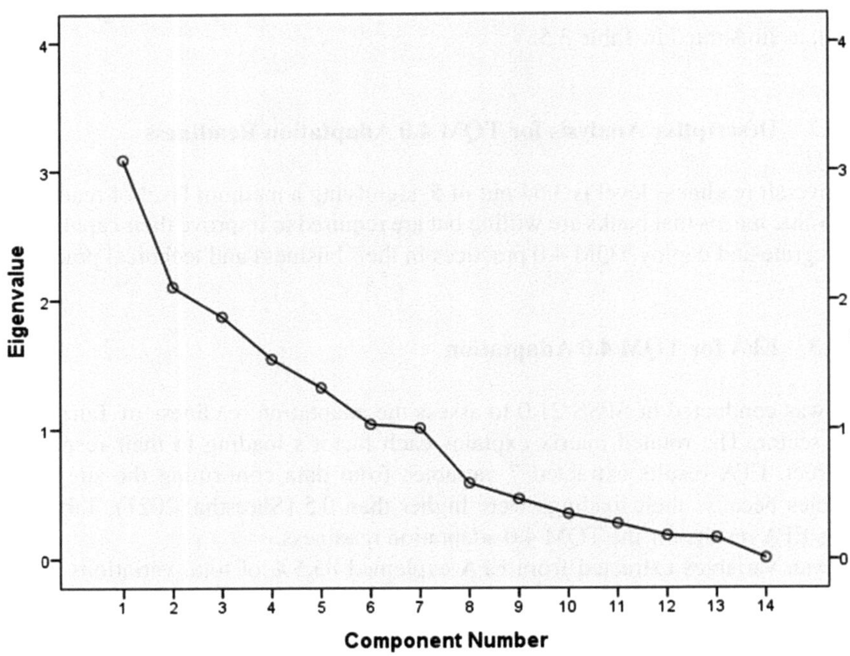

Fig. 3.3 Eigenvalues for TQM 4.0 adaptation readiness in Tanzania banking sector. *Source* Created by the authors

3.4.3.4 CFA for TQM 4.0 Adaptation Readiness in Tanzania Banking Sector

After conducting EFA, the next step was to confirm the extent to which each factor measures its respective constructs. A CFA model was built in AMOS 21.0 software for the variables and factors acquired from the EFA results. CFA was conducted based on minimum standardised factor loadings (SFLs) of 0.5 for each factor, explaining how each factor can affect the variations of the latent variable it measures (Marsh et al., 2020). The results of CFA confirmed all factors to be helpful in assessing the TQM 4.0 adaptation readiness in Tanzania's banking sector.

Thus the variables for adaptation of TQM 4.0 and their respective factors as revealed by both EFA and CFA include (i) Infrastructure with (I1) availability of tools and equipment needed to work effectively with I4.0 QM technologies (I2) existence of ICT systems to support data processing and decision making, (ii) Training and Skills with (TS1) sufficient skills to cope with adaptation of digital QM technologies and (TS2) training on how to adapt I4.0 QM technologies, (iii) Mission, vision and strategy with (VS1) organisation's clear strategies to ensure high quality of products/services and (VS2) alignment of I4.0 with organisation mission, vision, and strategy, (iv) Financial set-up with (FS1) a strong financial base for adaptation and use of I4.0 QM technologies and (FS2) financial strength for successful adaptation of advanced QM technologies, (v) Government set-up with (GS1) policy measures for importation and transfer of advanced QM technologies in Tanzania and (GS2) government's role in ensuring successful adaptation of I4.0 technologies for bank firms in Tanzania, (vi) Awareness with (AW1) awareness of the benefits of adopting I4.0 technologies and (AW2) aware of the current technologies associated with I4.0, and (vii) Technology Adoption with (TA1) digitisation of firm to facilitate quality of products and services (TA2) reliable IT set up in the organisation. Figure 3.4 illustrates the structural equation model path diagram.

The model fit test was conducted to understand how well a model generalises to data similar to that which it was supposed to measure. A well-fitted model matches the data too closely and produces a more accurate outcome. The TQM 4.0 adoption readiness model was tested based on the Comparative fit Index (CFI), root mean square error of approximation (RMSEA), good-of-fit index (GFI), standardised root mean square residual (SRMR), and adjusted good-of-fit index (AGFI). The criteria for the goodness of the model are RMSEA ≤ 0.06, CFI ≥ 0.95 (Shi et al., 2019), AGFI ≥ 0.90 (Afthanorhan et al., 2019), SRMR ≤ 0.08, GFI ≥ 0.90 (Cho et al., 2020). The initial model did not achieve a goodness of model with model indices values not matching the required values for a good model. The model was improved through the fitting process (covariance and regressions) and retested for its fitness, and the second test revealed a good model fit for all model fit indices. The convergent validity of the model was found to be acceptable, with AVE values above 0.5 for each construct (Zailani et al., 2018). This result establishes the model's reliability as all values meet the preset criterion (Table 3.7).

The discriminant validity (DV) is a measurement showing how unrelated constructs are truly unrelated; as opposed to convergent validity, the DV uses a

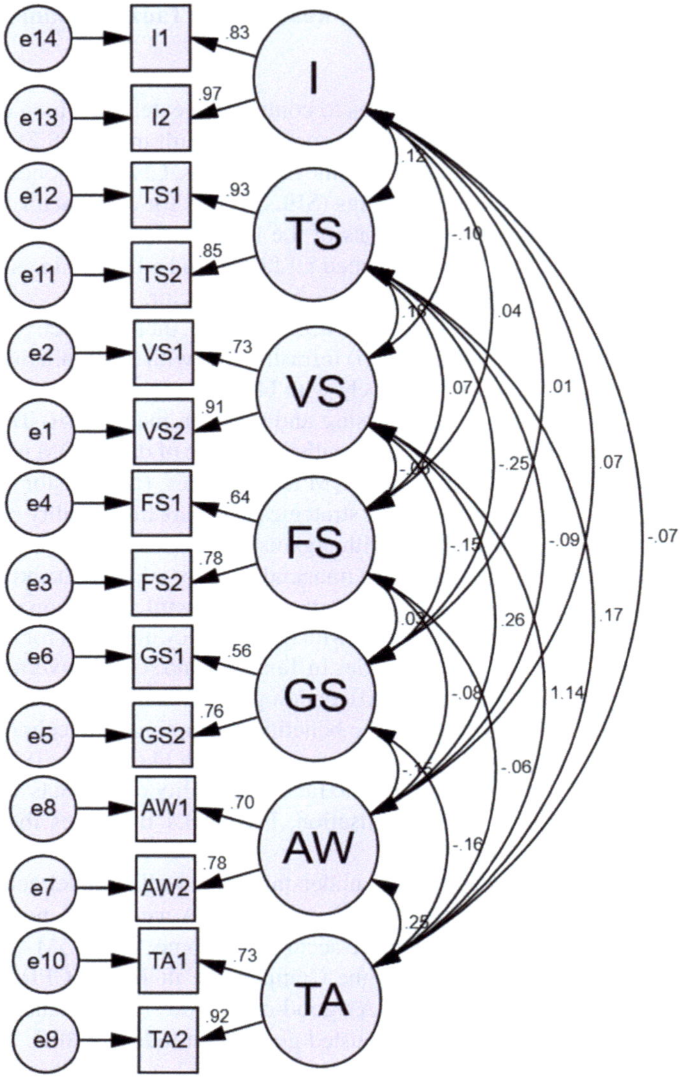

Fig. 3.4 Structural equation model path diagram adaptation readiness. *Source* Created by the authors

correlation coefficient to show the relationship among variables. The correlation coefficient between unrelated variables should be low for good DV. Moreover, the correlation coefficients for each construct must be less than the square root of AVE (bold diagonal values). As per Hodson (2021), there are limited studies which can prove the standard value for DV. However, a value less than 0.70 recommends that

Table 3.7 Reliability and convergent validity of TQM 4.0 adoption readiness model

Variable	CR	AVE	Initial Model	Revised Model
Awareness (AW)	0.707	0.548	CFI = 0.821 RMSEA = 0.149 GFI = 0.804 SRMR = 0.175 AGFI = 0.771	CFI = 0.953 RMSEA = 0.007 GFI = 0.960 SRMR = 0.067 AGFI = 0.920
Infrastructure (I)	0.897	0.814		
Training and Skills (TS)	0.885	0.794		
Vision and Strategy (VS)	0.813	0.687		
Financial Set-up (FS)	0.772	0.507		
Government Set-up (GS)	0.713	0.559		
Technology Adoption (TA)	0.813	0.683		

Source Created by the authors

Table 3.8 DV of the TQM 4.0 model

Variable	AW	I	TS	VS	FS	GS	TA
AW	**0.740**						
I	0.472	**0.902**					
TS	0.092	0.116	**0.891**				
VS	0.255	0.100	0.177	**0.829**			
FS	0.380	0.037	0.070	0.054	**0.712**		
GS	0.149	0.009	0.251	0.555	0.030	**0.748**	
TA	0.248	0.074	0.173	0.143	0.062	0.156	**0.829**

Source Created by the authors

DV probably exists between the measured items (Hodson, 2021). This criterion was met, as illustrated in Table 3.8, indicating an acceptable DV.

3.4.4 Driving Forces for TQM 4.0 Adaptation

Regression Analysis Results: The results from the model summary show a very positive relationship between the dependent variable and other independent variables, where R is 0.714 and R^2 is 0.507. The value of the Adjusted R Square was 0.479. Table 3.9 illustrates the model summary results. Table 3.10 summarizes the coefficient values of the obtained variables. The coefficient of determination (R^2) shows a number between 0 and 1 that measures how well a statistical model forecasts the results. When R-squared = 1, this indicates that the regression predictions perfectly fit the measured or collected data; R-squared = 0: the independent variables do not explain any of the variability, while R-squared = 0.50: the model's variables can explain nearly half of the observed differences. Therefore, the R^2 is acceptable because it is between 1 and 0.50. Also, all *t*-values are at least 1.96; thus, the predictors' values are acceptable because the higher the *t*-values, the greater the confidence of the analyzed data (Danguche & Taifa, 2023).

Top management commitment influences the adaptation of TQM 4.0 in the banking sector ($\beta = 0.249$). The study's findings confirmed that senior bank managers should control the implementation of TQM 4.0. *Continuous improvement* ($\beta = 0.256$) is another major driving force influencing the adaptation of TQM 4.0 in the banking sector. The major driving force influencing the adaptation of TQM 4.0 in the banking sector is *teamwork and collaboration* ($\beta = 0.266$). This is because the success of ensuring that every individual maintains quality at the source requires a high degree of collaboration between the management, staff, and clients.

Table 3.9 Model summary

Model	R	R Square	Adjusted R Square	Std. Error of the Estimate
1	0.714[a]	0.5097	0.479	0.781

[a] Predictors: (Constant), Top management commitment, Teamwork and Collaboration, Leadership, Leveraged Technology Adoption, Continuous Improvement, Customers and Suppliers integration, Organisation Policy, Customer Focus
Source Created by the authors

Table 3.10 Regression coefficients

Model		Unstandardised Coefficients		Standardised Coefficients	t	Sig
		B	Std. Error	Beta		
1	(Constant)	0.360	0.508		0. 000	0.000
	Organisation Culture	0.125	0.272	0.254	3.511	0.000
	Organisation Policy	0.321	0.242	0.246	2.691	0.000
	Leveraged Technology Adoption	0.142	0.246	0.194	6.631	0.000
	Teamwork and Collaboration	0.230	0.302	0.266	8.329	0.000
	Leadership	0.151	0.213	0.213	4.803	0.000
	Continuous Improvement	0.422	0.267	0.256	8.453	0.000
	Customer Focus	0.268	0.163	0.256	3.411	0.000
	Top management commitment	0.021	0.372	0.249	2.816	0.000

[a] Dependent Variable: TQM
Source Created by the authors

Leadership ($\beta = 0.213$) is also a driving force influencing the adaptation of TQM 4.0 in the banking sector. The study's findings showed that to keep up with the quick speed of technological change, bank managers are beginning to understand the value of cultivating a culture of continuous learning and equipping their staff with the abilities needed to thrive in the fiercely competitive business environment.

Organisation policy significantly influenced the adaptation of TQM 4.0 with (β value of.246). This study showed that some banks have explicitly included QN objectives in their employees' annual goals. Also, the study's results demonstrate a strong correlation between I4.0 banking service quality and *technology adoption* with (β value of.194). According to the respondents, using technology can help firms easily discover and prevent problems earlier, which improves customer happiness and product quality. Furthermore, most bank managers surveyed elucidated how I4.0 technologies enhance the efficacy of QM systems by providing instantaneous data insights and facilitating enhanced decision-making.

Organisation culture: How individuals behave within the firm (culture) significantly influenced adaptation of TQM 4.0 ($\beta = 0.254$). According to the respondents, a perfect organisational culture incorporates aspects of community culture: a creative and inventive culture and an inwardly-centred, familial culture prioritising employee relationships. The three most crucial efficiency requirements are taking risks, being creatively free, and innovating and developing.

3.4.5 CFA for Driving Forces

The minimum SFL for a CFA model is 0.5 (Marsh et al., 2020). (TC1) Interdisciplinary and interdepartmental collaboration within the organisation and (TC2) collaboration with partners, suppliers and clients to develop products and services had SFLs of 0.14 and 0.31, respectively, failing to meet the minimum SFL criteria; hence, they were dropped. Dropping those factors meant dropping their latent variable, i.e., Teamwork and collaboration (TC). Figure 3.5 depicts CFA results for driving forces.

The fitness of the driving force model was conducted in AMOS 21.0 with the same procedures as that of the readiness model. The initial mode did not achieve a good fit as its model fit indices did not match the recommended values as cited: RMSEA ≤ 0.06, CFI ≥ 0.95 (Shi et al., 2019), AGFI ≥ 0.90 (Afthanorhan et al., 2019), SRMR ≤ 0.08, GFI ≥ 0.90 (Cho et al., 2020). The model was fitted through a regression weight line from (CF1). All processes and operations at the organisation are aimed at meeting customers' demands to (CS1) services are data-driven, creating the association between the factors, i.e., which drastically improved the mode fit by 74 (M.I). The modified model had its indices improved and met the required goodness of the model, as seen in Table 3.11. Also, the convergent validity of the model was acceptable, with AVE values for each construct meeting the criterion of AVE ≥ 0.5. Likewise, the discriminant validity (DV) of the driving force model in Table 3.12 indicates a good DV since all values are above 0.7 (Hodson, 2021).

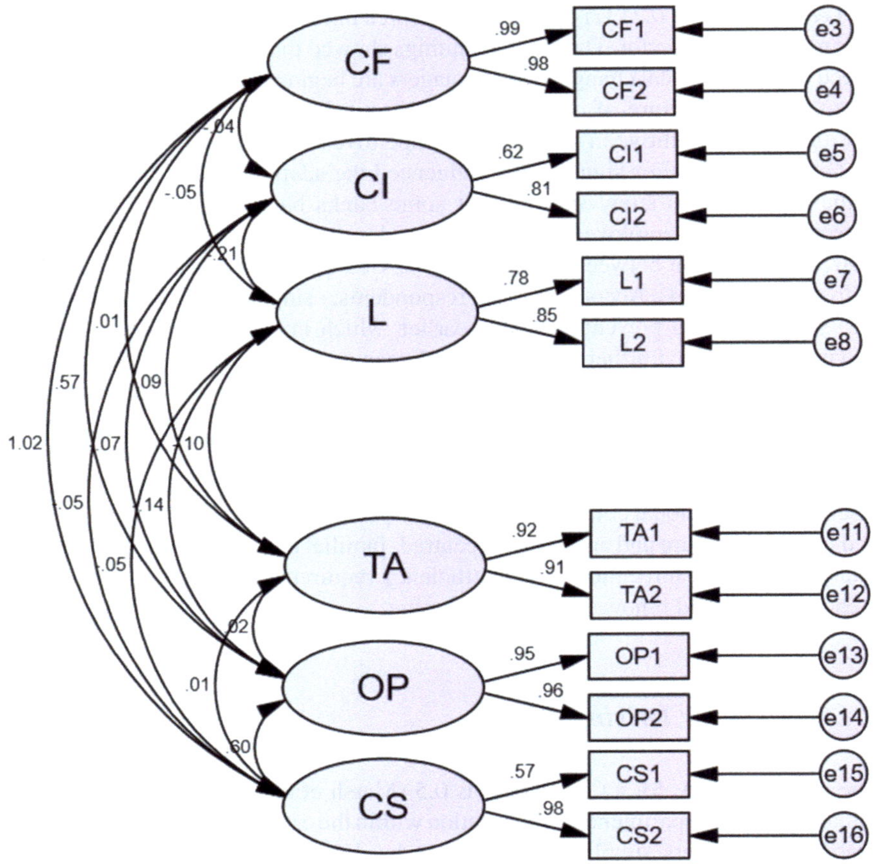

Fig. 3.5 Structural equation mod.el path diagram for driving forces. *Source* Created by the authors

Table 3.11 Reliability and convergent validity of driving force model

Variable	CR	AVE	Initial model	Fitted model
Organisation Policy (OP)	0.956	0.916	CFI = 0.940 RMSEA = 0.104 GFI = 0.892 SRMR = 0.1164 AGFI = 0.817	CFI = 1.000 RMSEA = 0.000 GFI = 0.967 SRMR = 0.0249 AGFI = 0.940
Customer Focus (CF)	0.988	0.976		
Continuous Improvement (CI)	0.779	0.519		
Leadership (L)	0.799	0.665		
Technology Adoption (TA)	0.915	0.843		
Customer supplier integration (CS)	0.816	0.839		

Source Created by the authors

Table 3.12 DV of driving force model

Variable	OP	CF	CI	L	TA	CS
OP	**0.957**					
CF	0.373	**0.988**				
CI	– 0.072	– 0.036	**0.720**			
L	– 0.136	– 0.049	−0.214	**0.816**		
TA	0.016	0.014	0.087	−0.095	**0.918**	
CS	0.290	0.107	−0.053	−0.049	0.011	**0.916**

Source Created by the authors

3.4.6 TQM 4.0 Adaptation Framework

Figure 3.6 illustrates the key steps that provide a framework for all banks in Tanzania to effectively implement TQM 4.0 by adapting I4.0 technologies in their business strategies and operations. The framework validation involved practitioners' views. Bank managers, quality experts, IT experts, and other bank staff were engaged in group discussions. This resulted in modification of the developed framework, which was returned to bank practitioners and experts for obtaining their views, comments and recommendations. Finally, the current framework was developed to adapt TQM 4.0 for the banking sector in Tanzania.

The proposed adaptation framework is designed for the collaborative application of managers, quality experts, IT experts, bank staff and customers. The implementation of the framework includes the following steps: First, the firm must ensure a high level of readiness to adapt I4.0 technologies in its business strategies and processes. This involves incorporating readiness factors, including awareness, infrastructure, technology adoption, training and skills, financial set-up and vision, mission, and strategies of the organisation. Initially, the firm must increase its awareness of the existence and benefits of deploying digital technologies. Then, I4.0 should be incorporated within the vision and core values of the organisation. In addition, there should be a strong financial base for adapting and implementing technologies. Moreover, the management must ensure regular training and skills development programs to equip staff with competencies to use I4.0 technologies.

Secondly, the firm should apply TQM 4.0 driving forces, including top management commitment, leadership, customer focus, continuous improvement, teamwork and collaboration, and supplier integration. A key component of implementing I4.0 in businesses is leadership. A banking leader manages the organisation's vision and strategy and ensures that the bank's goals follow client expectations, regulatory regulations, and market developments. Teamwork and collaboration are critical for bank employees. In the context of I4.0, teamwork is advantageous since it unites heterogeneous operations and procedures to work together toward a common goal. Eliminating departmental barriers, enhancing generalist skills, and expediting decision-making foster organisational learning.

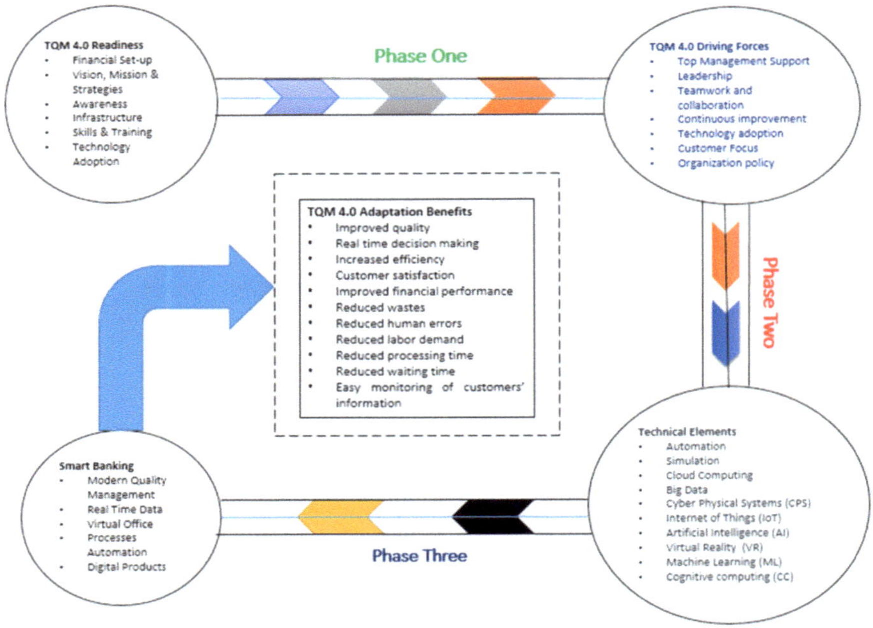

Fig. 3.6 TQM 4.0 adaptation framework. *Source* Created by the authors

Next, the organisation should establish a smart factory. This can be achieved by applying digital technologies like AI and VR in daily business operations. Additionally, smart factories include automation of processes, application of digital QM tools and methods, and establishment of user-friendly digital products and services. Lastly, the entire process should be monitored and evaluated to assess the achievement level and analyse major areas that need further improvement. The TQM adaptation framework comprises modern technologies. Modern technologies impact not only the banking sector but also the development of the state, changing the state control principles to meet modern conditions (Nedyalkova, 2023).

3.5 Concluding Remarks

Tanzanian banks' journey toward digital transformation is thrilling. The findings indicate that the overall readiness level is 3.54 out of 5, demonstrating a medium level of adaptation readiness. Such readiness level signifies that manual interventions augment some degree of I4.0 adaptation in implementing TQM in banks. The confirmed driving factors for the TQM 4.0 adaptation include legislation, political will, strategy, and policy. In addition, this study proposed a TQM 4.0 adaptation framework for the banking sector. This study examined the critical variables that characterise the successful adaptation of I4.0, thus suggesting TQM 4.0 implementation in Tanzania's banking service sector. Moreover, the adaptation framework for banks operating in the country is proposed. The process requires commitment from all stakeholders: banks, clients, financial services regulators, and the government. Banks need to extend their digital services, boost user experience, and strengthen cyber security. Moreover, more people need to be digitally literate, and digital banking services should be available to everyone, regardless of where they live or their socioeconomic standing. Technology stakeholders and employees in technology transfer instruments like R&D institutions must have sufficient skills and expertise to seek and adapt to new technologies.

References

African Economic Research Consortium. (2023). *Digital financial inclusion and market development in East African Community (EAC) Economies* (D. Ngui, A. Shimeles, N. Ndung'u, D. Cracknell, & J. Greenacre (eds.).

Afthanorhan, A., Awang, Z., Rashid, N., Foziah, H., & Ghazali, P. L. (2019). Assessing the effects of service quality on customer satisfaction. *Management Science Letters, 9*(1), 13–24.

Akhmatova, M. S., Deniskina, A., Akhmatova, D. M., & Prykina, L. (2022). Integrating quality management systems (TQM) in the digital age of intelligent transportation systems industry 4.0. *Transportation Research Procedia, 63*, 1512–1520. https://doi.org/10.1016/j.trpro.2022.06.163

Al-Shobaki, S. D., Fouad, R. H., & Al-Bashir, A. (2010). The Implementation of Total Quality Management (TQM) for The Banking Sector in Jordan. *Jordan Journal of Mechanical and Industrial Engineering, 4*(2), 304–313.

Ali, K., Johl, S. K., Muneer, A., Alwadain, A., & Ali, R. F. (2022). Soft and Hard total quality management practices promote industry 4.0 readiness: A SEM-neural network approach. *Sustainability, 14*, 1–23.

Ali, Smy., Enamul Haque, M., Zahid Hasan, M., & Author, C. (2019). *Implementation of TQM in banking sector of Bangladesh: A comparative Study between Public and private sector banks in Bangladesh, 21*(8), 1–07. https://doi.org/10.9790/487X-2108030107

Alsolamy, A. A., Albelad, K. S., & Hasan, S. H. (2013). Total quality management & service sector. *Journal of Advances in Mathematics, 6*(3), 880–884.

Amaechi, D. I., & Sylva, W. (2021). *Revisiting Total Quality Management in Service Organisations, 10*(7), 31–40. https://doi.org/10.35629/8028-1007013140

Antony, J., McDermott, O., & Sony, M. (2022). Quality 4.0 conceptualisation and theoretical understanding: A global exploratory qualitative study. *TQM Journal, 34*(5), 1169–1188. https://doi.org/10.1108/TQM-07-2021-0215

Baran, E., & Polat, T. K. (2022). Classification of Industry 4.0 for Total Quality Management: A Review. *Sustainability (Switzerland), 14*, 1–20.

Broday, E. E. (2022). The evolution of quality: From inspection to quality 4.0. *International Journal of Quality and Service Sciences, 14*(3), 368–382.

Cañas, H., Mula, J., & Campuzano-Bolarín, F. (2020). A General Outline of a Sustainable Supply Chain 4.0. *Sustainability (Switzerland), 12*(19), 1–17. https://doi.org/10.3390/su12197978

Cho, G., Hwang, H., Sarstedt, M., & Ringle, C. M. (2020). Cutoff criteria for overall model fit indexes in generalized structured component analysis. *Journal of Marketing Analytics, 8*(4), 189–202.

Danguche, I. H., & Taifa, I. W. R. (2023). Factors influencing total productive maintenance implementation for thermal generation plants. *Tanzania Journal of Engineering and Technology, 42*(1), 97–112. https://doi.org/10.52339/tjet.v42i1.892

Deshpande, V. A., Taifa, I. W. R., & Deresse, N. C. (2021). Deployment of the Taguchi technique for surface roughness optimisation. *International Journal of Industrial and Systems Engineering, 39*(1), 1–30. https://doi.org/10.1504/ijise.2020.10028682

Dias, A. M., Carvalho, A. M., & Sampaio, P. (2022). Quality 4.0: Literature review analysis, definition and impacts of the digital transformation process on quality. *International Journal of Quality & Reliability Management, 39*(6), 1312–1335.

Doko, F., & Miskovski, I. (2019). An overview of big data analytics in Banking: Approaches, challenges and issues. *UBT International Conference*, 11–17.

Ebiringa, O. T. (2018). Total quality management for service delivery By commercial banks: Analysis of critical success factors. *International Journal of Management Sciences and Business Research, 1*(3), 1–11.

Ezenyilimba, E., Ezejiofor, R. A., & Afodigbueokwu, H. E. (2019). Effect of Total quality management on organizational performance of deposit money banks in Nigeria. *Nternational Journal of Business & Law Research, 7*(3), 15–28.

Fang, X., Cao, C., Chen, Z., Chen, W., Ni, L., Ji, Z., & Gan, J. (2020). Using mixed methods to design service quality evaluation indicator system of railway container multimodal transport. *Science Progress, 103*(1), 1–27. https://doi.org/10.1177/0036850419890491

Fening, F. A. & Boateng-okrah, E. (2017). TQM implementation Concepts and Tools/Techniques. *International Journal of Social Science and Business, 2*(3), 13–24.

Gökalp, E., Gökalp, M. O., & Eren, P. E. (2018). Industry 4.0 revolution in clothing and apparel factories: Apparel 4.0. In *Industry 4.0 From the Management Information Systems Perspectives* (pp. 169–184). Peter Lang. https://doi.org/10.3726/b15120/21

Hodson, G. (2021). Construct jangle or construct mangle? Thinking straight about (nonredundant) psychological constructs. *Journal of Theoretical Social Psychology, 5*(4), 576–590.

Hussein, S. K., & Taifa, I. W. R. (2024). Six Sigma methodology implementation for minimising yarn breakages in the apparel industry. *International Journal of Industrial and Systems Engineering, 48*(2), 228–258. https://doi.org/10.1504/ijise.2023.10056743

Hyun Park, S., Seon Shin, W., Hyun Park, Y., & Lee, Y. (2017). Building a new culture for quality management in the era of the Fourth Industrial Revolution. *Total Quality Management and Business Excellence, 28*(9–10), 934–945. https://doi.org/10.1080/14783363.2017.1310703

Jakobo, E. P., & Taifa, I. W. R. (2025). Investigating the applicability of industry 4.0 technologies in road construction projects: A quantitative research design from construction 4.0 perspectives. *Engineering Reports, 7*(10), 1–24. https://doi.org/10.1002/eng2.70406

James, J. M., & Taifa, I. W. R. (2023). Quality improvement of long oil alkyd (LOA) resin requirements in the formulation of Hi-gloss paints. *International Journal of Quality and Reliability Management, 40*(7), 1753–1776. https://doi.org/10.1108/IJQRM-08-2022-0247

Jha, U. C. (2016). Effect of TQM on customer satisfaction in Indian Iron & Steel Industry. *RIET-IJSET: International Journal of Science, Engineering and Technology, 3*(2), 103. https://doi.org/10.5958/2395-3381.2016.00013.7

Kitsovi, J. K., & Taifa, I. W. R. (2024). Lean Six Sigma implementation: Results from the soft drinks industry. *International Journal of Industrial and Systems Engineering*, 1–31. https://doi.org/10.1504/IJISE.2024.10067284

Kothari, C. R. (2004). *Research methodology: Methods and techniques* (2nd ed.). New Age International (P) Limited.

Kulenović, M., Folta, M., & Veselinović, L. (2021). The analysis of total quality management critical success factors. *Quality Innovation Prosperity, 25*(1), 88–102.

Kumar, V. (2019). IoT Applications in Finance and Banking. *International Journal of Research and Analytical Reviews (IJRAR), 6*(2), 951–954.

Lawsky, S. B. M. (2014). *Financial Services Report on Cyber Security in the Banking Sector* (Issue May).

Maganga, D. P., & Taifa, I. W. R. (2023a). Quality 4.0 conceptualisation: An emerging quality management concept for manufacturing industries. *The TQM Journal, 34*(5), 1169–1188. https://doi.org/10.1108/tqm-11-2021-0328

Maganga, D. P., & Taifa, I. W. R. (2023b). Quality 4.0 transition framework for Tanzanian manufacturing industries. *The TQM Journal*, *35*(6), 1417–1448. https://doi.org/10.1108/TQM-01-2022-0036

Maganga, D. P., & Taifa, I. W. R. (2023c). The readiness of manufacturing industries to transit to Quality 4.0. *International Journal of Quality & Reliability Management*, *40*(7), 1729–1752. https://doi.org/10.1108/IJQRM-05-2022-0148

Maganga, D. P., & Taifa, I. W. R. (2024). Determining the maturity level for the selected manufacturing industries through Industry 4.0 perspectives. *International Journal of Management and Decision Making*, *23*(4), 480–504.

Magd, H., Negi, S., & Ansari, M. S. A. (2021). Effective TQM Implementation in the Service Industry: A Proposed Framework. *Quality Innovation Prosperity*, *25*(2), 95–129. https://doi.org/10.12776/qip.v25i2.1594

Magoti, E., & Mtui, J. M. (2020). The Relationship between economic growth and service sector in Tanzania: An empirical investigation. *African Journal of Economic Review, 8*(2), 219–238.

Mange, M. A., & Taifa, I. W. R. (2026). Service engineering 4.0 applicability: Results from stakeholders' engagement assessment in the public building construction projects. *Journal of Engineering*. 1–19. https://doi.org/10.1155/je/5557271

Marsh, H. W., Guo, J., Dicke, T., Parker, P. D., & Craven, R. G. (2020). Confirmatory Factor Analysis (CFA), Exploratory Structural Equation Modeling (ESEM), and Set-ESEM: Optimal Balance Between Goodness of Fit and Parsimony. *Multivariate Behavioral Research, 55*(1), 102–119. https://doi.org/10.1080/00273171.2019.1602503

McKinsey. (2019). Global AI Survey: AI proves its worth, but few scale impact. *McKinsey & Company*, 1–16.

McNeish, D., An, J., & Hancock, G. R. (2018). The thorny relation between measurement quality and fit index cutoffs in Latent variable models. *Journal of Personality Assessment, 100*(1), 43–52. https://doi.org/10.1080/00223891.2017.1281286

Mehdiabadi, A., Tabatabeinasab, M., & Spulbar, C. (2020). Are We Ready for the Challenge of Banks 4.0? Designing a Roadmap for Banking Systems in Industry 4.0. *International Journal of Financial Studies*, *8*(2), 1–29.

MoF. (2023). *The economic survey 2022*. https://www.mof.go.tz/uploads/documents/en-1691583449-THEECONOMIC%20SURVEY_2022.pdf

Nasrallah, N. M. (2023). Using Artificial Intelligence (AI) in Banking Services. In *Introductory Booklet Series* (Issue 24, pp. 56–73).

Nedyalkova, P. G. (2023). Principles of financial control in the Public Sector. *IGI Global Scientific Publishing*. https://doi.org/10.4018/978-1-6684-8883-6

Nguyen, T. A. Van, Nguyen, K. H., & Tucek, D. (2023). Total Quality Management 4.0 Framework: Present and Future. *Journal of Operations and Supply Chain Management*, *16*(3), 311–322.

Nhelekwa, L. B., Mollel, J. Z., & Taifa, I. W. R. (2024). Assessing the digitalisation level of the Tanzanian apparel industry: Industry 4.0 perspectives. *Research Journal of Textile and Apparel*, *28*(2), 185–205. https://doi.org/10.1108/RJTA-11-2021-0138

Ntamulyango, D. K. (2023). *Industry 4.0 readiness assessment in beverage industries*. Master of Engineering Management (Project Management) Dissertation, University of Dar es Salaam.

Nyangarika, A. (2016). An analysis of service quality for customer satisfaction at Tanzania posts corporation. *Journal of Marketing and Consumer Research, 20*, 1–12.

Nzumile, J. M., Mahabi, V., & Taifa, I. W. R. (2024). Contribution of Industry 4.0 Technologies in Adopting Metrology 4.0 in Manufacturing Industries. In C. Machado & J. P. Davim (Eds.), *Smart Engineering Management. Management and Industrial Engineering* (pp. 43–72). Springer. https://doi.org/10.1007/978-3-031-52990-0_3

Nzumile, J. M., Pastory, D., & Taifa, I. W. R. (2024b). Applicability of Metrology 4.0 Technologies for the Manufacturing Industries. *Mapan—Journal of Metrology Society of India, 39*, 559–571. https://doi.org/10.1007/s12647-024-00740-7

Osei, L. K., Cherkasova, Y., & Oware, K. M. (2023). Unlocking the full potential of digital transformation in banking: A bibliometric review and emerging trend. *Future Business Journal*, *9*(1). https://doi.org/10.1186/s43093-023-00207-2

Pakkala, D., & Spohrer, J. (2019). Digital service: Technological agency in service systems. *Annual Hawaii International Conference on System Sciences*, *2019-Janua*, 1886–1895. https://doi.org/10.24251/hicss.2019.229

Philip, W. W. (2021). The comparison of TQM practices and quality performance between manufacturing & service. *Polish Journal of Management Studies, 23*(1), 436–452.

Pog, C., & Dovleac, R. (2021). Implementation and impact of Industry 4.0 and Quality 4.0 in the banking sector. *MATEC Web of Conferences, 342*, 1–10.

Radziwill, N. (2018). Quality 4.0: Let's get digital—The many ways the fourth industrial revolution is reshaping the way we think about quality. *Quality Progress*, 24–29.

Rana, M. E. (2023). The role and potential applications of cloud computing in the banking industry. *15th International Conference on Developments in ESystems Engineering (DeSE)*, 292–297.

Rizvi, M. (2020). A review of IoT in banking industry. *International Peer Reviewed/refereed Multidisciplinary Journal (EIPRMJ), 9*(2), 42–46.

Rojko, A. (2017). Industry 4.0 Concept: Background and overview. *International Journal of Interactive Mobile Technologies, 11*(5), 77–90.

Sader, S., Husti, I., & Daróczi, M. (2019). Industry 4.0 as a key enabler toward successful implementation of total quality management practices. *Periodica Polytechnica Social and Management Sciences, 27*(2), 131–140.

Saha, P., Talapatra, S., Belal, H. M., & Jackson, V. (2022). Unleashing the Potential of the TQM and Industry 4.0 to Achieve Sustainability Performance in the Context of a Developing Country. *Global Journal of Flexible Systems Management, 23*(4), 495–513. https://doi.org/10.1007/s40171-022-00316-x

Shaaban, S. Y., & Athumani, H. I. (2020). Assessing Strategies to Create Cyber Security Awareness Among Employees in National Microfinance Bank in Tanzania. *International Journal of Economics, Commerce and Management*, *VIII*(12), 250–259.

Shi, D., Lee, T., & Maydeu-Olivares, A. (2019). Understanding the model size effect on SEM fit indices. *Educational and Psychological Measurement, 79*(2), 310–334.

Shrestha, N. (2021). Factor Analysis as a Tool for Survey Analysis. *American Journal of Applied Mathematics and Statistics*, *9*(1), 4–11. https://doi.org/10.12691/ajams-9-1-2

Sonono, B., & Ortstad, R. (2017). The effects of the digital transformation process on banks ' relationship with customers: Case study of a large swedish bank. *Uppsala Universitet Master's Thesis*, 62.

Taifa, I. W. R., Hayes, S. G., & Stalker, I. D. (2020). Computer modelling and simulation of an equitable order distribution in manufacturing through the Industry 4.0 framework. *2nd International Conference on Electrical, Communication and Computer Engineering (ICECCE), 12–13 June 2020*, 1–6. https://doi.org/10.1109/ICECCE49384.2020.9179275

Taifa, I. W. R., Hayes, S. G., & Stalker, I. D. (2021). Towards a digital revolution in the UK apparel manufacturing: An industry 4.0 perspective. In P. Bartolo, F. Silva, S. Jaradat, & H. Bartolo (Eds.), *Industry 4.0—Shaping the Future of the Digital World, 2nd International Conference on Sustainable Smart Manufacturing (S2M 2019), Manchester* (pp. 3–8). CRC Press, Taylor & Francis Group. https://doi.org/10.1201/9780367823085-01

Taifa, I. W. R., Makundi, E. D., & Mwaluko, G. S. (2021b). Production quality improvement for the soft drinks bottling industry through six sigma methodology. *International Journal of Industrial and Systems Engineering, 39*(4), 536–564. https://doi.org/10.1504/ijise.2020.10030896

Testa, M., D'Amato, A., Singh, G., & Festa, G. (2023). Innovative profiles of TQM in banking management. The relationship between employee training and risk mitigation. *TQM Journal*. https://doi.org/10.1108/TQM-01-2022-0043

Viharos, Z. J., Soós, S., Nick, G. A., Várgedő, T., & Beregi, R. J. (2017). Non-comparative, Industry 4.0 readiness evaluation for manufacturing enterprises. *15th IMEKO TC10 Workshop on Technical Diagnostics Technical Diagnostics in Cyber-Physical Era*, 181–187.

Yang, G. (2023). *Application of CAD Virtual Reality Technology in Bank Financial Business System, 20*, 13–23. https://doi.org/10.14733/cadaps.2023.S1.13-23

Zailani, S., Jafarzadeh, S., Iranmanesh, M., Nikbin, D., & Selim, N. I. I. (2018). Halal logistics service quality: Conceptual model and empirical evidence. *British Food Journal, 120*(11), 2599–2614.

Chapter 4
Integrating Decision Science and Fuzzy Logic to Evaluate and Improve Water Quality: A Pathway to Operational Excellence in Environmental Management

Ajoy Kanti Das, Nandini Gupta, Suman Das, Rakhal Das, Carlos Granados, and Suman Patra

Abstract This chapter presents a comprehensive study using a Fuzzy Soft Expert System (FSES) to evaluate and improve water quality in the Manu River, Tripura, India, focusing on the anthropogenic influences over the period 2020–2021. By integrating decision sciences with fuzzy logic, the study captures complex interactions between various water quality parameters and human activities. Multi-criteria decision-making (MCDM) models are employed to analyze pre-monsoon, monsoon, and post-monsoon seasonal variations, offering a dynamic and robust approach to water quality management. The results provide insights into key water quality indicators, such as pH, dissolved oxygen, and biochemical oxygen demand, allowing for the development of strategies aimed at operational excellence in environmental management. These findings contribute to both academic research and practical applications, emphasizing how decision sciences can enhance the quality and productivity of water resource management systems. Furthermore, the approach highlights how fuzzy logic-based systems can support policy-making and operational decision-making, ensuring sustainable environmental practices and improved water quality standards.

A. K. Das (✉) · S. Patra
Department of Mathematics, Tripura University, Agartala, India
e-mail: ajoykantidas@gmail.com

N. Gupta
Department of Environmental Science, Bir Bikram Memorial College, Agartala, India

S. Das
Department of Education (ITEP), NIT Agartala, Jirania, India

R. Das
Department of Mathematics, The ICFAI University Tripura, Mohanpur, India

C. Granados
Estudiante de Doctorado en Matemáticas, Magister en Ciencias Matemáticas, Universidad de Antioquia, Medellín, Colombia
e-mail: carlosgranadosortiz@outlook.es

I. Mukherjee et al. (eds.), *Decision Sciences for Quality and Productivity Improvement*,
https://doi.org/10.1007/978-981-95-7545-9_4

Keywords Decision sciences · Fuzzy soft expert system · Water quality assessment · Anthropogenic influences · Environmental management · River water quality · Productivity improvement

4.1 Introduction

The growing demands of industrialization, urbanization, and agricultural activities in North-East India have severely impacted the water quality of the region's rivers (Das et al., 2024, 2025a). This poses severe risks to the sustainability of the environment and public health. The Manu River stands out among these essential waterways since it provides most of the drinking water for several communities in Tripura (Das et al., 2025b). However, the health of the river is now seriously threatened by alarming pollution levels linked to agricultural runoff and untreated sewage discharge. To prevent pollution and protect public health, it is imperative that the Manu River's water quality be evaluated and that efficient management plans be created. These pressing issues spurred this study's implementation of an FSES to assess and enhance the Manu River's water quality. This novel method offers an innovative framework for handling the uncertainty and complexity present in environmental evaluations by fusing fuzzy logic (Zadeh, 1965) with decision sciences (Das, 2016, 2018; Das & Granados, 2021, 2022a, 2022b, 2022c; Das et al., 2022, 2023). Better resource management and operational excellence are promoted by FSES, which makes informed decision-making possible by improving the precision and dependability of water pollution assessments.

Molodtsov's development of Soft Set Theory (SSTH) (Molodtsov, 1999) also provides a strong mathematical framework designed to handle decision-making difficulties, particularly those with unclear definitions and unidentified components. SSTH excels at solving real-world decision problems by enabling flexible parameter definitions, especially when information is lacking. SSTH is a useful instrument in our pursuit of efficient water quality management because of its versatility, distinguishing it from other models that handle uncertainty. Building on this framework, Maji et al. (2002, 2003) improved the usefulness of SSTH in decision-making processes by further developing it by adding subset operations. Because of these developments, SSTH is a useful tool for streamlining complex decision-making tasks in various applications. By adding more mathematical operations and effectively illustrating the use of De Morgan's rules in this context, Ali et al. (2009) extended the operational framework of SSTH. This extension improved SSTH's theoretical stability. Al-cantud and Santos-García (2017) have shown the usefulness of SSTH in real-world applications by using it to enhance decision-making processes, particularly in situations where data is lacking. Additional developments in SSTH have expanded its use and reach. By introducing expanded methodologies that broaden its applicability and enable more complicated analyses and solutions to difficult decision-making situations, Chen et al. (2020) enhanced the theoretical foundation of SSTH. Dalkılıç (2021) showed how well SSTH works to solve decision-making problems in uncertain situations, especially in dynamic and unpredictable settings. Additionally, Dalkılıç and Demirtaş (2023) used SSTH to address the difficulties caused by the COVID-19 pandemic to optimize resource allocation and guide containment tactics. This highlights SSTH's applicability in various fields and demonstrates how it may be used to inform crucial public health choices.

By proposing fuzzy sets to manage data uncertainty efficiently, Zadeh (1965) made a substantial contribution to the fields of decision sciences and data analytics. Numerous extensions of this fundamental idea have resulted, such as intuitionistic fuzzy sets, hesitant fuzzy sets, interval-valued fuzzy sets, and fuzzy multisets. These advancements offer some innovative frameworks that go much beyond the capabilities of conventional crisp set theory for describing and understanding uncertainty (Mukherjee & Das, 2022, 2023). Fuzzy sets are used in many sectors, proving their adaptability and significance. Fuzzy sets in decision sciences enable better modeling in domains like operational excellence, productivity evaluation, and quality control (Paik & Mondal, 2021). Additionally, they are helpful in databases, multi-criteria decision-making, economics, pattern recognition, neural networks, and medicine (Das, 2018; Das & Granados, 2022c). Researchers and practitioners can more effectively negotiate the complexity and uncertainties present in data by integrating fuzzy logic into various fields, ultimately improving decision-making procedures and results. Fuzzy sets are helpful in technical applications, as demonstrated by recent developments by Darvish Falehi and Torkaman (2023), who investigated their usage for precise voltage restoration. Furthermore, Akram and Shumaiza (2023) improved the effectiveness of decision-making processes in practical situations by introducing a novel approach utilizing bipolar fuzzy set theory. These contributions demonstrate fuzzy sets' adaptability and growing significance in solving challenging issues in various domains.

These theoretical advancements in fuzzy logic (Zadeh, 1965) and SSTH (Molodtsov, 1999) offer crucial instruments for handling uncertainties and complexity in environmental assessments in assessing and enhancing water quality. Our work intends to improve the accuracy of water quality assessments by combining various approaches, which will ultimately support sound decision-making and operational excellence in managing water resources. Particularly after Roy and Maji (2007) introduced a novel paradigm for decision-making, fuzzy soft sets (Maji et al., 2001) have attracted a lot of attention. This paradigm makes better use of FSS's advantages to manage uncertainty. Weighted FSS theory was developed by researchers to refine FSS further, leading to new uncertainty measures that improve decision-making processes and techniques, including weighted hesitant FSS theory (Wen, 2023). Wen (2023) introduced a sophisticated approach to group decision-making by working on weighted hesitant fuzzy soft sets, highlighting the need to consider hesitations and uncertainties. The accuracy and dependability of decision results are improved by the model's incorporation of weighted components, which consider the varying degrees of importance given to various elements. This approach has potential in intricate decision-making situations where various parties and viewpoints must be balanced to arrive at sound findings. Feng et al. (2010) built on these developments by stressing the significance of developing adaptable approaches in FSS-based decision-making. Together, these contributions highlight the growing complexity and practical usefulness of FSS in handling challenging decision-making situations. Liu et al. (2023) demonstrated the usefulness of FSS in medical diagnostics and public health by creating expert systems based on it for COVID-19 prediction. Their method demonstrates how FSS can manage incomplete and ambiguous data, which is essential for handling medical emergencies. The idea of filters in FSS-based topological spaces was introduced by Gao and Wu (2021), who made important theoretical contributions. Their investigation into the uses of these filters has improved the theoretical underpinnings of FSS and expanded its range of applications in topological and mathematical research by opening the door to a deeper comprehension of its structural characteristics. Furthermore, Bhardwaj and Sharma (2021) presented a novel approach to decision-making that is based on FSS and illustrated how it may be used in actual decision-making situations. Making educated decisions in unpredictable situations requires a thorough framework for quantifying uncertainty, which their measure offers. This contribution demonstrates how flexible FSS is across various decision-making settings, including engineering and economics. Together, these advancements show how FSS is becoming more sophisticated and applicable in both theoretical and practical contexts, making it a vital tool for addressing real-world decision-making issues in various sectors.

A significant contribution by Das and Granados (2022a) involves the development of a fuzzy parameterized intuitionistic fuzzy soft multiset theory for group decision-making. Their investigation of FP-intuitionistic multi-fuzzy N-soft sets, which increase the adaptability of decision-making models, complements this work (Das & Granados, 2022b). They presented IFP-intuitionistic multi-fuzzy N-soft sets, further expanding this field of study and proving their usefulness in decision-making situations (Das & Granados, 2022c). Furthermore, Das (2018) suggested weighted fuzzy soft multisets as a novel tool for decision-making, while Das and Granados (Das, 2016; Das & Granados, 2023) explored intuitionistic fuzzy rough relations and preference intuitionistic fuzzy rough relations, highlighting their partial inclusion properties. Their collaborative work in 2021 also presented a fuzzy soft group decision-making approach based on weighted average ratings, further refining the theoretical and practical aspects of decision analysis (Das & Granados, 2021). Applications-wise, Das et al. (2022) suggested new operations on fuzzy soft sets, demonstrating their usefulness in situations involving decision-making. Similarly, Das et al. (2023) introduced the concept of weighted hesitant bipolar-valued fuzzy soft sets, which provide a more nuanced framework for evaluating alternatives. Das et al.'s (2024) development of a fuzzy MCDM model for examining human influences on urban river water quality is one of their noteworthy contributions to environmental decision-making. This research is extended in 2025 with weighted hesitant fuzzy soft set and fuzzy soft set models for rating water pollution and a case study applying fuzzy soft decision-making models to assess pollution levels in the Haora and Manu Rivers (Das et al., 2025a, 2025b). Granados et al. (2022) provided continuous neutrosophic distributions with neutrosophic parameters, offering a probabilistic approach to uncertainty modeling. In 2023, Granados et al. (2023) proposed a weighted neutrosophic soft multiset approach, demonstrating its application in decision-making problems that require handling multiple levels of uncertainty. Fuzzy soft multiset theories in decision-making have also benefited greatly from the contributions of Mukherjee and Das (2016a). Their work in 2015 applied interval-valued intuitionistic fuzzy soft multisets in real-world decision problems (Mukherjee & Das, 2015c), while their research explored the use of interval-valued intuitionistic fuzzy soft sets for investment decision-making (Mukherjee & Das, 2015a). In 2022, they invented Einstein operations for fuzzy soft multisets, further enhancing computing tools for decision analysis (Mukherjee & Das, 2022). Fuzzy soft multisets are thoroughly explored in their 2023 book, which covers both the theoretical underpinnings and real-world applications (Mukherjee & Das, 2023). The relational and topological structures of fuzzy and rough set models were further investigated by Mukherjee and Das (2015b, 2016b), and their 2025 collaboration presents an extended interval-valued neutrosophic rough soft set framework for water quality evaluation (Mukherjee et al., 2025). All things considered, these studies provide significant contributions to the development of fuzzy, soft, and neutrosophic set theories, which have applications in computational intelligence, environmental sustainability, and decision-making. Their work offers useful approaches for managing uncertainty, enhancing the precision of decisions, and tackling challenging real-world issues, especially in pollution assessment and water quality management.

Although there are several versions of the water quality index (WQI) for determining the consistency of surface water, WQI stands out for its precision and usefulness in determining river water quality. A thorough water quality index model was presented by Brown et al. (1970) and is now the industry standard for evaluating water quality. In their study of the effects of seasonal change on water sources in India, Kumar et al. (2017) noted notable variations in water quality and availability brought about by changing climatic patterns. Guettaf et al. (2017) evaluated the water quality of the Seybouse River in Algeria in regional studies, using WQI to thoroughly assess the river's state. Their study underlines the need for routine water quality monitoring for managing and safeguarding water resources. Miller and Hutchins (2017) also examined how urbanization and climate change affect water bodies in the UK. They talked about the difficulties in reducing these effects and how these elements lead to the deterioration of water quality. Together, these studies highlight the value and adaptability of WQI as a method for managing and monitoring water conditions in various geographical locations and under different environmental stressors. Shah and Joshi (2017) obtained the water quality index of the Sabarmati River in India, providing insights into the river's health and the impacts of numerous contaminants. An evaluation of the effects of climate change and land-use changes on the water resources of the Thames River basin was carried out by Hutchins et al. (2018). Their investigation brought to light the intricate relationships between human activity and natural elements affecting water quality. In their investigation of water condition trends in river basins throughout Europe, Diamantini et al. (2018) provided a comprehensive overview of the variables influencing water quality variations throughout the continent. The significance of long-term monitoring and the requirement for a unified water management policy among European countries was underlined by this study. The water quality of China's Min River's sea-entry segment was examined by Rao et al. (2019). Their research yielded important information about how upstream activities and natural processes affect water quality downstream as the river approaches the ocean. In their study on the impact of urbanization on the Sabarmati River, Patel et al. (2020) looked at how the fast urbanization of the area has impacted the river's quality. Their results highlight the difficulties in managing water supplies in metropolitan areas growing quickly. Together, these studies show how important WQI is to comprehending and controlling water quality in various settings and geographical regions. They underline the significance of comprehensive and continual water quality assessments to support effective water resource management and policy decisions. Ahmed et al. (2021) used machine learning techniques in conjunction with the WQI to perform a contamination assessment of the Rawal Dam in Pakistan. Their research demonstrates how well WQI works with sophisticated computational techniques to evaluate water quality and pinpoint pollution sources in intricate environmental systems. The flexibility of WQI-based methods and the incorporation of fuzzy set theory for more complex water quality evaluations were demonstrated by Patel and Chitnis (2022), who used fuzzy set theory in their simulation of the water conditions in the Sabarmati River. These studies demonstrate the importance of WQI in tackling the world's water pollution problems and the continuous need for better approaches, especially when handling data discrepancies and standardization needs across various environmental contexts. The issues raised, like the necessity for standardization and data variability, motivate continued study into improving WQI techniques and expanding their suitability for various situations. These developments ensure precise and trustworthy water quality evaluations, facilitating well-informed choices and successful environmental management plans.

The intricate process of assessing river water quality, which is influenced by several Water Quality Parameters (WQPs), and the inherent uncertainties involved are examined in this paper. We introduce the FSES, a methodology that combines fuzzy logic, soft set theory, and decision sciences for an all-encompassing assessment of water pollution to tackle this complexity. In particular, our study uses FSES to assess the pollution levels in the Manu River, which flows into Bangladesh from North-East Tripura, India, and is a crucial drinking water source. Essential water quality measures such as total coliform, fecal coliform, pH, dissolved oxygen, biochemical oxygen demand, total alkalinity, total hardness, and total dissolved solids are all included in the FSES framework. From February 2020 to January 2021, we gathered information on these characteristics at five carefully selected locations along the river. By employing pollution scores derived from the FSES methodology, we aim to provide critical indicators of water quality that facilitate effective evaluation and management of water pollution in the Manu River. This approach not only enhances the understanding of water condition dynamics but also has significant implications for operational excellence in environmental management and public health strategies.

The structure of this chapter is organized into three main sections:

Section 2: Conceptual Framework and Methodology

This section explores the foundational concepts essential for understanding the integrated methodology of decision sciences and fuzzy logic. Key topics include fuzzy sets, soft sets, and FSS, which are crucial for managing uncertainties in water quality assessment. We will also emphasize the significance of the Manu River as a study area, detailing the materials and methods employed for data collection and analysis. These concepts provide the necessary theoretical background to support subsequent discussions and applications related to evaluating and improving water quality.

Section 3: FSES for Water Quality Assessment

This section introduces the FSES as a water condition rating and evaluation instrument. FSES thoroughly evaluates water pollution levels by combining the concepts of fuzzy sets and soft sets. We will detail the methods and algorithms that support FSES, highlighting its benefits and practicality in water quality assessments. The goal of this creative strategy is to improve resource management and decision-making in the process of improving water quality.

Section 4: Conclusion and Future Research Directions

The main conclusions and ramifications of using FSES to evaluate the Manu River's water quality are outlined in the concluding section. We will emphasize how these insights support operational excellence in the management of water resources. Additionally, this section will outline potential avenues for future research and development, suggesting areas where further enhancements to FSES and related methodologies can be explored to advance water quality assessment techniques.

This structured approach ensures a systematic and comprehensive exploration of the proposed methodologies, starting from foundational concepts and culminating in practical applications and future directions that promote operational excellence in water management.

4.2 Conceptual Framework and Methodology

In this segment, we establish the conceptual framework and methodology for our study, focusing on soft sets, fuzzy sets, and fuzzy soft sets as foundational tools. We also outline the significance of the study area, detailing the materials and methods employed for data collection and analysis. Let's assume V symbolizes the original universe, while P(V) indicates its collection of subsets, and P represents a collection of criteria.

4.2.1 Preliminaries

Definition 2.1.1 (Molodtsov, 1999) A soft set defined over a universe V is denoted by the pair (ψ, P), where ψ is a function characterized by $\psi : P \rightarrow P(V)$. This function ψ systematically associates each element from the parameter set P with a subset of the universe V, thereby encapsulating the inherent degree of uncertainty or ambiguity linked to each parameter. This mapping enables a flexible and adaptive representation of information by representing the different degrees of uncertainty associated with various characteristics, which is crucial for improving decision-making processes. These representations are essential in operational contexts because they offer a strong foundation for evaluating and enhancing decision results in complex and unpredictable circumstances.

Definition 2.1.2 (Zadeh, 1965) Fuzzy sets are a generalization of classical sets where objects can have partial membership. A fuzzy set X defined on a universe V can be expressed as $X = \{(o, \mu_X(o)) : o \in V\}$, where the mapping $\mu_X : V \rightarrow [0,1]$ represents the membership function, also known as the fuzzy membership function. The degree of membership or membership value assigned to each element o in the universe V is indicated in this context by $\mu_X(o)$. To enable more nuanced representations of uncertainty and more informed decision-making in various operational contexts, this mapping is crucial for assessing the degree to which each object belongs to the fuzzy set.

Let FS(V) be the collection of all fuzzy sets over V.

Definition 2.1.3 (Maji et al., 2001) Given the universe V, a pair (ψ, P) is defined as an FSS, where ψ:P → FS(V) is a mapping function. A pair consisting of the mapping ψ and a non-empty subset P of parameters essentially defines an FSS. Each member from the parameter set P is effectively associated with a corresponding fuzzy set over the universe V by this mapping ψ. This paradigm effectively captures decision-making processes' fuzziness and intrinsic ambiguity by mapping each element of P to a fuzzy set. A thorough grasp of complicated events in operational contexts is promoted by this structured representation, which is crucial for improving the caliber and accuracy of analyses in various applications.

By offering a systematic framework for additional analysis and discussions surrounding uncertainty and ambiguity in parameter mapping, these definitions establish the foundation for comprehending and applying soft sets, fuzzy sets, and fuzzy soft sets in the research study.

4.2.2 Study Area

Significance: The Manu River is a crucial water resource for drinking water, agriculture, and maintaining aquatic habitats, making it of great ecological and socioeconomic importance.

Environmental Context: The research region includes various land uses and habitats, from urban settlements to agricultural fields, which can lead to different kinds and degrees of water contamination.

Hydrological Dynamics: Accurately interpreting water quality data requires an understanding of the Manu River's hydrological dynamics, which include flow patterns, sediment movement, and water retention.

Human Impact: Human endeavors like farming, manufacturing, urbanization, and waste management can have a significant influence on the quality of the water and cause pollution in rivers.

4.2.3 Materials and Methods

Sampling Strategy: The Manu River's sampling stations are carefully chosen to provide representative sampling throughout its many sections while considering geographic variability.

Sampling Period: Gathering water samples over a long period allows for recording seasonal fluctuations, which can affect water quality measures, particularly during the monsoon and post-monsoon seasons.

Analytical Techniques: Data accuracy, dependability, and compatibility with established standards are guaranteed when WQPs are measured using the standard procedures described in the APHA recommendations (American Public Health Association (APHA), 2005).

4.2.4 Fuzzy Soft Expert System

Fuzzy Membership Functions: By defining fuzzy membership functions for WQPs, real-world complexity can be reflected in how ambiguity and vagueness are represented in water quality evaluations.

Weighted Assessments: By giving WQPs weights according to their relative importance, a more thorough and nuanced calculation of pollution scores is made possible, considering the various effects of various factors on the overall quality of the water.

Mean Operation: The FSES's mean operation combines information from several specialists and sample locations to produce a comprehensive evaluation of water pollution that incorporates various inputs and viewpoints.

Data Interpretation: A thorough grasp of the Manu River's water quality dynamics, including temporal fluctuations and pollution trends, is made possible by the study's all-encompassing approach to data collection, analysis, and interpretation.

Comparative Analysis: By comparing measured values with regulatory bodies' stated requirements, we can evaluate compliance and identify areas of concern regarding variances in water quality.

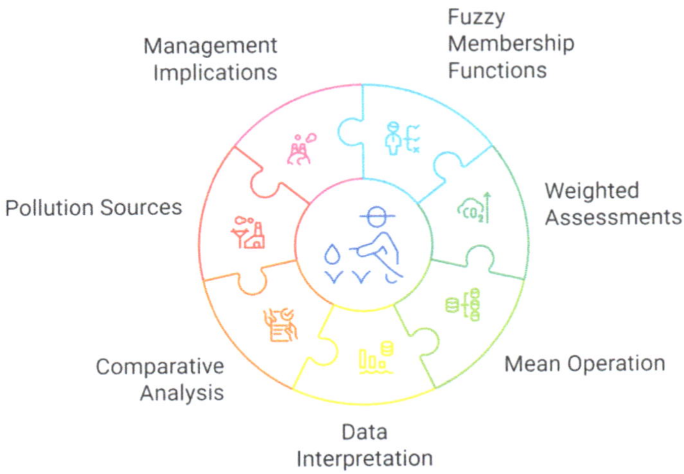

Fig. 4.1 Components of FSES in water quality assessment

Pollution Sources: The study can clarify the leading causes of water pollution in the Manu River by considering the sources of contamination, which include sewage inputs, industrial discharges, and agricultural runoff.

Management Implications: To effectively reduce the effects of water pollution, focused interventions, pollution control strategies, and sustainable practices are required. These findings have important ramifications for public health, environmental preservation, and water resource management (Fig. 4.1).

4.3 Fuzzy Soft Expert System and Assessment of Water Pollution of Manu River

We present a mathematical operation known as the mean operation on fuzzy soft sets in the framework of a fuzzy soft expert system for evaluating water contamination in the Manu River. For clarity, let's define a few terms and notations:

- Let's assume V symbolizes the original universe, P(V) indicates its collection of subsets, and P represents a collection of criteria related to water quality assessment.
- In the Manu River's water pollution assessment, assume that FSS(V) is the total of all fuzzy soft sets over V.

Definition 3.1 Let $(\psi_1, P), (\psi_2, P), \ldots, (\psi_q, P) \in FSS(V)$. Then the mean operation Θ on the FSSs $(\psi_1, P), (\psi_2, P), \ldots, (\psi_q, P)$ is denoted by $\Theta\big((\psi_1, P), (\psi_2, P), \ldots, (\psi_q, P)\big)$ and defined as a FSS $(\Psi, P) = \Theta\big((\psi_1, P), (\psi_2, P), \ldots, (\psi_q, P)\big)$ where $\forall s \in V, \forall pt_k \in P$,

$$\mu_{\Psi(pt_k)}(s) = \frac{1}{q}\Big(\mu_{\psi_1(pt_k)}(s) + \mu_{\psi_2(pt_k)}(s) + \cdots + \mu_{\psi_q(pt_k)}(s)\Big).$$

In this definition:

- q is the number of FSSs.
- $\mu_{\Psi(pt_k)}(s)$ represents the membership function of the resulting FSS at point $pt_k \in P$ for a particular grade of membership $s \in V$.
- $\mu_{\psi_i(pt_k)}$ (s)denotes the membership function of the ith FSS at point $pt_k \in P$ for the same grade of membership $s \in V$.

In simpler terms, the mean operation Θ computes the average membership value for each parameter $pt_k \in P$, across all the FSSs $(\psi_1, P), (\psi_2, P), (\psi_3, P), \ldots, (\psi_q, P)$. This average value is then used to construct a new FSS (Ψ, P), representing a consolidated assessment of water pollution based on the inputs from multiple fuzzy soft sets.

This mean operation Θ plays a crucial role in aggregating information and providing a comprehensive evaluation of water pollution in the Manu River by considering various parameters and their degrees of membership in different FSSs.

Building on the aforementioned concepts, we now present our FSES, which is designed to assess water quality for the purpose of rating pollution levels. This framework integrates fuzzy soft sets to provide a nuanced evaluation of water quality parameters, enabling a comprehensive assessment of pollution levels in aquatic environments.

4.3.1 Algorithm (FSES)

Step 1. Enter a set of sampling stations $S_S = \{ss_1, ss_2, ss_3, \ldots, ss_n\}$, a WQP set $P = \{pt_1, pt_2, pt_3, \ldots, pt_m\}$, and a group of experts $E = \{ex_1, ex_2, ex_3, \ldots, ex_q\}$. Entering parameters such as sampling stations, water quality parameters, and expert data is crucial for establishing a comprehensive assessment framework. This step ensures that all relevant factors and stakeholders are accounted for in the evaluation process.

Step 2. Enter the resulting crisp data summaries $DT = \{dt_1, dt_2, dt_3, \ldots, dt_q\}$ of WQPs for all the selected sampling stations $ss_1, ss_2, ss_3, \ldots, ss_n$ as provided by each expert $ex_k, k = 1, 2, 3, \ldots, q$. Inputting crisp data summaries from experts provides the initial dataset necessary for analysis. These data summaries serve as the foundation for generating fuzzy soft sets and computing pollution scores.

Step 3. Enter standard and ideal values of the WQPs according to any recommending agencies. Incorporating standard and ideal values of water quality parameters is essential for benchmarking and comparison purposes. These values help determine the deviation from optimal conditions and guide decision-making regarding pollution mitigation strategies.

Step 4. Utilizing the standard and ideal values of the water quality parameters outlined in Step 3, define fuzzy membership function $\mu_{pt_k}:R \to [0,1]$ for each WQP $pt_k \in P$, where R is a set of real numbers. Defining fuzzy membership functions enables the representation of uncertainty and vagueness inherent in water quality assessments. This step captures the nuances of parameter values and their degrees of membership in fuzzy sets.

Step 5. Following the establishment of fuzzy membership functions, convert the crisp data summaries $dt_1, dt_2, dt_3, \ldots, dt_q$ into FSSs (ψ_1, P), (ψ_2, P), (ψ_3, P), ..., $and\left(\psi_q, P\right)$ respectively and present them in tabular form. Converting crisp data summaries into FSSs facilitates a more flexible and nuanced representation of water quality data. Fuzzy soft sets allow for the consideration of uncertainty and ambiguity, enhancing the accuracy of pollution assessments.

Step 6. To compute the resultant fuzzy soft sets, we apply the mean operation, which integrates data collected from various experts and sampling locations. This consolidation of information provides a comprehensive view of water quality across different parameters and locations.

Step 7. Enter weight ϖ_k for each WQP $pt_k \in P$, where ϖ is a mapping from P to [0,1], such that $\varpi_k = \varpi\left(pt_k\right), k = 1, 2, 3, \ldots, m$. Assigning weights to WQPs reflects their relative significance in the assessment process. Weighted assessments ensure that critical factors contribute more significantly to the overall pollution score calculation.

Step 8. Compute the pollution score utilizing the formula.

$$\Omega_{\varpi}(ss_i) = \frac{\sum_{k=1}^{m}\left[\varpi\left(pt_k\right) \times \Omega\left(\mu_{\Psi(pt_k)}(ss_i)\right)\right]}{\sum_{k=1}^{m}\varpi\left(pt_k\right)}, pt_k \in P \text{and } \forall ss_i \text{ in } S_S$$

This score facilitates easy interpretation, with lower scores indicating better water quality and higher scores signaling potential pollution issues.

Step 9. Interpreting the pollution score helps stakeholders understand the overall water quality status. If pollution score $\Omega_{\varpi}(ss_k)$ approaches zero, it signifies excellent water quality; conversely, if it approaches one, it indicates poor water quality, i.e., indicate areas of concern that may require intervention or remediation measures.

This FSES offers a systematic approach to evaluating water pollution levels based on expert inputs, standard values, fuzzy membership functions, and weighted assessments of water quality parameters. Figure 4.2 demonstrates the flowchart of the FSES for water quality assessment. It outlines the systematic process of assessing pollution levels based on expert inputs, fuzzy membership functions, and weighted assessments of water quality parameters.

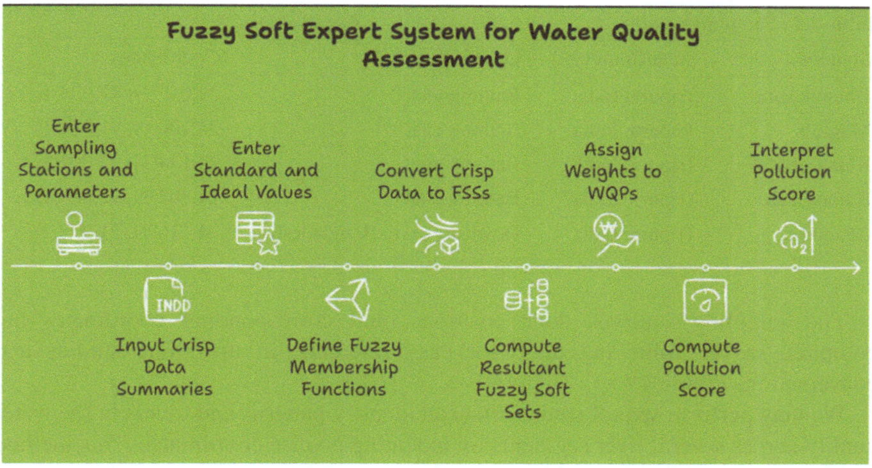

Fig. 4.2 Fuzzy soft expert system-based water quality assessment

4.3.2 Study Area and Data Collection

The assessment of water pollution in the Manu River using the FSES involved a comprehensive and systematic approach. Here's a detailed explanation of the methodology and process:

4.3.2.1 Site Selection and Sampling

In this study, we have included location coordinates in our analysis to enhance the accuracy and reliability of our data. For this study, five strategic sampling sites were carefully chosen along the Manu River to ensure a comprehensive representation of water quality across different locations. The locations that were chosen are Chandipur, which is close to the Indo-Bangladesh border (24.316°N, 91.992°E), and Dhumacharar (24.017°N, 91.974°E). The distribution of point sources of waste discharge in the region, including residential sewage, agricultural runoff, and industrial effluents, which are known to have a significant influence on water quality, was the basis for the precise selection of these sites.

We used a Garmin eTrex Vista Cx GPS device to record the geographic coordinates of every sampling location precisely. This instrument is renowned for its accuracy and dependability in capturing latitude and longitude, ensuring that the gathered data may be precisely plotted and subjected to spatial analysis. By acquiring accurate location data, we can associate the water quality metrics with particular environmental and anthropogenic factors present at each site.

Table 4.1 Sampling stations

Stations	State/Country	Location	Coordinates
Dhumacharar	Tripura, India	Bathing ghat	24.017°N, 91.974°E
Masauli	Tripura, India	Bathing ghat	24.100°N, 91.972°E
Kumarghat	Tripura, India	Bathing ghat	24.174°N, 92.002°E
Kailashahar	Tripura, India	Bathing ghat	24.302°N, 92.004°E
Chandipur	Tripura, India	Downstream to Bangladesh	24.316°N, 91.992°E

The sampling stations, their positions, and corresponding coordinates are compiled in the following table for easy reference in upcoming studies and conversations (Table 4.1):

We may perform spatial studies that can identify patterns and trends in the water quality across several river segments by including precise coordinates. This method makes our results more reliable and makes it easier to uncover possible sources of pollution and evaluate how they affect aquatic ecology. A more comprehensive understanding of the region's water quality problems is also made possible by the geographic data, allowing comparisons with other studies in comparable settings. We can more effectively interpret the findings and offer well-informed suggestions for water management and policy initiatives meant to enhance the well-being of the Manu River and the ecosystems around it by comparing the location data with the examined water quality metrics.

4.3.2.2 Sampling Period and Frequency

Between February 2020 and January 2021, three separate water samples were taken from each sampling location. This prolonged sampling period captures seasonal fluctuations and long-term trends in water quality. Pre-monsoon, monsoon, and post-monsoon evaluations were part of the sample sessions between February 2020 and January 2021. Each of these seasons is important for comprehending the changes in water quality characteristics.

2020 Pre-Monsoon Season (February–May): Because there is usually less rainfall, water levels are more constant, and contaminants are concentrated because of less diffusion. This season's sampling aids in determining the baseline water quality and locating any current sources of contamination, such as runoff from farms or household trash discharges.

Monsoon Season (June to September 2020): Water quality can be greatly impacted by the monsoon season's intense rains. Higher levels of turbidity and pollutants in the water are frequently the result of sediments and pollutants being mobilized by increased runoff. We may examine how rainfall affects water quality, including the effects of flooding and increased surface runoff on pollutant concentrations, by taking samples throughout this time.

Post-Monsoon Period (October 2020–January 2021): After the monsoon, water levels usually level off, and the impact of precipitation starts to fade. However, because of sediment resuspension and the delayed water quality recovery, this time frame can still exhibit high pollution levels. Understanding the monsoon's lingering effects on water quality and assessing the success of any post-rainy-season mitigating strategies require sampling during this period.

The study thoroughly explains how the Manu River's water quality varies over time by combining data from these three different seasonal periods, emphasizing the dynamic relationships between seasonal variations and water quality metrics.

4.3.2.3 Selected Water Quality Parameters

This study's choice of water quality measures was determined by examining pertinent literature, global norms, and local environmental issues. In particular, the metrics selected are representative of those frequently employed to assess anthropogenic impacts on water quality and the condition of water bodies. These parameters include physical, chemical, and biological indicators that are critical in assessing the suitability of water for various uses (e.g., drinking, irrigation, industrial processes).

Key references include guidelines from the World Health Organization (WHO), the Australian Water Quality Management Framework, and studies on water quality assessment in similar geographical and climatic conditions, particularly in the Indian subcontinent. Moreover, regional reports from local environmental agencies and academic research specific to North-East India were examined to ensure that the selected parameters are relevant to the unique environmental and anthropogenic factors affecting water quality in Tripura.

The specific parameters—pH, electrical conductivity, iron, dissolved oxygen, total hardness, total alkalinity, total dissolved solids, calcium, magnesium, and turbidity—were included due to their direct impact on water usability and their sensitivity to changes caused by human activity (such as industrial runoff, agricultural practices, and urbanization). These parameters are critical indicators of water pollution and ecosystem health, reflecting both the physical and biological conditions of water bodies.

4.3.2.4 Standard Methods for Measuring Water Quality Parameters and Analysis

Standard techniques for assessing water quality parameters were used in this study by the recommendations made by the WHO (2011) and the American Public Health Association (APHA, 2005). These methods ensure the accuracy and uniformity of water quality evaluations at various sampling sites.

1. **pH Measurement**: Using a calibrated pH meter and the APHA technique (APHA, 2005), we ascertained the pH levels of water samples. This technique

uses a glass electrode, which gives precise hydrogen ion concentration readings necessary to determine the water's acidic or alkaline.

2. **Dissolved Oxygen (DO)**: Using the Winkler titration method (APHA, 2005), we determined dissolved oxygen. This common practice is mixing chemicals with the water sample to create a residue that can be titrated to measure the amount of dissolved oxygen, a crucial sign of ecosystem health and water quality.
3. **Biochemical Oxygen Demand (BOD)**: The 5-day BOD test (APHA, 2005) was used to measure the BOD levels. This test provides information on the levels of organic pollution in water by measuring the amount of oxygen absorbed by microorganisms during the decomposition of organic matter in a water sample over a predetermined time.
4. **Total Hardness:** Titration was used to assess total hardness. The concentration of calcium and magnesium ions, essential for assessing water quality, is shown by the color shift that occurs when the water sample is treated with a chelating agent.
5. **Total Alkalinity:** The acid titration method (APHA, 2005) was used to measure alkalinity. This technique calculates the water's overall buffering capacity by titrating a sample of water with a strong acid until a predetermined endpoint is reached.
6. **Total Dissolved Solids (TDS):** APHA method 2540 gravimetric analysis was used to measure TDS. To ascertain the concentration of dissolved solids, which might affect aquatic life and water quality, the water sample is filtered, evaporated, and the residue is weighed.
7. **Total Coliform and Fecal Coliform:** The Most Probable Number (MPN) method (APHA method 9221) was used to determine the presence of coliform bacteria. This method allows for the quantification of possible fecal contamination by incubating water samples with certain media that promote the growth of coliform bacteria.

The APHA and WHO standard methodologies offer a comprehensive framework for assessing water quality criteria. The study ensures that the data gathered are reliable and can be dependably compared to other studies and regulatory criteria by following these principles. Additionally, the application of established procedures makes it easier to spot patterns and possible sources of contamination, which supports efficient water quality management plans (Fig. 4.3).

4.3.2.5 Measurement Units of Water Quality Parameters

To evaluate the condition of aquatic ecosystems and ensure that the water is safe for recreational and human use, water quality parameters are crucial. These parameters have different measurement units depending on the particular characteristic being evaluated. The standard measurement units for the important water quality metrics utilized in this investigation are listed below:

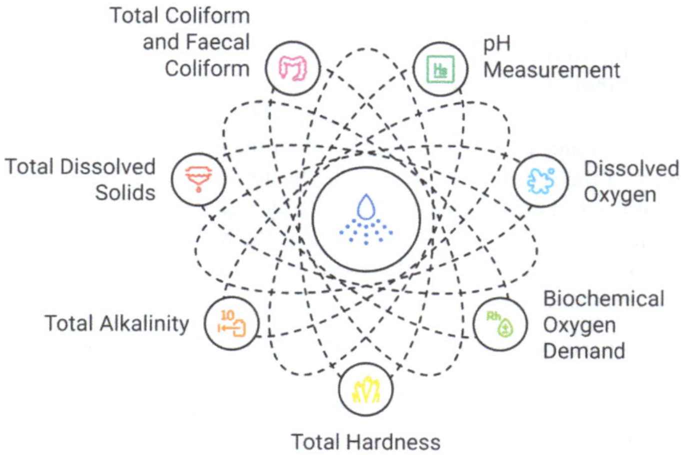

Fig. 4.3 Important water quality parameters

1. **pH**: The pH scale is a logarithmic scale used to specify the acidity or alkalinity of an aqueous solution. It ranges from 0 (highly acidic) to 14 (highly alkaline), with 7 being neutral. The pH of water is a crucial indicator of its quality, influencing chemical reactions, biological processes, and the solubility of minerals and metals.
2. **Dissolved Oxygen**: Measured in milligrams per liter (mg/L) or parts per million (ppm), dissolved oxygen is vital for aquatic life. It reflects the amount of oxygen available in the water for organisms to breathe. Higher levels of dissolved oxygen are generally associated with healthy ecosystems, while low levels can indicate pollution or eutrophication.
3. **Biochemical Oxygen Demand (BOD)**: BOD is measured in milligrams per liter (mg/L) or parts per million (ppm) and indicates the amount of oxygen that microorganisms will consume while decomposing organic matter in water at a specified temperature over a specified time (usually five days). Higher BOD values indicate lower water quality and higher amounts of organic contamination.
4. **Total Hardness**: Total hardness, which is measured in milligrams per liter (mg/L) as calcium carbonate ($CaCO_3$), indicates how much calcium and magnesium ions are present in water. The solubility of metals and the efficiency of detergents are two ways hardness can impact water quality.
5. **Total Alkalinity**: The water's ability to withstand pH variations, caused mainly by the presence of bicarbonates, carbonates, and hydroxides, is represented by total alkalinity, which is also measured in milligrams per liter (mg/L) as calcium carbonate (CaCO3). In aquatic habitats, it is essential for preserving constant pH levels.
6. **Total Dissolved Solids (TDS)**: TDS quantifies the total concentration of dissolved substances in water, such as salts, minerals, and organic matter, and is expressed in milligrams per liter (mg/L) or parts per million (ppm). The flavor

and usability of water may be impacted by elevated TDS levels, which can also be a sign of pollution.

7. **Total Coliform**: The MPN of coliform bacteria per 100 ml (mL) of water is used to calculate the total coliform bacteria. These bacteria serve as markers for both general water quality and fecal contamination. Their existence raises the possibility of the presence of pathogenic bacteria.
8. **Fecal Coliform**: Fecal coliform, specifically indicative of fecal contamination from warm-blooded animals, is measured as the MPN per 100 ml (mL) of water, just like total coliform. Finding these bacteria is essential to determining if water is safe to drink and use for pleasure.

These units have been standardized to facilitate communication and comparison across various investigations and regulatory contexts. Comprehending these metrics is crucial for assessing aquatic ecosystem health, ensuring potable water, and implementing efficient water management techniques.

4.3.2.6 Data Presentation and Comparison

Tables 4.2, 4.3, and 4.4 display the resulting clear data summaries of WQPs from the pre-monsoon, monsoon, and post-monsoon sessions (February 2020 to January 2021), respectively. These tables thoroughly summarize the measured values at each sample location throughout several time periods.

Following that, we contrasted the measured values with the benchmarks set by regulatory organizations such as the WHO (2011), Central Pollution Control Board (2008), Indian Council of Medical Research (1975), and Bureau of Indian Standards

Table 4.2 Crisp data summaries for the pre-monsoon session

Stations	wp_1	wp_2	wp_3	wp_4	wp_5	wp_6	wp_7	wp_8
Dhumacharar	6.12	6.45	3.35	41.43	58.97	119.95	234.25	183.94
Masauli	6.45	6.85	3.55	44.74	63.54	139.54	263.34	171.75
Kumarghat	6.75	6.54	3.97	49.95	62.55	142.67	278.43	196.54
Kailashahar	6.55	5.75	4.75	62.45	72.75	158.12	264.47	211.11
Chandipur	6.20	5.47	5.46	64.47	79.65	161.32	319.85	235.46

Table 4.3 Crisp data summaries for the monsoon session

Stations	wp_1	wp_2	wp_3	wp_4	wp_5	wp_6	wp_7	wp_8
Dhumacharar	6.57	6.95	4.46	44.65	55.45	103.85	245.87	173.10
Masauli	6.74	6.78	4.96	49.55	52.55	111.65	251.65	176.29
Kumarghat	6.48	6.71	4.91	55.65	57.80	119.34	271.48	191.38
Kailashahar	6.65	6.45	5.24	64.86	65.05	127.29	279.90	199.69
Chandipur	6.25	6.25	5.95	71.25	70.55	137.63	297.77	222.95

Table 4.4 Crisp data summaries for the post-monsoon session

Stations	wp_1	wp_2	wp_3	wp_4	wp_5	wp_6	wp_7	wp_8
Dhumacharar	6.35	6.75	4.45	48.87	53.90	112.85	241.66	179.92
Masauli	6.60	6.86	4.56	53.25	59.58	123.79	265.58	188.86
Kumarghat	6.56	6.95	4.91	61.56	61.25	136.15	282.93	197.75
Kailashahar	6.37	5.96	6.24	60.98	71.75	146.54	315.19	212.95
Chandipur	6.51	5.34	6.75	65.55	77.95	159.37	354.25	234.55

(2012). Based on established norms and thresholds, this comparison aids in evaluating the current state of the water quality and identifying any pollution risks.

4.3.2.7 Assessment of Water Pollution of Manu River Using FSES

Step 1. Let the set of sample stations be represented as Station = $\{s_1 =$ Dhumacharar, $s_2 =$ Masauli, $s_3 =$ Kumarghat, $s_4 =$ Kailashahar, $s_5 =$ Chandipur$\}$ along the Manu River, as shown in Table 4.2. We define the set P of WQPs as follows:

$$P = \left\{ \begin{array}{c} wt_1 = pH,\, wt_2 = Dissolve\ oxygen,\, wt_3 = Biochemical\ oxygen\ demand, \\ wt_4 = Total\ hardness,\, wt_5 = Total\ alkalinity,\, wt_6 = Total\ dissolved\ solid, \\ wt_7 = Total\ Coliform,\, wt_8 = Fecal\ coliform \end{array} \right\}$$

Step 2. We analyze the derived crisp data summaries of water quality parameters for all eight designated sites during the pre-monsoon, monsoon, and post-monsoon periods, as shown in Tables 4.2, 4.3, and 4.4, respectively.

Step 3. We reference the standard and ideal values of the water quality parameters based on recommendations from relevant agencies, as presented in Table 4.5.

Step 4. Drawing from the ideal and standard values of the water quality indicators presented in Table 4.5, we formulate fuzzy membership functions for diverse water quality indicators as outlined below:

1. pH: $\mu_{wt_1}(x) = \begin{cases} \frac{7.0-x}{7.0-6.5};\ when\ 6.5 \le x \le 7.0 \\ \frac{x-7.0}{8.5-7.0};\ when\ 7.0 \le x \le 8.5 \\ 1;\ otherwise \end{cases}$

2. Dissolve oxygen: $\mu_{wt_2}(x) = \begin{cases} \frac{14.6-x}{14.6-5};\ when\ 5 \le x \le 14.6 \\ 1;\ when\ x \le 5 \\ 0;\ when\ x \ge 14.6 \end{cases}$

3. Biochemical oxygen demand: $\mu_{wt_3}(x) = \begin{cases} \frac{x-0}{5-0};\ when\ 0 \le x \le 5 \\ 1;\ when\ x \ge 5 \end{cases}$

4. Total hardness: $\mu_{wt_4}(x) = \begin{cases} \frac{x-0}{300-0};\ when\ 0 \le x \le 300 \\ 1;\ when\ x \ge 300 \end{cases}$

5. Total alkalinity: $\mu_{wt_5}(x) = \begin{cases} \frac{x-0}{200-0}; \textit{when}\ 0 \leq x \leq 200 \\ 1; \textit{when}\ x \geq 200 \end{cases}$
6. Total dissolved solid: $\mu_{wt_6}(x) = \begin{cases} \frac{x-0}{500-0}; \textit{when}\ 0 \leq x \leq 500 \\ 1; \textit{when}\ x \geq 500 \end{cases}$
7. Total Coliform: $\mu_{wt_7}(x) = \begin{cases} \frac{x-0}{50-0}; \textit{when}\ 0 \leq x \leq 50 \\ 1; \textit{when}\ x \geq 50 \end{cases}$
8. Fecal coliform: $\mu_{wt_8}(x) = \begin{cases} \frac{x-0}{20-0}; \textit{when}\ 0 \leq x \leq 20 \\ 1; \textit{when}\ x \geq 20 \end{cases}$

These functions represent the degree of membership of a parameter value to a specific category.

Step 5. After establishing fuzzy membership functions for various WQPs, the crisp data summaries are transformed into FSSs denoted as $(\psi, P), (\varphi, P), and (\sigma, P)$, as illustrated in Tables 4.6, 4.7, and 4.8, respectively.

Step 6. We then calculate the resultant FSS denoted as $(\Psi, P) = (\psi, P)\Theta(\varphi, P)\Theta(\sigma, P)$, as shown in Table 4.9.

Step 7. The weight ϖ_i for each water quality parameter $p_i \in$ P is determined using the formula $\alpha_i = \frac{1}{S_i}$ where S_i recommended standard value of ith water quality parameter $p_i \in P$. According to this calculation, the relative weights assigned to the water quality parameters in $P$are as follows:

$$\{\varpi = \varpi_1 = \varpi(wt_1) = 0.118; \varpi_2 = \varpi(wt_2) = 0.2; \varpi_3 = \varpi(wt_3) = 0.2; \varpi_4 = \varpi(wt_4) = 0.003; \varpi_5 = \varpi(wt_5) = 0.005; \varpi_6 = \varpi(wt_6) = 0.002; \varpi_7 = \alpha(wt_7) = 0.02; \varpi_8 = \varpi(wt_8)) = 0.05\}$$

The approach of defining the weight of a water quality parameter using the reciprocal of its standard value is rooted in the understanding that lower concentrations of certain pollutants indicate better water quality, while higher concentrations are detrimental. This method serves several purposes and is justified in the following ways:

1. **Inverse Relationship**: The underlying logic is that the quality of water improves as the concentration of harmful substances decreases. Thus, parameters with lower standard values—indicating better water quality—are assigned higher weights. Conversely, parameters with higher standard values (indicating poorer quality) receive lower weights. This inverse relationship helps in ranking parameters based on their impact on overall water quality.
2. **Standard Values as Benchmarks**: Standard values for water quality parameters, established by regulatory bodies like the WHO and the Environmental Protection Agency, provide benchmarks for acceptable levels. We ensure that parameters that are more important for preserving water quality are given more weight in the final evaluation by employing the reciprocal of these values.
3. **Normalization of Units**: The ranges and units of measurement for many water quality parameters vary. This method normalizes the parameters by utilizing the standard value's reciprocal, enabling comparisons across other metrics.

This guarantees that every parameter's significance is assessed consistently, irrespective of its unit or natural range.

4. **Focus on Water Quality Improvement**: The method emphasizes the need for improvement in water quality. For example, the assessment model assigns a lower weight to a high concentration of a pollutant that harms human health or aquatic life, emphasizing the need for activities to lessen that concentration.
5. **Prioritization of Management Efforts**: By assigning weights in this manner, decision-makers can prioritize management efforts toward parameters that have the most significant negative impact on water quality. This aligns with a strategic approach to environmental management, where resources can be allocated effectively to areas that require urgent attention.

Defining weights based on the reciprocal of standard values provides a logical and systematic way to prioritize water quality parameters. It underscores the relationship between concentration levels and water quality, ensuring that critical indicators of pollution and ecosystem health are appropriately emphasized in the analysis.

Step 8. Based on the FSS (Ψ, P) presented in Table 4.9 and the relative weight ϖ outlined in step 6, we calculate the pollution score $\Omega_{\varpi}(ss_i)$ for each $ss_i \in S_S$ as follows: $\Omega_{\varpi}(ss_1)$=0.857018769, $\Omega_{\varpi}(ss_2)$=0.835870538, $\Omega_{\varpi}(ss_3) = 0.859481786$, $\Omega_{\varpi}(ss_4) = 0.919630082$, $\Omega_{\varpi}(ss_5) = 0.963362771$.

Step 9. Based on the data provided, the pollution scores reflecting the water quality in the Manu River at the sampling stations Dhumacharar, Masauli, Kumarghat, Kailashahar, and Chandipur were 0.857018769, 0.835870538, 0.859481786, 0.919630082, and 0.963362771, respectively. It is noteworthy that all these pollution scores (varying from 0.843442901 to 0.963362771) categorize the water condition of the Manu River at all data collection sites as unsatisfactory, mainly owing to the arrival of wastewater characterized by higher total coliform and fecal coliform. Of particular interest is Station Masauli, specifically the Bathing Ghat point (24.100°N, 91.972°E), which has a pollution score of 0.835870538, indicating comparatively

Table 4.5 Ideal and standard values of water quality parameters

WQPs	Parameter name	Standard value	Ideal value	Recommending agencies
wt_1	pH	6.5–8.5	7	ICMR (1975)/BIS (2012)
wt_2	Dissolved Oxygen (mg/l)	5.00	14.6	WHO (2011)
wt_3	Biological Oxygen Demand (mg/l)	5.00	0	ICMR (1975)
wt_4	Total Hardness(mg/l)	300	0	ICMR (1975)/BIS (2012)
wt_5	Total Alkalinity (mg/l)	200	0	BIS (2012)
wt_6	Total Dissolved Solids (mg/l)	500	0	ICMR (1975)/BIS (2012)
wt_7	Total Coliform (MPN/100 ml)	50	0	CPCB (2008)
wt_8	Fecal Coliform (MPN/100 ml)	20	0	CPCB (2008)

Table 4.6 The FSS (ψ, P)

Stations	wt_1	wt_2	wt_3	wt_4	wt_5	wt_6	wt_7	wt_8
Dhumacharar	1.0	0.848958	0.670	0.1381	0.29485	0.23990	1	1
Masauli	1.0	0.807292	0.710	0.1491	0.31770	0.27908	1	1
Kumarghat	0.5	0.839583	0.794	0.1665	0.31275	0.28534	1	1
Kailashahar	0.9	0.921875	0.950	0.2082	0.36375	0.31624	1	1
Chandipur	1.0	0.951042	1.000	0.2149	0.39825	0.32264	1	1

Table 4.7 The FSS (φ, P)

Stations	wt_1	wt_2	wt_3	wt_4	wt_5	wt_6	wt_7	wt_8
Dhumacharar	0.86	0.796875	0.892	0.1488	0.27725	0.20770	1	1
Masauli	0.52	0.814583	0.992	0.1652	0.26275	0.22330	1	1
Kumarghat	1.00	0.821875	0.982	0.1855	0.28900	0.23868	1	1
Kailashahar	0.70	0.848958	1.000	0.2162	0.32525	0.25458	1	1
Chandipur	1.00	0.869792	1.000	0.2375	0.35275	0.27526	1	1

Table 4.8 The FSS (σ, P)

Stations	wt_1	wt_2	wt_3	wt_4	wt_5	wt_6	wt_7	wt_8
Dhumacharar	1.00	0.817708	0.890	0.1629	0.26950	0.22570	1	1
Masauli	0.80	0.806250	0.912	0.1775	0.29790	0.24758	1	1
Kumarghat	0.88	0.796875	0.982	0.2052	0.30625	0.27230	1	1
Kailashahar	1.00	0.900000	1.000	0.2033	0.35875	0.29308	1	1
Chandipur	0.98	0.964583	1.000	0.2185	0.38975	0.31874	1	1

Table 4.9 The FSS (Ψ, P)

Stations	wt_1	wt_2	wt_3	wt_4	wt_5	wt_6	wt_7	wt_8
Dhumacharar	0.9533	0.82118	0.8173	0.1499	0.2805	0.22443	1	1
Masauli	0.7733	0.80937	0.8713	0.1639	0.2928	0.24999	1	1
Kumarghat	0.7933	0.81944	0.9193	0.1857	0.3027	0.26544	1	1
Kailashahar	0.8667	0.89028	0.9833	0.2092	0.3493	0.28797	1	1
Chandipur	0.9933	0.92847	1.0000	0.2236	0.3803	0.30555	1	1

better water quality at this location than others. Conversely, our analysis reveals that the water quality at station Chandipur (located at the Indo-Bangla border area) downstream into Bangladesh (24.316°N, 91.992°E) is notably poorer than at other stations.

4.3.3 *Result Analysis*

The pollution scores derived from the FSES provide valuable insights into the water condition of the Manu River at different data collection sites. Let's delve deeper into the explanations behind these pollution scores:

4.3.3.1 Overall Water Quality Assessment

The pollution scores varying from 0.843442901 to 0.963362771 categorize the water quality of the Manu River at all data collection sites as poor. This categorization is primarily attributed to higher levels of total coliform and fecal coliform, indicating contamination from wastewater sources. The following analysis provides a detailed overview of water conditions at each data collection site along the Manu River, highlighting the specific pollution scores and potential sources of contamination.

Dhumacharar: Pollution score of 0.857018769 indicates poor water quality due to elevated levels of pollutants, particularly coliform bacteria, possibly from local human activities or agricultural runoff.

Masauli: Notably, the pollution score of 0.835870538 suggests comparatively better water quality at this location, particularly at the Bathing Ghat point. This improvement could be attributed to lower levels of pollutants or better water management practices in this area.

Kumarghat: A pollution score of 0.859481786 signifies poor water quality, similar to other upstream stations, and indicates consistent pollution levels along the river stretch.

Kailashahar: The pollution score of 0.919630082 indicates deteriorating water quality, possibly influenced by additional pollution sources or reduced dilution capacity downstream.

Chandipur (Indo-Bangla Border): Notably, the pollution score of 0.963362771 at this station indicates significantly poorer water quality than other locations. This drop in water quality may result from localized pollution sources close to the border or cumulative pollution inputs along the iver course (Fig. 4.4).

4.3.3.2 Factors Influencing Pollution Scores

Coliform Levels: Elevated levels of fecal and total coliform are the main cause of higher pollution scores at all stations. These bacteria indicate the presence of sewage or organic waste in the river water and are markers of fecal pollution.

Human Activities: Anthropogenic activities that affect the overall water quality throughout the river stretch include industrial discharge, agricultural runoff, and inappropriate trash disposal.

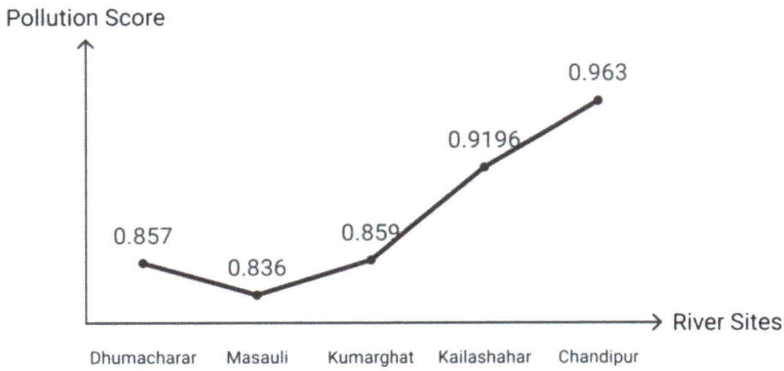

Fig. 4.4 Pollution scores of Manu River sites

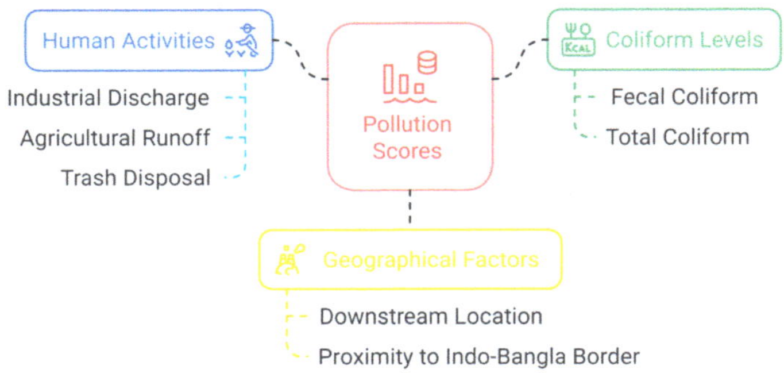

Fig. 4.5 Factors influencing pollution scores

Geographical Factors: Chandipur's downstream location and close proximity to the Indo-Bangla border may expose it to additional sources of pollution, which could contribute to the water quality degradation that has been reported (Fig. 4.5).

4.3.3.3 Impact of pH, Dissolved Oxygen, and Biochemical Oxygen Demand on Water Quality

The analysis of pH, dissolved oxygen, and biochemical oxygen demand from the results presented in Table 4.9 provides critical insights into the water quality at the five sampling stations along the Manu River. Here's a detailed observation of each parameter based on the provided FSS:

pH (Weight: wt_1): The pH values across the stations show several fuzzy scores, with the highest at Chandipur (0.9933) and the lowest at Dhumacharar (0.9533). This suggests that the water quality is generally alkaline or neutral across these sites. Maintaining a pH within the acceptable range (typically 6.5–8.5) is crucial for aquatic life, as extreme pH levels can adversely affect biodiversity, metabolic processes, and the solubility of pollutants. The relatively high scores indicate that the water quality is favorable concerning pH, which is essential for the health of aquatic ecosystems.

Dissolved Oxygen (Weight: wt_2): The dissolved oxygen levels also reflect significant variations among the sampling sites, with scores ranging from 0.82118 in Dhumacharar to 0.92847 in Chandipur. These scores indicate relatively good oxygen availability, essential for sustaining fish and other aquatic organisms. Higher dissolved oxygen levels are indicative of healthier ecosystems, as they support aerobic respiration in aquatic life. The results suggest that the oxygen levels at all stations are adequate, though slightly lower scores at Dhumacharar may warrant monitoring for potential oxygen depletion due to pollution or organic matter decomposition.

Biochemical Oxygen Demand (Weight: wt_3): BOD values are crucial for assessing organic pollution levels in water bodies. The scores for BOD range from 0.8173 in Dhumacharar to 1.0000 in Chandipur, reflecting varying levels of organic matter present in the water. A higher BOD score indicates more significant organic pollution and a higher demand for oxygen by microorganisms. This can lead to reduced dissolved oxygen levels, especially in areas with high organic waste. According to the results, Chandipur has a high BOD, which may indicate that organic pollutants have increased due to anthropogenic activities.

The findings show that although the dissolved oxygen and pH levels are generally within acceptable ranges, the fluctuating BOD levels point to localized organic pollution problems. Higher BOD concentrations can have a detrimental effect on overall water quality by lowering dissolved oxygen levels and endangering aquatic ecosystems. Therefore, monitoring and management efforts should concentrate on these areas.

To stop ecological deterioration, these metrics must be continuously monitored, especially in places like Chandipur where BOD levels are high. Adopting waste management and pollution prevention measures could improve the Manu River's water quality and sustain the well-being of its aquatic life.

4.3.3.4 Significance of Results to Stakeholders

For several stakeholders, including local communities, legislators, environmental organizations, and businesses, the findings of the Manu River's water quality evaluation have significant ramifications. Knowing the importance of these results can help with strategic planning and well-informed decision-making to enhance water quality and manage resources responsibly.

Local Communities

- **Health Implications:** The identification of poor water quality, particularly concerning elevated levels of total coliform and fecal coliform, highlights immediate health risks to local communities that depend on the river for drinking water, bathing, and other domestic uses. Communities can benefit from awareness programs about waterborne diseases and the importance of safe water practices.

- **Livelihoods:** Many local communities rely on the river for fishing and agriculture. Water quality deterioration can negatively impact crop irrigation and fish populations, endangering economic stability and food security. To create sustainable practices that reduce pollution and save livelihoods, stakeholders can work together.

Policymakers and Government Agencies

- Regulatory Frameworks: The findings highlight the need for more stringent laws and regulations on agricultural runoff and wastewater discharge. Policymakers can use this information to create and carry out laws that support improved waste management techniques and safeguard water supplies.
- Resource Allocation: The evaluation results might direct the distribution of funds and resources for initiatives aimed at improving the water quality. Policymakers might prioritize locations with the highest pollution scores for intervention and remediation.

Environmental Organizations

- Conservation Initiatives: The findings can be used by environmental non-governmental organizations to promote the preservation of the Manu River and its ecology. Campaigns to restore the health of the river through reforestation, habitat restoration, and pollution mitigation measures can be supported by the data.
- Public Awareness Campaigns: The crucial results can mobilize community participation and awareness campaigns. Organizations can raise public awareness of the need to preserve water quality and the harm pollution does to biodiversity.

Industries and Businesses

- Corporate Social Responsibility (CSR): Through CSR initiatives, businesses that operate close to the river can be persuaded to embrace more environmentally friendly practices. Businesses can lessen their environmental effect by investing in waste treatment and cleaner technology as a result of the findings.
- Risk management: Businesses that depend on the river must know how water quality affects their operations. The findings can help advise industries in creating backup plans for possible water-related problems and improve risk assessments.

Academia and Research Institutions

- Opportunities for Additional Research: The results may encourage more investigation into the causes and effects of pollution on water quality. Academic institutions can work with local governments and communities to monitor continuous changes in water quality and investigate creative solutions.
- Data for Model Development: Using the data, researchers may create prediction models that evaluate the effects of various pollution sources over time, allowing for the developing of more efficient management plans for the river's health.

The Manu River's water quality assessment results are important to many stakeholders because they draw attention to pressing environmental and public health problems that require attention. By comprehending and implementing these findings, stakeholders can collaborate to restore the river's ecosystem, enhance public health, and implement sustainable water management techniques. This cooperative strategy can ensure the long-term sustainability of this vital water supply and build resilience against upcoming pollution concerns.

4.3.3.5 Management Implications

To improve the Manu River's water quality, the FSES-based assessment identifies problem regions and stresses the need for efficient pollution management measures, especially those that target coliform contamination.

To reduce the adverse effects of pollution and protect water resources for the health of ecosystems and human welfare, it also emphasizes the significance of ongoing monitoring, prompt actions, and sustainable management techniques.

The pollution ratings provide a thorough assessment of the dynamics of the water condition along the Manu River, directing focused actions and management plans for environmental preservation and protection.

4.3.3.6 Urgent Action Needed

The water quality of the Manu River exhibits hazardous levels of microbiological pollution. The high Total Coliform and fecal coliform concentrations in the Manu River water samples from all monitoring locations and sessions indicate a severe health risk. Total coliform bacteria indicate fecal pollution and the possible presence of dangerous pathogens in water sources. The risk of waterborne illnesses and diseases is further highlighted by fecal coliform derived from human and animal waste.

Communities that depend on the Manu River for drinking water and other household needs are particularly in danger from this type of microbial pollution. Many waterborne illnesses, such as cholera, typhoid fever, hepatitis, and gastrointestinal infections, can be brought on by these bacteria. These health risks are more likely to affect vulnerable groups, including children, older people, and people with weakened immune systems.

To address these issues, prompt and all-encompassing actions are needed, such as:

- Water Treatment: Using efficient methods to remove microbiological contaminants from water, such as disinfection using UV radiation or chlorine. Water treatment procedures face difficulties when microbiological pollutants are present. To ensure the safety of drinking water supplies, sophisticated treatment technologies and vigilant monitoring are required, as traditional water treatment procedures may not eradicate all germs.

- Source Protection: Policies should be implemented to stop untreated sewage discharge and agricultural runoff from further contaminating the Manu River.
- Monitoring and Testing: To identify and quickly treat contamination, the water quality is regularly monitored and tested at several locations along the river.
- Public Awareness: Teaching nearby people about the dangers of drinking tainted water and encouraging hygienic habits like boiling water before drinking it. Public health is directly threatened by the high concentrations of the bacteria Total Coliform and Fecal Coliform found in water samples from the Manu River. One of the leading causes of waterborne illnesses and even deaths globally is microbial contamination of water sources, which is particularly problematic in places with poor access to sanitary facilities and clean water.
- Cooperation: Governmental institutions, environmental groups, local communities, and other stakeholders must work together to effectively mitigate the microbial contamination in the Manu River. Implementing thorough water quality monitoring programs, upholding laws, and encouraging community involvement in pollution control projects require cooperative efforts. They are working with local communities, environmental organizations, and government agencies to create and execute long-term solutions for improving water quality.
- Contamination Sources: The high concentrations of coliform bacteria are a sign of contamination from several sources, including industrial discharges, agricultural runoff that contains animal waste, and untreated sewage from human settlements. These sources must be located and addressed for pollution control and water quality management to be effective.
- Environmental Consequences: Microbial pollution has a negative impact on aquatic ecosystems in addition to human health. Marine plants and animals may suffer from oxygen depletion caused by high coliform bacteria concentrations. It can further deteriorate water quality and aid in the growth of toxic algal blooms.
- Community Vulnerability: The health hazards linked to microbial contamination are especially dangerous for communities that depend on the Manu River for bathing, cooking, and drinking. Prioritizing mitigation activities is necessary for vulnerable groups, like the elderly, pregnant women, and children, who are more susceptible to waterborne illnesses.
- Long-Term Solutions: Reducing microbiological contamination necessitates a multifaceted strategy that includes policy interventions, community education, water treatment enhancements, and pollution avoidance. To offer safe and dependable water supplies, long-term solutions should prioritize infrastructure development, source protection, and sustainable water resource management techniques.

These initiatives are essential for ensuring access to safe and clean drinking water, a fundamental human right, and protecting public health. Prompt intervention and continuous monitoring and management are necessary to reduce the health concerns associated with microbial pollution in the Manu River and other comparable water bodies worldwide.

4.4 Conclusions

The Manu River in Tripura, India, is the specific subject of the study, which explores the intricacies of assessing river water quality. Our study's use of the FSES, a groundbreaking system for measuring water pollution, yielded concerning pollution scores that show the river's declining water quality. The leading cause of this deterioration is the high concentrations of total and fecal coliform bacteria, mainly caused by household wastewater's discharge into the river. These findings have significant ramifications, indicating the urgent need for swift action to reduce pollution sources and safeguard the public's health in the area. Building on these discoveries, our study aims to improve the pollution score function to make FSES more valuable and applicable. This enhancement attempts to produce more precise and valuable assessments to support informed decision-making and focused pollution management and remediation interventions.

The FSES's evaluation of the Manu River's water pollution provides crucial new information about the dynamics of water quality, the sources of pollution, and possible health hazards. Water quality at measured stations is classified as poor by the pollution ratings obtained from the FSES, mainly because of high fecal and total coliform levels. This emphasizes how urgent it is to deal with microbiological contamination and implement efficient pollution control strategies.

The study's main findings include:

- Poor Water Quality Status: The pollution scores from the examined stations, which range from 0.843 to 0.963, show poor water quality, which poses severe threats to human health and ecological health.
- Microbial Contamination: High levels of fecal and total coliform indicate sewage, agricultural runoff, and other sources of contamination, underscoring the necessity of water treatment and source protection.
- Effect on Public Health: Vulnerable groups that depend on the Manu River for household and drinking water are particularly at risk for health problems due to the presence of microbiological pollutants.
- Urgent Action Needed: Immediate and thorough actions are needed to combat microbiological contamination. These actions include water treatment, source protection, monitoring, public awareness, and stakeholder collaboration.
- Long-Term Solutions: To improve water quality over the long run, sustainable methods of managing water resources, pollution control techniques, infrastructure upgrades, and legislative actions are necessary.
- Cooperation: Effective pollution reduction and water quality management depend on cooperation between governmental institutions, environmental groups, other stakeholders, and local populations.
- Community Vulnerability: To protect public health, mitigation activities must prioritize vulnerable populations, emphasizing supplying safe and dependable water sources.

The study's result emphasizes how critical it is to address microbial contamination in the Manu River and other comparable water bodies worldwide. To ensure access to safe and clean drinking water, safeguard ecosystems, and reduce health risks related to water pollution, it urges quick action, continuous monitoring, and sustainable management techniques.

In the future, our research will go beyond water quality evaluation. We see broader uses for FSES in various fields, such as computer science and medical diagnostics. By incorporating modern circumstances and utilizing technological developments like artificial intelligence and data analytics, FSES can be modified to tackle intricate problems and provide insightful information in various industries. In areas where water pollution is a problem, this continued research and development of FSES is a big step toward bettering environmental management techniques, increasing public health outcomes, and encouraging sustainable development.

References

Ahmed, M., Mumtaz, R., & Rafia Zaidi, S. M. H. (2021). Analysis of water quality indices and machine learning techniques for rating water pollution: A case study of Rawal Dam, Pakistan. *Water Supply, 21*(6), 3225–3250.

Akram, M., Shumaiza, & Alcantud, J. C. R. (2023) *Multi-criteria decision-making methods with bipolar fuzzy sets* (Forum for Interdisciplinary Mathematics). Springer.

Alcantud, J. C. R., & Santos-García, G. (2017). A new criterion for soft set-based decision-making problems under incomplete information. *International Journal of Computational Intelligence Systems, 10*, 394–404.

Ali, M. I., Feng, F., Liu, X. Y., Min, W. K., & Shabir, M. (2009). On some new operations in soft set theory. *Computer & Mathematics with Applications, 57*(9), 1547–1553.

American Public Health Association (APHA). (2005). *Standard methods for the examination of water and wastewater* (21st ed.). American Public Health Association.

Bhardwaj, N., & Sharma, P. (2021). An advanced uncertainty measure using fuzzy soft sets: Application to decision-making problems. *Big Data Mining and Analytics, 4*(2), 94–103.

Bureau of Indian Standards (BIS). (2012). *Indian standards specification for drinking water* (BIS: 10500).

Brown, R. M., McClelland, N. I., Deininger, R. A., & Tozer, R. G. (1970). A water quality index—Do we dare? *Water Sewage Works, 117*, 339–343.

Chen, Y., Liu, J., Chen, Z., & Zhang, Y. (2020). Group decision-making method based on generalized vague N-soft sets. In *Chinese control and decision conference* (pp. 4010–4015).

Central Pollution Control Board (CPCB). (2008). *Guidelines for water quality management*.

Dalkılıç, O. (2021). A novel approach to soft set theory in decision-making under uncertainty. *International Journal of Computer Mathematics*.

Dalkılıç, O., & Demirtaş, N. (2023). Algorithms for Covid-19 outbreak using soft set theory: Estimation and application. *Soft Computing, 27*, 3203–3211.

Darvish Falehi, A., & Torkaman, H. (2023). Optimal fractional order interval type-2 fuzzy controller for upside-down asymmetric multilevel inverter based dynamic voltage restorer to accurately compensate faulty network voltage. *Journal of Ambient Intelligence and Humanized Computing*.

Das, A. K., & Granados, C. (2022a). A new fuzzy parameterized intuitionistic fuzzy soft multiset theory and group decision-making. *Journal of Current Science and Technology, 12*(3), 547–567. https://doi.org/10.14456/jcst.2022.42

Das, A. K., & Granados, C. (2022b). FP-intuitionistic multi fuzzy N-soft set and its induced FP-Hesitant N soft set in decision-making. *Decision Making: Applications in Management and Engineering, 5*(1), 67–89. https://doi.org/10.31181/dmame181221045d

Das, A. K., & Granados, C. (2022c). IFP-intuitionistic multi fuzzy N-soft set and its induced IFP-hesitant N-soft set in decision-making. *Journal of Ambient Intelligence and Humanized Computing, 14*, 10143–10152. https://doi.org/10.1007/s12652-021-03677-w

Das, A. K. (2016). On partially included intuitionistic fuzzy rough relations. *Afrika Matematika, 27*, 993–1001. https://doi.org/10.1007/s13370-016-0395-2

Das, A. K. (2018). Weighted fuzzy soft multiset and decision-making. *International Journal of Machine Learning and Cybernetics, 9*, 787–794. https://doi.org/10.1007/s13042-016-0607-y

Das, A. K., & Granados, C. (2021). An advanced approach to fuzzy soft group decision-making using weighted average ratings. *SN Computer Science, 2*, 471. https://doi.org/10.1007/s42979-021-00873-5

Das, A. K., Granados, C., & Bhattacharya, J. (2022). Some new operations on fuzzy soft sets and their applications in decision-making. Songklanakarin *Journal of Science and Technology, 44*(2), 440–449. https://doi.org/10.14456/sjst-psu.2022.61

Das, A. K., Gupta, N., & Granados, C. (2023). Weighted hesitant bipolar-valued fuzzy soft set in decision-making. *Songklanakarin Journal of Science and Technology, 45*(6), 681–690. https://sjst.psu.ac.th/journal/45-6/10.pdf

Das, A. K., Gupta, N., Mahmood, T., Tripathy, B. C., Das, R., & Das, S. (2024). An innovative fuzzy multi-criteria decision making model for analyzing anthropogenic influences on urban river water quality. *Iran Journal of Computer Science*. https://doi.org/10.1007/s42044-024-00211-x

Das, A. K., Gupta, N., Mahmood, T., Tripathy, B. C., Das, R., & Das, S. (2025a). An efficient water quality evaluation model using weighted hesitant fuzzy soft sets for water pollution rating. In A. Kumar, P. Kumar, S. Rathee, & B. Kumar (Eds.), *Mechatronics: Concepts, tools, applications, and new trends* (1st ed., p. 17). CRC Press. https://doi.org/10.1201/9781003494478

Das, A. K., Gupta, N., Patra, S., Tripathy, B. C., Das, R., & Datta, R. (2025b). An effective fuzzy soft decision-making model for rating water pollution: A case study of Manu, the longest river in Tripura, India. *Vietnam Journal of Science and Technology*.

Das, A. K., & Granados, C. (2023). Preference intuitionistic fuzzy rough relation and its theoretical approach. *Journal of the Indian Mathematical Society, 90*(3–4), 199–212.

Diamantini, E., Lutz, S. R., Mallucci, S., Majone, B., Merz, R., & Bellin, A. (2018). Driver detection of water quality trends in three large European river basins. *Science of the Total Environment, 612*, 49–62.

Feng, F., Jun, Y. B., Liu, X., & Li, L. (2010). An adjustable approach to fuzzy soft set based decision making. *Journal of Computational and Applied Mathematics, 234*, 10–20.

Gao, R., & Wu, J. (2021). Filter with its applications in fuzzy soft topological spaces. *AIMS Mathematics, 6*(3), 2359–2368.

Granados, C., Das, A. K., & Das, B. (2022). Some continuous neutrosophic distributions with neutrosophic parameters based on neutrosophic random variables. *Advances in the Theory of Nonlinear Analysis and its Applications, 33*(2), 293 https://doi.org/10.31197/atnaa.1056480

Granados, C., Das, A. K., & Osu, B. (2023). Weighted neutrosophic soft multiset and its application to decision making. *Yugoslav Journal of Operations Research, 33*(2), 293–308. https://doi.org/10.2298/YJOR220915034G

Guettaf, M., Maoui, A., & Ihdene, Z. (2017). Assessment of water quality: A case study of the Seybouse River (North East of Algeria). *Applied Water Science, 7*, 295–307.

Hutchins, M. G., Abesser, C., Prudhomme, C., Elliott, J. A., Bloomfield, J. P., Mansour, M. M., & Hitt, O. E. (2018). Combined impacts of future land-use and climate stressors on water resources and quality in groundwater and surface waterbodies of the upper Thames River basin, UK. *Science of the Total Environment*, 962–986.

Indian Council of Medical Research (ICMR). (1975). *Manual of standards of quality for drinking water supplies* (Special Report No. 44:27).

Kumar, N., Tischbein, B., Kusche, J., Laux, P., Beg, M. K., & Bogardi, J. J. (2017). Impact of climate change on water resources of upper Kharun catchment in Chhattisgarh, India. *Journal of Hydrology: Regional Studies, 13*, 189–207.

Liu, W., Khalil, A. M., Basheer, R., & Lin, Y. (2023). Prediction system for diagnosis and detection of coronavirus disease-2019 (COVID-19): A fuzzy-soft expert system. *CMES-Computer Modeling in Engineering & Sciences, 135*(3), 2715–2730.

Maji, P. K., Biswas, R., & Roy, A. R. (2001). Fuzzy soft sets. *Journal of Fuzzy Mathematics, 9*(3), 589–602.

Maji, P. K., Biswas, R., & Roy, A. R. (2002). An application of soft sets in decision-making problem. *Computers & Mathematics with Applications, 44*(8–9), 1077–1083.

Maji, P. K., Biswas, R., & Roy, A. R. (2003). Soft set theory. *Computers & Mathematics with Applications, 45*(4–5), 555–562.

Miller, J. D., & Hutchins, M. (2017). The impacts of urbanization and climate change on urban flooding and urban water quality: A review of the evidence concerning the United Kingdom. *Journal of Hydrology: Regional Studies, 12*, 345–362.

Molodtsov, D. (1999). Soft set theory-first results. *Computers & Mathematics with Applications, 37*(4–5), 19–31.

Mukherjee, A., & Das, A. K. (2015a). Application of interval valued intuitionistic fuzzy soft set in investment decision making. In *2015 Fifth International Conference on Advances in Computing and Communications (ICACC)* (pp. 61–64). https://doi.org/10.1109/ICACC.2015.37

Mukherjee, A., & Das, A. K. (2015b). Relations on intuitionistic fuzzy soft multi sets. In K. Kim (Ed.), *Information Science and Applications. Lecture Notes in Electrical Engineering* (vol. 339). Springer. https://doi.org/10.1007/978-3-662-46578-3_71

Mukherjee, A., & Das, A. K. (2015c). Interval valued intuitionistic fuzzy soft multi set theoretic approach to decision making problems. In *2015 International Conference on Computer, Communication and Control (IC4)* (pp. 1–5). https://doi.org/10.1109/IC4.2015.7375640

Mukherjee, A., & Das, A. K. (2016a). Application of fuzzy soft multi sets in decision-making problems. In Nagar, A., Mohapatra, D., Chaki, N. (Eds.), *Proceedings of 3rd International Conference on Advanced Computing, Networking and Informatics. Smart Innovation, Systems and Technologies* (vol. 43). Springer. https://doi.org/10.1007/978-81-322-2538-6_3

Mukherjee, A., & Das, A. K. (2016b). Topological structure formed by intuitionistic fuzzy rough relations. *Journal of the Indian Mathematical Society, 83*(1–2), 135–144.

Mukherjee, A., & Das, A. K. (2022). Einstein operations on fuzzy soft multisets and decision making. *Boletim Da Sociedade Paranaense De Matematica, 40*, 1–10. https://doi.org/10.5269/bspm.32546

Mukherjee, A., & Das, A. K. (2023). *Essentials of fuzzy soft multisets: Theory and applications* (pp. 1–151). Springer Nature Singapore. https://doi.org/10.1007/978-981-19-2760-7

Mukherjee, A., Das, A. K., Gupta, N., Patra, S., Mahmood, T., Das, S., & Das, R. (2025). A novel generalized interval-valued neutrosophic rough soft set framework for enhanced decision-making: Application in water quality assessment. *Transactions on Fuzzy Sets and System.*

Paik, B., & Mondal, S. K. (2021). A distance-similarity method to solve fuzzy sets and fuzzy soft sets based decision-making problems. *Soft Computing, 24*, 5217–5229.

Patel, A., & Chitnis, K. (2022). Application of fuzzy logic in river water quality modeling for analysis of industrialization and climate change impact on Sabarmati river. *Water Supply, 22*(1), 238–250.

Patel, P., Bablani, S., & Patel, A. (2020). Impact assessment of urbanization and industrialization using Water Quality Index on Sabaramati River, Ahmedabad. In *International Conference on Innovative Advancement in Engineering and Technology (IAET).* (pp. 1–7). Elsevier.

Rao, Q., Qiu, Y., & Li, J. (2019). Water quality assessment and variation trends analysis of the Min River sea-entry section, China. *Water, Air, Soil, & Pollution, 230*(12), 1–11.

Roy, A. R., & Maji, P. K. (2007). A fuzzy soft set theoretic approach to decision-making problems. *Journal of Computational & Applied Mathematics, 203*, 412–418.

Shah, K. A., & Joshi, G. S. (2017). Evaluation of water quality index for River Sabarmati, Gujarat, India. *Applied Water Science, 7*, 1349–1358.

Wen, X. (2023). Weighted hesitant fuzzy soft set and its application in group decision making. *Granul Comput, 8*, 1583–1605.

World Health Organization (WHO). (2011). *Guidelines for drinking water quality* (4th ed.). World Health Organisation.

Zadeh, L. A. (1965). Fuzzy sets. *Information and Control, 8*(3), 338–353.

Chapter 5
A Solution Framework to Address Model Parameter Uncertainties in ANN-Based Response Surface Models for Multivariate Process Quality Control

Abhinav Kumar Sharma and Anagha Savit

Abstract Multivariate manufacturing process output involves multiple correlated critical quality characteristics called 'responses.' These responses must be monitored, controlled, and optimised simultaneously to maintain the desired overall product quality. Due to dynamic and complex behaviour in multivariate manufacturing processes, researchers and practitioners prefer data-driven empirical models, so-called response surface (RS) models. An empirical RS model provides a mapping function(s) between dependent responses and independent controllable variables. RS models are developed based on offline experimentation or real-time 'as-is' process data, or a combination of both. In this context, due to inherent sampling or process uncertainties, the estimated parameters of the RS model can deviate from their actual values. Thus, such uncertainties in model parameters need to be quantified while developing the RS model(s). Due to the influence of outliers and complex nonlinear relationships between independent and dependent variables, many researchers recommend artificial neural networks (ANN) to generate the RS. However, no specific research considered model parameter uncertainties to develop the RS, using ANN, for multivariate manufacturing processes. Thus, this study attempts to demonstrate and compare three popular approaches, viz. Approximate Bayesian Ensembling (ABE), Monte Carlo Dropout (MCD), and Bayes by Backprop (BBB) to address model parameter uncertainties for ANN-based RS models. The performance of these approaches is evaluated using simulated, real-life manufacturing and experimental case data. The key metrics used for performance assessment are average test mean square error and signal-to-noise (S/N) ratio. A multi-criteria decision-making (MCDM) technique is further used to rank the approaches. The

A. K. Sharma (✉)
Operations and Quantitative Techniques Area, Indian Institute of Management Shillong, Shillong, Meghalaya, India
e-mail: abhinav@iimshillong.ac.in

A. Savit
Department of Mechanical Engineering, Indian Institute of Technology Bombay, Mumbai, Maharashtra, India

I. Mukherjee et al. (eds.), *Decision Sciences for Quality and Productivity Improvement*,
https://doi.org/10.1007/978-981-95-7545-9_5

results indicate the superiority of Approximate Bayesian Ensembling in providing credible confidence intervals.

Keywords Machine learning · Quality control · Artificial neural network · Model parameter uncertainty · Response surface · Multivariate manufacturing process

5.1 Introduction

One of the goals of any multivariate manufacturing process is to produce desired quality products for its customers, whether internal or external. The overall quality of the product is assessed based on its process output measurement on multiple interdependent 'critical-to-quality (CTQ) characteristics' or 'responses.' As an example, in multivariate manufacturing of steel strips (Kim & Lin, 2000), the overall quality of the final product is determined based on process output measures of tensile strength, yield strength and elongation. However, monitoring and control of these multiple responses is considered a challenging problem. These problems are generally referred to as multivariate process control (MPC). Simultaneous optimisation of correlated responses, which is an integral part of MPC, is specifically referred to as a multiple response optimisation (MRO) problem.

Mukherjee and Ray (2006) emphasised six important steps for complex MRO solution, (i) identify 'critical-to-quality' responses, (ii) collect relevant data based on an appropriate data collection scheme, (iii) develop appropriate empirical RS model(s), (iv) formulate the overall MRO problem, (v) generate trade-off solutions using an appropriate metaheuristic search strategy, and (vi) evaluate the derived solution(s) for real-life implementation. In MPC (Maji & Mukherjee, 2024; Sikder et al., 2020), an MRO solution specifically addresses the adjustment phase of real-time process control.

Various researchers have emphasised the criticality of the RS model in mapping the functional relationship between responses and independent variables (Montgomery, 2005; Mukherjee & Routroy, 2012). An appropriate response function can precisely estimate the responses for a given multivariate process condition. Real-time best process control or adjustment settings depend on the adequacy of the RS model, so as to provide global or near-optimal solutions.

Generally, the RS model(s) are developed based on a sequence of experiments [e.g. Design of Experiments (DOE)] or 'as-is' manufacturing process data or a combination of both (Coit et al., 1998; Mukherjee & Ray, 2006). In a mass manufacturing (discrete or continuous) environment, estimating the response function using sequential DOE is generally difficult, if not impossible. This can be attributed to additional costs due to scraps generated in experiments in certain offline trial conditions, risk associated with trials in unknown experimental regions due to interaction effects, extra time demanded from the workforce, and production loss in a shift due to offline trials (Goh, 1988; Sharma et al., 2023). In addition, experimental or 'as-is' process data may consist of unusual, missing or outlier observations that can call for approximation while developing the RS models based on classical parametric approaches (Lee & Kim, 2008). The outliers can be removed if there is strong non-statistical evidence (Montgomery & Peck, 1992). However, excluding outliers without due consideration might lead to underestimating the inherent variability of the process. As highlighted by researchers (Anderson-Cook & Prewitt, 2005; Shi et al., 2004), the OLS-based parametric model may lack accurate estimation of the RS model for complex nonlinear relationships with outliers, particularly when there is no statistical justification for removing those outliers. Additionally, a statistically significant correlation between independent variables and varied model assumptions can create hindrances in model building based on parametric approaches (Montgomery & Peck, 1992).

As the RS is developed using sample data, it is also essential to incorporate response predictive uncertainty and/or model parameter uncertainties (Chapman et al., 2014; Sharma et al., 2022). Due to model parameter uncertainties, the optimal process setting conditions, as determined from the fitted RS model(s), may not guarantee global or near-optimality for a different set of RS model(s) developed using different samples collected from the same process (Chapman et al., 2014). Ignoring the predictive uncertainty of the RS model can result in a deviation between the point estimate of responses at a specific process setting condition and the realised true response values. Consequently, the actual response values of the identified best solution can be suboptimal (or local optimal) and even exceed the desired customer specification limits. Very few researchers (Chapman et al., 2014; He et al., 2012, 2021; Ouyang et al., 2017, 2020; Sharma & Mukherjee, 2020; Sharma et al., 2022) have attempted to analyse the RS model parameter and/or predictive uncertainties, considering their influence on point estimate. However, all these studies are restricted to parametric RS models.

To mitigate the limitations of parametric models, several researchers have advocated non-parametric (or distribution-free) approaches [such as artificial neural networks (ANN), patient rule induction method (PRIM), multivariate adaptive regression splines (MARS), and support vector regression (SVR)] to derive appropriate RS models (Coit et al., 1998; Feng & Wang, 2003; Jack Feng & Wang, 2004; Khan et al., 2020; Lee & Kim, 2008; Lee et al., 2021a; Mukherjee & Routroy, 2012; Paliwal & Kumar, 2009; Sharma et al., 2023; Zhang & Huang, 1995). Most of these works suggest ANN as an important RS model-building approach. Zhang and Huang (1995) further claim that ANN is one of the most efficient RS modelling approaches for multivariate manufacturing processes. This is attributed mainly because of (i) their capability to represent intricate non-linear dynamics between dependent and independent variables in the presence of outliers, (ii) their effectiveness in processing interactions among predictor variables, and (iii) their ability to handle significant correlations within independent and dependent variables. Researchers (Sharma et al., 2023; Sikder et al., 2020) have also attempted to analyse the impact of ANN model uncertainty on the point estimates of responses. However, their work is restricted to response predictive uncertainties only.

As per the critical review of the literature (refer to Sect. 5.2), there is no evidence in the open literature that evaluates and compares varied approaches that deal with model parameter uncertainties of ANN in the context of multivariate manufacturing processes. Thus, considering the criticality and importance of ANN-based prediction model under parameter uncertainties, in the context of MRO and MPC problem for complex and nonlinear multivariate manufacturing processes, this study attempts to fill the said research gaps based on the following research questions:

RQ1: What are the existing approaches that can deal with parameter uncertainties of ANN, while developing the RS models?

RQ2: How can decision-makers specifically identify the most suitable approach to develop the RS models, using ANN, considering model parameter uncertainties?

RQ3: How do these approaches perform on multivariate test functions, experimental data and real-life multivariate manufacturing data sets?

The three suggested approaches identified in this study to address model parameter uncertainties in an ANN model are (i) Bayes by Backprop (BBB) (Blundell et al., 2015), (ii) Monte-Carlo Dropout (MCD) (Gal & Ghahramani, 2015), and (iii) Approximately Bayesian Ensembling (ABE) (Pearce et al., 2020). This study explores all these approaches and compares their performance using three different problem contexts, viz., multiobjective test functions, real-life lab experimental data and a real-life multivariate manufacturing case data.

The remainder of this paper is organised as follows. In Sect. 5.2, a critical review of the literature is presented to identify the research gaps and define the research objectives. Section 5.3 elaborates on an eight-step solution framework to address model parameter uncertainties in ANN-based RS models for multivariate process. Section 5.4 details the datasets considered in the study. Section 5.5 discusses the analysis and findings based on the implementation of the solution framework on three different problem contexts, viz. multiobjective test functions, real-life lab experimental dataset, and real-life multivariate manufacturing data set. Section 5.6 highlights the implications of the study in manufacturing context. Section 5.7 highlights the conclusions, limitations, and scope for future investigations.

5.2 Literature Review

Mukherjee and Ray (2006) categorise RS modelling into parametric and non-parametric (or distribution-free) approaches. Some of the widely used parametric methods for the development of the RS model are ordinary least squares (OLS) regression, seemingly unrelated regression, multivariate regression, and generalised linear models (Das & Lee, 2009; Derringer & Suich, 1980; Khuri & Mukhopadhyay, 2010; Kim & Lin, 2000; Shah et al., 2004).

Using parametric RS models, some researchers have addressed model parametric and/or response predictive uncertainties. He et al., (2012, 2017) used OLS and simultaneous confidence interval (CI)-based approach to estimate the response predictive uncertainty. Park (2013) suggested a bootstrap re-sampling-based approach to construct simultaneous CI so as to incorporate response predictive uncertainties. Ouyang et al. (2016a) proposed a robust parameter design approach, considering regression model parameter uncertainties. Ouyang et al. (2016b) further considered the prediction region of multiple responses to address the response uncertainties. However, the approach requires all the response functions to be fitted with the same polynomial order and with the same predictor. In many situations, a subset of predictor variables may be significant for a particular response. Using a common set of predictor variables to fit responses may result in model overfitting and decrease predictive accuracy. Ouyang et al. (2016c) and Wang et al., (2019, 2021) proposed Bayesian inference-based procedure for estimating model parameter uncertainties in RS model development using seemingly unrelated regression and standard multivariate regression models. In their approaches, the posterior distribution of the model parameter is derived from Jefferey's non-informative prior to constructing a credible region for model predictions. Chapman et al. (2014) incorporated model parameter uncertainties and response predictive uncertainties for estimating the responses. In this study, model parameter uncertainty is addressed by simulating multiple model parameters based on the point estimate of fitted response models and the standard error of regression. Furthermore, prediction uncertainty is incorporated by constructing prediction intervals of the responses. Han et al. (2022) consider predictive uncertainties in RS models, developed based on seemingly unrelated regression, by sampling new response values from the point estimate of responses and the simulated error term. The error term is assumed to be multivariate normal with mean zero and the covariance of error distribution is estimated from the variance–covariance matrix of responses. Sharma and Mukherjee (2020) address response predictive uncertainty associated with the OLS-based regression model by constructing simultaneous prediction intervals for multiple responses. Sharma et al. (2022) simultaneously address model parameters and response predictive uncertainty for OLS-based RS models. In their study, the model predictive uncertainty is addressed by constructing a confidence interval on model parameters and response predictive uncertainty is addressed as per Sharma and Mukherjee (2020) approach.

Although parametric methods to develop the RS model may work satisfactorily in certain scenarios, they may not be adequate to describe an underlying complex nonlinear relationship. Parametric models also require few prior assumptions on the functional form of the model (such as linear, quadratic, and higher-order polynomials) between response and predictors. Furthermore, parametric methods have restrictive distribution assumptions (Sharma et al., 2023).

In the context of non-parametric or distribution-free RS models, many researchers recommended ANN for mapping multivariate manufacturing processes (Mukherjee & Routroy, 2012; Noorossana et al., 2009; Onler et al., 2022; Tong & Hsieh, 2001). Lee and Kim (2008) and Lee et al. (2020) used the multi-response patient rule induction method (MR-PRIM) to develop the RS models. Kwak et al. (2010) used an MR-PRIM approach to develop RS models for multistage manufacturing processes. Lee et al. (2021a) used multi-response classification and regression trees (MR-CART) to develop an RS model for a steel manufacturing process. However, their approach requires a sample with a number of observations greater than 5000 and a number of variables less than 15. Lee et al. (2021b) used MR-CART to develop RS models for a multi-stage steel manufacturing process. Jaypuria et al. (2023) developed RS models for predicting electron beam weld quality from weld bead surface using SVR. Denkena et al. (2019) used SVR to develop RS models for process time and quality characteristics of a helical flute grinding process. García et al. (2019) propose nearest neighbour regression, distance-weighted k-nearest regression, and SVR to predict the inner and outer diameter in a tubing extrusion process. A summary of key literature on modelling multivariate manufacturing processes is provided in Table 5.1.

As evident from the review of literature and Table 5.1 summary, there is no study on non-parametric RS models that address model parameter uncertainties in multivariate manufacturing process. Sharma et al. (2023) attempt to incorporate response predictive uncertainties for RS models developed using ANN, SVR and multivariate adaptive regression splines (MARS). They use a bootstrap sampling approach to construct simultaneous prediction intervals for the responses and show

Table 5.1 Summary of the key literature on modelling variate manufacturing processes considering uncertainties

Article	Modelling approach		Type of data		Type of uncertainty	
	P	NP	D	A	PR	M
He et al. (2012)	✓		✓		✓	
Park (2013)	✓		✓		✓	
Chapman et al. (2014)	✓		✓		✓	✓
Ouyang et al. (2016a)	✓		✓			✓
Ouyang et al. (2016b)	✓		✓		✓	
Ouyang et al., (2016c)	✓		✓			✓
He et al. (2017)	✓		✓		✓	
Wang et al. (2019)	✓		✓			✓
Sharma and Mukherjee (2020)	✓		✓		✓	
Wang et al. (2021)	✓		✓			✓
Han et al. (2022)	✓		✓		✓	
Sharma et al. (2022)	✓		✓		✓	✓
Lee and Kim (2008)		✓		✓		
Kwak et al. (2010)		✓		✓		
Mukherjee and Routroy (2012)		✓		✓		
Denkena et al. (2019)		✓	✓			
García et al. (2019)	✓	✓		✓		
Lee et al. (2021a)		✓		✓		
Lee et al. (2021b)		✓		✓		
Sharma et al. (2023)		✓		✓	✓	

P – Parametric, NP – Non – parametric, D – DOE data, A – 'As – is' data, PR – Response predictive uncertainty, M – Model uncertainty the superior performance of ANN to develop the RS model. However, their study did not consider model parameter uncertainties.

There are few instances of research that incorporate model parameter uncertainties using ANN models in other areas of manufacturing. Benker et al. (2021) suggest Bayesian deep learning models trained with Hamiltonian Monte Carlo (HMC) to estimate the remaining useful life (RUL) of simulated turbofan engines and compare the performance of HMC with variational inference (VI) method (Graves, 2011). However, the authors did not consider MCD and ABE for developing prediction models. McNaught and Chan (2011) developed a decision-support system combining Bayesian networks with an intelligent user interface to help Motorola operators diagnose and correct faults during product system testing. Vehtari and Lampinen (1999) evaluated the performance of Bayesian neural networks on prediction of the quality properties of concrete. In their study, Bayesian neural networks consistently provided better results than other methods. Jones et al. (2010) used Bayesian neural networks for modelling maintenance planning in a manufacturing industry. Nannapaneni et al. (2016) introduced a framework that utilises Bayesian neural networks to combine uncertainties from various sources and aims to predict the performance of injection moulding. Giannetti and Ransing (2016) proposed an algorithm to incorporate risk-based thinking into quantifying uncertainty in manufacturing operations. This approach employed a probabilistic method, specifically the likelihood ratio test with bootstrapping, to achieve accurate uncertainty estimation.

Based on the above discussion, critical review of literature, and summary of literature provided in Table 5.1, following research gaps are identified:

(i) Mukherjee and Routroy (2012), Sikder et al. (2020), and Sharma et al. (2023) recommended ANN-based RS models for nonlinear multivariate manufacturing processes. However, all these studies ignored the effect of model parameter uncertainties on predicted response. There is no evidence of literature that explored ANN-based RS model parameters uncertainties and their influence on prediction accuracy.
(ii) There is no open literature that provides a solution framework to address model parameter uncertainties for nonparametric RS model in multivariate manufacturing process.

Thus, this research attempts to provide answers to RQ1, RQ2, and RQ3 (refer to Sect. 5.1). The novel contributions of this work are:

(i) Provides a systematic step-by-step solution framework to deal with parameter uncertainties of ANN-based RS models for multivariate manufacturing process.
(ii) Provides a guideline to evaluate performance of RS models, using ANN, considering model parameter uncertainties.
(iii) Validates the framework and provides evidence on performance evaluation of three different approaches (BBB, MCD, and ABE), to address uncertainties in ANN-based RS models, using classical multivariate test functions, multiple response experimental data, and real-life multivariate manufacturing data.

5.3 A Solution Framework

Sharma et al. (2023) discussed steps to select appropriate nonparametric RS modelling approach for an MRO problem. This study proposes and details a tailored eight-step framework based on their solution framework, to develop an appropriate ANN model, considering model parameter uncertainties, for multivariate manufacturing processes. The proposed new framework is divided into three phases and includes comparative performance analysis and ranking of various RS models. The three-phase process of model development and performance comparison is illustrated in Fig. 5.1. Each phase is detailed in subsequent sub-sections.

5.3.1 *Phase 1: Identification of Independent and Response Variables, Data Collection, and Data Pre-Processing*

In the first step (**Step 1 in** Fig. 5.1) of phase 1, independent variables (X) and response variables (R) are identified using cause-and-effect diagrams, experimental data, past evidence, process knowledge, and preliminary correlation analysis. The feasible operating range of the independent (controllable) variables, along with the target values and specification limits for each response, is also defined in this step. Subsequently, an appropriate data collection scheme is selected to gather the relevant data required for developing an empirical response surface (RS) model for each response variable (**Step 2 in** Fig. 5.1). Data collection may be based on experimental design (Montgomery, 2005), 'as-is' process data, or a combination of both. It is essential to ensure that the process remains statistically stable during the data collection phase and that the collected data sufficiently covers the feasible operating range of the independent variables. In the next step, the collected data is cleaned and standardised (**Step 3 in** Fig. 5.1). The standardised data, excluding the extreme values of the independent variables, are then split into K folds. From these, K distinct data partitions are created by treating one of the folds as test data and the remaining K–1 folds as training data. During the training process, the extreme values of the independent variables are included in the training data. This is done to ensure that training data contains extreme values for developing RS models.

5.3.2 *Phase 2: Development of ANN-Based RS Models Considering Model Uncertainty*

ANNs are considered as one of the best choices for developing multivariate process models (Coit et al., 1998; Zhang & Huang, 1995). This is primarily due to the intrinsic capacity of ANNs to approximate any continuous function (Hornik et al.,

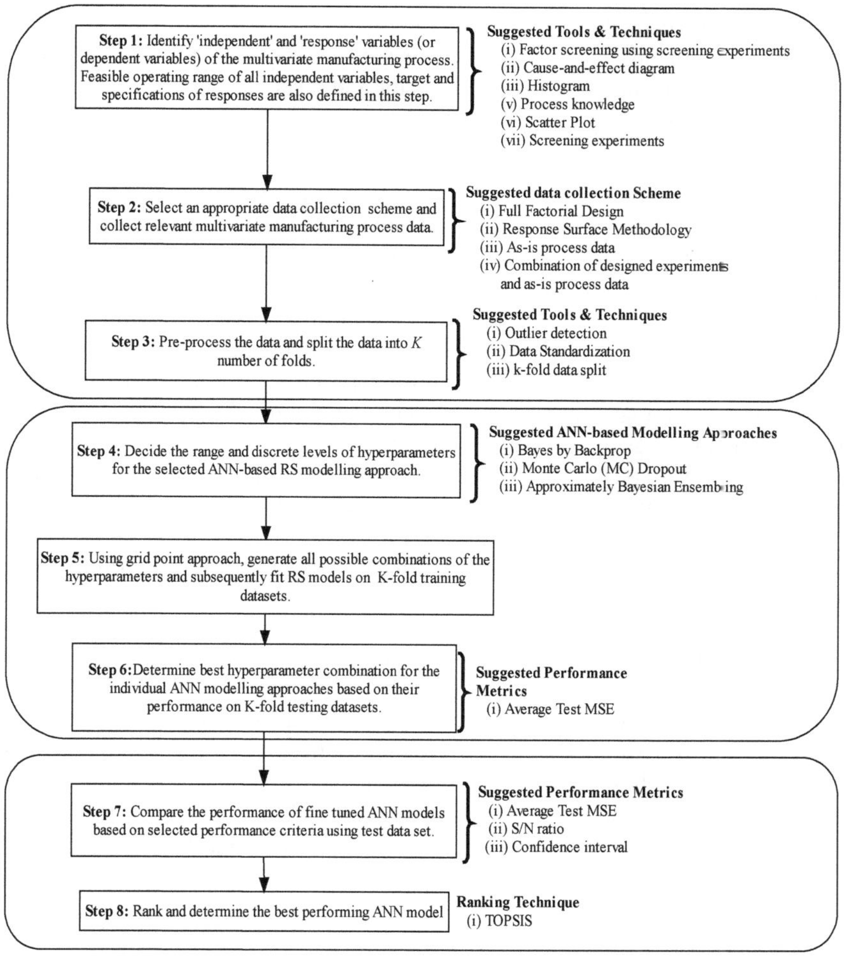

Fig. 5.1 The eight-step framework to develop and select an appropriate ANN model considering model parameter uncertainties

1989). Hagen et al. (2002) mentioned various advantage of neural networks, and few are highlighted below:

(i) ANNs offer a high degree of flexibility in modelling intricate, high-dimensional relationships between predictor and response variables that may be difficult or even impossible for polynomial OLS regression models or nonlinear regression models to capture effectively.
(ii) ANN can be trained without making specific assumptions about the functional form (e.g., linear, quadratic, or higher-order polynomial) or the underlying data distribution.

(iii) ANNs are capable of approximating highly complex, non-linear relationships in a computationally efficient manner using the backpropagation algorithm. The relationship between the predictor and response vectors is determined by the weights and biases within the network, which are tuned during the training process.

The training of an ANN (Hagen et al., 2002) consists of two passes, (i) a forward pass and (ii) a backward pass. In the forward pass, the input is passed through the hidden layer of the ANN in order to predict the output(s). The input consists of a vectorised data fed into the network, and the output(s) refers to the result produced by the output layer(s) of the ANN. The forward pass involves two critical steps: (i) weighted summation for each neuron by the calculation of the weighted sum of its inputs, and (ii) passing weighted sum from each neuron through an appropriate activation function such as sigmoid, linear, and hyperbolic tangent to produce the neuron's output(s) as desired.

In the backward pass or backpropagation, the error between the ANN predictions and the actual values for given inputs are calculated. Subsequently using a chain rule, the gradient of the error with respect to each weight in the ANN is calculated. The weights of the network are then optimised using a learning algorithm, typically gradient descent or its variants, and a learning rate, to find the combination of weights resulting in minimal error (e.g. mean square error). During the training, the forward and backward passes are repeated for several iterations until termination criteria is met.

The performance of a specific ANN modelling approach depends upon the selection of its intrinsic parameters. In phase 2, the best hyperparameters for selected ANN modelling approaches are determined to fit the dataset. In this study, the best hyperparameter combination for the selected ANN modelling techniques are determined using grid search and K-fold cross-validation method (**Step 4– Step 6** in Fig. 5.1). The average test mean square error $\left(\overline{MSE}_{test}\right)$ is selected as the performance criterion and is determined as follows,

$$\overline{MSE}_{test}=\frac{\sum_{k=1}^{K} MSE_{k,test}}{K} \tag{5.1}$$

In Eq. (5.1), $MSE_{k,test}$ is the test fold MSE for k^{th} data split and K is the total number of data splits. The hyperparameter combination with lowest $\overline{MSE}_{test}$ is selected as the best combination. The detailed procedure for K-fold cross-validation is outlined in Fig. 5.2. Brief details on selected ANN modelling approaches are provided in subsequent subsections.

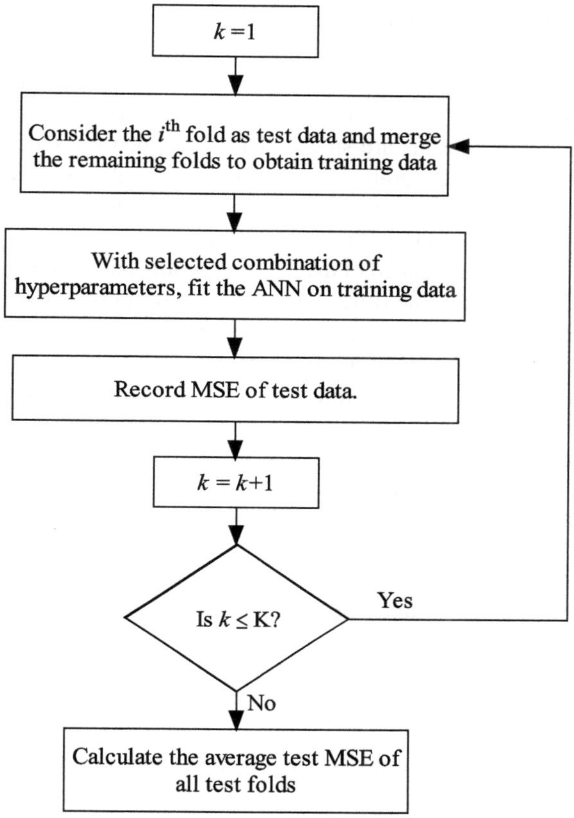

Fig. 5.2 The K-fold cross-validation method

5.3.2.1 Bayes by Backprop (BBB)

BBB (Blundell et al., 2015) combines the principles of Bayesian inference with backpropagation. This approach involves approximating the posterior distribution over the weights of a neural network, thereby facilitating the quantitative assessment of model uncertainty in the network's predictions. The key idea is to parameterise the posterior distribution of the weights using a distribution with learnable parameters, such as a Gaussian distribution. This is achieved by variational learning, which consists of specifying a prior distribution over the model parameters. Learnable counterparts are introduced for each model parameter, which are optimised during training using backpropagation.

5.3.2.2 Monte Carlo Dropout (MCD)

Gal and Ghahramani (2015) proposed MCD to estimate model uncertainty in neural network. In standard dropout method (Srivastava et al., 2014), during training, random neurons are stochastically dropped out (set to zero) with a certain probability at each iteration. This helps reduce the complexity of a network and reduce overfitting by forcing the neural network to learn more robust features. While testing, neurons are kept with their original weights.

In MCD, instead of using dropout only once, as in standard dropout, MCD applies dropout multiple times with different dropout masks and computes predictions for each sample. The final prediction is the average of the predictions from all the dropout samples. The motivation behind MCD technique is that a neural network with arbitrary depth and non-linearities, with dropout applied before every weight layer, is mathematically equivalent to an approximation to the probabilistic deep Gaussian process. The dropout objective, in effect, minimises the Kullback–Leibler (KL) divergence between an approximate distribution and the posterior of a deep Gaussian process. By using dropout during testing, the network effectively becomes a probabilistic model, and the multiple dropout samples can be seen as samples from a distribution over predictions. This ensemble of predictions allows us to estimate the model's uncertainty or confidence in its predictions.

5.3.2.3 Approximately Bayesian Ensembling (ABE)

ABE (Pearce et al., 2020) is a technique used to approximate Bayesian inference in deep learning models by combining the principles of ensembling with Bayesian modelling to estimate model uncertainty. The goal is to achieve robust predictions and obtain uncertainty estimates without incurring the computational cost of full Bayesian inference. Conventional Bayesian modelling, while effectively quantifying model uncertainty, is often very computationally expensive, especially in deep learning models with a large number of parameters. On the other hand, ensembling methods can improve generalisation and robustness but typically cannot provide reliable information about model uncertainty. ABE aims to strike a balance between these two approaches. This technique consists of a modification to the usual neural network ensembling process that results in a predictive distribution that is closer to the Bayesian distribution. This is accomplished by regularising parameters about values drawn from an anchor distribution, which can be set to be equal to the prior distribution. This method is dubbed anchor ensembling, and falls into a family of Bayesian inference methods. A summary of applications, advantages, and limitations of all three approaches, as per open literature, is provided in Table 5.2.

Table 5.2 A summary of applications, advantages, and limitations of all three approaches

RS modelling approach	Application areas	Pros	Cons
BBB	Image classification (Shridhar et al., 2019); time series forecasting (Németh & Hadházi, 2024); fatigue damage prediction (Fernández et al., 2022)	(i) BBB regularises the network by minimising the expected lower bound on the marginal likelihood. This provides a more principled form of regularisation compared to heuristic techniques like dropout (Blundell et al., 2015) (ii) By learning a probability distribution over the weights, BBB can capture the uncertainty in the network's predictions in regions with little training data (Blundell et al., 2015)	(i) The variational inference methods used in BBB may underestimate uncertainty, which could lead to under-exploration and premature convergence in practice (Blundell et al., 2015) (ii) The choice of variational family may poorly approximate true posterior leading, limiting uncertainty quality (Blundell et al., 2015)
MCD	Myocardial infarction diagnosis (Jahmunah et al., 2023); Fuel property prediction (Yalamanchi et al., 2023); Geochemical data imputation (Puzyrev & Duuring, 2025)	(i) MCD allows uncertainty quantification without changing the model or the optimisation process (Gal & Ghahramani, 2015) (ii) MCD allows uncertainty quantification without sacrificing computational complexity (Gal & Ghahramani, 2015)	(i) MCD is highly influenced by accuracy of assumed distribution of parameters (Song et al., 2024) (ii) MCD requires careful tuning of the dropout probability and the number of forward passes at inference time. Both hyperparameters have a significant impact on the quality of the predictive uncertainty (Gal & Ghahramani, 2015)

(continued)

Table 5.2 (continued)

RS modelling approach	Application areas	Pros	Cons
ABE	Image classification; sentiment analysis; (Pearce et al., 2020); material property modelling (Ghorbanian et al., 2025);	(i) ABE offers scalability with respect to number of model parameters and data for uncertainty quantification compared to Bayesian frameworks (Pearce et al., 2020)	(i) The marginal variance of the approximate posterior is generally underestimated compared to the true Bayesian posterior (Pearce et al., 2020) (ii) Even with large number of ensemble neural network, the ABE does not fully capture the posterior parameter distributions (Pearce et al., 2020)

5.3.3 Phase 3: Comparison of the Performance of Selected Modelling Techniques

In this phase, the quality of the prediction of ANN models, based on three different approaches (viz. BBB, MCD, ABE), is compared using classical multivariate test functions, laboratory pin-on-disc experimental data and a real-life multivariate process data (**Step 7–Step 8** in Fig. 5.1). Metric for comparison is the average test fold mean squared error (MSE). Two-way ANOVA, Tukey's multiple comparison test, signal-to-noise (SN) ratio, and a multi-criteria decision-making technique are used to select the best RS model considering uncertainties.

5.4 Data Generation Mechanism

In this study, three different types of data (e.g. simulated, experimental, and as-is) are selected to develop the RS models for analysis. In manufacturing environment, these three types of data are common source for process quality monitoring, improvement and control. Simulation data are generated using a total of 19 multi-objective test functions. Experimental data used were generated from a pin-on-disc machine and collected based on full factorial DOE trials. Finally, one real-life multivariate honing machining process 'as-is' data is considered to assess the performance of selected ANN modelling approaches. A summary of the selected data sets is provided in Table 5.3, and a brief description is provided in subsequent sub-sections.

Table 5.3 Summary of selected datasets

Data set	Data source	Data type	Data details	Number of independent variables	Number of responses
1	Huband et al. (2006)	Simulation	Multi-objective test functions	7–30	2–5
2	Mukherjee (2012)	Laboratory experiments	DOE data to map multivariate functional relationship of tribological responses and control factors in sliding contact experiment in pin-on-disc	3	4
3	Mukherjee (2007)	'As-is' from machining process	Rough honing process data of engine cylinder liner bore to understand multivariate functional relationship between responses and controllable variables	12	3

5.4.1 Dataset 1: Multi-objective Test Functions

In this study, multi-objective test functions comprising of five ZDT test functions (two objectives) and seven DTLZ test functions (each scaled to three and five dimensions) (Huband et al., 2006) are considered to generate the data. Selected multivariate test functions are listed in Table 5.4, and a brief description of independent variables and responses for the experimental and real-life case (Steps **1–2** in Fig. 5.1) is provided in subsequent paragraphs.

5.4.2 Dataset 2: Experimentation to Analyse Tribological Responses in Sliding Contact (Mukherjee, 2012)

The tribological properties of materials in sliding contact were collected using a wear and friction tester machine. Data were collected based on a full factorial design of experiments (DOE). The objective was to model the relationship between three independent variables and four specific response characteristics [i.e., coefficient of friction under sliding contact (y_1), frictional force (y_2), wear rate (y_3), and surface temperature (y_4)]. A summary of the controllable factors and response variables is presented in Tables 5.5 and 5.6.

Table 5.4 List of multi-objective test functions

Function name	Number of variables	Bounds on variables	Objective function expressions
ZDT1	30	[0,1]	$f_1(x) = x_1$ $f_2(x) = g(x)[1 - \sqrt{x_1/g(x)}]$ $g(x) = 1 + 9(\sum_{i=2}^{n} x_i)/(n-1)$
ZDT2	30	[0,1]	$f_1(x) = x_1$ $f_2(x) = g(x)[1 - (x_1/g(x))^2]$ $g(x) = 1 + 9(\sum_{i=2}^{n} x_i)/(n-1)$
ZDT3	30	[0,1]	$f_1(x) = x_1$ $f_2(x) = 1 - \sqrt{f_1/g} - (f_1/g)\sin(10\pi f_1)$ $g(x) = 1 + 9(\sum_{i=2}^{n} x_i)/(n-1)$
ZDT4	10		$f_1(x) = x_1$ $f_2(x) = g(x)[1 - \sqrt{x_1/g(x)}]$ $g(x) = 1 + 10(n-1) + \sum_{i=2}^{n}[x_i^2 - 10\cos(4\pi x_i)]$
ZDT6	10	[0,1]	$f_1(x) = 1 - \exp(-4x_1)\sin^6(6\pi x_1)$ $f_2(x) = g(x)[1 - (f_1(x)/g(x))^2]$ $g(x) = 1 + 9[(\sum_{i=2}^{n} x_i)/(n-1)]^{0.25}$
DTLZ1	M + k-1 M = no. of objectives, k = |A| = 5	[0,1]	$f_1(\mathrm{x}) = (1/2)x_1x_2......x_{M-1}(1 + g(x_M))$ $f_2(\mathrm{x}) = (1/2)x_1x_2......(1 - x_{M-1})(1 + g(x_M))$ $\vdots$ $f_{M-1}(\mathrm{x}) = (1/2)x_1(1 - x_2)(1 + g(x_M))$ $f_M(\mathrm{x}) = (1/2)(1 - x_1)(1 + g(x_M))$ $g(\mathrm{x}_M) = 100\left[\,\lvert x_M\rvert + \sum_{x_i \in \mathrm{x}_M} \begin{matrix}(x_i - 0.5)^2 - \\ \cos(20\pi(x_i - 0.5))\end{matrix}\right]$
DTLZ2	M + k-1 k = |A| = 10	[0,1]	$f_1(\mathrm{x}) = (1 + g(x_M))cos(x_1\pi/2)cos(x_2\pi/2)...$ $cos(x_{M-2}\pi/2)cos(x_{M-1}\pi/2)$ $f_2(\mathrm{x}) = (1 + g(x_M))cos(x_1\pi/2)cos(x_2\pi/2)...$ $cos(x_{M-2}\pi/2)sin(x_{M-1}\pi/2)$ $\vdots$ $f_{M-1}(\mathrm{x}) = (1 + g(x_M))cos(x_1\pi/2)sin(x_2\pi/2)$ $f_M(\mathrm{x}) = (1 + g(x_M))sin(x_1\pi/2)$ $g(\mathrm{x}_M) = \sum_{x_i \in \mathrm{x}_M}(x_i - 0.5)^2$

(continued)

Table 5.4 (continued)

Function name	Number of variables	Bounds on variables	Objective function expressions
DTLZ3	M + k-1 k = |A| = 10	[0,1]	$f_1(x) = (1 + g(x_M))cos(x_1\pi/2)cos(x_2\pi/2)...$ $cos(x_{M-2}\pi/2)cos(x_{M-1}\pi/2)$ $f_2(x) = (1 + g(x_M))cos(x_1\pi/2)cos(x_2\pi/2)...$ $cos(x_{M-2}\pi/2)sin(x_{M-1}\pi/2)$ $\vdots$ $f_{M-1}(x) = (1 + g(x_M))cos(x_1\pi/2)sin(x_2\pi/2)$ $f_M(x) = (1 + g(x_M))sin(x_1\pi/2)$ $g(x_M) = 100\left[\|x_M\| + \sum_{x_i \in x_M} \begin{matrix}(x_i - 0.5)^2 - \\ \cos(20\pi(x_i - 0.5))\end{matrix}\right]$
DTLZ4	M + k-1 k = |A| = 10	[0,1]	$f_1(x) = (1 + g(x_M))cos(x_1^\alpha\pi/2)cos(x_2^\alpha\pi/2)...$ $cos(x_{M-2}^\alpha\pi/2)cos(x_{M-1}^\alpha\pi/2)$ $f_2(x) = (1 + g(x_M))cos(x_1^\alpha\pi/2)cos(x_2^\alpha\pi/2)...$ $cos(x_{M-2}^\alpha\pi/2)sin(x_{M-1}^\alpha\pi/2)$ $\vdots$ $f_{M-1}(x) = (1 + g(x_M))cos(x_1^\alpha\pi/2)sin(x_2^\alpha\pi/2)$ $f_M(x) = (1 + g(x_M))sin(x_1^\alpha\pi/2)$ $g(x_M) = \sum_{x_i \in x_M} (x_i - 0.5)^2$
DTLZ5	M + k-1 k = |A| = 10	[0,1]	$f_1(x) = (1 + g(x_M))cos(\theta_1\pi/2)cos(\theta_2\pi/2)...$ $cos(\theta_{M-2}\pi/2)cos(\theta_{M-1}\pi/2)$ $f_2(x) = (1 + g(x_M))cos(\theta_1\pi/2)cos(\theta_2\pi/2)...$ $cos(\theta_{M-2}\pi/2)sin(\theta_{M-1}\pi/2)$ $\vdots$ $f_{M-1}(x) = (1 + g(x_M))cos(\theta_1\pi/2)sin(\theta_2\pi/2)$ $f_M(x) = (1 + g(x_M))sin(\theta_1\pi/2)$ $\theta_i = \frac{\pi}{4(1+g(r))}(1 + 2g(r)x_i),\ i = 2, 3, ..., (M-1)$ $g(x_M) = \sum_{x_i \in x_M} (x_i - 0.5)^2$

(continued)

Table 5.4 (continued)

Function name	Number of variables	Bounds on variables	Objective function expressions
DTLZ6	M + k-1 k = |A| = 10	[0,1]	$f_1(\mathrm{x}) = (1 + g(x_M))cos(\theta_1\pi/2)cos(\theta_2\pi/2)\ldots cos(\theta_{M-2}\pi/2)cos(\theta_{M-1}\pi/2)$ $f_2(\mathrm{x}) = (1 + g(x_M))cos(\theta_1\pi/2)cos(\theta_2\pi/2)\ldots cos(\theta_{M-2}\pi/2)sin(\theta_{M-1}\pi/2)$ $\vdots$ $f_{M-1}(\mathrm{x}) = (1 + g(x_M))cos(\theta_1\pi/2)sin(\theta_2\pi/2)$ $f_M(\mathrm{x}) = (1 + g(x_M))sin(\theta_1\pi/2)$ $\theta_i = \frac{\pi}{4(1+g(r))}(1 + 2g(r)x_i),\ i = 2, 3, \ldots, (M - 1)$ $g(\mathrm{x}_M) = \sum_{x_i \in \mathrm{x}_M} x_i^{0.1}$
DTLZ7	M + k-1 k = |A| = 20	[0,1]	$f_1(\mathrm{x}_1) = x_1$ $f_2(\mathrm{x}_2) = x_2$ $\vdots$ $f_{M-1}(\mathrm{x}_{M-1}) = x_{M-1}$ $f_M(\mathrm{x}) = (1 + g(x_M))h(f_1, f_2, \ldots, f_{M-1}, g)$ $g(\mathrm{x}_M) = 1 + \frac{9}{\lvert x_M \rvert}\sum_{x_i \in \mathrm{x}_M} x_i$ $h(f_1, f_1, \ldots, f_1, g) = M - \sum_{i=1}^{M-1}\left[\frac{f_i}{1+g}(1 + \sin(3\pi f_i))\right]$

Table 5.5 Summary of controllable factors and uncontrollable covariates for dataset 2

Controllable factors	Unit	Bounds in scaled value [min, max]/ levels
Type of material	Brass/Aluminium	{–1, 1}
Load (kgf)	kgf	[–1, 1]
Velocity (m/s)	m/s	[–1, 1]

Table 5.6 Summary of response variables for dataset 2

Response	Unit	Type of response	Bounds [min, max]
Coefficient of friction	No units	STB	[0.187, 0.518]
Friction force	N	STB	[6.48, 58.94]
Rate of wear	Mm	STB	[0.1056, 3.4596]
Temperature	^{O}C	STB	[34, 92]

5.4.3 Dataset 3: Engine Liner Bore Machining (Honing) Process Data (Mukherjee, 2007)

This case involved RS model development for a rough honing machining process on the engine liner bores of a six-cylinder diesel engine of a heavy-duty commercial automobile. The rough honing process is a numeric-controlled, hydraulic oil-pressure-based machining operation. In particular, the objective was to determine functional relationship of twelve in-process parameters, such that the degrees of customer satisfaction related to three specific response characteristics [i.e. average finish liner bore diameter (y_1), maximum finish liner bore ovality (y_2), and maximum finish liner bore diameter taper (y_3)] are simultaneously optimised. Three uncontrollable covariates are also considered that affect the responses. A summary of the controllable factors, uncontrollable input covariates, and response variables is presented in Tables 5.7 and 5.8.

The data standardisation process involves subtracting the variable's mean from the variable's actual values and then dividing by the variable's standard deviation. After

Table 5.7 Summary of controllable factors and uncontrollable input covariates for dataset 3

Controllable factors	Unit	Bounds in scaled value [min, max]
Hydraulic oil temperature	°C	[–2.2493, 1.8169]
Cutting oil temperature	°C	[–2.1593, 1.6113]
Sensor-based air pressure	Kg/cm^2	[–1.6718, 1.5735]
Sensor-based air filter pressure	N/m^2	[–0.25338, 3.9271]
Rough one-pass honing time	s	[–1.6041, 2.2299]
Sensor-based zero setting correction	μm	[–3.719, 1.7328]
Sensor-based total cutting correction	μm	[–1.6874, 2.8084]
Sensor-based tool radial expansion	μm	[–5.643, 0.17600]
Dog length (reverse point range)	mm	[–0.73721, 3.8243]
Uncontrollable Input Covariates		
Average liner bore diameter	mm	[0.26284, 1.42665]
Maximum liner bore ovality	mm	≤ -0.3725
Maximum liner bore taper	mm	≤ -0.3951

Table 5.8 Summary of response variables for dataset 3

Output responses	Unit	Type of response	Bounds in scaled values (min, max)
Average liner bore diameter	mm	NTB	[−1.74563, 0.81415]
Maximum liner bore ovality	mm	LTB	$\leq$ 1.2067
Maximum liner bore taper	mm	LTB	$\leq$ 0.85207

standardisation, the dataset is partitioned into K folds. In this study, K is selected as 5 (**Step 3** in Fig. 5.1). This is due to ability of fivefold cross-validation to achieve good balance between computational efficiency and estimation accuracy, particularly when dataset size and computational resources are limited (Kohavi, 1995).

5.5 Analysis and Findings

5.5.1 Fine-Tuning the Selected ANN Modelling Approaches

After standardising and partitioning the data into K number of folds, fine-tuned ANN models are developed with optimal combination of hyperparameters. All the computational runs are done on Tesla T4 GPU on Google Colab notebooks coded in Python 3.

For a specific dataset, the performance of ANN modelling approach depends upon selection of its intrinsic hyperparameters. The intrinsic parameters of each ANN modelling approach and their selected ranges are listed in Table 5.9. In all ANN modelling techniques, a single hidden layer was used, with the number of neurons in the hidden layer ranging from 1 to 50 (Sharma et al., 2023). In this study, a grid search method was used to find the best hyperparameter combination for each ANN approach for a specific dataset and its performance was tested on test data (**Step 4–6** in Fig. 5.1). Comparative analysis of performance of selected ANN modelling approaches is provided in the following sub-sections.

5.5.2 Performance Comparison Based on Multivariate Multi-objective Test Functions

The performance of ANN models is evaluated on the test data of multivariate multi-objective test functions. A two-way ANOVA (Montgomery, 2005) is conducted to assess whether the performance of RS modelling techniques differ significantly in terms of average fivefold cross-validation test MSE. The results of the two-way ANOVA are presented in Table 5.10. In this analysis, the average fivefold cross-validation MSE is treated as the response variable, while the RS modelling techniques

Table 5.9 Intrinsic parameters of selected RS modelling techniques and range of selected values

RS modelling technique	Hyperparameter	Range of values	Source
BBB	Learning rate	$\{10^{-3}, 10^{-4}, 10^{-5}\}$	Blundell et al. (2015)
	Number of samples	{1, 2, 5, 10}	
	Mixture weight	{1/4, 1/2, 3/4}	
	Prior variance parameter σ_1	{0, 1, 2}	
	Prior variance parameter σ_2	{6, 7, 8}	
MCD	Dropout rate	[0.1, 0.5]	Gal and Ghahramani (2015)
	Number of MC samples	[10,100]	
ABE	Number of ensemble members	[5–10]	Pearce et al. (2020)

are considered as factor levels. To eliminate the effect of variability in response values introduced by different multivariate test functions in the statistical comparison of RS modelling approaches, the multivariate test function is treated as a block factor. In two-way ANOVA with *a* number of factor treatments (levels) and *b* number of blocks in the blocking factor, the sum of squares for the treatments is calculated as given below

$$\mathrm{SS}_{\mathrm{Treatments}}=\frac{1}{\mathrm{b}}\sum_{\mathrm{i}=1}^{\mathrm{a}}\mathrm{y}_{\mathrm{i.}}^{2}-\frac{\mathrm{y}_{..}^{2}}{\mathrm{N}} \tag{5.2}$$

in Eq. (5.2), $y_{i.}$ is the sum of all observations taken under treatment level *i*, $y_{..}$ is the sum of all observations, and *N* is the total number of observations. Subsequently, the sum of squares for block factor is calculated as given below

$$SS_{Blocks}=\frac{1}{a}\sum_{j=1}^{b}y_{.j}^{2}-\frac{y_{..}^{2}}{N} \tag{5.3}$$

Table 5.10 Results of two-way ANOVA on multivariate test functions

Source	DF	Sum of squares	Mean square	F ratio	p-value
RS modelling approaches	2	5.3893638	2.6946819	58.5822	< 0.0001
Multivariate Test Functions [as Block]	18	2.1221929	0.117899606	2.5631	0.0080
Error	36	1.6559396	0.045998322		
Total	56	9.1674963			

in Eq. (5.3), $y_{.j}$ is the sum of all observations in block *j*. The total sum of squares is calculated as follows

$$SS_T = \sum_{i=1}^{a}\sum_{j=1}^{b} y_{ij}^2 - \frac{y_{..}^2}{N} \quad (5.4)$$

The error sum of squares is obtained as

$$SS_E = SS_T - (SS_{Treatments} + SS_{Blocks}) \quad (5.5)$$

The mean square for treatments, blocks, and error is calculated by dividing the respective sum of squares by their corresponding degrees of freedom (DF). The DF for treatments and blocks are $a - 1$ and $b - 1$, respectively. Subsequently, the F-ratios for treatments and blocks are computed by dividing their respective mean squares by the mean square of the error term. Based on the p-value reported in Table 5.10, it is evident that the performance of modelling approaches significantly differs, considering $\alpha = 0.05$ (level of significance).

Post two-way ANOVA, Tukey's multiple comparison test (Tukey, 1991) is employed to identify which specific RS modelling approaches differ significantly in terms of average fivefold cross-validation test MSE. The results from the Tukey's multiple comparison test are presented in Table 5.11. The results further confirm that there is significant difference in performance of the best-fit models. Models that do not share the common alphabets (e.g. A and B) indicate significant differences in average fivefold cross-validation test error. It is evident that there is no statistically significant difference in the performance of ABB and BBB at the 5% level of significance, and both models outperform MCD.

The main effects plot of S/N ratio (Ross, 2005) is provided in the Fig. 5.3. Average fivefold cross-validation test error is smaller-the-better (STB) type of response. Thus, the S/N ratio for a particular RS modelling approach is calculated based on the following expression:

Table 5.11 Tukey's multiple comparison test on multivariate test functions

RS modelling approach	Grouping code (at 5% level of significance)	Average fivefold cross-validation test error	Lower 95% confidence limit	Upper 95% confidence limit
MCD	A	1.0197456	0.91995670	1.1195345
ABE	B	0.3768593	0.25866214	0.4582400
BBB	B	0.35854511	0.27707039	0.4766482

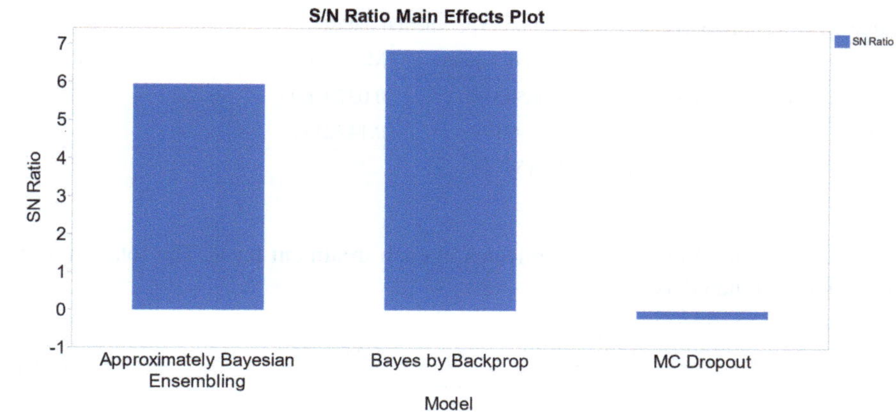

Fig. 5.3 Main effects plot of S/N ratio at different levels (or modelling approaches) for the multivariate multi-objective test functions

$$(\mathrm{S/N})_i = -10 \times \log_{10}\left(\frac{\sum_{j=1}^{T} MSE_{ji}}{T}\right) \tag{5.6}$$

where i represents a specific model, j is the test function, and T is total number of test functions. Higher S/N ratio indicates better performance in terms of consistently lower fivefold test MSE across test functions.

From the results, it is evident that Bayes by Backprop resulted in models with lowest average fivefold test MSE, followed by Approximately Bayesian Ensembling and MC Dropout. The S/N ratio is also highest for Bayes by Backprop.

5.5.3 Performance Comparison Based on Laboratory Experimental Data

The performance of ANN models is evaluated on the test data from an experimental dataset (Mukherjee, 2012). The results of the one-way ANOVA are presented in Table 5.12. In this analysis, the average fivefold cross-validation MSE is treated as the response variable, while the RS modelling techniques are considered as factor levels. In one-way ANOVA, the sum of squares of treatments is calculated as per the following expression,

$$SS_{Treatments} = \frac{1}{n}\sum_{i=1}^{a} y_{i.}^2 - \frac{y_{..}^2}{N} \tag{5.7}$$

Table 5.12 Results of one-way ANOVA on experimental dataset

Source	DF	Sum of squares	Mean squares	F ratio	p-value
RS modelling technique	2	0.0659539	0.03297695	0.2319	0.7976
Error	9	1.2799179	0.1422131		
Total	11	1.3458718			

where n is the total number of replicates in each treatment level. The total sum of squares is calculated as follows

$$SS_T = \sum_{i=1}^{a}\sum_{j=1}^{n} y_{ij}^2 - \frac{y_{..}^2}{N} \tag{5.8}$$

The mean square for treatments and error is calculated by dividing the respective sum of squares by their corresponding degrees of freedom (DF). The DF for treatments and error are a - 1 and N-a, respectively. Subsequently, the F-ratios for treatments are computed by dividing their respective mean squares by the mean square of the error term.

Based on the p-value reported in Table 5.12, no statistically significant difference is observed in the performance of the RS modelling techniques considering $\alpha = 0.05$.

The main effects plot of S/N ratio for fivefold cross-validation test MSE of individual responses is provided in Fig. 5.4. S/N ratio for a particular RS modelling approach is calculated based on following expression:

$$(\mathrm{S/N})_i = -10 \times \log_{10}\left(\frac{\sum_{y=1}^{Y} MSE_{ji}}{Y}\right) \tag{5.9}$$

where i represents a specific model, y is the response number, and Y is total number of response functions.

The S/N ratio is highest for MCD followed by BBB, and ABE. Higher S/N ratio indicates better performance in terms of lower fivefold test MSE across responses.

5.5.4 *Performance Comparison Based on Real-Life Honing Process Data*

The performance of ANN models is further evaluated on the test data from a real-life honing dataset (Mukherjee, 2007). The results of the one-way ANOVA are presented in Table 5.13. In this analysis, the average fivefold cross-validation MSE is treated as the response variable, while the RS modelling techniques are considered as factor

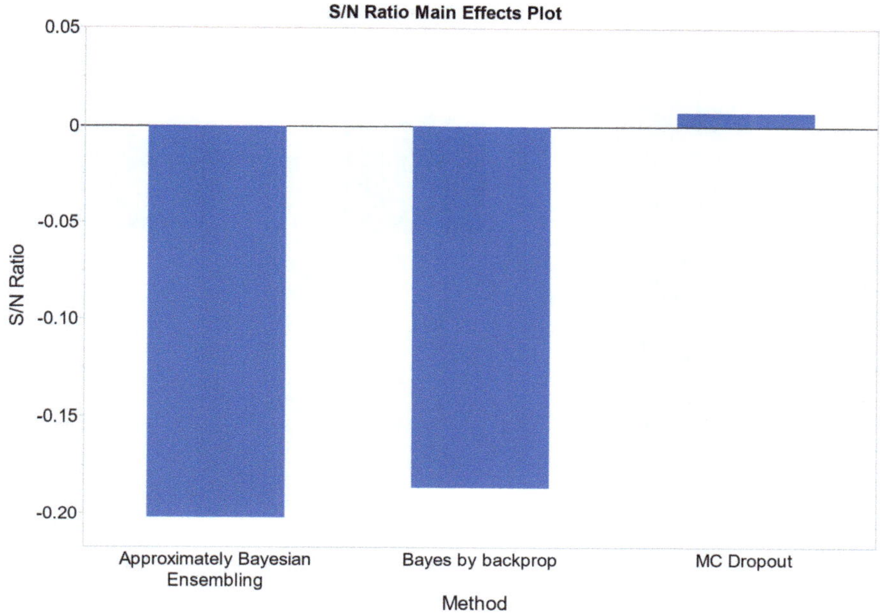

Fig. 5.4 Main effects plot of S/N ratio at three different factor levels (modelling approaches) for the experimental data set

levels. Based on the p-value reported in Table 5.13, no statistically significant difference is observed in the performance of the RS modelling techniques considering $\alpha = 0.05$.

The main effects plot of S/N ratio for fivefold cross-validation test MSE of individual responses is provided in Fig. 5.5. S/N ratio for a particular RS modelling approach is calculated based on expression given in Eq. 5.3. The S/N ratio is highest for MCD followed by BBB, and ABE.

Table 5.13 Results of one-way ANOVA on the real-life honing process dataset

Source	DF	Sum of squares	F ratio	p-value
RS modelling technique	2	0.37946657	3.511	0.0978
Error	6	0.32423715		
Total	8	0.70370372		

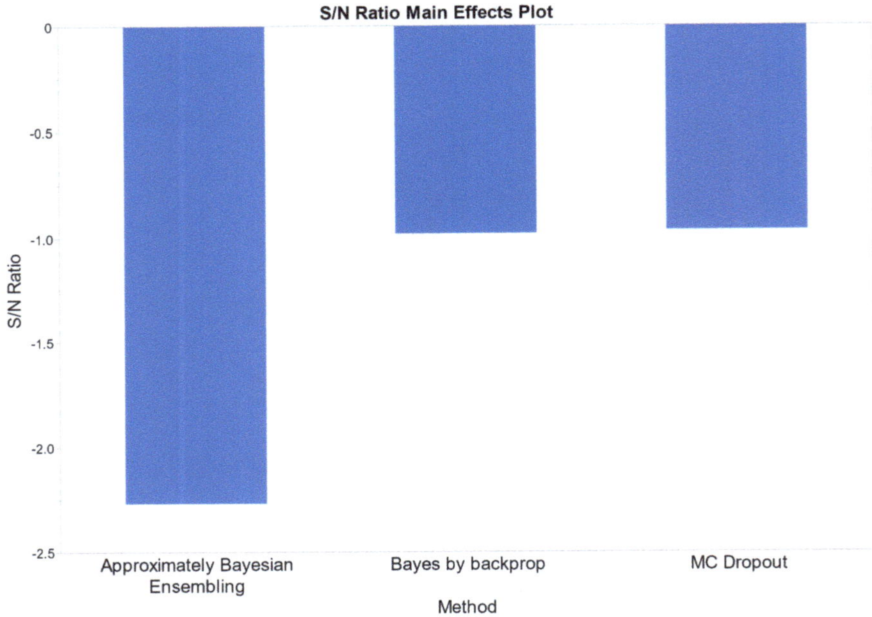

Fig. 5.5 Main effects plot of S/N ratio at three different factor levels (modelling approaches) for the real-life honing process data set

5.5.5 Ranking of ANN-Based RS Modelling Approaches Using MCDM Technique

Based on the MSE and S/N ratio values in three different datasets, the ANN-based RS approaches are ranked using a popular multi-criteria decision-making (MCDM) technique, so-called 'Technique for Order of Preference by Similarity to Ideal Solution (TOPSIS)' (Tzeng & Huang, 2011). A six-step procedure to rank the solutions using TOPSIS is provided below.

Step 1: Arrange the set of alternatives (ANN RS modelling techniques) and criterion (MSE and S/N ratio) in the form of a decision matrix given in Table 5.14.

In Table 5.14, there are M criteria and N number of alternatives. $A_{n,m}$ $\forall n \in 1, 2, ..., N ; M \in 1, 2, ..., M$, is the value of nth alternative for m^{th} criterion.

Step 2: Normalise the values of alternatives in each criterion using the following expression

$$r_{nm} = \frac{A_{nm}}{\sqrt{\sum_{n=1}^{N} A_{nm}^2}}, \quad \forall n \in 1, 2, ..., N ; M \in 1, 2, ..., M \tag{5.10}$$

Table 5.14 Arrangement of alternatives and criteria in the form of a decision matrix

	Criteria			
Alternative	Criterion 1	Criterion 2	…	Criterion M
1	$A_{1,1}$	$A_{1,2}$	…	$A_{1,M}$
2	$A_{2,1}$	$A_{2,2}$	…	$A_{2,M}$
3	$A_{3,1}$	$A_{3,2}$	…	$A_{3,M}$
⋮	⋮	⋮	⋮	⋮
N	$A_{N,1}$	$A_{N,2}$	…	$A_{N,M}$

Step 3: Calculate the weighted normalised value of each alternative as follows,

$$v_{\mathrm{nm}} = w_{\mathrm{m}} \times r_{\mathrm{nm}} \tag{5.11}$$

Step 4: Obtain the positive ideal solution (PIS), and negative ideal solution (NIS) corresponding to the weighted normalised values, as given in Step 3. PIS is determined from below expression,

$$\mathrm{PIS} = \mathrm{A}^{+} = \left\{v_{1}^{+}, v_{2}^{+}, \ldots, v_{\mathrm{M}}^{+}\right\} \tag{5.12}$$

where $v_{\mathrm{m}}^{+}\ \forall \mathrm{m} = 1, 2, \ldots, \mathrm{M}$ is the best alternative value among all alternatives for m^{th} criterion. For LTB criterion, the best alternative value corresponds to maximum alternative value in m^{th} criterion. For STB, the best alternative value corresponds to minimum alternative value in m^{th} criterion. For NTB criterion, the best alternative value is the one that has minimum deviation from target value. NIS is determined as,

$$\mathrm{NIS} = \mathrm{A}^{-} = \left\{v_{1}^{-}, v_{2}^{-}, \ldots, v_{\mathrm{M}}^{-}\right\} \tag{5.13}$$

where $v_{\mathrm{m}}^{-}\ \forall \mathrm{m} = 1, 2, \ldots, \mathrm{M}$ is the worst alternative value among all alternatives for mth criterion. For the LTB criterion, the worst alternative value corresponds to the minimum alternative value in mth criterion. For STB, worst alternative value corresponds to maximum alternative value in mth criterion. For NTB criterion, the worst alternative value is the one that has a maximum deviation from the target value.

Step 5: Obtain distance from PIS and NIS of each alternative using the following distance measures,

$$D_{n}^{+} = \sqrt{\sum_{\mathrm{m}=1}^{\mathrm{M}} \left[v_{\mathrm{nm}} - v_{\mathrm{m}}^{+}\right]^{2}}, \ \forall \mathrm{n} = 1, 2, \ldots, \mathrm{N} \tag{5.14}$$

$$D_{n}^{-} = \sqrt{\sum_{\mathrm{m}=1}^{\mathrm{M}} \left[v_{\mathrm{nm}} - v_{\mathrm{m}}^{-}\right]^{2}}, \ \forall \mathrm{n} = 1, 2, \ldots, \mathrm{N} \tag{5.15}$$

Table 5.15 Ranking of methods by TOPSIS

Method	TOPSIS Ranking
BBB	1
MCD	2
ABE	3

In Eqs. (5.8) and (5.9), D_n^+ and D_n^- are the separations of nth alternative from PIS and NIS, respectively.

Step 6: The closeness to PIS of each alternative can be calculated from following equation,

$$C_{\mathrm{n}}^{+} = \frac{D_{\mathrm{n}}^{-}}{D_{\mathrm{n}}^{-} + D_{\mathrm{n}}^{+}} \tag{5.16}$$

The alternatives are arranged in the order of increasing C_{n}^{+}. The alternative with highest C_{n}^{+} is regarded as the best alternative.

The best ranked ANN-based RS modelling approaches by TOPSIS are summarised in Table 5.15. From Table 5.15**,** it is evident that Bayes by Backprop is ranked the best using TOPSIS.

Plots of observed values in test data, corresponding predicted values and confidence intervals obtained by different methods in manufacturing case studies are provided in Figs. 5.6, 5.7, 5.8, 5.9, 5.10 and 5.11.

The percentage of observed testing data points falling within confidence interval limits for each modelling approach is provided in Table 5.16.

From Table 5.16, it is evident that the percentage of test data points falling within confidence interval limits is highest for ABE and followed by Bayes by Backprop (BBB). Thus, it can be concluded that ABE has resulted in wider and credible confidence intervals. Therefore, the likelihood of the actual response value falling within confidence interval limits is higher. Also, Tables 5.12 and 5.13 show that there is no significant difference in performance of ABE and BBB (in terms of mean square error).

5.6 Research Implications

In this work, different ANN-based RS modelling approaches for multivariate manufacturing process are studied to incorporate parameter uncertainty. The performance of the modelling approaches is compared on varied multi-objective test functions, experimental data, and real-life multivariate manufacturing case data. Incorporating model parameter uncertainties provides a confidence interval in which the actual

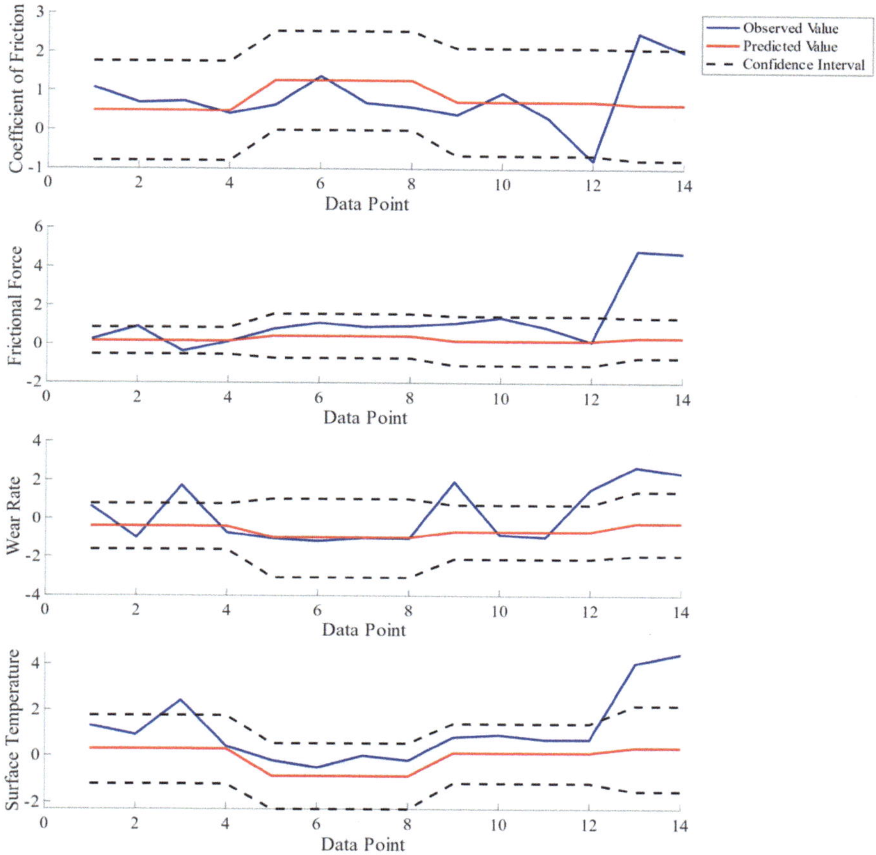

Fig. 5.6 Plots of observed values in test data, corresponding predicted values and confidence intervals obtained using ABE on laboratory experimental data

values of responses are likely to fall. Decision-maker can make quantitative assessment of the variability associated with point estimate of the responses. Such information helps to determine appropriate process settings conditions that have higher likelihood to adhere to customer specification in real-time. This paper provides a critical review of the existing approaches that can deal with parameter uncertainties of ANN, while developing the RS models. Subsequently, this study proposed a step-by-step solution framework, which the decision-makers can specifically use to identify the most suitable approach to develop the ANN-based RS models, considering model parameter uncertainties in specific multivariate manufacturing scenario. The implementation of the framework is also demonstrated using three different type of data set prevalent in multivariate manufacturing process quality control (e.g. simulation, experimentation, and 'as-is'). The suggested top-ranked model(s) can be further modified or tested in varied multivariate process modelling scenarios. The

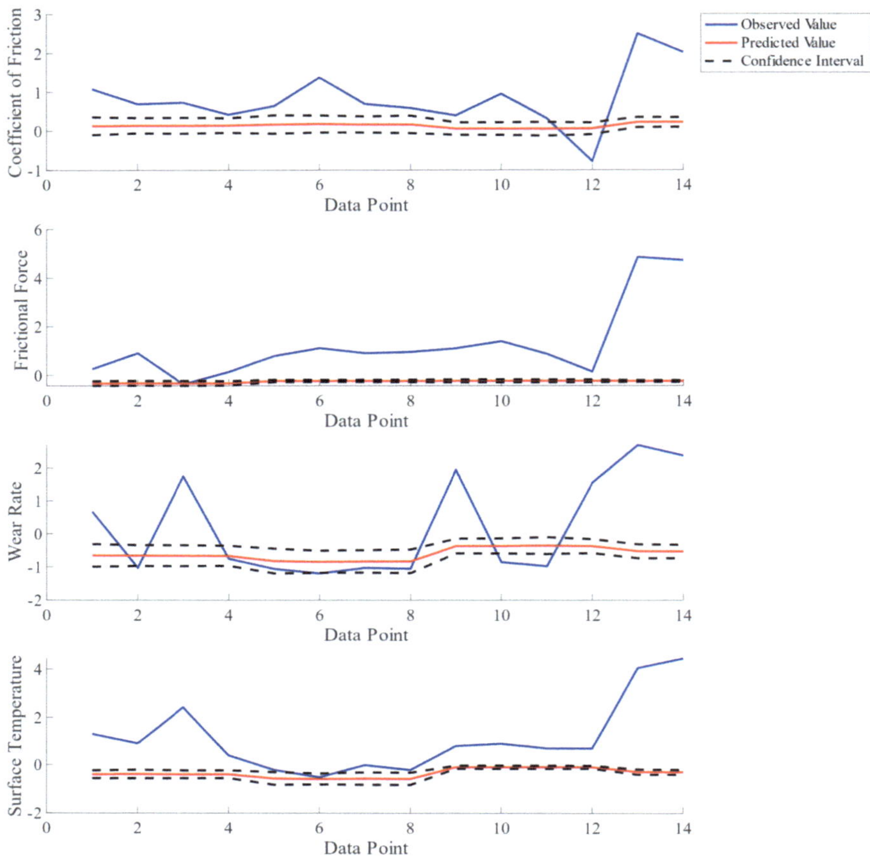

Fig. 5.7 Plots of observed values in test data, corresponding predicted values and confidence intervals obtained using MCD on laboratory experimental data

results and insights are expected to help practitioners and instigate researchers for the appropriate selection of ANN-based RS model(s), considering model parameter uncertainties.

5.7 Conclusions

This study provides a comprehensive solution framework to compare and contrast different ANN-based RS models for multivariate manufacturing processes, considering model parameter uncertainties. Some key highlights from the study are:

(i) The study results with multivariate test functions show similar performance (w.r.t. average fivefold test error) of BBB and ABE.

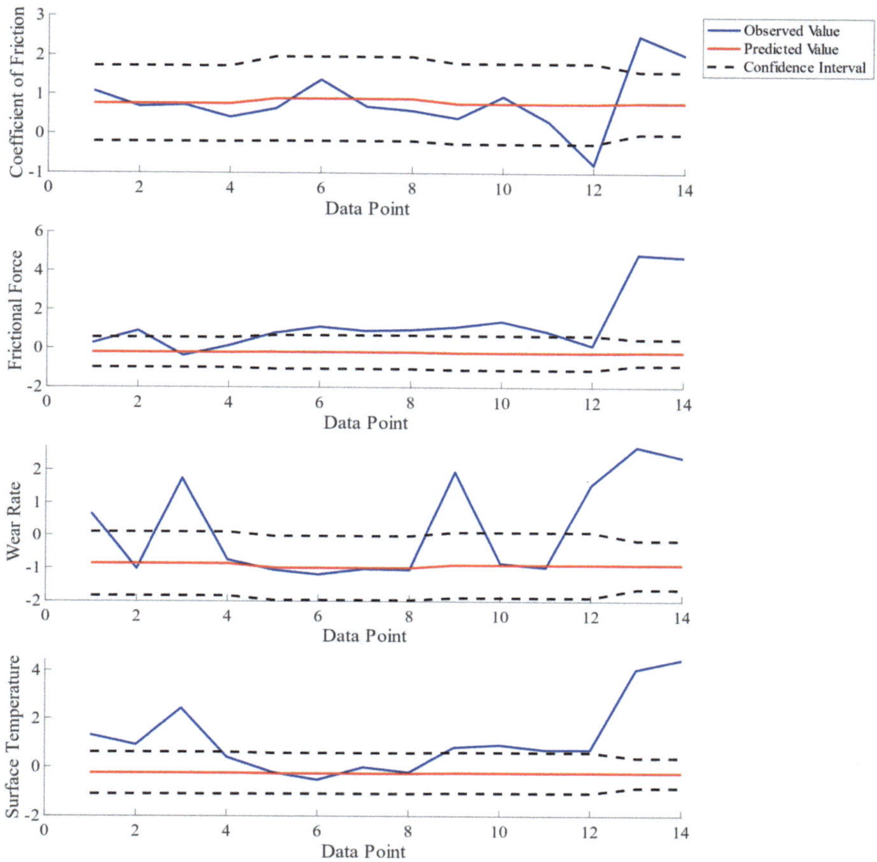

Fig. 5.8 Plots of observed values in test data, corresponding predicted values and confidence intervals obtained using BBB on laboratory experimental data

(ii) The study results with laboratory experimental dataset and honing process dataset show similar performance (w.r.t. average fivefold test error) of BBB, MCD, and ABE.
(iii) Overall ranking, using TOPSIS and based on varied data sets shows superiority of BBB.
(iv) Confidence interval analysis of the predicted responses with actual responses shows that BBB is less credible than the ABE.

The study also has some limitations. This study lacks confirmatory trial validation to assess the estimates of interval associated with a point estimate. Generalisation ability and performance of the approaches can be further tested with real-life and experimental data. The impact of model parameter uncertainty on ANN-based RS models developed through experimental data collected from a stable process can be

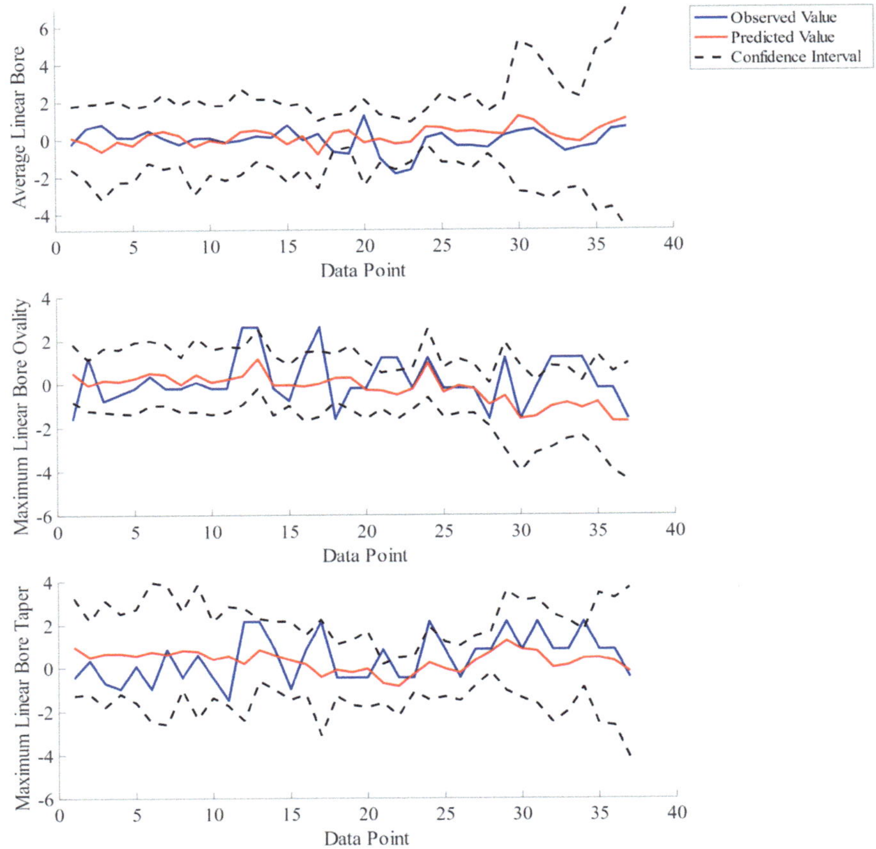

Fig. 5.9 Plots of observed values in test data, corresponding predicted values and confidence intervals obtained using ABE on honing process data

further analysed. Furthermore, enhancement of ANN RS models, considering both model parameters and predictive uncertainties, can also be attempted.

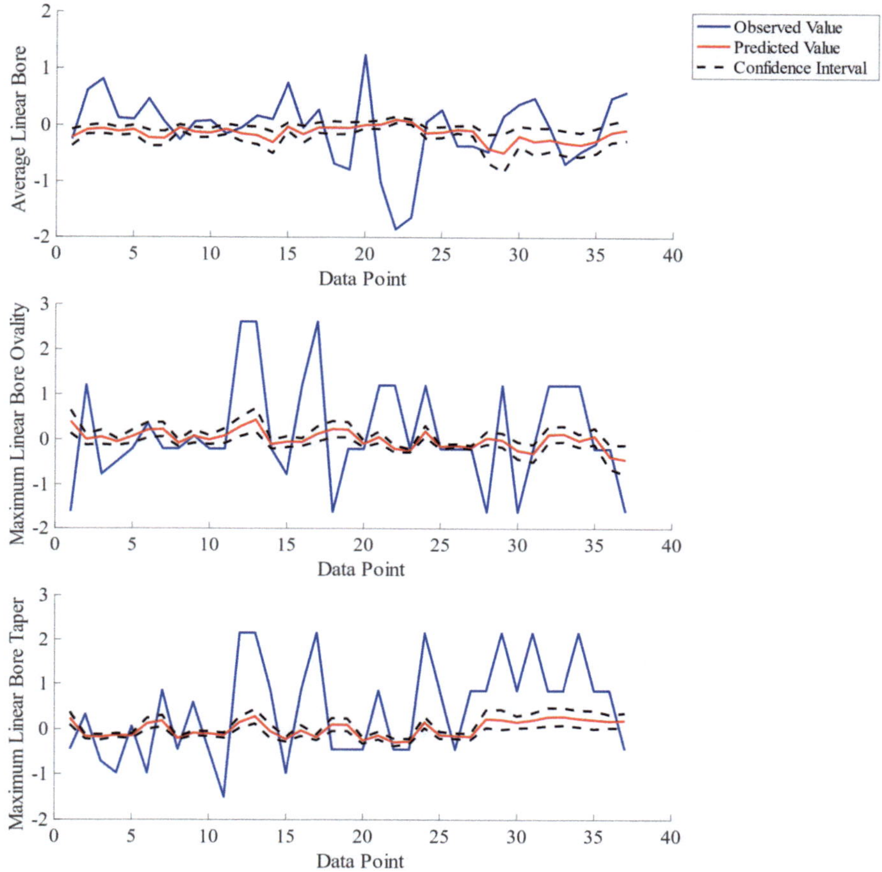

Fig. 5.10 Plots of observed values in test data, corresponding predicted values and confidence intervals obtained using MCD on honing process data

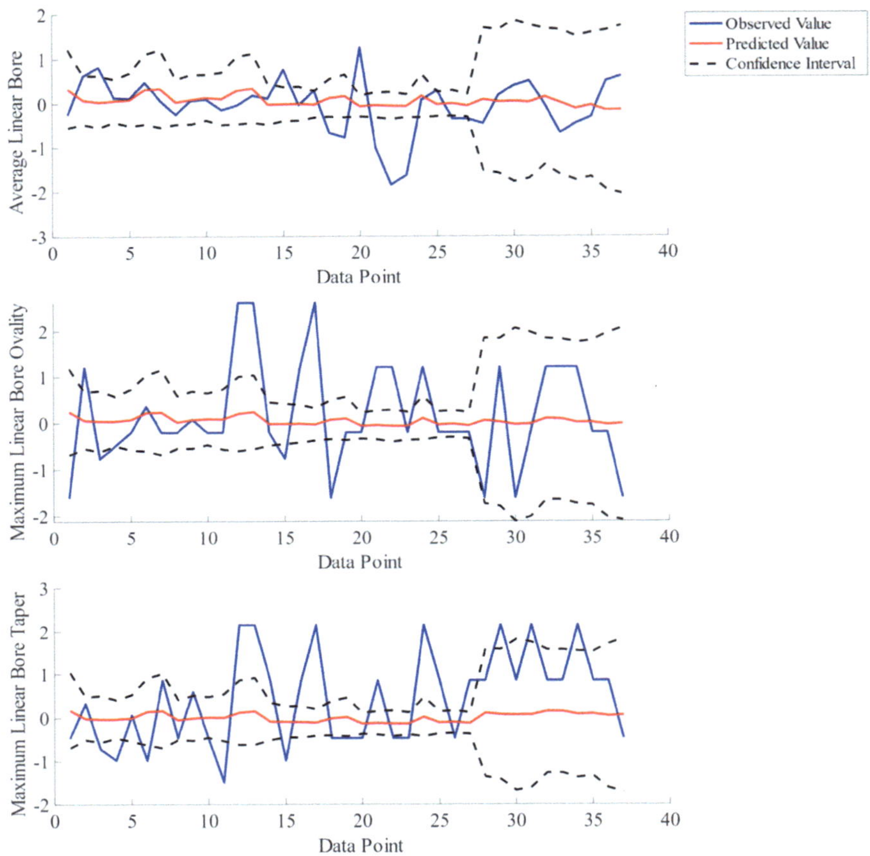

Fig. 5.11 Plots of observed values in test data, corresponding predicted values and confidence intervals obtained using BBB on honing process data

Table 5.16 Percentage of actual data points falling within confidence interval limits for each modelling technique in each manufacturing case

Data set	ANN-based modelling approach	Percentage of test data points falling within the confidence interval limits
Laboratory experiment data	ABE	62.16
	MCD	0
	BBB	27.02
Honing process data	ABE	57.14
	MCD	0
	BBB	7.14

References

Anderson-Cook, C. M., & Prewitt, K. (2005). Some guidelines for using nonparametric methods for modeling data from response surface designs. *Journal of Modern Applied Statistical Methods, 4*, 106–119. https://doi.org/10.22237/jmasm/1114906320

Benker, M., Furtner, L., Semm, T., & Zaeh, M. F. (2021). Utilizing uncertainty information in remaining useful life estimation via Bayesian neural networks and Hamiltonian Monte Carlo. *Journal of Manufacturing Systems, 61*, 799–807. https://doi.org/10.1016/j.jmsy.2020.11.005

Blundell, C., Cornebise, J., Kavukcuoglu, K., & Wierstra, D. (2015). Weight uncertainty in neural networks. In *32nd international conference on machine learning* (pp 1613–1622).

Chapman, J. L., Lu, L., & Anderson-Cook, C. M. (2014). Incorporating response variability and estimation uncertainty into Pareto front optimization. *Computers & Industrial Engineering, 76*, 253–267. https://doi.org/10.1016/j.cie.2014.07.028

Coit, D. W., Jackson, B. T., & Smith, A. E. (1998). Static neural network process models: Considerations and case studies. *International Journal of Production Research, 36*, 2953–2967. https://doi.org/10.1080/002075498192229

Das, R. N., & Lee, Y. (2009). Log-normal versus gamma models for analyzing data from quality-improvement experiments. *Quality Engineering, 21*, 79–87. https://doi.org/10.1080/08982110802317372

Denkena, B., Dittrich, M. A., Böß, V., et al. (2019). Self-optimizing process planning for helical flute grinding. *Production Engineering, 13*, 599–606. https://doi.org/10.1007/s11740-019-00908-0

Derringer, G., & Suich, R. (1980). Simultaneous optimization of several response variables. *Journal of Quality Technology, 12*, 214–219. https://doi.org/10.1080/00224065.1980.11980968

Feng, C. X., & Wang, X. F. (2003). Surface roughness predictive modeling: Neural networks versus regression. *IIE Transactions (Institute of Industrial Engineers), 35*, 11–27. https://doi.org/10.1080/07408170304433

Fernández, J., Chiachío, M., & Chiachío, J. et al. (2022). Uncertainty quantification in neural networks by approximate Bayesian computation: Application to fatigue in composite materials. *Engineering Applications of Artificial Intelligence, 107*. https://doi.org/10.1016/j.engappai.2021.104511

Gal, Y., & Ghahramani, Z. (2015). Dropout as a Bayesian approximation: representing model uncertainty in deep learning.

García, V., Sánchez, J. S., Rodríguez-Picón, L. A., et al. (2019). Using regression models for predicting the product quality in a tubing extrusion process. *Journal of Intelligent Manufacturing, 30*, 2535–2544. https://doi.org/10.1007/s10845-018-1418-7

Ghorbanian, J., Casaprima, N., & Olivier, A. (2025). Empowering approximate Bayesian neural networks with functional priors through anchored ensembling for mechanics surrogate modeling applications. *Computer Methods in Applied Mechanics and Engineering*. https://doi.org/10.1016/j.cma.2024.117645

Giannetti, C., & Ransing, R. S. (2016). Risk based uncertainty quantification to improve robustness of manufacturing operations. *Computers & Industrial Engineering, 101*, 70–80. https://doi.org/10.1016/j.cie.2016.08.002

Goh, T. N. (1988). Statistical methodologies for quality and production improvement. *Industrial Management & Data Systems, 88*, 21–24. https://doi.org/10.1108/eb057523

Graves, A. (2011). Practical variational inference for neural networks. In *Advances in neural information processing systems.*

Hagen, M. T., Demuth, H. B., Beale, M. H., & De, J. O. (2002). *Neural network design.* PWS Publishing.

Han, Y., Tu, Y., Ouyang, L., et al. (2022). Economic quality design under model uncertainty in micro-drilling manufacturing process. *International Journal of Production Research, 60*, 1086–1104. https://doi.org/10.1080/00207543.2020.1851792

He, Y., He, Z., Kim, K. J., et al. (2021). A robust interactive desirability function approach for multiple response optimization considering model uncertainty. *IEEE Transactions on Reliability, 70*, 175–187. https://doi.org/10.1109/TR.2020.2995752

He, Y., He, Z., Lee, D. H., et al. (2017). Robust fuzzy programming method for MRO problems considering location effect, dispersion effect and model uncertainty. *Computers & Industrial Engineering, 105*, 76–83. https://doi.org/10.1016/j.cie.2016.12.021

He, Z., Zhu, P. F., & Park, S. H. (2012). A robust desirability function method for multi-response surface optimization considering model uncertainty. *European Journal of Operational Research, 221*, 241–247. https://doi.org/10.1016/j.ejor.2012.03.009

Hornik, K., Stinchcombe, M., & White, H. (1989). Multilayer feedforward networks are universal approximators. *Neural Networks, 2*, 359–366. https://doi.org/10.1016/0893-6080(89)90020-8

Huband, S., Hingston, P., Barone, L., & While, L. (2006). A review of multiobjective test problems and a scalable test problem toolkit. *IEEE Transactions on Evolutionary Computation, 10*, 477–506.

Jack Feng, C. X., & Wang, X. F. D. (2004). Data mining techniques applied to predictive modeling of the knurling process. *IIE Transactions (Institute of Industrial Engineers), 36*, 253–263. https://doi.org/10.1080/07408170490274214

Jahmunah, V., Ng, E. Y. K., Tan, R.-S., et al. (2023). Uncertainty quantification in DenseNet model using myocardial infarction ECG signals. *Computer Methods and Programs in Biomedicine, 229*, Article 107308. https://doi.org/10.1016/j.cmpb.2022.107308

Jaypuria, S., Bondada, V., & Kumar Gupta, S., et al. (2023). Prediction of electron beam weld quality from weld bead surface using clustering and support vector regression. *Expert Systems with Applications, 211*. https://doi.org/10.1016/j.eswa.2022.118677

Jones, B., Jenkinson, I., Yang, Z., & Wang, J. (2010). The use of Bayesian network modelling for maintenance planning in a manufacturing industry. *Reliability Engineering and System Safety, 95*, 267–277. https://doi.org/10.1016/j.ress.2009.10.007

Khan, W. A., Chung, S. H., Awan, M. U., & Wen, X. (2020). Machine learning facilitated business intelligence (Part I): Neural networks learning algorithms and applications. *Industrial Management and Data Systems, 120*, 164–195. https://doi.org/10.1108/IMDS-07-2019-0361

Khuri, A. I., & Mukhopadhyay, S. (2010). Response surface methodology. *Wiley Interdiscip Rev Comput Stat, 2*, 128–149.

Kim, K. J., & Lin, D. K. J. (2000). Simultaneous optimization of mechanical properties of steel by maximizing exponential desirability functions. *Journal of the Royal Statistical Society: Series C: Applied Statistics, 49*, 311–325. https://doi.org/10.1111/1467-9876.00194

Kohavi, R. (1995). A study of cross-validation and bootstrap for accuracy estimation and model selection. In *Proceedings of the 14th international joint conference on artificial intelligence (IJCAI)* (pp. 1137–1143).

Kwak, D. S., Kim, K. J., & Lee, M. S. (2010). Multistage PRIM: Patient rule induction method for optimisation of a multistage manufacturing process. *International Journal of Production Research, 48*, 3461–3473. https://doi.org/10.1080/00207540902791827

Lee, D. H., Kim, S. H., Kim, E. S., et al. (2021a). MR-CART: Multiresponse optimization using a classification and regression tree method. *Quality Engineering, 33*, 457–473. https://doi.org/10.1080/08982112.2021.1888120

Lee, D. H., Kim, S. H., & Kim., K. J. (2021b). Multistage MR-CART: Multiresponse optimization in a multistage process using a classification and regression tree method. *Computers & Industrial Engineering, 159*. https://doi.org/10.1016/j.cie.2021.107513

Lee, D. H., Yang, J. K., & Kim, K. J. (2020). Multiresponse optimization of a multistage manufacturing process using a patient rule induction method. *Quality and Reliability Engineering International, 36*, 1982–2002. https://doi.org/10.1002/qre.2669

Lee, M. S., & Kim, K. J. (2008). MR-PRIM: Patient rule induction method for multiresponse optimization. *Quality Engineering, 20*, 232–242. https://doi.org/10.1080/08982110701778468

Maji, A., & Mukherjee, I. (2024). An efficient adaptive r-MD multivariate single control chart for nonlinear multiple quality characteristics. *International Journal of Production Research, 62*, 784–822. https://doi.org/10.1080/00207543.2023.2173508

McNaught, K., & Chan, A. (2011). Bayesian networks in manufacturing. *Journal of Manufacturing Technology Management, 22*, 734–747. https://doi.org/10.1108/17410381111149611

Montgomery, D. C. (2005). *Design and analysis of experiments.* Wiley.

Montgomery, D. C., & Peck, E. A. (1992). *Introduction to linear regression analysis.* John Wiley & Sons.

Mukherjee, I. (2012). Simultaneous optimization of mean and variances of multi-stage and multi-response manufacturing process.

Mukherjee, I. (2007). *Modelling and optimization of abrasive metal cutting processes.* Indian Institute of Technology Kharagpur

Mukherjee, I., & Ray, P. K. (2006). A review of optimization techniques in metal cutting processes. *Computers & Industrial Engineering, 50*, 15–34. https://doi.org/10.1016/j.cie.2005.10.001

Mukherjee, I., & Routroy, S. (2012). Comparing the performance of neural networks developed by using Levenberg-Marquardt and Quasi-Newton with the gradient descent algorithm for modelling a multiple response grinding process. *Expert Systems with Applications, 39*, 2397–2407. https://doi.org/10.1016/j.eswa.2011.08.087

Nannapaneni, S., Mahadevan, S., & Rachuri, S. (2016). Performance evaluation of a manufacturing process under uncertainty using Bayesian networks. *Journal of Cleaner Production, 113*, 947–959. https://doi.org/10.1016/j.jclepro.2015.12.003

Németh, K., & Hadházi, D. (2024). Generating density nowcasts for U.S. GDP growth with deep learning: Bayes by Backprop and Monte Carlo dropout.

Noorossana, R., Davanloo Tajbakhsh, S., & Saghaei, A. (2009). An artificial neural network approach to multiple-response optimization. *International Journal of Advanced Manufacturing Technology, 40*, 1227–1238. https://doi.org/10.1007/s00170-008-1423-7

Onler, R., Koca, A. S., Kirim, B., & Soylemez, E. (2022). Multi-objective optimization of binder jet additive manufacturing of Co-Cr-Mo using machine learning. *International Journal of Advanced Manufacturing Technology, 119*, 1091–1108. https://doi.org/10.1007/s00170-021-08183-z

Ouyang, L., Chen, J., Ma, Y., et al. (2020). Bayesian closed-loop robust process design considering model uncertainty and data quality. *IISE Trans, 52*, 288–300. https://doi.org/10.1080/24725854.2019.1636428

Ouyang, L., Ma, Y., Byun, J. H., et al. (2016a). An interval approach to robust design with parameter uncertainty. *International Journal of Production Research, 54*, 3201–3215. https://doi.org/10.1080/00207543.2015.1078920

Ouyang, L., Ma, Y., Byun, J. H., et al. (2016b). A prediction region-based approach to model uncertainty for multi-response optimization. *Quality and Reliability Engineering International, 32*, 783–794. https://doi.org/10.1002/qre.1790

Ouyang, L., Ma, Y., Chen, J., et al. (2016c). Robust optimisation of Nd: YLF laser beam micro-drilling process using Bayesian probabilistic approach. *International Journal of Production Research, 54*, 6644–6659. https://doi.org/10.1080/00207543.2016.1154212

Ouyang, L., Ma, Y., Wang, J., & Tu, Y. (2017). A new loss function for multi-response optimization with model parameter uncertainty and implementation errors. *European Journal of Operational Research, 258*, 552–563. https://doi.org/10.1016/j.ejor.2016.09.045

Paliwal, M., & Kumar, U. A. (2009). Neural networks and statistical techniques: A review of applications. *Expert Systems with Applications, 36*, 2–17. https://doi.org/10.1016/j.eswa.2007.10.005

Park, C. (2013). Determination of the joint confidence region of the optimal operating conditions in robust design by the bootstrap technique. *International Journal of Production Research, 51*, 4695–4703. https://doi.org/10.1080/00207543.2013.792963

Pearce, T., Leibfried, F., & Brintrup, A., et al. (2020). Uncertainty in neural networks: Approximately Bayesian ensembling. In *Proceedings of the 23rdinternational conference on artificial intelligence and statistics* (pp 234–244).

Puzyrev, V., & Duuring, P. (2025). Uncertainty quantification of geochemical data imputation using Monte Carlo dropout. *Journal of Geochemical Exploration, 272*. https://doi.org/10.1016/j.gexplo.2025.107695

Ross, P. J. (2005). *Taguchi techniques for quality engineering* (2nd ed.). McGraw Hill.
Shah, H. K., Montgomery, D. C., & Carlyle, W. M. (2004). Response surface modeling and optimization in multiresponse experiments using seemingly unrelated regressions. *Quality Engineering, 16*, 387–397. https://doi.org/10.1081/QEN-120027941
Sharma, A. K., & Mukherjee, I. (2020). Enhanced multi-objective solution approach for multiple quality characteristics optimisation problems considering predictive uncertainties. *International Journal of Quality and Reliability Management, 37*, 112–144. https://doi.org/10.1108/IJQRM-01-2019-0011
Sharma, A. K., Mukherjee, I., & Bera, S. (2023). A novel machine learning-based multiobjective robust optimisation strategy for quality improvement of multivariate manufacturing processes. *International Journal of Production Research, 61*, 4322–4340. https://doi.org/10.1080/00207543.2022.2093683
Sharma, A. K., Mukherjee, I., Bera, S., & Sengupta, R. N. (2022). A robust multiobjective solution approach for mean-variance optimisation of correlated multiple quality characteristics. *International Journal of Quality and Reliability Management, 39*, 2205–2232. https://doi.org/10.1108/IJQRM-12-2020-0409
Shi, X., Schillings, P., & Boyd, D. (2004). Applying artificial neural networks and virtual experimental design to quality improvement of two industrial processes. *International Journal of Production Research, 42*, 101–118. https://doi.org/10.1080/00207540310001602937
Shridhar, K., Laumann, F., & Liwicki, M. (2019). A comprehensive guide to Bayesian convolutional neural network with variational inference. abs/1901.02731
Sikder, S., Mukherjee, I., & Panja, S. C. (2020). A synergistic Mahalanobis-Taguchi system and support vector regression based predictive multivariate manufacturing process quality control approach. *Journal of Manufacturing Systems, 57*, 323–337. https://doi.org/10.1016/j.jmsy.2020.10.003
Song, Y., Li, F., & Wang, Z. et al. (2024). Uncertainty quantification of data-driven quality prediction model for realizing the active sampling inspection of mechanical properties in steel production. *International Journal of Computational Intelligence Systems, 17*. https://doi.org/10.1007/s44196-024-00451-6
Srivastava, N., Hinton, G., Krizhevsky, A., & Salakhutdinov, R. (2014). Dropout: A simple way to prevent neural networks from overfitting.
Tong, L. I., & Hsieh, K. L. (2001). A novel means of applying neural networks to optimize the multiresponse problem. *Quality Engineering, 13*, 11–18. https://doi.org/10.1080/08982110108918619
Tukey, J. W. (1991). The philosophy of multiple comparisons. *Statistical Science, 6*. https://doi.org/10.1214/ss/1177011945
Tzeng, G.-H., & Huang, J.-J. (2011). *Multiple attribute decision making*. Chapman and Hall/CRC.
Vehtari, A., & Lampinen, J. (1999). Bayesian neural networks for industrial applications. In *1999 IEEE midnight - sun workshop on soft computing methods in industrial applications* (pp. 63–68). IEEE.
Wang, J., Ma, Y., Tsung, F., et al. (2019). Economic parameter design for ultra-fast laser microdrilling process. *International Journal of Production Research, 57*, 6292–6314. https://doi.org/10.1080/00207543.2019.1566660
Wang, J., Mao, T., & Tu, Y. (2021). Simultaneous multi-response optimisation for parameter and tolerance design using Bayesian modelling method. *International Journal of Production Research, 59*, 2269–2293. https://doi.org/10.1080/00207543.2020.1730011
Yalamanchi, K. K., Kommalapati, S., & Pal, P., et al. (2023). Uncertainty quantification of a deep learning fuel property prediction model. *Applications in Energy and Combustion Science, 16*. https://doi.org/10.1016/j.jaecs.2023.100211
Zhang, H. C., & Huang, S. H. (1995). Applications of neural networks in manufacturing: A state-of-the-art survey. *International Journal of Production Research, 33*, 705–728. https://doi.org/10.1080/00207549508930175

Chapter 6
Role of Digital Technologies in Quality Improvement for a Sustainable Healthcare System

Prince Kumar Tiwari and Cherian Samuel

Abstract Digital technologies like blockchain, internet of things, smart devices, artificial intelligence, machine learning, cloud computing, digital health records, and big data are transforming the sustainable healthcare system. The chapter discusses the different digital technologies in the sustainable healthcare, the link between digital transformation and sustainable healthcare, the challenges in the adoption of digital technologies for sustainable healthcare, and the key solutions for adoption to overcome the challenges in sustainable healthcare. In nutshell, the role of digital technologies in quality improvement for a sustainable healthcare system is addressed along with a future outlook.

Keywords Digital technologies · Quality improvement · Sustainable · Healthcare system

6.1 Introduction

Digital technologies have been critical in healthcare industries since the 1990s, when the term "e-health" was coined. Digital transformation in healthcare has become steadily more relevant over the last two decades. In a recent study, Ferrigno et al. (2023) identified digital transformation as a future research area relevant to the topic of Industry 4.0. Due to rapid digital advancements, healthcare organizations are undergoing a unique kind of transformation, especially in the adoption and application of digital technologies like blockchain, artificial intelligence (AI), cloud computing, and digital twins, owing to patient needs, the pandemic response, and new government regulations. Worldwide, medical systems are under pressure to enhance

P. K. Tiwari · C. Samuel (✉)
Mechanical Engineering Department, IIT (BHU), Varanasi, UP, India
e-mail: csamuel.mec@itbhu.ac.in

P. K. Tiwari
e-mail: princekumartiwari.rs.mec23@itbhu.ac.in

I. Mukherjee et al. (eds.), *Decision Sciences for Quality and Productivity Improvement*,
https://doi.org/10.1007/978-981-95-7545-9_6

quality in the pharmaceutical supply chain. A significant part of digital transformation in medical areas is designed to make medical services more efficient, accessible, and meet high standards.

Digital transformation has the potential to benefit society and make the healthcare industry more sustainable. Healthcare systems must utilize digital technology to develop innovative solutions that enhance quality, address medical issues, and establish sustainable healthcare supply chain systems. Healthcare data should be leveraged to transform traditional medical systems into technologically advanced healthcare systems. Additionally, enhancing the quality of the healthcare supply chain will be beneficial, including cost savings, addressing counterfeit drug issues, promoting transparency, and ensuring accountability in hospitals. Meaningful adoption and application of digital technologies are possible if data collection is proper in hospitals. Medical education in medical colleges can also benefit from advanced digital transformation in the healthcare system. It can enable professionals to create more innovative solutions to medical problems. In this way, practitioners will now face new opportunities to learn and apply their knowledge to healthcare problems (Laurenza et al., 2018).

The digitalization of the healthcare system has the potential to reduce wasteful aspects of healthcare services and is increasingly impacting healthcare quality, including faster diagnosis, treatment initiation, and continuous monitoring, as well as supply chain visibility. Digital transformation in the pharmaceutical sector enables healthcare providers to access the information they need to deliver high-quality care rapidly.

The healthcare area can achieve sustainable goals. It can improve healthcare by making services more effective, efficient, and crucial to individual needs digital transformation of healthcare can also make the pharmaceutical supply chain more sustainable by reducing waste, increasing cost-effectiveness, optimizing resources, and lowering carbon emissions. For example, digital tools like telemedicine lessen the need for patients and healthcare providers to travel, thereby reducing carbon emissions. Electronic health records (EHRs) and decision support systems also help use resources more efficiently and improve patient care outcomes. The pandemic, like COVID-19, accelerated the adoption of digital transformation in healthcare by enhancing the reliability and sustainability of healthcare.

Healthcare systems worldwide are undergoing rapid changes due to the increasing application and adoption of new digital technologies. This change is not just about using electronic tools in medical work—it's a significant shift in how healthcare is planned, delivered, and measured. This chapter presents a novel and integrated perspective on how digital technologies—such as artificial intelligence, blockchain, internet of things, digital twins, big data analytics, cloud computing, robotics, and telemedicine—collectively contribute to quality improvement within a sustainable healthcare framework., this work develops a unified conceptual model linking digital innovation to the core dimensions of healthcare quality—Counterfeit of drugs, Transparency in healthcare supply chain, patient-care effectiveness etc., while simultaneously addressing the application, challenges of the adoption of digital technologies and solutions. Digital tools in the healthcare system can enhance healthcare functions by reducing errors and optimizing resource utilization. They also make healthcare more accessible through telehealth and mobile health apps, which help people in remote areas get the care they need. Additionally, using data to inform decisions helps forecast health problems before they occur, allowing doctors to control costs better and support individuals in maintaining their health.

While several studies have explored the digitalization of healthcare, many have mainly remained descriptive—focusing on listing technologies rather than analyzing how these innovations collectively contribute to sustainable quality improvement.

Blockchain technology plays a vital role in enhancing data protection, transparency, controlling counterfeit of drugs and traceability throughout the healthcare supply chain. Blockchain enables safe storage and sharing of electronic health records (EHRs) among hospitals, clinics, labs, and patients. This strengthens the authenticity of patient information, minimizes medical fraud, and maintains cold-chain integrity in pharmaceutical logistics. (Govindarajan et al., 2025; McGhin et al., 2019).

Blockchain emerges as particularly transformative due to its foundational role in ensuring the control of counterfeit drugs, transparency in the pharmaceutical supply chain, and data security. It reduces the need for paperwork and also helps with route optimization—critical elements of sustainable healthcare systems.

Collectively, these technologies create a synergistic ecosystem where blockchain upholds trust and data integrity, Digital Twins enable ongoing prediction and optimization, and the Metaverse fosters immersive training, collaboration, and knowledge sharing. Figure 6.1 depicts the digital technologies in sustainable healthcare.

6.2 Digital Technologies Transforming Healthcare

6.2.1 Artificial Intelligence (AI) and Machine Learning (ML)

When scientists first considered robots that could replicate human thinking in the early days of computing, the concept of using AI in healthcare began to emerge. In the healthcare sector, the adoption of AI is not a new concept and has already been used properly. More and more pharmaceutical organizations are using AI because it can significantly improve patient care, treatment outcomes, and the accuracy of medical diagnoses. One example of how AI is being utilized is in creating tools that aid in diagnosis. For instance, AI can analyze medical images, such as CT scans and X-rays, to identify signs of illness or injury. (Olawade et al., 2024). However, improvements in machine learning techniques, increased processing power, and the accessibility of large datasets marked the beginning of its widespread usage. From early expert systems to sophisticated neural networks that surpass human specialists in specific tasks, artificial intelligence has evolved over time. With a variety of

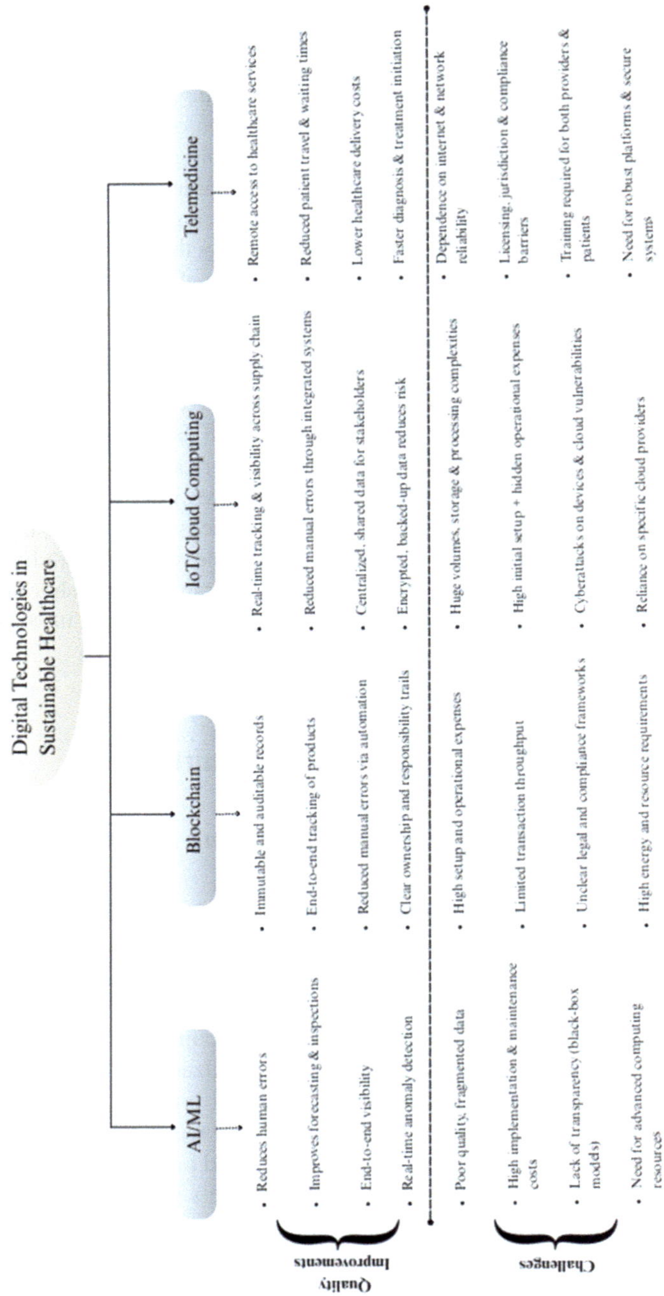

Fig. 6.1 Digital technologies in sustainable healthcare

applications, including illness diagnosis, patient outcome prediction, and individualized treatment planning in clinical settings, artificial intelligence is currently revolutionizing healthcare (Kumah, 2025). Computational models are used by artificial intelligence and machine learning to automate repetitive operations, support clinical decision-making, and identify patterns in clinical and operational data. In real-world applications, AI/ML enhances quality by facilitating earlier and more precise diagnosis (as in medical imaging), forecasting the likelihood of deterioration or readmission, streamlining triage and resource allocation, and using predictive models to customize treatment regimens. Additionally, AI facilitates process improvement (e.g., automated documentation, coding, and workflow anomaly detection), which lessens physicians' cognitive burden and error rates. Algorithmic bias, inconsistent generalizability across people and environments, reliance on data quality, and ethical and legal issues with explainability and implementation are significant drawbacks. See systematic studies of ML applications in healthcare for in-depth analyses and debates on the advantages and disadvantages (Ullah & Ali, 2025).

6.2.2 Internet of Things (IoT) and Smart Devices

The internet of things, or IoT for short, is a cutting-edge and quickly developing technology. One of the industries expected to benefit the most from this expansion is the healthcare sector. By automating administrative tasks, IoT technologies simplify healthcare operations, reduce costs by eliminating the need for a large administrative staff, and save time. Additionally, regular duties like prescription dispensing and vital sign monitoring can be automated, lowering the possibility of mistakes and reducing the cost of labor (Li et al., 2024). The internet of things (IoT) is the result of sophisticated information and communications technology research. It might improve the standard of living for city dwellers. Given that the world's population is growing at a startling rate, and the number of chronic illnesses is also increasing, there is a rising need to create affordable healthcare systems that can effectively administer and offer a variety of medical services while lowering overall costs (Abdulmalek et al., 2022). The internet of things (IoT) enables continuous sensing and networked connectivity for patients, devices, and facilities through wearable devices, bedside sensors, smart infusion pumps, and environmental monitors. IoT supports quality improvement by enabling remote patient monitoring (RPM), early detection of physiological decline, real-time tracking of device performance, and automated alerts (Parihar et al., 2024). Key challenges include device interoperability, data security/privacy, and the need for robust edge/cloud architectures to handle streaming data.

6.2.3 Blockchain for Data Integrity and Supply-Chain Transparency

In 2009, the technology and architecture platform known as blockchain was introduced. Blockchain technology stores data in decentralized ledgers that are dispersed throughout all of the computer machines that make up the blockchain infrastructure (McGhin et al., 2019).

The potential of blockchain technology to address significant challenges within the healthcare sector has been widely acknowledged. Its robust capabilities are particularly relevant for enhancing data security, safeguarding patient privacy, and fostering seamless interoperability between systems. The inherent transparency and unchangeable nature of its decentralized ledger architecture empower individuals with greater control over their personal health information. This model allows patients to own their medical data and selectively grant authorized healthcare providers access, thereby facilitating the secure management of electronic health records (EHRs). Such an approach not only has the potential to reduce administrative overheads but also significantly bolsters data privacy and simplifies the exchange of critical information across disparate healthcare systems. However, a primary impediment to widespread adoption remains the intricate challenge of managing the diverse, complex, and often multidimensional nature of medical data itself.

Therefore, when combined with a blockchain-based platform, other enablers like cloud computing offer a means of managing electronic medical information while safeguarding patient privacy and reducing the risks of unauthorized access. Blockchain has not been widely adopted as quickly as anticipated, despite its potential in the healthcare industry. Scholars who study the discrepancy between theoretical promise and real-world application have voiced concerns about this "failure of translation." However, blockchain technology has a lot of potential to help with the digital transformation of healthcare (Govindarajan et al., 2025).

Blockchain and distributed ledger technologies provide tamper-evident, append-only records and smart contract automation, enhancing trust, provenance, and traceability in healthcare data and supply chains. In supply-chain contexts, blockchain enhances quality by enabling the immutable tracking of pharmaceuticals, medical devices, and biologics, thereby reducing counterfeit risk, improving recall efficiency, and strengthening cold-chain verification. For clinical data, permissioned ledgers can support auditable consent management and provenance for shared records without necessarily exposing raw patient data.

6.2.4 Digital Twin Technologies

Digital Twin Technologies (DTT) are virtual models that replicate real-world systems, objects, or processes, and are continually updated with live data from them. These digital versions utilize information from sensors, artificial intelligence, and machine learning to simulate, track, and predict the behavior of their real counterparts.

This technology has transformed many industries by enabling people to study and improve physical systems in real-time. As automation and digital technologies continue to grow under Industry 4.0, Digital Twins are becoming increasingly popular across sectors—including healthcare.

In healthcare, Digital Twins aim to create comprehensive digital representations of patients. These virtual models help improve disease prevention, diagnosis, and treatment by simulating different aspects of the human body. They can be used to study how drugs interact, assess the effectiveness of treatments, and design personalized care for each patient.

Digital twins enable doctors and researchers to predict how the body or a medical system will respond under various conditions. This makes them a powerful and evolving tool for tailoring medical treatments and preventive strategies to each individual's unique needs (Sun et al., 2023).

6.2.5 Big Data and Predictive Analytics

"Big data" in healthcare refers to the aggregation of large, heterogeneous datasets—EHRs, imaging, genomics, claims, device telemetry, and social determinants—which, together with predictive analytics, enable population-level insights and patient-level risk stratification. Predictive analytics improves quality by identifying high-risk patients for targeted interventions (reducing readmissions and adverse events), supporting precision public-health responses, and informing capacity planning and demand forecasting. Effective use requires careful problem framing, feature engineering, validation (especially temporal and external validation), and attention to bias and fairness. Reviews demonstrate multiple clinical success stories but also emphasize rigorous methodological standards and governance frameworks to translate analytics into improved outcomes.

6.2.6 Cloud Computing and Digital Health Records

Cloud platforms provide scalable storage, compute resources, and managed services that underpin modern electronic health records (EHRs), data lakes, and analytics pipelines. Although the rapid advancement of internet of things (IoT) has significantly improved patient care and health outcomes, it has also resulted in stricter requirements for data storage and analysis (Calabrese & Cannataro, 2015). The increasing amount of clinical, analytical laboratory, and "-omics" data generated by the integration of IoT technologies raises several concerns, including data management, sharing, confidentiality, security, and high-performance computing. Additionally, by leveraging cloud computing to distribute and store data at scale in a more structured, organized, and transparent way, the risk of data loss can be decreased (Xie et al., 2022). This technology can increase the scalability of healthcare resources and activities by giving access to more computational power and storage capacity at a cheaper cost than traditional grid technologies. For instance, in India, tertiary healthcare facilities' electronic medical record (EMR) systems are connected to a remote health cloud, enabling desktop sharing and immediate order and note entry because EMRs are accessible from any location (Clifford et al., 2016).

6.2.7 Robotics and Automation

Robotics in healthcare spans surgical robots, robotic-assisted rehabilitation, autonomous delivery robots, and disinfection/UV robots. These systems improve quality by increasing procedural precision (reducing complications and recovery time), automating repetitive tasks (medication or specimen transport), and augmenting workforce capacity where labor shortages exist (Khinvasara & Hearing, 2024). Surgical and rehabilitation robots have shown measurable improvements in specific clinical outcomes and patient throughput in many settings; logistics robots can reduce contamination risk and free clinical staff for higher-value care. Challenges include high capital cost, training and credentialing needs, regulatory oversight, and variable evidence on cost-effectiveness across contexts.

6.2.8 Telemedicine and Mobile Health (mHealth)

Telemedicine and mHealth use digital communication (video, asynchronous messaging, apps) and smartphones/wearables to extend care beyond physical facilities. They improve quality by increasing access (particularly in remote or underserved areas), enabling timely follow-ups and chronic-disease management, supporting patient self-management and adherence, and reducing unnecessary emergency visits (Aceto et al., 2020). mHealth interventions have been shown to improve outcomes in areas such as diabetes and hypertension management when combined with clinician oversight and behavioral interventions (Egbewande et al., 2023). Equity issues (digital divide, literacy), reimbursement models, clinical integration, and data privacy are recurring implementation barriers. For recent evidence on the impacts and design considerations of telemedicine and mHealth interventions, consult systematic reviews.

6.3 Link Between Digital Transformation and Sustainable Healthcare

6.3.1 Patient and Health Professional Engagement for Sustainable Healthcare

Patient engagement typically refers to a prosumer of healthcare, where the coproduction of pharmaceutical services and the co-creation of value take a central place. Patient commitment is defined as a process in which patients and healthcare professionals work together as equal stakeholders, share their skills to exchange information, and generate innovative ideas. Patient engagement is seen as a strategy to maintain the sustainability of the National Health Service healthcare and promote health equity for the entire population. Active patient engagement plays a crucial role in sustainable value creation by improving health outcomes qualitatively. The critical components of patient engagement include information sharing, shared decision-making, patient education, communication, self-management, and access to healthcare services. Additionally, with this transformed healthcare system, patients become more proactive, taking responsibility for their own health and well-being. By learning and practicing digital health tools, healthcare professionals can significantly optimize resources, including waste management, workforce management, time savings, and operational cost savings, ultimately leading to a more sustainable healthcare environment. Overall, this literature suggests that patient and health professional contributions to sustainable healthcare are highly significant.

Digital transformation refers to the systematic adoption of digital tools and technologies (AI, IoT, blockchain, cloud computing, automation, etc.) in healthcare workflows, decision-making, and service delivery. Sustainable healthcare refers to systems that balance environmental protection, economic viability, and social equity, while delivering high-quality care (Koebe, 2025) (Table 6.1).

Table 6.2 provides examples of how digital technologies help in achieving the sustainable healthcare goals.

6.3.2 How Each Technology Concretely Supports Sustainability Goals

Table 6.2 portrays how each technology concretely supports sustainability goals.

Table 6.1 Examples of how digital technologies help

Mechanism	How digital technologies help	Evidence/research examples
Reducing environmental footprint	Digital/virtual services reduce patient and staff travel, reducing carbon emissions. Also, digitization reduces paper use, physical infrastructure needs, and waste from tests/reports	Telemedicine reduces CO_2 emissions from travel (e.g. ~ 6,655 tons CO_2 avoided in one provider via digital appointments. A systematic review confirms that telemedicine reduces carbon footprint, primarily through reduced transport emissions (Rodler et al., 2023). Telemedicine in China: Replacing in-person visits led to substantial reductions in greenhouse gas emissions (e.g. ~ 85.5 kg CO_2 per replaced session) (Z. Li et al., 2025)
Improved efficiency and reduced costs	Digital tools and analytics streamline administrative tasks, optimize resource allocation (e.g. staff, beds, equipment), reduce duplicative diagnostics, and cut down waiting times. This preserves economic resources and supports sustainability	Digital transformation and big data/AI in Jordan: Improved diagnostic accuracy and operational efficiency (Al-Dmour et al., 2025). Clinical laboratories: Digitalization reduces waste and costs while maintaining quality (Fung, 2025)
Enhanced quality of care and patient outcomes	AI, blockchain, decision-support systems, and data analytics enable earlier detection, better predictions, and personalized medicine, leading to fewer complications and readmissions. This reduces resource waste and improves social equity	AI & big data analytics in jordan: Positive impact on treatment planning and diagnostic accuracy (Al-Dmour et al., 2025). Review on digital transformation for sustainable health argues that ICT can improve access, treatment quality, and equity (F. Hameed & Hameed, 2023b)

(continued)

Table 6.1 (continued)

Mechanism	How digital technologies help	Evidence/research examples
Access, equity, and social sustainability	Digital health (telehealth, remote monitoring, mobile health) expands access to underserved populations (rural, remote, mobility-limited), which supports social justice and avoids overburdening centralized facilities	"Digital transformation for sustainable health & well-being: A review…" points out ICTs' role in improving access and fair health outcomes (F. Hameed & Hameed, 2023a). Telehealth in ambulatory settings during the COVID-19 pandemic avoided travel burdens, costs, and time, especially for patients residing far from facilities (Shaver, 2022)
Supporting policy and strategic alignment to SDGs	Many digital interventions align with the Sustainable Development Goals (especially SDG 3: Good Health & Well-being) and enable the monitoring, measurement, and reporting of health & environmental metrics. Digital platforms assist in data collection, transparency, and accountability	AI for sustainability in healthcare: Mapping studies showing how AI helps achieve SDGs (Sajwani, 2024). Digital transformation & sustainability literature: Integrating sustainable health considerations into policy frameworks (K. Hameed et al., 2024)

6.4 Challenges in the Adoption of Digital Technologies for Sustainable Healthcare

Table 6.3 presents the challenges in the adoption of digital technologies in sustainable healthcare.

6.4.1 Implications of the Factors and Subfactors?

Table 6.4 illustrates the implications due to factors and subfactors in sustainable healthcare.

6.5 Global Digital Healthcare Practices

Amid the growing need for digitalization, the Indian government launched the Ayushman Bharat Digital Mission in September 2021. It creates and utilizes digital tools to increase the accessibility, affordability, and acceptability of healthcare. The

Table 6.2 How technology supports sustainability goals in healthcare

Technology	How it supports sustainability in healthcare
(AI/ML)	Predictive models for disease outbreaks or patient deterioration → early intervention → reduces wasted resources Optimizing hospital operations (staffing, bed allocation, supply usage) → **lowers energy consumption, lowers costs**
Blockchain	Secure, immutable patient data reduces duplicative tests and **redundant paperwork**. Transparent supply chains reduce counterfeit drugs and wastage reducing administrative overhead and cost
Digital Twin Technologies	Virtual replicas allow simulation of treatment plans → reduce failed treatments, and fewer hospitalizations Hospital workflows improve **resource utilization** (beds, staff) → **better energy** and cost efficiency Helps in training and education → reduces risk, errors, **and waste from real-world practice**
Big Data	Aggregated data (population health, epidemiology) allows better planning, preventive care, → reduced disease burden Identify inefficiencies in systems (which departments overuse resources, etc.)
Cloud Computing	Shared infrastructure reduces the need for physical hardware in every hospital, **lowering the carbon footprint and energy use** Scalable computing for heavy workloads (imaging, analytics) Easier collaboration, data sharing, remote work → less travel
Robotics / Automation	Robots can do repetitive/hazardous tasks (e.g., cleaning, supply transport) → faster, safer, less human fatigue Automated systems reduce errors, speeding up processes and resulting **in less waste (in terms of time and materials)** Surgical robots enable minimally invasive procedures → shorter hospital stays, faster recovery**, less resource use**
IoT (internet of things)	Remote patient monitoring → fewer hospital visits, early detection, and reduced travel and resource consumption Sensors in hospitals for energy**/environmental monitoring** → reduce waste Device and equipment tracking prevents loss and misuse
Telemedicine	Access to care without travel → **reduces carbon emissions and cost** Helps underserved or rural populations obtain care Reduces the burden on physical infrastructure, allowing remote management Can reduce hospital-acquired infections by **avoiding in-person visits**

purpose of this mission is to establish a national digital health ecosystem that is coordinated, effective, and comprehensive. Enable citizens, public and private healthcare organizations, digital innovations, and other partners to come together and handle the digitization of healthcare nationwide.

The NHS of the UK, one of the highest-ranked health service models, has adopted digitization, beginning with the introduction of NHS electronic care records, which enable the sharing of patient records with their permission. This process enables physicians and other primary care staff to schedule hospital appointments and facilitates the electronic transmission of prescriptions.

Table 6.3 Challenges in the adoption of digital technologies in sustainable healthcare

Factors	Subfactors	References
Regulatory and policy challenges	Legal problems and lack of policies Lack of concrete clinical guidelines for digital health applications Classification and risk assessment Lack of standardization	Borges do Nascimento et al. (2023)
Organizational and corporate culture challenges	Lack of management willingness Lack of awareness about the need for digital technologies (DTs) The inflexibility of the corporate culture structure Many drugs (e.g., vaccines, insulin) require cold chain or temperature-controlled logistics	Ashish A. Adhikari (2021) Zaman et al. (2024) Kulkov et al. (2023)
Technological and infrastructure challenges	Lack of IT Infrastructure for data collection and processing System interoperability Data management and data storage Underdeveloped technological infrastructure	Manish Shashi (2022), Sadiku, Eze et al. (2018), Steinwandter et al. (2019)
Financial and investment challenges	High investment cost of digital technologies (DTs) High initial implementation cost Increment in unit cost of medicines Maintenance costs	Bhuiyan et al. (2020), Rohan, Laya et al. (2018), Degryse (2016)
Operational and process challenges	Complexity in operational processes Lack of scalability and flexibility Counterfeiting and corruption in pharmaceutical companies	Ghadge et al. (2023), Zulfiqar et al. (2022)

(continued)

Table 6.3 (continued)

Factors	Subfactors	References
Human resource and knowledge challenges	Lack of knowledge and experience about digital skills Difficulty in training Lack of motivation towards new system adoption	Alina, Eldar et al. (2017), Abugabah et al. (2020), Chandra-Mouli et al. (2019)
Ethical and security challenges	Privacy and confidentiality risk Vulnerabilities in digital technologies Lack of transparency	Arden et al. (2021)

Australia was the first country to adopt a population-centric strategy for implementing My Health Record (MHR), a national repository of electronic health histories of patients, built to ease patients' journeys. This strategy transmits significant insights for developing countries, where data protection, and health data privacy are concern issues.

About two decades ago, South Korea's Ministry of Health formulated an excellent plan for National Healthcare Information and Communication Technology (ICT). Since then, healthcare institutions in Korea have undergone extensive digitized, with almost all hospitals implementing computerized provider order entry systems, patient management systems, electronic health record systems. The successful ICT initiatives in Korean healthcare institutions offer valuable lessons for developing countries, which is in process of developing a digitally enabled health claims platform.

About 25 years ago, Estonia initiated its digital transformation of its healthcare systems by introducing unified health information system. This system integrated public and private medical records, allowed patients access to their own information's, and registered them to public information systems—E-health technologies, including electronic health records (EHRs), digital imaging, and digital registration.

6.6 Key Solutions for Adoption Challenges in Sustainable Healthcare

Table 6.5 portrays the key solutions for adoption challenges in sustainable healthcare.

6.7 Conclusions

Digital technologies are rapidly becoming foundational to quality improvement in healthcare, especially as sustainability becomes a central objective for health systems worldwide. Across many settings, from high-income countries to low- and

Table 6.4 Implications due to factors and subfactors

Factors	Implications due to factors	Subfactors	Implications due to subfactor
Regulatory and policy challenges	Slows the adoption of digital health by creating regulatory uncertainty	Legal problems and lack of policies Lack of concrete clinical guidelines for digital health applications Classification and risk assessment Lack of standardization	Increases risk of disputes and discourages innovation Leads to inconsistent clinical practices Delays approval and safe use of technologies Prevents interoperability between systems
Organizational and corporate culture challenges	Weakens organizational readiness for digital transformation	Lack of management Willingness Lack of awareness about the need for digital technologies (DTs) The inflexibility of the corporate culture structure Many drugs (e.g., vaccines, insulin) require cold chain or temperature-controlled logistics	Restricts leadership support for new initiatives Digital health is deprioritized in planning Creates resistance to innovation Adds operational and cost burdens in logistics
Technological and infrastructure challenges	Creates unequal access to digital healthcare	Lack of IT infrastructure for data collection and processing System interoperability Data management and data storage Underdeveloped Technological Infrastructure	Limits the capacity to collect and process health data Causes duplication of records and delays in care Leads to errors and compromised data security Restricts adoption in smaller or rural facilities

(continued)

Table 6.4 (continued)

Factors	Implications due to factors	Subfactors	Implications due to subfactor
Financial and investment challenges	Limits adoption in resource-constrained settings	High Investment cost of digital technologies (DTs) High initial implementation cost Increment in unit cost of medicines Maintenance costs	Hospitals avoid committing to advanced technologies Slows scaling of digital health solutions Reduces affordability for patients Creates a recurring financial burden
Operational and process challenges	Increases inefficiencies in healthcare delivery	Complexity in operational processes Lack of scalability and flexibility Counterfeiting and corruption in pharmaceutical companies	Staff face confusion and higher error rates Prevents expansion of successful pilots Undermines trust in pharmaceutical supply chains
Human resource and knowledge challenges	Creates uneven adoption across the workforce	Lack of knowledge and experience about digital skills Difficulty in training Lack of motivation towards new system adoption	Increases errors in technology use Prolongs the transition to digital systems, Causes low acceptance of new tools
Ethical and security challenges	Reduces patient trust in digital healthcare	Privacy and confidentiality Risk Vulnerabilities in digital technologies Lack of transparency	Data leaks expose sensitive health information Increases risks of cyberattacks Lowers accountability and patient acceptance

middle-income contexts, evidence shows that tools such as electronic health records, telemedicine, mobile health applications, AI/ML algorithms, IoT devices, blockchain systems, and semantic web technologies can enhance patient access, reduce delays, improve accuracy of diagnosis and treatment, enable better patient engagement, and support more efficient use of resources (Zamstein et al., 2024).

Quality improvement through digital means contributes to sustainability in several linked ways: reducing waste (of time, materials, and redundancies), improving operational efficiency, lowering costs, enhancing preventive care (thus reducing the

Table 6.5 Key solutions for adoption challenges in sustainable healthcare

Challenge	AI/ML	Blockchain	Digital Twin	Big Data	Cloud Computing	Robotics/ Automation	IoT	Telemedicine
Regulatory and policy	Compliance monitoring, predictive regulation alerts	Immutable records, smart contracts enforce rules	Simulate compliance under regulations	Track metrics for reporting	Secure central storage, easier audits	Automate documentation and reporting	Monitor devices, drugs, environmental standards	Audit trails for remote consultations
Organizational and corporate culture	Data-driven decision making	Transparent cross-department records	Visualize workflows to encourage collaboration	Shared analytics dashboards	Remote collaboration and knowledge sharing	Standardize repetitive tasks, free staff	Real-time operational updates	Promote patient-centric remote care culture
Technological and infrastructure	Enhances legacy systems, predictive maintenance	Interoperability between siloed systems	Model and optimize infrastructure usage	Integrate heterogeneous data sources	Reduce on-site infrastructure, scalable	Improve efficiency using existing systems	Connect devices and equipment	Reduces dependence on physical infrastructure
Financial and investment	Optimize resource allocation, predict costs	Reduce billing fraud	Simulate cost-saving workflows	Identify inefficiencies	Lower hardware & IT maintenance costs	Reduce labor costs, errors	Optimize energy and device management	Reduce travel and unnecessary admissions
Operational and process	Optimize scheduling, patient flow, reduce errors	Transparent supply and procedure tracking	Identify bottlenecks, optimize resources	Analytics for workflow improvement	Centralized data speeds decisions	Handle repetitive tasks, faster processing	Real-time monitoring of equipment, beds, patients	Streamline consultations and triage

(continued)

Table 6.5 (continued)

Challenge	AI/ML	Blockchain	Digital Twin	Big Data	Cloud Computing	Robotics/Automation	IoT	Telemedicine
Human resource and knowledge	Decision support for staff, knowledge augmentation	Secure credential verification	Virtual training and simulation	Identify training gaps	Access to online education and collaboration	Reduce manual labor dependency	Real-time alerts and guidance	Remote mentoring and consultation
Ethical and security	Anonymize data, detect security breaches	Secure, decentralized access; consent management	In silico testing reduces patient risk	Aggregate anonymized research data	Encryption and centralized security	Automate sensitive procedures	Detect unauthorized access	Secure, encrypted communication and consent management

burden of acute exacerbations), and delivering more equitable care. For example, digital transformation that improves diagnostic efficiency or remote monitoring can prevent hospitalizations, reduce travel, reduce environmental footprint, and maintain continuity of care.

Yet, this promise is tempered by persistent challenges: infrastructure gaps, interoperability barriers, data privacy, regulatory complexities, workforce skills shortages, and issues of equity and access. Also, after initial pilots or deployments, scaling up digital solutions without sacrificing quality or introducing new disparities remains difficult.

All things considered, AI, blockchain, IoT, big data, and telemedicine have the potential to improve the quality of the healthcare supply chain and can lead to sustainability.

6.8 Future Outlook

In the future, a number of emerging technologies can transform the pharmaceutical supply chain for enhancing the contribution in healthcare operations to quality enhancement in sustainable healthcare systems:

- Digital Twins for Predictive Care:

Digital twin technologies—copies of patients or organs—can facilitate real-time monitoring, accurate modeling of disease development, and response to treatment. By simulating hospital operations and selecting the most accurate treatments, these tools help doctors reduce waste and improve quality and sustainability. (Sun et al., 2023)

- Metaverse and Immersive Environments for Care, Education, and Patient Engagement:

The potential of the healthcare metaverse for immersive training and education, virtual clinics, and therapeutic settings is being investigated. These immersive systems have the potential to increase patient engagement, reduce expenses, and enhance accessibility, particularly in remote areas (Wang et al., 2024).

- Integration of Predictive Analytics & Telemedicine Platforms for Chronic Disease Management:

PrediHealth and other recent initiatives demonstrate how telemonitoring, environmental sensors, and predictive models can be used to optimize resource use, prevent hospitalizations, and forecast exacerbations of chronic illnesses, such as heart failure.

References

Abdulmalek, S., Nasir, A., Jabbar, W. A., Almuhaya, M. A. M., Bairagi, A. K., Khan, M. A. M., & Kee, S. H. (2022). IoT-Based Healthcare-Monitoring System towards Improving Quality of Life: A Review. In *Healthcare (Switzerland)* (Vol. 10, Issue 10). MDPI. https://doi.org/10.3390/healthcare10101993

Abugabah, A., Nizamuddin, N., & Abuqabbeh, A. (2020). A review of challenges and barriers implementing RFID technology in the Healthcare sector. *Procedia Computer Science, 170*, 1003–1010. https://doi.org/10.1016/j.procs.2020.03.094

Aceto, G., Persico, V., & Pescapé, A. (2020). Industry 4.0 and Health: Internet of Things, Big Data, and Cloud Computing for Healthcare 4.0. In *Journal of Industrial Information Integration* (Vol. 18). Elsevier B.V. https://doi.org/10.1016/j.jii.2020.100129

Al-Dmour, R., Al-Dmour, H., Basheer Amin, E., & Al-Dmour, A. (2025). Impact of AI and big data analytics on healthcare outcomes: An empirical study in Jordanian healthcare institutions. *Digital Health, 11*. https://doi.org/10.1177/20552076241311051

Arden, N. S., Fisher, A. C., Tyner, K., Yu, L. X., Lee, S. L., & Kopcha, M. (2021). Industry 4.0 for pharmaceutical manufacturing: Preparing for the smart factories of the future. *International Journal of Pharmaceutics, 602*, 120554. https://doi.org/10.1016/j.ijpharm.2021.120554

Bhuiyan, A. B., Ali, Md. J., Zulkifli, N., & Kumarasamy, M. M. (2020). Industry 4.0: Challenges, opportunities, and strategic solutions for Bangladesh. *International Journal of Business and Management Future, 4*(2), 41–56. https://doi.org/10.46281/ijbmf.v4i2.832

Borges do Nascimento, I. J., Abdulazeem, H., Vasanthan, L. T., Martinez, E. Z., Zucoloto, M. L., Østengaard, L., Azzopardi-Muscat, N., Zapata, T., & Novillo-Ortiz, D. (2023). Barriers and facilitators to utilizing digital health technologies by healthcare professionals. *Npj Digital Medicine, 6*(1), 161. https://doi.org/10.1038/s41746-023-00899-4

Calabrese, B., & Cannataro, M. (2015). Cloud computing in healthcare and biomedicine. *Scalable Computing: Practice and Experience, 16*(1). https://doi.org/10.12694/scpe.v16i1.1057

Chandra-Mouli, V., Ferguson, B. J., Plesons, M., Paul, M., Chalasani, S., Amin, A., Pallitto, C., Sommers, M., Avila, R., Eceéce Biaukula, K. V., Husain, S., Janušonytė, E., Mukherji, A., Nergiz, A. I., Phaladi, G., Porter, C., Sauvarin, J., Camacho-Huber, A. V., Mehra, S., & Engel, D. M. C. (2019). The political, research, programmatic, and social responses to adolescent sexual and reproductive health and rights in the 25 years since the international conference on population and development. *Journal of Adolescent Health, 65*(6), S16–S40. https://doi.org/10.1016/j.jadohealth.2019.09.011

Clifford, A., Lang, L., Chen, R., Anstey, K. J., & Seaton, A. (2016). Exposure to air pollution and cognitive functioning across the life course – A systematic literature review. *Environmental Research, 147*, 383–398. https://doi.org/10.1016/j.envres.2016.01.018

Degryse, C. (2016). Digitalisation of the economy and its impact on labour markets. *SSRN Electronic Journal*. https://doi.org/10.2139/ssrn.2730550

Egbewande, O. M., Oladipo, H. J., Olowolagba, S. A., & Iyiola, K. H. (2023). Application of telemedicine in the provision of healthcare in Nigeria: An insight from COVID-19. *Journal of Health Reports and Technology, 9*(1). https://doi.org/10.5812/jhrt-130916

Fung, A. W. S. (2025). Establishing sustainable quality improvement in the clinical laboratory: Redesign of the total testing process and digital transformation of routine quality assurance activities. *Clinical Biochemistry, 137*, Article 110915. https://doi.org/10.1016/j.clinbiochem.2025.110915

Ghadge, A., Bourlakis, M., Kamble, S., & Seuring, S. (2023). Blockchain implementation in pharmaceutical supply chains: A review and conceptual framework. *International Journal of Production Research, 61*(19), 6633–6651. https://doi.org/10.1080/00207543.2022.2125595

Govindarajan, U. H., Narang, G., Singh, D. K., & Yadav, V. S. (2025). Blockchain technologies adoption in healthcare: Overcoming barriers amid the hype cycle to enhance patient care. *Technological Forecasting and Social Change, 213*. https://doi.org/10.1016/j.techfore.2025.124031

Hameed, F., & Hameed, K. (2023a). *A Sustainable Digital Transformation in Healthcare and Well-Being: An Overview, Integration, Design and Security Challenges, Blockchain Technology, Applications, and Future Research Directions*. https://doi.org/10.20944/preprints202308.0867.v2

Hameed, F., & Hameed, K. (2023b). *The Role of Digital Transformation in Healthcare: A Sustainability Perspective, Design and Integration Challenges, Security and Privacy Challenges, Blockchain Technology, Applications, Future Research Directions*. https://doi.org/10.20944/preprints202308.0867.v1

Hameed, K., Naha, R., & Hameed, F. (2024). Digital transformation for sustainable health and well-being: a review and future research directions. In *Discover Sustainability* (Vol. 5, Issue 1). Springer Nature. https://doi.org/10.1007/s43621-024-00273-8

Khinvasara, T., & Hearing, S. (2024). Issue 3 www.jetir.org (ISSN-2349–5162). *JETIR2403131 Journal of Emerging Technologies and Innovative Research, 11*. https://doi.org/10.5281/zenodo.10828703

Koebe, P. (2025). How digital technologies and AI contribute to achieving the health-related SDGs. *International Journal of Information Management Data Insights, 5*(1), Article 100298. https://doi.org/10.1016/j.jjimei.2024.100298

Kumah, E. (2025). Artificial intelligence in healthcare and its implications for patient centered care. *Discover Public Health, 22*(1), 524. https://doi.org/10.1186/s12982-025-00924-9

Laurenza, E., Quintano, M., Schiavone, F., & Vrontis, D. (2018). The effect of digital technologies adoption in healthcare industry: A case based analysis. *Business Process Management Journal, 24*(5), 1124–1144. https://doi.org/10.1108/BPMJ-04-2017-0084

Li, Z., Xiang, L., Ning, J., Li, W., Huang, Y., & Xiao, X. (2025). Pathways to sustainable health care development: Study on the carbon reduction potential of telemedicine in China. *Journal of Medical Internet Research, 27*, Article e63927. https://doi.org/10.2196/63927

Li, C., Wang, J., Wang, S., & Zhang, Y. (2024). A review of IoT applications in healthcare. *Neurocomputing, 565*. https://doi.org/10.1016/j.neucom.2023.127017

McGhin, T., Choo, K. K. R., Liu, C. Z., & He, D. (2019). Blockchain in healthcare applications: Research challenges and opportunities. In *Journal of Network and Computer Applications* (Vol. 135, pp. 62–75). Academic Press. https://doi.org/10.1016/j.jnca.2019.02.027

Olawade, D. B., David-Olawade, A. C., Wada, O. Z., Asaolu, A. J., Adereni, T., & Ling, J. (2024). Artificial intelligence in healthcare delivery: Prospects and pitfalls. *Journal of Medicine, Surgery, and Public Health, 3*, Article 100108. https://doi.org/10.1016/j.glmedi.2024.100108

Parihar, A., Prajapati, J. B., Prajapati, B. G., Trambadiya, B., Thakkar, A., & Engineer, P. (2024). Role of IOT in healthcare: Applications, security & privacy concerns. In *Intelligent Pharmacy* (Vol. 2, Issue 5, pp. 707–714). KeAi Publishing Communications Ltd. https://doi.org/10.1016/j.ipha.2024.01.003

Rodler, S., Ramacciotti, L. S., Maas, M., Mokhtar, D., Hershenhouse, J., De Castro Abreu, A. L., Fuchs, G., Stief, C. G., Gill, I. S., & Cacciamani, G. E. (2023). The impact of telemedicine in reducing the carbon footprint in health care: A systematic review and cumulative analysis of 68 million clinical consultations. *European Urology Focus, 9*(6), 873–887. https://doi.org/10.1016/j.euf.2023.11.013

Sajwani, R. A. (2024). *Artificial Intelligence for Sustainability Development in Healthcare* (pp. 264–272). https://doi.org/10.1007/978-3-031-56121-4_26

Sharma, R. S., Rohatgi, A., Jain, S., & Singh, D. (2023). The Ayushman Bharat Digital Mission (ABDM): Making of India's Digital Health Story. *CSI Transactions on ICT, 11*(1), 3–9. https://doi.org/10.1007/s40012-023-00375-0

Shaver, J. (2022). The state of telehealth before and after the COVID-19 pandemic. *Primary Care: Clinics in Office Practice, 49*(4), 517–530. https://doi.org/10.1016/j.pop.2022.04.002

Sun, T., He, X., & Li, Z. (2023). Digital twin in healthcare: Recent updates and challenges. *Digital Health, 9*. https://doi.org/10.1177/20552076221149651

Ullah, W., & Ali, Q. (2025). Role of artificial intelligence in healthcare settings: a systematic review. In *Journal of Medical Artificial Intelligence* (Vol. 8). AME Publishing Company. https://doi.org/10.21037/jmai-24-294

Wang, Y., Zhu, M., Chen, X., Liu, R., Ge, J., Song, Y., & Yu, G. (2024). The application of metaverse in healthcare. *Frontiers in Public Health, 12*. https://doi.org/10.3389/fpubh.2024.1420367

Xie, L., Zhang, S., Xin, M., Zhu, M., Lu, W., & Mo, P.K.-H. (2022). Electronic health literacy and health-related outcomes among older adults: A systematic review. *Preventive Medicine, 157*, Article 106997. https://doi.org/10.1016/j.ypmed.2022.106997

Zamstein, N., Nanyonga, S., Morel, E., Wayne, R., Nottebaum, S., & Kozlakidis, Z. (2024). *Future Developments of Digital Health and Considerations on Sustainability* (pp. 231–238). https://doi.org/10.1007/978-3-031-62332-5_23

Part II
Productivity Management

Chapter 7
Pearl Millet Yield Prediction: A Comparative Analysis for Forecasting Models

Nikita Dhankar, Srikanta Routroy, and Satyendra Kr. Sharma

Abstract The crop yield estimation is an important aspect in agri-supply chain and forms the basis of decision-making for its different functional areas. The crop yield has a direct impact on farmer income, logistics planning and its infrastructure development. In the current study, pearl millet yield in Indian context is predicted considering available secondary data (rainfall, year, temperature, soil moisture, and pressure) for six districts (Nagaur, Jodhpur, Alwar, Barmer, Churu, and Jaipur) of Rajasthan from 1966 to 2020. The pearl millet yield is predicted using various predictive analytics tools such as multivariate adaptive regression splines (MARS), random forest (RF), multiple regression, TreeNet, and classification and regression tree (CART) in Minitab version 21. The root mean square error (RMSE), correlation factor (*R*), and adjusted *R*-squared were the three accuracy measures utilized to validate the models. All models were statistically tested using out-of-bag or with fivefold cross-validation. The results show that fairly accurate prediction was obtained The results of the study indicate that the TreeNet model outperformed other predictive models, achieving an *R*-squared value of 74.59%, demonstrating its superior capability in predicting pearl millet yield. Temperature has the highest relative importance based on the predicted model, followed by pressure, rainfall, and soil moisture. The present work will be a valuable addition to the pearl millet yield for casting literature in specific.

Keywords Pearl millet · Machine learning algorithms · Yield prediction · Multiple regression · CART · Random forest · MARS · TreeNet

N. Dhankar
Amity Global Business School, Noida, India

S. Routroy (✉)
Department of Mechanical Engineering & Joint Faculty, School of Interdisciplinary Research and Entrepreneurship (SIRE), BITS Pilani, Pilani Campus, Pilani, India
e-mail: srikanta@pilani.bits-pilani.ac.in

S. Kr. Sharma
Department of Management, BITS Pilani, Pilani Campus, Pilani, India
e-mail: satyendrasharma@pilani.bits-pilani.ac.in

I. Mukherjee et al. (eds.), *Decision Sciences for Quality and Productivity Improvement*,
https://doi.org/10.1007/978-981-95-7545-9_7

7.1 Introduction

Agriculture is one of the most significant economic sectors in India. It employs over 500 million people and contributes 18.3% of India's total GDP (MoSPI, 2023; Niti Aayog, 2023). It is therefore one of the most critical economic industries, and any disruptions can seriously impact the Indian as well as global economy. Farming data-driven industry has lately experienced a significant growth with regard to the adoption of predictive analytics in farming as regards many factors like the climate, health of crops, and profitability of farming activities (Medida et al., 2023). Predictive analytics is a very strong tool. It helps by using past information with complex methods and artificial intelligence in order to arrive at a better decision for resource use in farming.

Many sectors have had the practice researched—from healthcare to water treatment, even banking industries, and its trend is upwards in application. Its adoption has also been on the rise in the agricultural industry because the current research works indicate how it can be used to enhance productivity and make the execution of sustainable practices more effortless (Ak Muhammet Fatih et al., 2020; Bencheikh et al., 2020; Mundada, 2023; Nishant et al., 2020).

Since the COVID-19 pandemic, supply chains have promised to redesign and transform their operations with the intention of greater resilience in handling disruption and shock events (Govindan et al., 2020). The agricultural sector was significantly impacted and thus sparked much interest in the improved resilience of the agricultural supply chain (Okolie & Ogundeji, 2022). There is an important need, therefore to identify and embrace new methodologies in the design and construction of more resilient agricultural supply chains for potential future crises. Machine learning techniques mainly deal with analyzing vast volumes of data. Another sub field of machine learning was predictive analytics; in which it can do more than just fit data-analyzing the same patterns into the future. That makes it a very useful tool for analysis, and thus highly prominent (Mccarthy & Mccarthy, 2022).

In places with arid and semi-arid climates, pearl millet is highlighted as a key farming crop, especially within India and numerous areas across Africa (Nguyen & Blum, 2004). The yield of crops is a vital component of the agricultural supply chain. The assessment of crop yield serves as the basis for various forms of decision-making across multiple functional areas (Basavaraj et al., 2010). Precise production forecasts exert a substantial influence on the effective organization of administrative responsibilities, enhancement of infrastructure, and the financial stability of farmers. In the context of Indian agriculture, the prediction of pearl millet yield holds considerable importance, given that pearl millet constitutes a staple crop in numerous regions (Dhankar & Routroy, 2024; Dhankar et al., 2023). This endeavor would result in a highly accurate estimation of pearl millet yields, which could guarantee food availability, improve agricultural practices, and facilitate informed decision-making (Sitohang & Karnadi, 2021). In contrast to conventional models, it has been demonstrated that Minitab performs comparably regarding the accuracy of yield predictions; however, its application is relatively more user-friendly.

This paper mainly focuses on the application of machine learning in agriculture. The process deals with the estimation of yields for pearl millet through Minitab 21.0 version. It has been proved that machine learning is able to provide support toward better decision-making. The motivation to conduct research in machine learning comes from its ability to address very complex, nonlinear relationships found in agricultural data that have sources with many sources of environmental and agricultural impacts. These machine learning models could include a variety of sources such as weather, soil attributes, and crop health in data inputs. Such complex interdependencies provide the model to come up with better, flexible yield forecasts than traditional time series techniques might get muddled with that. Advanced tools in these above categories promise accuracy and flexibility besides being scalable. In so many ways, they're quite pretty good for predicting outcomes from agricultural activities. This research work aims at finding the best model to predict pearl millet yields through using different models: Multivariate Adaptive Regression Splines, Random Forest, Multiple Regression, TreeNet, and Classification and Regression Tree. Such models take into consideration detailed agricultural data and fluctuations in the environment. This means that with the best forecasting model for predicting pearl millet yield, farmers and agricultural workers can get useful information on how to improve crop management, utilize resources better, and enhance their ability to deal with environmental changes. This also forms part of a wider vision of improving predictive outcomes for agriculture. The comparison itself underlines those areas that need improvement: it's precision farming, sustainability in agriculture, and food system resilience. Through the unification of empirical analysis and advanced computational techniques within Minitab version 21.0, this study sets forth to empower agricultural stakeholders with the knowledge and tools necessary for navigating the complexities of pearl millet yield prediction.

7.2 Literature Review

There is ample literature that studies and predicts of yield of crops using data-driven techniques. Application of statistical methods and analytics tools has become a growing area of interest within the last 5 years. In a post-COVID world, the importance of supply chain analytics and managing supply chain disruptions has become more important than ever (Raj et al., 2022; Valiya & Mishra, 2023). A variety of new challenges have emerged, and it is important more than ever that supply chains be designed to handle future problems (Govindan, 2020). Traditional methods of managing supply chains are no longer as effective when dealing with large scale industries, as they are limited in scope. We thus see that there is great scope for the use and implementation of analytics tools in supply chain design and management. A growing sub area of major importance is the sector of predictive analytics. Traditionally used in the field of business analytics (Mccarthy & Mccarthy, 2022) or medicine (Ak Fatih et al., 2020), these techniques have shown great success. They are highly accurate, easy to understand and able to handle complex data and give us working models to better understand how even slight variations in input data can give us dramatically different results. One of the most popular tools to implement methods of predictive analytics is the Minitab software. Minitab has been used in a variety of scientific and industrial projects (Okolie & Ogundeji, 2022). Minitab is thus the ideal software for our usage, as it is easy to implement and its models can be easily understood, allowing us to analyze the full nature of our final outcome. Techniques of predictive analytics have been used in the past in a variety of sectors of agriculture and crop management such as crop productivity (Kofi et al., 2023), organic crop yield, weather data (Hachimi et al., 2023), livestock management (Mouzakitis et al., 2021) and price forecasting (Dang et al., 2021). Commonly, predictive analytics were not only found to be far more efficient than other alternatives, they are also able to deliver tangible results that prove useful for not only researchers, but also farmers and policymakers. A topic of major interest has been yield prediction using predictive analytics. Yield has consistently been shown to be the most important factor for all farmers (Kaur & Kumar, 2022). Rice has a large amount of publicly available data, so there are many studies analyzing it and determining possible supply chain modifications and production pipelines (Alfred et al., 2021). However, most of these papers are reliant on building external tools, making them unfeasible for ordinary farmers. An important gap in the vast majority of literature is that most yield prediction models neglect the input of all type of farmer-controlled and non-farmer-controlled factors (Dhankar et al., 2023). There is thus a major research gap in understanding the full impact of all factors on agriculture. Most studies that seek to understand this look at the issue through very narrow lenses. As such they are unable to fully understand its impact. There is thus the need for a study that goes into greater depth. Most current literature is focused on building new models, and is often too broad in scope for individual farmers to draw conclusions. Thus, it is important for researchers to pursue models that are able to provide more useful results for farmers and policymakers. Numerous investigations carried out in this domain are further summarized in Table 7.1.

The applicability of several Minitab prediction models in agriculture has been determined after a thorough analysis of the literature. The pearl millet supply chain was found to have limited access to Minitab for the comparative study of different predictive models. However, there are only a few number of predictors taken into account in the majority of the studies. Our study uses Minitab version 21 to predict pearl millet yield in the Indian context, taking into account secondary data (rainfall, year, temperature, soil moisture, and pressure) that is available for six districts (Nagaur, Jodhpur, Alwar, Barmer, Churu, and Jaipur) of Rajasthan from 1966 to 2020. These tools include multivariate adaptive regression splines (MARS), random forest (RF), multiple regression, TreeNet, and classification and regression tree (CART). This helps to fill in these research gaps. Despite the urgent necessity for such a thorough investigation to fully understand the predictors' influence, it is rarely documented in the literature. The present investigation aims to close these research gaps and contribute significantly to the body of knowledge on the supply chain of pearl millet.

Table 7.1 Related research of implementation of various Minitab predictive models in agriculture

Authors	Crop	Research methodology	Results	Conclusions
Iwańska et al. (2018)	Wheat yield	CART model is applied to Poland wheat datasets to determine their yield variations in winter	Factors such as lack of crop rotation, poor quality of soil, application of wrong herbicide etc. found to damage wheat yield	By following sustainable practices and practicing proper soil conservation, wheat yield can be greatly improved
Tittonell et al. (2008)	Maize	The productivity of the maize crop was determined by using CART techniques to tie crop yields to parameters related to soil and crop management	Soil fertility was found to have major impact on maize crop yield. High- and medium-income farmers were found to have higher yields on average	Farmers with lower income and poor soil fertility can practice crop rotation to mitigate poor yields
Studnicki (2021)	Triticale (Wheat Hybrid)	CART analysis to determine variation of triticale yield throughout the year	Triticale yield found to vary throughout the season depending on various factors, such as fungicide in spring and water in winter	By adjusting outputs on a seasonal basis, farmers can expect more improved and consistent yield
Monjezi (2021)	Sugar beet	CART analysis was conducted to determine efficiency of sugar beet crop production	CART algorithms generated up to 95% accuracy when predicting yield	CART method is well-suited for large datasets, can get more resource intensive with time
Patil et al. (2018)	Agriculture crop	CART and IDC methodologies were used and contrasted to analysis satellite data to determine variations in crop yield with water productivity	CART on average was found to have 15–20% better performance than IDC, correctly identifying up to 80% of crop data	CART can be used to monitor efficiency of irrigation systems for various crops
Shukla et al. (2018)	Agriculture crop	Various machine learning algorithms were comparatively analyzed for ten different regions of India	TreeNet model was found to have good performance for single crop analysis	TreeNet model is desirable when analyzing large datasets for single output

(continued)

Table 7.1 (continued)

Authors	Crop	Research methodology	Results	Conclusions
Shepherd and Walsh (2007)	Agriculture crop	Effect of IR spectroscopy on crop yield was measured to establish an improvement in performance	IR spectroscopy monitoring was found to be useful to identify performance of individual inputs	TreeNet algorithm performs well when utilizing unconventional inputs
Moradi et al. (2022)	Pomegranate	TreeNet algorithm was used to identify improvements in pomegranate fruit on treatment with hot water or salicylic acid	Application of salicylic acid or hot water postharvest could help preserve pomegranate fruit quality	TreeNet is good when analyzing data over longer time period
Narasipura (2017)	Mango	TreeNet and other convolutional learning networks were used to monitor growth of mango tree in a variety of conditions	TreeNet had higher accuracy than convolutional networks and successfully eliminated noise from datasets	TreeNet is useful to eliminate noise from large datasets
Sankey et al. (2008)	Soil clay, Organic C and Inorganic C	Nature of various types of soil was analyzed with TreeNet to determine their impact on efficiency	Clayey and organic soil had high impact on crop yield and efficiency	TreeNet can be used as preliminary analysis to identify most important variables from data
Everingham et al. (2016)	Sugarcane	Application of Random Forest to determine yield of sugarcane	The random forest regression model's R-squared improved over time, rising from 66.76 to 79.21	Random Forest method shows accuracy even with simplified assumptions
Krause et al. (2020)	Corn and Soybean	Random Forest approach was developed to measure input factors such as planting rate, hybrid/variety, topography, soil characteristics, weather variables, and understand their effects on yield	The impact of the random forest regression variable for planting rate was quite high. shown to have the least influence on yield output	Random Forest model is good for simple datasets, but can hide underlying complexities

(continued)

Table 7.1 (continued)

Authors	Crop	Research methodology	Results	Conclusions
Ok et al. (2007)	Agricultural crops	Using pixel-based and parcel-based methods, the paper offers a thorough review of the Random Forest algorithm	Random Forest method found to have 85.89% accuracy for the given datasets	Random Forest method is useful for datasets of all types and sizes
Jeong et al. (2016)	Wheat, Potato and Maize	Random Forest method applied to a variety of US and global based datasets to determine efficiency of crops such as wheat, potato and maize	Random Forest gave up to 14% to 49% accuracy for a very diverse dataset	Random Forest highly versatile and applicable to different models, can struggle with extreme and noise values
Nayana et al. (2022)	Wheat	MARS model applied on national and state level to determine overall wheat yield	MARS able to provide highly accurate model that can be adjusted for individual states	MARS is useful to understand individual variations in datasets
Shan et al. (2020)	Summer maize	MARS model used to study evapotranspiration in maize crop during Chinese summers and determine how yield may fluctuate	Evapotranspiration can cause great changes in yield if unaccounted for during irrigation	MARS model strong at identifying hidden relationships
Dhaliwal (2024)	Sweet corn	A range of machine learning techniques are examined and tested to forecast the yield of sweet corn	MARS model found to outperform most models after multiple iterations	MARS model accurate but resource and time intensive
Wu et al. (2022)	Sunflower	Various machine learning methods such as Random Forest, SVM and MARS applied to determine impact of sunflower root length and density on yield in saline soil	MARS highly accurate, but found to no longer be relevant after finetuning data parameters	MARS model carries risk of overfitting

7.3 Methodology

7.3.1 Study Area and Data Collection

The present research involves six districts situated in the state of Rajasthan, including Alwar, Barmer, Churu, Jaipur, Jodhpur, and Nagaur. The temporal scope for data collection across these districts spanned from June to October, coinciding with the cultivation period of Kharif crops, such as pearl millet, within the region. Information on yield was extracted from the Bajra database curated by the National Informatics Centre, Ministry of Communication and IT, Government of India. Additional variables were acquired from the Copernicus Climate Data Store. The data gathered spans the years 1998–2020 across the aforementioned six districts, constituting the foundational raw panel data utilized in the model training process. Nonetheless, it is pertinent to acknowledge that numerous factors could be classified as environmental. However, as a result of the dependence on secondary sources for the acquisition of data, merely a few selected variables are represented in this investigation. The variables considered for analysis between the years 1966 and 2020 include rainfall, year of production, temperature, soil moisture, and atmospheric pressure, contingent upon the availability of data sources. Among the six selected districts, Alwar and Jaipur are characterized by relatively high precipitation levels, whereas the districts of Jodhpur, Barmer, Churu, and Nagaur experience low rainfall, akin to the broader state, attributed to their positioning within the rain shadow region of the Aravalli hill range. As established by Li et al. (2019), precipitation is essential for determining millet crop yields, like maize; also, their analysis revealed that drought conditions influence yield more than rainfall. The dataset pertaining to the dependent variable has incorporated temperature metrics derived from satellite observations, which include mean, standard deviation, maximum, and minimum annual temperatures. Lobell et al. (2014) conduct an empirical study to assess how temperature responded in twelve crops in the state of California, describing how such crops responded differently to shifts in temperature. Consequently, a variety of temperature statistics has been employed to comprehensively assess its influence on the yield of pearl millet. To evaluate the implications of extended direct sunlight, which can promote plant growth yet may be detrimental to certain crops, both "cloud fraction" and "surface solar radiation received at the surface" have been taken into account. Cloud fraction refers to the ratio of a specific grid box that is obscured by clouds (whether liquid or ice), and it ranges from zero to one. The amount of solar radiation falling on the Earth's surface directly and diffused is determined as the difference between this amount and that reflected by the Earth's surface. The remainder reaches the Earth's surface, where it is subject to reflection. Net solar radiation at the surface is described as the variation between incoming solar radiation and the reflected radiation. Units are in joules per square meter (W/m^2). The atmospheric pressure present at the Earth's surface may significantly influence the growth dynamics of plant species. Fluctuations in atmospheric pressure are also recognized as a critical determinant, as evidenced by the work of Michaels (1982), which demonstrated that approximately 40% of the variation in crop yield could be attributed to internal pressure deviations across a substantial expanse of the Great Plains in the United States, thereby enhancing the predictive accuracy of wheat yields. Atmospheric pressure refers to the force per unit area imposed on land, ocean, and the other water bodies. It quantifies the cumulative weight of the air column situated vertically above a specific point on the Earth's surface. The annual mean and standard deviation of this dataset were derived from the Copernicus satellite observations. Research by Grange and associates in 1987 reveals that relative humidity between 55 and 90% does not greatly affect plant growth; however, when humidity levels go beyond this, plants may become more vulnerable to diseases, leading to potential crop yield reductions. Consequently, it was imperative to incorporate this variable into the analysis to investigate its impact on the annual millet yield. Humanize Relative humidity is the ratio of the pressure of water vapor in air to the saturation vapor pressure expressed as a percentage at which point the air saturated that is, reaches its saturation point from where water vapor starts to condense into liquid or ice. For temperatures exceeding 0 °C (273.15 K), saturation is calculated over liquid water. For temperatures less than −23 °C, the saturation is calculated on ice. For temperatures between −23 °C and 0 °C, the parameter is calculated by quadratic interpolation between saturation values on ice and on water. Relative humidity and absolute humidity metrics were obtained from the Copernicus Climate Data Store (CDS) dataset pertaining to the six districts under investigation; however, only relative humidity was utilized to circumvent the complications associated with multicollinearity. As noted by Chan et al. (2022), machine learning solutions tend to outperform econometric solutions in reducing the impacts of multicollinearity, yet they suggest omitting any variables that could inadvertently embody its effect on the dataset. Wind speed constitutes a significant variable influencing crop growth, as evidenced by the research conducted by Cleugh et al. (1998). The force exerted by the wind has the capacity to dislodge leaves or completely detach them from the plant. Lush plant canopies may experience abrasion through either intermittent or continuous contact. Soil particles that are elevated into suspension by wind currents possess the potential to erode and inflict damage upon plant tissues. The mechanical force of the wind can physically topple plants, thereby complicating the harvesting process for crops. The direction of the wind can play a pivotal role through the implementation of windbreaks. The judicious application of local windbreaks to shield crops from wind exposure can yield enhanced agricultural outputs, as demonstrated by Cleugh et al. (1998). Arguably, the most important factor in agriculture is the soil itself. To account for the influence of soil, soil moisture data was procured from the CDS database. A study was made by Rossato et al. (2017) to find out the effect of the soil moisture content in the upper layer in the semi-arid region of north-eastern Brazil, which our study area also belongs to. The findings indicating that plants exhibited improved responses to moisture content in the surface layer of the soil suggest that examining the influence of soil moisture on pearl millet yields in Rajasthan would be a valuable area of inquiry.

7.3.2 Data Analysis

In predictive models, five different methodological frameworks were used in yield prediction for pearl millet. For such work, this article considers as a basis the output by these modelling techniques: classification and regression trees; (Marc et al., 2000), multiple regression; (Analysis, 1990), random forest; (Zhang et al., 2022), multivariate adaptive regression splines; (Leathwick et al., 2006), and tree net; (Friedman, 2002). The methodologies employed were grounded in the theoretical models established by Meißner et al. (2014), Thuiller et al. (2009) along with Hardy et al. (2011). To investigate the correlation between a singular response variable, hereafter referred to as the dependent variable, and two or more manipulated variables categorized as independent variables, the application of a multiple linear regression statistical technique is deemed appropriate. The selected methodology for this scholarly inquiry is characterized by the inclusion of various variables that can be systematically controlled within a scientific paradigm. CART are a useful decision-tree algorithm for predictive analysis and data mining. This makes it possible to find hidden structure in complicated datasets. The application of the CART method, which is part of the statistical methodology, is intended to assist in determining the best predictors and their interactions for the explanation of a specific event. Due to their non-parametric nature, CARTs are well-suited to a broad range of datasets. They are applicable on both categorical and continuous variables. It needs quite low pre-processing, and is therefore applicable for exploratory data analysis. A major risk in CART models is overfitting. Since they rely on binary splits, they are poor at handling nonlinearly separable data. Depending on splitting conditions, sub-optimal trees may be built. If the data chosen is noisy, CART can give poor results, and may entirely ignore certain edge conditions. Classes formed after analysis may also be skewed and unbalanced, especially if poor splitting criteria are chosen. CART is one of the most commonly used tools in predictive analytics. It is efficient and simple to understand, being useful to identify preliminary results. TreeNet models use stochastic gradient boosting in order to allow for slight adjustments to ensemble error, thus vastly improving accuracy. Unlike traditional ensembles like bagging and boosting, TreeNet is non-sensitive to data errors and extraneous outliers. It thus provides accurate insight into data interdependence. As data does not need to be pre-processed, we save time. TreeNet also avoids the overfitting problem, as it builds hundreds of trees using the raw data, and only outputs the most relevant information. TreeNet is very computationally expensive, as it often builds several hundred trees. If data is unevenly distributed, TreeNet may not provide many useful insights in comparison to other predictors. As such, it is most useful for a large amount of well-distributed data points. TreeNet can be seen as a complementary model to CART. It is highly accurate and is able to easily handle boundary conditions. The main disadvantage is that it needs to build several hundred trees, thus making it relatively time-consuming. TreeNet is useful in cases where CART has been determined to be inefficient, or we need further analysis to complement results from CART. Random Forests are quite useful when there are a large number of variables and we have comparatively limited observations. The model avoids overfitting as it does not need to perform a preliminary train-test split. Below we have taken a simple model to illustrate the working of random forest model, and how it uses input training data and applies Random Forests method to it in order to get desired result. Random Forest thus divides the entire data into random subsets and applies the CART model to each of these subsets. It then takes the average of all these predictions to give us an aggregate prediction tree. This method of applying aggregate predictors is known as ensemble machine learning, as different models are working together to obtain the best result. The type of ensemble learning used by Random Forest is also known as bagging. Here, multiple models are trained on different subsets of training data. Random Forests are particularly useful when we have an incredibly limited number of data points. Unlike other models, Random Forests does not over fit as different trees are built with different analyses. Random Forests work best with non-clustered data, where there is a large diversity of data points. It is a very simple model to apply and understand, making it very popular for multiple use cases. It is also quite flexible, being useful in various type of classification and regression-based problems. These models tend to perform poorly with large datasets, and can become very slow the more data points we need to analyze. If the model is unable to eliminate noise, it may cause overfitting, leading to inaccurate results. Random Forest is thus highly desirable for our use case. MARS is able to adjust distribution patterns based on data clusters. Unlike traditional regression models which fit an external function and not the data, MARS adjusts itself based on the dataset, thus giving highly accurate plots. Its accuracy is measured by both Mean Squared Error (MSE) and Generalized Cross-Validation (GCV). In the MARS algorithm, we determine the best fit set of piecewise linear predictors that characterize the data. We then take their aggregate, and use them to make general predictions based on our input data. MARS can therefore be seen as a generalization of piecewise linear functions. What makes MARS quite effective compared to other models is that instead of generating a single best fit equation, which may overgeneralize for a given dataset, MARS creates piecewise linear functions, which change for different cut points or knots. MARS is able to not only ensure proper fit; it can also avoid overfitting by using backstage to remove any functions that map to outlier data. Thus, MARS ensures that the regression plot represents only the most important clusters, and is not adversely affected by outliers unlike traditional methods. Further, by fitting multiple linear equations for different cut points, MARS is able to give a very accurate equation of best fit. Thus, MARS is excellent to find the best fit equation and curve for a given dataset. The main issue with MARS models is that they have to rely on finding linear relationships between variables. If data is nonlinearly distributed, with multiple clusters then MARS models yield poor results. Furthermore, while MARS is excellent at fitting for training data, it is very poor at finding generalized linear relationships for new, unseen data. MARS thus has application for specific use cases, mainly where we have identified strong trend of linear distribution for given data points within the broader dataset. While all these models are similar, they have slight variations in their internal working, thus making them appropriate for different cases. In order to identify the most precise prediction model for pearl millet yield, this study applied each of these models. The selection of optimal hyperparameters for each model was achieved through systematic grid search and iterative testing to enhance model accuracy and robustness (Gualtieri et al., 2020). It was noted that the number of basis functions also was not excessive in relation to the requirements for the model to be interpretable and not too flexible. The penalty for the knots was intended to prevent the overfitting of the model, by which only fundamental nonlinear relationships modeled are captured. For the Random Forest model, the most recommended hyperparameters are the number of trees and the maximum level of depth per tree. When a number of these were taken as the configurations, they were termed as the one that may lead to overfitting but at the same time they are still capable of pattern recognition in the data. With regard to the CART model, some parameters were adjusted for this, the maximum depth of the tree and the minimum amount of samples needed at a node for that node to split to decrease overfitting were among these parameters. Likewise but for the TreeNet model, the most relevant learning rate, boosting iterations and maximum tree depth hyperparameters were also adjusted. The learning rate variable was set at a low value, this was intended to help in slowly building the accuracy of the targeted variable. This, together with a sufficient number of boosting iterations and a specified maximum depth, was aimed at enhancing the stability and accuracy of predictive targets across various runs of FSS-ML. All the models were fitted with the use of fivefold cross-validation. These choices were made after testing various configurations and evaluating their impact on model performance, aiming to achieve an accurate and generalizable model.

7.4 Results and Discussion

The results are obtained by utilizing various tools. The predictive models such as CART, Multiple Regression, MARS, TreeNet, and Random Forest implemented as part of the Predictive Models of Minitab® 21.1 are employed for yield predictions. The best model across all model types with maximum *R*-squared (Table 7.2). The results of the study indicate that the TreeNet model outperformed other predictive models, achieving an *R*-squared value of 74.59%, demonstrating its superior capability in predicting pearl millet yield. This research provides valuable insights into yield prediction methodologies and contributes significantly to the literature on pearl millet yield forecasting. Output for the best model (TreeNet) are presented in Figs. 7.1 and 7.2. Figure 7.1 depicted the normalized importance of the predicted yield variables chosen in this study. Whereas, Fig. 7.2 shows the actual versus predicted yield parameters for the TreeNet model. As per TreeNet model the normalized importance among the chosen factors are temperature > pressure > rainfall > soil moisture (Fig. 7.1). The various hyperparameters used to obtain the best TreeNet models are presented in Table 7.3. And the MSE and MAPE values for the test set of datasets for TreeNet model, is presented in Tables 7.4.

Table 7.2 Performance measure of five predictive models of Minitab for yield prediction

Best model within type	R-squared (%)	Mean absolute deviation
TreeNet®*	74.59	0.2358
MARS®	73.40	0.2449
Random Forests®	71.78	0.2443
Multiple Regression	66.45	0.2664
CART®	53.46	0.2944

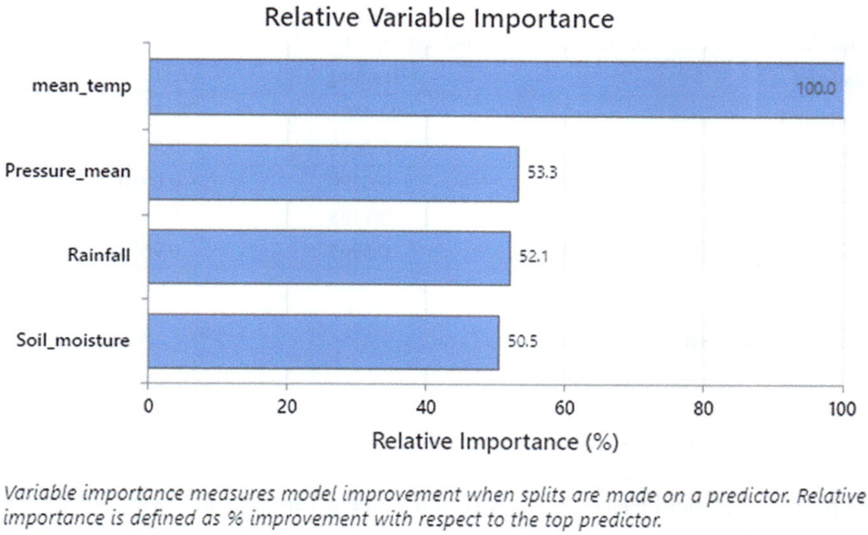

Fig. 7.1 Normalized importance graph for pearl millet yield

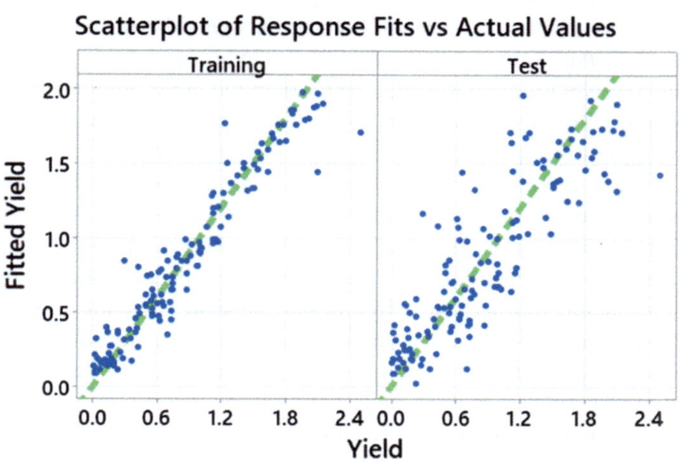

Fig. 7.2 Predicted yield versus actual yield

Table 7.3 Hyperparameters for best TreeNet® model

Number of trees grown	300
Optimal number of trees	49
Learning rate	0.1
Subsample fraction	0.7
Maximum terminal nodes per tree	6
Number of predictors selected for node splitting	Total number of predictors = 4

Table 7.4 Performance metrics for training and test sets of the TreeNet® model

Statistics	Training	Test
R-squared	92.45%	74.59%
Root mean squared error (RMSE)	0.1672	0.3067
Mean squared error (MSE)	0.0280	0.0940
Mean absolute deviation (MAD)	0.1185	0.2358
Mean absolute percent error (MAPE)	0.5967	0.9653

7.5 Conclusion

This study uses a novel forecasting approach by leveraging MR, CART, MARS, RF, and TreeNet models, each applied individually to enhance predictive accuracy. The method assisted in the development of the most significant model for predicting the pearl millet yield based on the best independent variables that were selected. It is possible that the proposed model would produce accurate predictions as a result of the systematic modelling of TreeNet through the utilization of optimal embedding parameters and the construction of a prediction model from the most effective independent variables. In terms of both mean squared error and mean absolute percentage error, the findings obtained from the hybrid forecasting approach indicate that the TreeNet model performed better than the other predictive models. The superiority of the TreeNet model may result in its implementation in a wide variety of different agricultural products, taking into consideration a variety of other sorts of elements, such as farmer-controlled and non-farmer controlled variables. Each model was tested using out-of-bag or fivefold cross-validation. The findings indicate an adequate prediction. Tree Net's R-squared achieve of 74.59% indicates its superiority in pearl millet production prediction. It is observed that temperature is the prominent factor, followed next by rainfall, pressure, and soil moisture, as the factors selected for this study are confined to non-farmer-controlled factors. Since the factors selected for this study are restricted to non-farmer controlled factors, the prediction of yield can be done more precisely by incorporating more variables like seed type, irrigation, pesticides, fertilizers, and crop rotation. This will lead to better results when the model used in this study is applied. Organized bodies can control their agricultural activities in order to obtain higher yield as a farmer cannot be able to control these factors rather understand their significance Social measures would ensure efficiency in forecasting model As a result of comparative evaluation of forecasting models of yield prediction of pearl millet using Minitab Version 21.0 predictive tools, mentioning also the benefit each of them has over the other and the drawbacks as well in conclusions of the discussion stage. In particular, it should be noted that such a capability of the technique allows researchers to enhance, by using Minitab Version 21.0 predictive models, precision agriculture, sustainable crop management, and food security across arid regions of the world.

7.6 Implications and Future Directions

The results derived from our comparative investigation of forecasting models for the prediction of pearl millet yields unveil multiple promising directions for forthcoming research, each possessing practical implications for agricultural decision-making, resource optimization, and policy development. Firstly, enhancing these models to incorporate region-specific variables—such as local soil characteristics, historical yield statistics, and distinct climatic trends—could yield predictions that are more aligned with the specific requirements of particular regions, thereby facilitating more focused agricultural practices and resource distribution. Furthermore, the amalgamation of diverse data sources, encompassing real-time meteorological data, satellite imagery, soil moisture metrics, and socioeconomic variables, would permit a more comprehensive approach to yield forecasting, addressing the entirety of factors that influence yield results. Future investigations may also examine sophisticated machine learning methodologies, including reinforcement learning and hybrid frameworks that integrate machine learning with conventional statistical techniques, to enhance the resilience and adaptability of yield forecasts. Such advancements could generate models that evolve and enhance their precision over time, yielding progressively trustworthy insights with each agricultural cycle. Furthermore, the development of user-centric, real-time advisory instruments predicated on these advanced models may empower agricultural producers by delivering actionable insights pertinent to planting, fertilization, and harvesting decisions via mobile platforms. Such instruments would facilitate informed decision-making for farmers, ultimately enhancing crop management and productivity. Ultimately, the adaptation of this predictive framework to encompass various crops and climatic conditions could disseminate its advantages across a multitude of agricultural environments, thereby amplifying its impact and contributing to overarching food security initiatives. Collectively, these prospective research trajectories not only augment the scientific comprehension of yield forecasting but also possess the potential to engender transformative instruments for farmers, researchers, and policymakers in the endeavor of fostering sustainable and productive agricultural practices.

Acknowledgements This work is funded by Ministry of Science and Technology, Department of Science and Technology, SEED Division, Government of India, New Delhi and is funded through the project Sanction No: SEED/ASACODER-018/2018(G) dated 25.06.2021 entitled, "Doubling Farm Women's income: Entrepreneurship development through postharvest processing and technology integration in arid zone."

References

Alfred, R., Obit, J. O. E. H., & Chin, C. P. (2021). Towards paddy rice smart farming: A review on big data, machine learning, and rice production tasks. *9*. https://doi.org/10.1109/ACCESS.2021.3069449

Ak, M. F. (2020). A comparative analysis of breast cancer detection and diagnosis using data visualization and machine learning applications. *Healthcare, 8*(2), 111. https://doi.org/10.3390/healthcare8020111

Analysis, R. (1990). Multiple Regression 2.1. 2–3.

Basavaraj, G., Rao, P. P., Bhagavatula, S., & Ahmed, W. (2010, December). Availability and utilization of pearl millet in India. *SAT EJournal, 8*, 1–6.

Bencheikh, I., Mabrouki, J., Azoulay, K., Moufti, A., & El Hajjaji, S. (2020). Predictive analytics and optimization of wastewater treatment efficiency using statistic approach. In *Big data and networks technologies 3* (pp. 310–319). Springer International Publishing.

Chan, J. Y., Mun, S., Leow, H., Bea, K. T., Cheng, W. K., Phoong, S. W., Hong, Z., & Chen, Y. (2022). Mitigating the multicollinearity problem and its machine learning approach: A review.

Cleugh, H. A., Miller, J. M., & Böhm, M. (1998). Direct mechanical effects of wind on crops*1*, 85–112.

Climate Research & Services, Pune. Available at: https://www.imdpune.gov.in/. Accessed: 24 June 2024.

Copernicus Climate Data Store | Available at: https://cds.climate.copernicus.eu/#!/home. Accessed: 24 June 2024.

Dang, C., Liu, Y., Yue, H., Qian, J., & Zhu, R. (2021). Autumn crop yield prediction using data-driven approaches: - Support vector machines, random forest, and deep neural network methods autumn crop yield prediction using data-driven approaches : - Support vector machines, random forest, and deep neural network methods es : - machines a. *Canadian Journal of Remote Sensing, 47*(2), 162–181. https://doi.org/10.1080/07038992.2020.1833186

Dhaliwal, D. S. (2024). *And field-level data*. 51–64.

Dhankar, N., & Routroy, S. (2024). Analyzing predictors of pearl millet supply chain using an artificial neural network. *19*(4), 1291–1315. https://doi.org/10.1108/JM2-09-2023-0202.

Dhankar, N., Routroy, S., & Sharma, S. K. (2023). Impact of seed type and fertilizer on pearl millet yield: A descriptive study in selected districts of Rajasthan. In *Handbook of evidence based management practices in business* (pp. 360–367). Routledge.

Everingham, Y., Sexton, J., Skocaj, D., & Inman-bamber, G. (2016). Accurate prediction of sugarcane yield using a random forest algorithm. *Agronomy for Sustainable Development*. https://doi.org/10.1007/s13593-016-0364-z

Friedman, J. H. (2002). *Stochastic gradient boosting 38*, 367–378.

Grange, R. I., & Hand, D. W. (1987). A review of the effects of atmospheric humidity on the growth of horticultural crops. *Journal of Horticultural Science, 62*(2), 125–134.

Goel, N., Kaur, S., & Kumar, Y. (2022). Machine learning-based remote monitoring and predictive analytics system for crop and livestock. In S. Singh, R. Garg & A. Sharma (Eds.), *AI, edge and IoT-based smart agriculture* (pp. 395–407). Academic Press. https://doi.org/10.1016/B978-0-12-824491-9.00025-2

Govindan, K., Mina, H., & Alavi, B. (2020). A decision support system for demand management in healthcare supply chains considering the epidemic outbreaks: A case study of coronavirus disease 2019 (COVID-19). *Transportation Research Part E, 138*, 101967. https://doi.org/10.1016/j.tre.2020.101967

Gualtieri, M., Carlsson, K., Sridharan, S., & Perdoni, R. (2020). The Forrester Wave TM: Multimodal predictive analytics and machine learning, Q3.

Hachimi, C. E., Belaqziz, S., Khabba, S., Sebbar, B., Dhiba, D., & Chehbouni, A. (2023). Smart weather data management based on artificial intelligence and big data analytics for precision agriculture, 1–22.

Hardy, S. M., Lindgren, M., Konakanchi, H., & Huettmann, F. (2011). Predicting the distribution and ecological niche of unexploited snowcrab (Chionoecetes opilio) populations in Alaskan waters: A Firstopen-access ensemble model. *Integrative and Comparative Biology, 51*, 608–622. https://doi.org/10.1093/icb/icr102

Iwańska, M., Oleksy, A., Dacko, M., Skowera, B., & Oleksiak, T. (2018). Use of classification and regression trees (CART) for analyzing determinants of winter wheat yield variation among fields in Poland, *55*(2), 197–214. https://doi.org/10.2478/bile-2018-0013

Jeong, J. H., Resop, J. P., Mueller, N. D., & Fleisher, D. H. (2016). Random forests for global and regional crop yield prediction*s*. 1–15. https://doi.org/10.1371/journal.pone.0156571

Kofi, I., Zaman, A., Nyarko-boateng, O., & Felix, A. (2023, April). A predictive analytics model for crop suitability and productivity with tree-based ensemble learning. *Decision Analytics Journal, 8*, 100311. https://doi.org/10.1016/j.dajour.2023.100311

Krause, M. R., Swede, J., Robbins, R., Dumond, T., Ochs, D., Gore, M. A., & Arliss, S. (2020, August). Random forest regression for optimizing variable planting rates for corn and soybean using topographical and soil data. 5045–5066. https://doi.org/10.1002/agj2.20442

Leathwick, J. R., Elith, J., & Hastie, T. (2006). Comparative performance of generalized additive models and multivariate adaptive regression splines for statistical modelling of species distributions. *9*, 188–196. https://doi.org/10.1016/j.ecolmodel.2006.05.022

Li, Y., Guan, K., Schnitkey, G. D., DeLucia, E., & Peng, B. (2019). Excessive rainfall leads to maize yield loss of a comparable magnitude to extreme drought in the United States. *Global Change Biology, 25*(7), 2325–2337. https://doi.org/10.1111/gcb.14628

Lobell, D. B., Nicholas, K., & Field, C. B. (2014). *On California crop yieldsa. March 2007*. https://doi.org/10.1007/s10584-006-9141-3

Marc, P., Richard, E., & Barbara, H. (2000). Classification trees: An alternative non-parametric approach for predicting species distributions. 679–694.

Mccarthy, R. V., & Mccarthy, M. M. (2022). *Applying predictive analytics* (pp. 199–232). Springer International Publishing. https://doi.org/10.1007/978-3-030-14038-0

Medida, L. H., Khang, A., & Kumar, G. L. N. V. S. (2023). Predictive analytics for high-tech agriculture. In *Handbook of RESEARCH on AI-equipped IoT applications in high-tech agriculture* (pp. 336–346). IGI Global.

Meißner, K., Fiorentino, D., Schnurr, S., Martinez, P., Huettmann, F., Holst, S., Brix, S., & Svavarsson, J. (2014). Distribution of benthic marine invertebrates at northern latitudes—An evaluation applying multi-algorithm species distribution models. *Journal of Sea Research, 85*, 241–254. https://doi.org/10.1016/j.seares.2013.05.007

Ministry of Statistics and programme implementation, government of India/Ministry of Statistics and Program Implementation. (2023). Available at: https://www.mospi.gov.in/. Accessed: 27 May 2024.

Michaels, P. J. (1982). Atmospheric pressure patterns, climatic change and winter wheat yields in North America. *Geoforum, 13*(3), 263–273.

Monjezi, N. (2021). The application of the CART and CHIAD algorithms in sugar beet yield prediction. *The Basrah Journal of Agricultural Sciences*.

Moradi, S., Zamani, Z., Moghadam, M. F., & Koushesh, M. (2022, June). Scientia Horticulturae Combination effects of preharvest tree net-shading and postharvest fruit treatments with salicylic acid or hot water on attributes of pomegranate fruit. *Scientia Horticulturae, 304*, 111257. https://doi.org/10.1016/j.scienta.2022.111257

Mouzakitis, S., Tsapelas, G., Pelekis, S., Ntanopoulos, S., Askounis, D., Osinga, S., Athanasiadis, I. N., Mouzakitis, S., Tsapelas, G., Pelekis, S., Ntanopoulos, S., & Askounis, D. (2021). Investigation of common big data analytics and decision-making requirements across diverse precision agriculture and livestock farming use cases to cite this version: HAL Id: hal-03361883. 0–12.

Mundada, M. R. (2023). Optimized farming: Crop recommendation system using predictive analytics. *International Journal of Intelligent Engineering & Systems, 16*(3).

National Informatics Centre | Govt. of India. Available at: https://www.nic.in/. Accessed: 24 June 2024.

Narasipura, O. (2017). *Semantic segmentation and individual crown.*

Navigation WDRA. Available at: https://wdra.gov.in/web/wdra/bajra. Accessed: 24 June 2024.

Nayana, B. M., Kumar, K. R., & Chesneau, C. (2022). Wheat yield prediction in India using principal component analysis-multivariate adaptive regression splines (PCA-MARS), pp. 461–474.

Nguyen, H. T., & Blum, A. (2004). Physiology and biotechnology integration for plant breeding edited by.

Nishant, P. S., Venkat, P. S., Avinash, B. L., & Jabber, B. (2020). Crop yield prediction based on Indian agriculture using machine learning. 5–8.

Niti Aayog. (2023). Available at: https://www.niti.gov.in/taxonomy/term/219. Accessed: 29 October 2024.

Ok, A. O., Akar, O., & Gungor, O. (2007). Evaluation of random forest method for agricultural crop classification. *Mlc*, 421–432. https://doi.org/10.5721/EuJRS20124535

Okolie, C. C., & Ogundeji, A. A. (2022). *And food security: A scientometric analysis.* 1–13. https://doi.org/10.1057/s41599-022-01080-0

Patil, V. C., Al-gaadi, K. A., Madugundu, R., Tola, E., Zeyada, A. M., Marey, S., & Biradar, C. M. (2018). CART and IDC—Based classification of irrigated agricultural fields using multi-source satellite data. *Geocarto International, 6049*, 1–19. https://doi.org/10.1080/10106049.2016.1232312

Raj, A., Anjan, A., Beatriz, A., Sousa, L. De, & Srivastava, S. K. (2022, January). Supply chain management during and post-COVID-19 pandemic: Mitigation strategies and practical lessons learned. *Journal of Business Research, 142*, 1125–1139. https://doi.org/10.1016/j.jbusres.2022.01.037

Rossato, L., Regina, C., Alvalá, S., Marengo, J. A., Zeri, M., Ana, P. M., Cunha, A., Pires, L. B. M., & Barbosa, H. A. (2017, November). *Impact of soil moisture on crop yields over Brazilian Semiarid. 5*, 1–16. https://doi.org/10.3389/fenvs.2017.00073

Sankey, J. B., Brown, D. J., Bernard, M. L., & Lawrence, R. L. (2008). Geoderma comparing local vs. global visible and near-infrared (VisNIR) diffuse reflectance spectroscopy (DRS) calibrations for the prediction of soil clay, organic C and inorganic C. *Geoderma, 148*(2), 149–158. https://doi.org/10.1016/j.geoderma.2008.09.019

Shan, X., Cui, N., Cai, H., Hu, X., & Zhao, L. (2020). Estimation of summer maize evapotranspiration using MARS model in the semi-arid region of northwest China. *Computers and Electronics in Agriculture, 174*(November 2019), 105495. https://doi.org/10.1016/j.compag.2020.105495

Shepherd, K. D., & Walsh, M. G. (2007). Infrared spectroscopy—Enabling an evidence-based diagnostic surveillance approach to agricultural and environmental management in developing countries. *19*, 1–19. https://doi.org/10.1255/jnirs.716

Shukla, G., Garg, R. D., Srivastava, H. S., & Kumar, P. (2018). Performance analysis of different predictive models for crop classification across an aridic to ustic area of Indian states. *Geocarto International, 6049*, 1–20. https://doi.org/10.1080/10106049.2016.1240721

Sitohang, S., & Karnadi, V. (2021). Forecasting method using the Minitab program. *Technium Social Sciences Journal, 16*, 618.

Studnicki, M. (2021). Long-term yield variability of triticale (× Triticosecale Wittmack) tested using a CART model.

Thuiller, W., Lafourcade, B., Engler, R., & Araújo, M. B. (2009). BIOMOD–a platform for ensemble forecasting of species distributions. *Ecography, 32*(3), 369–373.

Tittonell, P., Shepherd, K. D., Vanlauwe, B., & Giller, K. E. (2008). Unravelling the effects of soil and crop management on maize productivity in smallholder agricultural systems of western Kenya—An application of classification and regression tree analysis. *123*, 137–150. https://doi.org/10.1016/j.agee.2007.05.005

Using, D., Visualization, D., & Applications, L. (2020). *A comparative analysis of breast cancer detection and diagnosis using data visualization and machine.*

Valiya, A., & Mishra, A. K. (2023). Quantifying thresholds for advancing impact-based drought assessment using classification and regression tree (CART) models. *Journal of Hydrology, 625*(PA), 129966. https://doi.org/10.1016/j.jhydrol.2023.129966

Wu, L., Zeng, W., Lei, G., Ma, T., Wu, J., & Huang, J. (2022, March). Simulating root length density dynamics of sunflower in saline soils based on machine learning. *Computers and Electronics in Agriculture, 197*, 106918. https://doi.org/10.1016/j.compag.2022.106918

Zhang, L., Sun, P., Huettmann, F., & Liu, S. (2022). Where should China practice forestry in a warming world ? November 2021, 2461–2475. https://doi.org/10.1111/gcb.16065

Chapter 8
A Relationship Analysis of Digital Training of Students and Their Influence on Efficiency and Productivity in Control Institutions

Plamena Nedyalkova, Iliyan Hristov, and Gergana Tsoncheva-Petkova

Abstract In today's world, where digital technologies are part of our everyday lives, forming students' digital competencies is a top priority in every European educational system. This study aims to identify and investigate the problems in training students to form digital competence to meet the requirements and needs of public (government) sector organizations. The public sector is the leading employer that provides young people with various opportunities to realize and improve their professional knowledge and teachings. The symbiosis between education and the public sector has recently become established as an employer to enhance processes in one sphere and the other. However, there are still several problems in the relevant sectors of the economy, especially when forming a well-prepared workforce that can work in the new digital environment. The purpose of the overall research is to establish what is the relationship and dependence between the training and preparation of students and their subsequent influence on the effectiveness of the productivity of control institutions. In this abstract, we will not fully reveal all the research results. However, I will leave that to the readers to familiarize themselves with the development and reach the conclusion with their scientific curiosity. Here, we only emphasize that such a relationship was found. The results are more than definitive that state institutions should advertise their activities more among young people so that they know they can work for them and be better prepared for work in the public administration sector, which is much more complex and specific than the private sector. The problems of training students and forming digital competence will be tested and investigated with the help of mathematical and statistical methods to determine its influence and impact on their

P. Nedyalkova (✉) · I. Hristov · G. Tsoncheva-Petkova
University of Economics—Varna, Varna, Bulgaria
e-mail: plnedyalkova@ue-varna.bg

I. Hristov
e-mail: ilian_hristov@ue-varna.bg

G. Tsoncheva-Petkova
e-mail: gergana.thoncheva@ue-varna.bg

I. Mukherjee et al. (eds.), *Decision Sciences for Quality and Productivity Improvement*,
https://doi.org/10.1007/978-981-95-7545-9_8

preparation for professional realization in the public sector. This article is an NPI project No. 64/2023, approved by the University of Economics—Varna, Bulgaria.

Keywords Compactness · Digital competence · Training · Public sector · Control · Economy · Analysis · Decision · Productivity improvement

JEL CODE M40 · M41 · M42 · M48

8.1 Introduction

As easy as it may seem, acquiring and forming digital knowledge and skills among adolescents is tricky. In today's environment, handling different information retrieval platforms can be easily accessible but also significantly tricky due to the different approaches to handling this information and the specifics of working on these platforms. This situation also brings to the fore the problems of learning in today's environment, as the development of technology and information systems outpaces the overall learning process.

In the face of all public organizations, the public sector (state sector), including control institutions, which are part of the country's executive power, is lagging in their development compared to the private sector in digitizing processes. There are many reasons for this, but it can be assumed that one of the most significant and leading causes is the weak or not-so-good staffing in the public sector. The conservative and cumbersome state system, the lack of systematic training and retraining of staff, the lack of sufficient state financial resources, the lack of innovative ideas and approaches, etc., are all problems that slow down the dynamics in the development of an organization. It has been observed that the recruited personnel do not develop and remain with their initial professional capacity of knowledge and skills acquired during their training or from previous jobs and positions.

The control institutions work "directly with individuals and legal entities from the private sector and oversee business development." (Nedyalkova, 2023b, p. 69). On the other hand, the private sector resists how the control institutions and the overall state apparatus work, which is not expeditious, innovative, and creative. In reality, there is an opposition between two separate parties, which parties participate in a control process (one is the object of control, and the other is the control institution itself), and one of the reasons for this opposition is the cumbersome control process, due to the lack of established professional staff with formed digital competences that they have already acquired in the process of their education.

Due to this problematic relevance, the presented paper aims to investigate the influence and impact of students' digital compact formation for the purposes and needs of control institutions, which are public (state) sector organizations. To achieve the so-stated objective, the following main tasks are set:

1. To define the nature, meaning, and characteristics of digital competence[1].
2. To consider the problems in the education of students and the formation of their digital literacy.
3. To analyze the problem of professional compactness of the staff in the control institutions and their preparation for the digitization of processes.
4. To investigate the relationship and dependence between students' training and their professional realization in control institutions to support the digitization of control processes. The scope of the study includes the independent variables of process digitization, the size of the control institution, and the financial backing of employees in control institutions, which influence the dependent variable of student learning.

To achieve the stated aim and objectives, the following hypotheses are set for testing in the development:

1. H0: No exact relationship between the specified independent and dependent variables is found.
2. H1: A relationship between the specified dependent variable and the independent variables tested is established.

In testing hypothesis H1, the exact relationship between the dependent and independent variables is also established.

The article's theoretical part reveals the specifics and importance of digital competence in modern society. It also outlines the problematic areas of students' education in Bulgaria and the necessity of forming digital literacy. The empirical part explores the relationship between the digital development of the public sector as a working environment, the provision of digital services to society, and their impact on student learning.

8.2 Theoretical

8.2.1 Meaning and Characteristics of Digital Competence.

8.2.1.1 The Importance of Digital Literacy.

Digital competence is constantly evolving along with the development of modern society, contributing to more opportunities and perspectives for people. The global pandemic of COVID-19 and the established distance learning of school and university students have imparted new fundamental and core competencies to all, significantly pushing the development of digital literacy.

Digital competency is inherently a set of knowledge, skills, and attitudes that are required when using information and communication technologies and digital media

[1] In this paper, digital literacy and digital skills will be used as synonyms for digital competence.

for task performance, problem-solving as a means of communication, information management, collaboration, content creation and sharing, and knowledge-building effectively, efficiently, efficiently, appropriately, critically, creatively, autonomously, flexibly, ethically, and reflectively for work, leisure, participation, learning, socializing, and needing In other words, digital literacy is essential for all people in today's dynamic world because through it they can use digital technologies effectively and appropriately for various activities. In this way, "people cope adequately with the challenges of the new era by understanding the information presented by mass media, seeking to evaluate data critically, and communicating with others through various means" (Ferrari, 2012, p. 36).

Of course, digital competence needs to be developed in people, with education being one of the essential and crucial factors. Ilomaki, Paavola, Lakkala, and Kantosalo define digital competence as the set of "skills and practices necessary to use new technologies in meaningful ways and as a tool for learning, work, and leisure, an understanding of the essential phenomena of digital technologies in society as well as in one's own life, and the motivation to participate in the digital world as an active and responsible participant" (Ilomaki et al., 2016, pp. 44–46). According to the World Economic Forum report, "digital literacy is one of the critical skills that modern companies require from their employees to adapt to the changing job market successfully" (Word Economy Forum, 2020). Today's workplaces impose demands related to digital communication and information technology skills.

According to this, "digital competency can be defined as the attitudes, skills, and practices needed to use digital technologies in meaningful ways for learning or digital literacy and is a competency that includes not only the knowledge of how to use digital technologies but also the attitudes toward them and the behaviors associated with their use" (Pedaste et al., 2023, p. 3). Therefore, to use and apply digital technologies for learning effectively, it is necessary to know how to use them and have the motivation and positive attitude to collaborate and work with them.

In 2006, the European Parliament and the Council (European Parliament and the Council, 2006) identified digital competence as one of the essential eight competencies that all individuals need for personal fulfillment and development, social activity, and engagement. The competency combines knowledge, skills, and attitudes based on basic ICT skills by using digital competence to retrieve, evaluate, store, create, present, and share information, and communicate and participate in collaborative networks via the Internet. Digital competence involves the confident and critical use of information and communication technologies for work, leisure, and communication.

In this regard, the European Parliament and the Council emphasize that digital competence requires knowledge, skills, and attitudes (European Parliament and the Council, 2006). Knowledge is seen as knowledge related to the functioning of basic computer applications, defining risks in online communication, the role of technology in supporting creativity and innovation, the validity and reliability of online information, and the legal and ethical principles behind the use of collaborative tools. Skills required include seeking, gathering, and processing information and using it critically and systematically, assessing and distinguishing the virtual from the real world while recognizing the connections. People must use their skills to present and understand information and use ICT confidently, critically, and creatively in their everyday lives. Attitudes are identified as the essentials that citizens are critical and reflective of information, responsible users, and interested in engaging online communities and networks.

The European Digital Competence Framework (DigComp) provides a common understanding of digital literacy and provides a basis for digital skills policy formulation (Vuorikari et al., 2022). DigComp outlines five competency areas: information and media literacy, communication and collaboration skills, digital content creation, safety, and problem-solving. It plays a central role in terms of confident, critical, and responsible use and engagement of digital technologies for increased digital literacy requirements of citizens, increased environmental aspects, employment and education of the population, and lifelong, conscious learning.

Digital competence, therefore, encompasses a much broader range of skills for seeking, evaluating, and using information, communicating and collaborating through electronic means, and critical thinking, creativity, and innovation. It is thus becoming an unavoidable necessity in today's technological world for all people.

8.2.1.2 The Importance of Digital Literacy.

D. Belshaw (Belshaw, 2014) "identifies eight interrelated core capabilities in digital literacy, with some having different weights in particular contexts and situations." He defines and ranks them in the following order: (1) cultural capability (understanding context); (2) cognitive (thinking) capability (evaluating, interpreting, analyzing, and drawing conclusions); (3) constructive capability (creating meaningful and informative messages); (4) communicative capability (communicating with purpose); (5) confidence (problem-solving and managing one's own learning in a digital environment); (6) creative capability (using digital technologies and techniques to create or achieve impossible things previously); (7) critical capability (critical thinking related to analyzing and verifying data and facts); (8) civic capability (literate practices that support the development of civil society). These abilities represent essential skills and competencies one must possess to succeed in the digital age. Furthermore, Belshaw focuses on the challenges in digital literacy and how we can develop competencies to address them successfully.

In doing so, Belshaw expands the traditional notion of digital literacy by presenting it as a multilayered domain involving a combination of multiple capabilities. Technological developments are changing how people interact with information, which raises the question, "How can we be active participants in this dynamic digital world?" Belshaw draws that digital competence should not be seen as a static set of knowledge and skills but as a holistic and continuous development and learning process. This requires constant adaptation to new technologies, understanding their interaction with cultural and social contexts, and active participation in the digital literacy community.

Other authors "argue that developing digital literacy is a prerequisite for a fulfilling life" (Sefton-Green et al., p. 108). In support of this, the European Commission encourages Member States to invest in digital technologies by developing the digital skills of the population and encouraging digital innovation, which in symbiosis with innovation and entrepreneurship, will lead to economic growth in the European Union as well as the competitiveness of the European economy (European Union, 2010). The relationship between "the economic sphere and the understanding of communication, the aspects considered, such as mass media, socio-culture, and media industry, are essential for the economic sector of any country" (Hartley, 2002, p.23). Moreover, the Organisation for Economic Co-operation and Development (OECD) argues that digital literacy is the "key to success in the twenty-first century" and therefore, information and communication technologies (ICTs) should be actively used in schools, necessitating changes in the educational environment (OECD, 2001, p.4.). The European Community has its vital place, role, and responsibility in providing perspective for young people, enabling the link between education and business through digital opportunity for students, and creating digital innovation hubs and centers for cyber-specialists (Gabriel, 2018). This means that school education should provide knowledge and competencies in digital competence and provide training for students in accordance with successful realization in society and according to business needs. "Thus, the quality and efficiency of knowledge, skills, and competencies for the development, preparation, and culture of each person, the flexibility and openness that the school should provide to students, as well as accessibility and learnability, tailored to the age characteristics of students, their needs, interests, opportunities and abilities" (Lyubenova & Lyubenov, 2019, p. 65). Therefore, the following steps aim to identify the criteria and indicators to highlight innovative ideas and achieve the expected developmental effect (Gerdzhikova, 2019). Thus, for the last decade, "digital competence has been seen as a necessary 'life skill' comparable to literacy" (Ferrari, 2012, p. 87).

More broadly, digital literacy is the key to improving the lives of every individual, enabling everyone to participate fully in the economy and giving them a serious advantage, especially where technology takes center stage in all aspects of life. Through it, people will adapt much more quickly to the digital environment, cope with various technological challenges, and make the most of the opportunities offered by modern technology.

Digital competence should be understood and considered as a multifaceted concept. It appears as a cornerstone in European society because each country has an important task to embed digital literacy in the education of young people, thus meeting the needs of business and providing a better opportunity for the development of the individual in society. Challenges are related to developing digital literacy in countries driven by different understandings of digital literacy in different national contexts. Moreover, the challenge is compounded by different access to technology and the unclear role of educational institutions in the digital age.

8.2.1.3 Challenges Faced in Education Institutions and by Employers, and the Actions by Governments Across the World.

Increasingly, the social context and the vital role of schools are prevalent, and they need to carry out a series of actions to support and develop digital literacy. A challenge in this "situation is the opposition regarding the knowledge held by teaching staff versus that held by young people" (Green & Bigum, 1993, p.120). Moreover, research in this area highlights "this problem in literacy and identifies the need to strengthen the fragile base on which teachers should build and develop their digital literacies" (Hennessy et al., 2005; p.156). This forces young people to seek and acquire digital literacies outside of knowledge-building institutions. Emphasis needs to be placed on changing "the role of educational institutions in our society so that young people can be better prepared for the challenges of the digital age by advocating the need for digital competence in practical learning activities as a new kind of foundational skill" (Sefton-Green et al., 2009, p.110). Exactly how this should happen in schools remains a problematic and highly debated question, the answer depends on multiple factors and is immensely subject to further research in this area.

It is necessary to summarize that in order to overcome these challenges in the new era of development, as well as to ensure that all young people will have the opportunity to build and develop digital competencies, we accept as authors that this is possible by achieving: (1) equal access to digital technologies; (2) global rethinking of the role of educational institutions in the digital sphere; (3) to actively support the teaching staff in the development of their digital skills; and (4) developing and implementing effective digital literacy programs.

Evidence of the growing importance of digital competence is also provided by future actions being taken at both global and national levels. In the US, in 2021 will launch a new digital literacy initiative. President Joe Biden is meeting with leading technology companies to discuss approaches to improving digital literacy in the US. As a result, many programs are being initiated to promote digital literacy in US education and society. In 2023, a national strategy was signed to ensure that all Americans have access to digital literacy skills in school, the workplace, and society (The White House, 2023). In 2023, China officially launched an ICDL Foundation program (ICDL-Asia, 2023) to improve digital literacy among Chinese students and the country's adult population. Establishing the program highlights the crucial role and essential contribution to digital competence as a prerequisite for advancing and developing the digital economy.

The requirement for digital competence in public sector organizations, including control institutions, has been made a condition of employment. This condition has created a new challenge for job applicants as they have to present their digital competencies to their future employers during the job application process. The unsatisfactory results that employers directly received from the respective job competitions were one of the main reasons for looking for ways of joint cooperation between educational institutions and employers to improve the quality of training toward digital literacy through using new technologies in the training process.

A new procedure, "Modernization of Higher Education Institutions," has been launched nationally to modernize curricula and introduce digital educational content, electronic resources, and cloud technologies in the educational process, as well as professional development of teachers and improve their skills in using ICT-based innovative educational technologies, as well as internationalization of higher education institutions and participation in networks (Ministry of Education and Science of Bulgaria, 2022; Simeonov & Lambovska, 2012). In addition, the 2022 National Reform Programme includes a program for enterprise competitiveness and innovation to contribute to "accelerating digital transformation and transition to a circular economy, targeted support for the development of sectors in high-tech and medium-to high-tech industries and knowledge-intensive services, promoting the digital transformation of SMEs, strengthening research and innovation capacity and the introduction of advanced technologies" (Information provided by Ministry of Finance of Bulgaria).

8.2.2 Problems of Students' Education in Bulgaria and the Formation of Digital Competence.

The continuous development of technology, particularly digitalization, inevitably impacts the education of students worldwide. In the last few years, digitization has encompassed almost all areas of the economy, and education, as one of any country's most important priorities, is invariably part of this dynamic and rapidly growing process.

Higher education, as the last stage in the education system in Bulgaria, is expected to meet the challenges of scientific and technological progress. The main task facing teachers in higher education institutions is the formation and development of competencies that will help students in their professional realization after graduation, and why not during their studies, to meet business needs. (Strategy for developing higher education in the Republic of Bulgaria for the period 2021–2030). This necessitates a change in the focus of education from teaching knowledge to mastering key competencies and developing problem-solving abilities. The competency-based approach plays an important role here as it requires the application of integrated interdisciplinary interaction between different fields of science, a strong practical orientation of training, and the application of innovative approaches and practices in the teaching process. Therefore, education is a factor in a new quality of economy and society. As researchers and scientists, we accept that education and science are two sides of the same coin, as they have the same subject (a system of knowledge used in different ways—by the scientist directly in practice and by the teacher to train to handle the educational product and subject—people). Thus, a closed cycle of "science—education—practice" is formed (Lyubenova & Lyubenov, 2019, p. 90). Business as a significant factor in the economy, in turn, requires young specialists to possess a range of professional knowledge, skills, and competencies. In a world subdued by artificial intelligence and digitization, students must possess computer skills, excellent knowledge of office applications and business management software, and communication and organizational skills. The development of students' digital competencies is now at the forefront, as one of the main priorities of the European Union is to enforce the integration and support the introduction of information and communication technologies in education. The European Commission has adopted an eLearning Action Plan1, and the main components in it are related to acting to introduce information and communication technologies in the Bulgarian education system:

- Training of teachers in the use of digital technologies;
- Develop European educational services and software;
- Accelerating the development of a unified academic network.

In today's digital society, mastery and use of information and communication technologies are essential components of functional literacy, a prerequisite for personal and professional realization and growth.

The measures imposed at the beginning of COVID-19 have faced the education system with a challenging task: to quickly organize the learning process so that the negative consequences for the learners are minimal. The most "common problems during this period were the lack of certain professional experience of teachers, the poor provision of devices for students, the limited access to quality Internet, and the number of electronic learning materials" (Sergeieva et al., 2022, p. 102). This, in turn, has led to new forms of collaboration, data processing, and personal and institutional organization. Studies have shown that both students and faculty were not prepared for the sudden shift to virtual learning at the beginning of COVID-19 (Garrett et al., 2020), which impacted students in terms of their academic learning. Many academic institutions switched to virtual learning using the Zoom app and Google Meet. For this sudden transition, faculty were given significant "*flexibility*" in teaching their courses. Based on their "online teaching knowledge and skills, faculty members use various forms of virtual teaching ranging from fully synchronous to fully asynchronous instruction and anything in between" (Lone et al., 2023, p.1).

In this regard, the University of Economics—Varna was one of the most prepared universities in Bulgaria, as it had implemented the eLearning platform years earlier. Thus, students studying at the University of Economics—Varna could adapt very quickly to the rapidly changing situation. For most students, several main problems arose initially: whether they would be able to handle the online platform, whether they would have enough study materials, how to compensate for the personal communication with the teaching team, and the conduct of the exams. The digitization process at the University of Economics Varna has been a major management goal for many years now, investing in the organization of many trainings, seminars, public lectures, and discussions on this topic. The University of Economics—Varna independently develops, implements, maintains, and continuously improves much of the software required for documenting and information provision of its processes. The University has established a Centre for Research and Application of New Information and

Communication Technologies, which is engaged in developing new software products or extending the functions of existing ones. The Centre has been established as an important element of implementing the strategy adopted in 2012 to transform the University into a high-tech I-zone where teaching, research, and administrative processes are carried out using state-of-the-art information and communication technologies.

The introduction of digital learning in Bulgaria is not only a result of the COVID-19 pandemic but also follows the European Union's 2020–2030 digital development strategy, which envisages providing a secure digital environment for consumers and businesses to access goods across Europe, developing digital networks and services, and optimizing and growing the digital economy (Dimitrova, I. 2023, p. 214). In addition to the main priorities for developing digital technologies, the European Commission also focuses on training its citizens in their use and creating an action plan for digital education (2021–2027). It represents "a renewed EU policy initiative to support the sustainable and effective adaptation of EU Member States' education and training systems to the digital age" (Ratcliff et al., 2022, p.1).

The adopted European Framework for Digital Competence of Teachers invariably plays a key role in eliminating problems in Bulgaria's student education. It responds to a growing awareness among EU Member States that teachers need a set of specific digital skills to raise the level and incorporate innovation in education. The framework aims to capture and describe these teacher-specific digital competencies organized into six areas.

Thanks to the Recommendation of the Council of the European Union and of the European Parliament on 22 May 2018 on key competencies for lifelong learning (Text with EEA relevance) (2018/C 189/01), eight key competencies have been identified, including digital competencies, namely: communicative competence; linguistic competence; personal competence, social competence and competence; mathematical competence and competence in science, technology and engineering; entrepreneurial competence; civic competence; co These core competences are very important and need to be mastered for students to be successful.

In an effort to respond appropriately to dynamically changing conditions, educators are looking for ways to integrate the platforms in which learners are most active in the learning process. Approaches to using Pinterest in the learning process are discussed by (Schroeder et al., 2019, Holmes & Rasmussen, 2018), and (Staudt et al., 2020) even attempt to teach on Reddit. The conclusion is that to successfully adapt learning content to the givens and needs of the digital generation students, additional learning micro-resources need to be developed in a format that learners are already accustomed to. The aim is that "these resources develop specific skills, arouse interest, provoke curiosity and critical thinking, increase motivation, and make it easier to master the learning macro-resources" (Ivanova & Ibryamova, 2023, p. 123).

Thanks to the European Community's 2015 Education Development Strategies, students can determine their level of digital competence using a self-assessment card.

The self-assessment card has four components, each containing three proficiency levels: basic (basic), independent, and fluent.

Students can apply for the Digital Competencies Self-Assessment Card during their studies and careers. The digital competencies of individuals develop over time with the help of the technologies that are applied. The process does not end in the learning process but is further developed in the respective working environment. Employers wish to obtain highly skilled staff in order not to invest additional resources in the further training of their employees. However, the rapid pace of development of the working environment is outpacing the established training process and the established curricula, respectively. This puts an extreme dependency on the educational process and the evolving digital work environment, both in the public (government) and non-public (private) sectors.

8.3 Research Methodology

8.3.1 Procedure

Based on the above and presented so far, it can be assumed that the training of students to form digital competencies and their subsequent implementation in the public sector are two variables. This paper aims to determine whether the digital development of the public sector as a working environment and the provision of digital services to society affect students' learning. The working environment and working conditions in the public sector should be considered the independent variable, and students' learning and obtaining digital competence should be the **dependent variable**. Students' grades from their final training are not derived from their university studies. However, the actual professional grade is obtained from the employer and their practical implementation.

The public sector is one of the main employers in Bulgaria. According to the National Statistical Institute (NSI), the total number of employees in the public sector in Bulgaria in 2022 is 631 thousand people, of which 215.70 thousand people are employed in public administration, and 108.90 thousand people are employed in organizations with administrative and auxiliary activities. Other interesting data that the National Institute of Statistics of Bulgaria presents is that for the year 2022, employees according to the share of working time spent on digital devices is as follows:

Also, from the National Institute of Statistics for 2022, other interesting data and facts are presented, namely that in the public sector, including control institutions, in recent years, employees in these sectors have been engaged in the application of relatively complex calculations in their work, despite the availability of digital devices that support the work process, namely:

Therefore, considering the data presented in Table 8.1 and Table 8.2, it can be established that many employees work with digital devices and perform relatively complex computations in public sector organizations. The presented data also proves that the digitization of processes in the Bulgarian public sector has started, but these

Table 8.1 Employees by share of working time spent working with digital devices

Economic activities	Total	Half-time and more	Less than half the working time	No part of working time
Administrative and support activities	108.9	19.1	26.7	63.2
State management	215.7	89.8	81.0	44.4

Table 8.2 Employees, by a proportion of working time spent on relatively complex calculations

Economic activities	Total	Half-time and more	Less than half the working time	No part of working time
Administrative and support activities	108.9	(1.6)	14.4	92.9
State management	215.7	19.4	71.7	124.0

processes need the appropriate personnel with relevant knowledge and skills. Therefore, very often, public sector organizations, including controlling institutions, place relevant requirements on training organizations to prepare professional staff.

Control institutions, as public sector organizations, have certain obligations to fulfill. These institutions, as well as exercising control, are controlled by other institutions, such as the Court of Auditors, the State Financial Inspection Agency, the Ministry of Finance, etc. These institutions have changed over the years under the influence of various external factors; on the other hand, the training of students, which is aimed at the narrowly profiled preparation of staff for the relevant control institutions, depends precisely on them, on the professional requirements set by the relevant control institutions. Researchers have studied the problems in control institutions. Yolova et al. (2023), Nedyalkov et al. (2021) and others, but in these studies, the problem of the influence of control institutions as an employer on the training of students is studied.

Hence, we denote the dependent variable, i.e., student learning, by **y,** and the independent variable, **control institutions, which are studied as working environment and working conditions**, by **x.**

8.3.2 Research Methodology

The study applied regression analysis as a method to show the influence of the independent variables on the dependent variable. Regression analysis shows a statistical relationship (correlation) between variables but does not in itself prove causation. Since we have inferred statistical aggregated data from the institutions, for this reason we stop the attention of this method. The main purpose of regression analysis is to represent their correlation relationship. Also, with the help of this study, we aim to determine whether the test objects, namely the control institutions of the public sector that are changing through the digitization of their processes, impact the requirements for the acquisition of professional digital competencies by students. We will investigate this through a correlogram, i.e., a diagram representing the relationship between the relevant factor and the dependent variable. Correlogram is not shown in the findings.

The general regression model is presented as follows:

$$\hat{Y}_k = f(\varphi_k, \theta) \tag{8.1}$$

where:
$\hat{Y}_k$ regression model;
φ_k, θ—vector of regressions and vector of parameters;

The overall relationship between the two variables will be tested to determine the impact of changing working conditions in public sector organizations, including control institutions, on student learning. The study is built on the following constraints:

1. The study covers the year 2022, this period is one of the significant periods for the development of control institutions and their gradual digitization. In this period, there is the most reported data and information from the control institutions regarding the digitization processes and the competence of the personnel who work in these control institutions.
2. The reports on the activities of the Bulgarian control institutions entirely provide the information necessary for the empirical study on the status and provision of professional staff.
3. The study defines the following independent components that influence the dependent, viz:

   - The size of the controlling institution as an organizational unit (CI). We assume that the larger an organization is as a structural unit of individual units and components, the more highly qualified staff it needs. The three largest control institutions, which in recent years have been gradually implementing new information technologies in practice and striving to digitize their processes, have been considered for the study: the National Revenue Agency (NRA), the Customs Agency, and the General Labor Inspectorate Executive Agency.
   - Digitization of processes and digitization of documents in control institutions (D). This is one of the factors influencing the dependent variable, as digital working conditions pose corresponding challenges to students' training and future preparation for their respective jobs.
   - The financial backing for recruiting higher-skilled staff (F). Hiring well-trained and highly qualified staff requires significant salary costs. Young people's motivation is mainly the remuneration offered by employers, and their choice of training in the relevant fields depends on this factor.

The dependence between these variables can be represented as follows:

$$OS = f(TS,\ CI,\ D,\ F) \tag{8.2}$$

OS—the Dependent Variable Affected by the Independent Variable Components OE, D, and F.

TS—the Training of Students

CI—the Size of the Controlling Institution

D—digitization of Processes and Ization of Documents

F—The Financial Backing to Hire Highly Skilled Staff

The overall regression model is presented as follows:

$$OS = \alpha_0 + \alpha_1 TS + \alpha_2\, CI + \alpha_3\, D + \alpha_4\, F, \tag{8.3}$$

where:

$\alpha_0, \alpha_1, \alpha_2, \alpha_3,$ *and* $\alpha_4,$ *are* regression parameters that denote the coefficients of the independent variables.

The study's scope also considered the influence of contextual, mediating, and moderating variables to the extent that the statistical relationship could be presented more clearly. Context variables actually provide the context or setting in which a relationship is viewed, which is why they are so important. Mediating (mediator) variables explain how the independent variable (i.e., student learning in our study) affects the dependent variable. For the studied variables, it can be mentioned as examples:

1. Contextual variables of "The size of the control institution" (CI)—Economic environment, the purpose of the control institution, the scope of the activity of the control institution, etc.
2. Contextual variables of "digitization of processes and ization of documents" (D)—technological development and innovations in Bulgaria, the established strategy for digital development in the relevant economic spheres, etc.
3. Contextual variables of "Financial provision for hiring highly qualified personnel" (F)—Bulgaria's social policy regarding the accepted minimum thresholds for labor remuneration, social security, tax burdens, etc.
5. Moderating variables of "The size of the control institution" (CI)—organizational structure, continuity between new and old personnel, management policies, etc.
6. Moderating variables "Digitization of processes and the digitization of documents" (D)—the built digital infrastructure, the degree of digital competence of individuals, duration of the confirmation of digitization processes, etc.
7. Moderating variables of "Financial support for hiring highly qualified staff" (F)—include competitiveness of pay, opportunities for professional development provided by the institutions, and the ethical environment.

8.3.3 Research Results

All variables are calculated on the basis of the data extracted from the activity reports of the control institutions. Furthermore, the specificity of this study is that even if the same methodology is applied as a research approach, the final results derived will be different due to the following circumstances:

1. The study period may vary;
2. The institutions surveyed may be from both the private and public sectors. We believe that the sector's specificity is a prerequisite for different results.
3. The primary data used in the respective research can be derived using both the quantitative and qualitative approaches.
4. The final interpretation of the data is essential because different subjects (persons) may apply their different interpretations of the final results.

What is specific about this research approach is that it allows for its multipurpose purpose and representation of variables in different ways to represent the relationship from a separate set of factors. The factors may be more than specified, but we identify three main factors due to the present study's limitations.

Another significant feature of the study is that we use the descriptive approach to present the mean and standard deviation of the different variables within the study's scope. In the study, we present the minimum and maximum values of the variables through which one can get an idea of the actual possible variation they allow. A variation that is beyond the specified norms means that there is a negative effect on the dependent variable. Instead of observing motivation among the students, which is directed toward their development in the control institutions and applying their skills, it is possible to observe a negative effect if any of the dependencies and factors are not within their permissible values and limits. The research data is presented with the help of Table 8.3.

For the example considered, the value of the free term is **-55.63**, which is statistically significant P-value = 0.8, and the corresponding 95% confidence interval is **(–74.97; 63.84)**. The regression coefficient in front of the independent attribute (size

Table 8.3 Data description

Variables	Minimum	Maximum	Average value	Standard deviation
Student Training (**TS**)	–74,97	63,84	26.89	25,00
The size of the controlling institution (***CI***)—data on the total number of employees are taken into account	–1,6011	2,5238	1.689	0,74,284,576
Digitization of processes and ization of documents (**D**)	–73,7181	83,50	54.25	28,31
The financial backing to hire highly skilled staff (**F**)	–0,066	1,4498	1.23	0,2730

of the control institution) is 0.461. It is statistically significant, i.e., P-value = 0.5682, and the corresponding confidence interval is (–1.601; 2.5238). The study found that the regression coefficient in front of the independent variable process digitization is 4.8943. It is statistically significant, i.e., P-value = 0.871, and the corresponding confidence interval is (–73.718; 83.506). Regarding process digitization and document digitization, which are also independent variables, their regression coefficient before the independent variable is 4.894**,** its significance is P-value = 0.8711. The last independent factor influencing the dependent variable of student learning is "*Financial backing for hiring highly qualified staff*." For this factor, the regression coefficient in front of the independent variable is 0.691, and the corresponding 95% confidence interval is (–0.06631; 1.44982).

In regression analysis, it is not necessary to calculate a **y-mean** since the main purpose is to determine the relationship between the dependent and independent variables. For this reason, the graphical method is used to represent the relationship between the dependent and independent variables:

Hence, from Fig. 8.2, it is found that the regression equation has the form of $y = 469.05x + 5785.70$, i.e., linear regression is observed. The change in the dependent variable **y, i.e., students' learning, is by 469.05 units,** which means that for every change in x, the dependent variable y increases by 469.05. Therefore, the factors of the size of the control institution, digitization of processes and digitization of documents, and the financial provision for hiring highly qualified staff by the control institution in their change will increase the dependent variable by 469.05 units.

Also, with the help of Fig. 8.1, it is found that the main factor influencing students' learning as a motive is the reward they are expected to receive upon their realization. In today's mercantile society, remuneration is the main incentive for choosing a vocational field of study and major. For students, external environmental factors strongly influence the first steps to choosing a major. The respective institutions' size, development opportunities, and increasing administrative capacity are also leading motives. However, the main dependence in the choice of profession and professional realization depends on the factors governing the labor market: remuneration, realization, good working environment, etc. It is confirmed that students are drawn to those university courses that provide good career opportunities. An employer-student solid relationship is built through the labor market by external factors and not so much by internal factors within the educational institutions themselves.

The study's innovativeness is that these three factors—the size of the control institution, the digitization of the processes, and the financial provision for the recruitment of highly qualified staff—are examined as a common influence on the training of students who have directed their professional development in control institutions, which are public sector organizations. For these organizations, it is much easier to derive estimates from which the change in **y** and its predicted value can be determined (Fig. 8.3).

With the help of a new network model, the dependence on the relationship between student learning and the working conditions offered by the controlling institutions of the public sector as an employer:

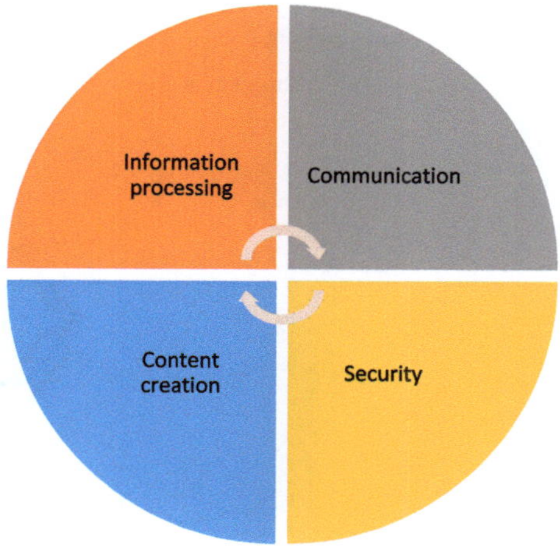

Fig. 8.1 Digital competencies self-assessment card

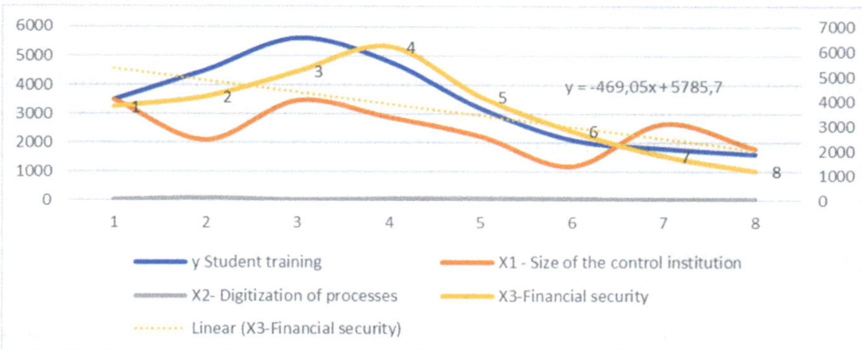

Fig. 8.2 Representation of the relationship between the dependent variable and the independent variable

This network relationship between the dependent and independent variables represents the radial extent of the variables. The radial extent of the variables represents the distance from the center of the graph to the specific lines that are the values of the variables for that particular study. This graph illustrates the overall study of the situation, namely how far the relevant variables can go and, therefore, the intensity of the relevant variables. Even with the relevant variables tested in this network manner, we conclude that the third factor, financial security, is the strongest; it impacts the other two factors and the dependent variable **y** accordingly.

For the analyzed period, 8 full reports for 2022 were found, in which data were extracted and presented regarding the digitalization of the control institutions and the training of personnel, especially the newly appointed personnel with little experience

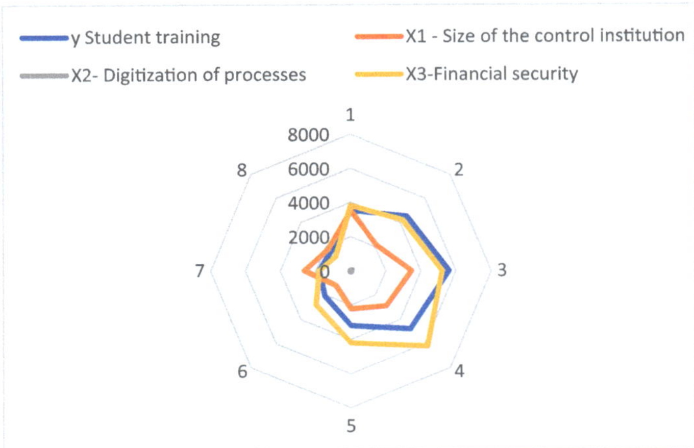

Fig. 8.3 The network relationship between student learning as the dependent variable and the work environment with its independent variables

in the control institutions and their preparation for direct work in the control institutions. Therefore, in graph 3, the 8-degree network is visible because of 8 reports from which the information for the relevant control institutions is derived.

8.4 Discussion

Issues of digitization as a factor that influences the learning process have been studied by various researchers, such as Kornienko and Mishina (2023), who studied the implementation of digital educational tools in institutions, also Cruz et al. (2022), Lo Iacono (2022) Shutenko et al. (2020), Nedyalkova (2020, 2023a) and others all of them present the problems in training students in terms of their preparation, the need for changes in the training process, and the implementation of technology in training. The relationship between the three factors size of the controlling institution (studied institution, as an employer), the second factor—digitalization of processes and digitalization of documents; and the third factor, financial provision for the recruitment of highly qualified manpower is strong, as a dependence on the training of students. This paper presents the issues in a different way and builds on all the other discussions and research. It can be assumed to be an extension of all the researchers who have worked in this area. However, it presents the regression relationship between training and external factors that influence training. This study also raises many new questions for future research, such as how digital transformation affects the development of society, the new professions that will be related to digitalization and digital transformation processes, etc.

8.5 Conclusions

Based on the presented study, the following main conclusions are drawn:

1. Digital competence is a complex set of knowledge, skills, and attitudes that are necessary when using information and communication technologies and digital media to perform tasks and solve problems.
2. Digital competence is a set of skills that are acquired not only in the process of learning but also during a professional career.
3. Student training is an important process that aims to meet employers' needs for the necessary professional staff. The training process is dynamic, aimed at renewing the training environment and validating new curricula and curricula relevant to their time and working conditions.
4. The Self-Assessment Card is an important means by which any person can determine their competency. This card can also be applied in a work environment, not only during training. The Self-Assessment Card provides direction for the development of each individual and identifies the professional qualities and skills that a person possesses at a given time. For this reason, it can be assumed that this card is suitable for use as a self-monitoring tool during training and when testing professional digital competence during one's professional career.
5. The literature talks about the multidimensional nature of digital literacy (Ilomäki et al., 2011; Belshaw, 2014) at different levels (Ferrari, 2012). The hypothesis can be considered to provide a clearer explanation of the reasons for not considering the other dimensions or levels.
6. On testing and proving hypotheses. Based on the research presented, hypothesis H1 is proven, as there is a solid linear relationship between the dependent variable of student learning and the independent variables: the size of control institutions, digitalization of processes, and financial backing to recruit highly qualified staff. This strong relationship means that the dependent variable changes significantly when these three factors change. The degree of change is the dependent variable, which is in the positive direction. That is, when the factors change positively, it correspondingly increases the motivation of students to improve their digital competencies and vice versa, when the factors change in a negative change, especially this point is observed when a change in the size of the control institution concerned changes the educational activity of students. This problem is also observed in the choice of occupational field when the relevant occupational sector has problems, i.e., the demand for employees and/or workers is reduced, and wages are significantly reduced.
7. In the study, it is proved that all the 95% confidence levels contain Zero; this means that the confidence interval of the correlation contains 0, which means that the study is not exhausted with this study. More research needs to be done with more data, and this research should be done over a longer period of time. As scientists, we believe the results will be different in the long rather than the short term. We accept that it is precisely in the long-term period that it is possible to determine how the detour interval changes most accurately. The confidence

interval of the correlation coefficient indicates the range within which the true correlation coefficient is expected to fall with a certain degree of certainty. This degree of security cannot be given and set at 100% in a short-term period as a guarantee. This can be done in a long-term period.

References

Belshaw, D. (2014). *The essential elements of digital literacies*. https://dougbelshaw.com/essential-elements-book.pdf.

Council of Ministers of the Republic of Bulgaria. (2022). Retrieved August 31, 2023, from https://www.strategy.bg/

Cruz, P. D., Covarrubias, L. P., & Pérez, P. A. (2022). The effect of resilience on entrepreneurial intention in higher education students in a post-covid stage 19. *Journal of Higher Education Theory and Practice*. https://doi.org/10.33423/jhetp.v22i18.5695

Dimitrova, I. (2023). Development of information society and integration of digital tools in the educational process during the pandemic—Problems and Precautions. *Strategies for Policy in Science and Education*, 31(4).

European Commission. (2023). Europass: Digital tools for skills and career management. Retrieved August 31, 2023, from https://europa.eu/europass/en

European Commission, Joint Research Centre. (2017). European framework for the digital competence of educators: DigCompEdu. Publications Office of the European Union. Retrieved August 31, 2023, from https://publications.jrc.ec.europa.eu/repository/handle/JRC107466

European_Parliament_and_the_Council. (2006). Recommendation of the European Parliament and of the council of 18 December 2006 on key competencies for lifelong learning. *Official Journal of The European Union*, L394/310.

European_Union. (2010). *Europe's digital competitiveness report*. http://ec.europa.eu/information_society/digital-agenda/documents/edcr.pdf

Ferrari, A. (2012). *Digital competence in practice: An analysis of frameworks*. Retrieved from Publications Office of the European Union. https://data.europa.eu/doi/10.2791/82116

Gabriel, M. (2018). Zaedno definirame proekta na badeshteto. [Strategies for Policy in Science and Education], *26*(1), 20–27.

Gerdzhikova, N. (2019). Inspektiraneto kato realizatsia na politika za poddarzhane na kachestvoto na uchilishtata. [Strategies for Policy in Science and Education], *27*(1), 51–57.

Garrett, R., Legon, R., Fredericksen, E. E., & Simunich, B. (2020). *CHLOE 5: The pivot to remote teaching in Spring 2020 and its impact*. https://www.qualitymatters.org/qa-resources/resource-center/articles-resources/CHLOE-project

Green, B., & Bigum, C. (1993). Aliens in the classroom. *Australian Journal of Education, 37*(2).

Hartley, J. (2002). *Communication, cultural and media studies: The key concepts* (3rd ed.). Routledge.

Hennessy, S., Ruthven, K., & Brindley, S. (2005). Teacher perspectives on integrating ICT into subject teaching: Commitment, constraints, caution, and change. *Journal of Curriculum Studies*, *37*(2), 155–192.

Holmes, A. F., & Rasmussen, S. J. (2018). Using Pinterest to stimulate student engagement, interest, and learning in managerial accounting courses. *Journal of Accounting Education, 43*, 43–56. https://doi.org/10.1016/j.jaccedu.2018.03.001

ICDL-Asia. (16 March 2023). *ICDL the digital skills standard*. https://icdlasia.org/icdl-programmes/

Ilomaki, L., Paavola, L., Lakkala, M., & Kantosalo, A. (2016). Digital competence—An emergent boundary concept for policy and educational research. *Education and Information Technologies, 21*(3), 655–679.
In Science and Education. (2023). 31(4s), p. 214. https://doi.org/10.53656/str2023-4s-18-de
Ivanova, A., & Ibryamova, E. (2023). The role of social networks and micro-earning in education digitalisation. *Strategies for Policy in Science and Education, 31*(4).
Kornienko, D. V., & Mishina, S. V. (2023). Implementation of digital education tools in the pedagogical community. *Journal of Higher Education Theory and Practice, 23*(13). https://doi.org/10.33423/jhetp.v23i13.6370
Lo Iacono, M. (2022). A model for a conscious digital citizenship. *Journal of e-learning and Knowledge Society, 18*(3), 111–116. https://doi.org/10.20368/1971-8829/1135683
Lone, T., Xu, P., Sun, Q., Davis, L., & Levi, A. (2023). An empirical analysis of agricultural college students' perceptions of virtual learning. *Journal of Higher Education Theory and Practice, 23*(13), 1–2.
Lyubenova, A., & Lyubenov, L. (2019). Sastoyanie na balgarskoto obrazovanie [Strategies for Policy in Science and Education] *27*(1), 88–109.
Ministry_of_ Education_and_Learning. The benefits of the "Modernisation of the Higher Education Institutions" program will be extended. https://sf.mon.bg/?go=news&p=detail&newsId=990
Ministry of Education and Science of Bulgaria. (2022). Modernization of higher education institutions. Retrieved August 31, 2023, from https://web.mon.bg/bg/100770
Ministry of Finance of Bulgaria. (2022). National reform programme of the Republic of Bulgaria 2022. Retrieved August 31, 2023, from https://www.minfin.bg
National Statistical Institute—https://www.nsi.bg/bg/
Nedyalkova, P. (2020). Specificities and characteristics of the assessment bases in the context of internal audit. In *Quality of Internal Auditing in the Public Sector.* Contributions to Management Science. Springer. https://doi.org/10.1007/978-3-030-29329-1_2
Nedyalkova, P., Andreeva, A., & Yolova, G. (2021). Digitalization and the new legal and economic challenges to employers in implementing internal control. *Economic Studies*, Economic Research Institute Bulgarian Academy of Sciences, *30*(5), 158–175.
Nedyalkova, P. (2023a). Testing and defining the effectiveness of the supervisory institution executive agency "General Labour Inspectorate." *IGI Global.* https://doi.org/10.4018/978-1-6684-9067-9.ch010
Nedyalkova, P. (2023b). *Principles of financial control in the public sector* (pp.1–300). IGI Global. ISBN, 978–166–84–8883–6.
OECD. (2001). *Learning to change.* Paris.
Pedaste, M., Kallas, K., & Baucal, A. (2023). Digital competence test for learning in schools: Development of items and scales. *Computers & Education* 203.
Ratcliff, ch., Martinello b., & Litos, V. (2020). *Digital agenda for Europe.* https://www.europarl.europa.eu/factsheets/en/sheet/64/digital-agenda-for-europe, [10.03.2023].
Sefton-Green, J., Nixon, H., & Erstad, O. (4:2 2009). Reviewing approaches and perspectives on "Digital Literacy". *Pedagogies: An International Journal*, *4*(2), 107–125.
Sergeieva, l., Stoichuk, T., Tarasova, O., Sulyma, T., & Tarasiuk, I. (2022) Developing a modern educational environment in the digital space at the institution of professional (Vocational-Technical) education. *Journal of Higher Education Theory and Practice. 22*(7), 102. https://doi.org/10.33423/jhetp.v22i7.5273
Schroeder, S., Curcio, R., & Lundgren, L. (2019). Expanding the learning network: How teachers use Pinterest. *Journal of Research on Technology in Education, 51*, 1–21. https://doi.org/10.1080/15391523.2019.1573354
Shutenko, A. I., Shutenko, E. N., Derevyanko, J. P., Kanishcheva, M. A., Kovtun, J. J., & Lokteva, A. V. (2020). Motivational and personal differences of students with dissimilar degrees of self-realization in higher school education. *Perspectives of Science and Education, 6*(48), 345–357.
Simeonov, O., & Lambovska, M. (2012). A suggestion about potentialities for the SWOT analysis's development concerning threats. *Economics and Management, 2*, 94–103.

Staudt W. K. B., & Carpenter, J. P. (2020). Teachers on Reddit? Exploring contributions and interactions in four teaching-related subreddits. *Journal of Research on Technology in Education, 52*(2), 216–233. https://doi.org/10.1080/15391523.2020.1722978

Strategy for developing higher education in the Republic of Bulgaria for the period 2021–2030. https://dv.parliament.bg/DVWeb/showMaterialDV.jsp?idMat=154629

The_White_House. (31 07 2023). *National cyber workforce and education strategy*. https://www.whitehouse.gov/wp-content/uploads/2023/07/NCWES-2023.07.31.pdf

University of Economics—Varna. (n.d.). Centre for Research and Application of New Information and Communication Technologies (CIPNICT). Retrieved August 31, 2023, from https://ue-varna.bg/bg/p/7811/struktura/universitetski-tsentrove/tsentar-za-izsledvane-i-prilagane-na-novi-informatsionni-i-komunikatsionni-tehnologii-tsipnikt

Vuorikari, R., Kluzer, S., & Punie, Y. (2022). *DigComp 2.2: The digital competence framework for citizens—With new examples of knowledge, skills and attitudes*. Publications Office of the European Union.

Yolova, G. O., Andreeva, A., Dimitrova, D. N., Blagoycheva, H. V., Nedyalkova, P., & Bogdanov, H. (2023). Legal and economic aspects of state control over compliance with Labor legislation. *IGI Global*. https://doi.org/10.4018/978-1-6684-9067-9

Word_Economi_Forum. (2020). *The future of jobs report*. https://www.weforum.org/reports/the-future-of-jobs-report-2020

Chapter 9
Enhancing Quality and Productivity: A Deep Dive into Technology Adoption Models for Operational Excellence

Ved Prabha Toshniwal, Rakesh Jain, Gunjan Soni, Bharti Ramtiyal, Shrishti Gupta, and Vijay Raj

Abstract The importance of technology adoption theories is unmatched when it comes to discovering the barriers and enablers in consumer behavior in adoption of a new technology. Various theories are available in literature within the realm of consumer behavior study, each emphasizing different facets of adoption, be it behavioral or technological. While analyzing the adoption of emerging technology, a theory that considers both technological and human behavioral factors is essential. Most studies do not have a clear approach to selecting a technology adoption model for their research. In this study, our main focus is to compare the models that predominantly focus on the technological aspects and identify a best fit model to study the adoption of emerging technologies in the pharmaceutical sector. To achieve this, we employed a combination of Multi-Criteria Decision Making (MCDM) methods. Seven criteria were formulated in collaboration with experts from the pharmaceutical industry. Five technology adoption models were chosen that focused on technology-related aspects. The weights of the criteria were determined using the PIvot Pairwise RElative Criteria Importance Assessment method, while the technology adoption

V. P. Toshniwal (✉) · R. Jain · G. Soni · S. Gupta · V. Raj
Department of Mechanical Engineering, Malaviya National Institute of Technology, Jaipur, Rajasthan, India
e-mail: 2021RME9074@mnit.ac.in; veda.toshniwal@gmail.com

R. Jain
e-mail: rjain.mech@mnit.ac.in

G. Soni
e-mail: gsoni.mech@mnit.ac.in

S. Gupta
e-mail: 2020ume2020@mnit.ac.in

V. Raj
e-mail: 2020ume1660@mnit.ac.in

B. Ramtiyal
Faculty of Management and Commerce Poornima University, Jaipur, India
e-mail: bharti.mnit2022@gmail.com

I. Mukherjee et al. (eds.), *Decision Sciences for Quality and Productivity Improvement*,
https://doi.org/10.1007/978-981-95-7545-9_9

models were ranked based on ratings provided by experts, utilizing multiple methods such as MARCOS, TOPSIS, EDAS, ELECTRE and CODAS. The obtained rankings were subsequently compared to validate the methodologies employed. Notably, the Task Technology Fit (TTF) model emerged as the top choice across all three MCDM methods, showcasing its efficacy in examining technology-related factors influencing the adoption of Pharma 4.0.

Keywords Technology adoption model · TOPSIS · MCDM · Task technology fit · Pharma 4.0 · CODAS

9.1 Introduction

Industry 4.0 denotes the fourth revolution to have taken place in manufacturing. The changing of the manufacturing process into digital intrusion into the procedure of manufacture characterizes the digitization of manufacture and fundamentally, the onset of Industry 4.0. It is the era of smart, automated systems, driven by tools like data analytics and machine learning. Industry 4.0 is the revolution of advanced connectivity and interaction of machines, systems, and people. It is built on the foundation of the Internet of Things (IoT), Internet of Systems, and cyber-physical systems (Sahi et al., 2020). At the current times, the machines become interconnected not only with each other but also to communicate, analyze, and diagnose issues, all without human interventions. As a result, it becomes much more efficient, productive, and flexible to execute the processes (Zhang et al., 2022).

For instance, big data and analytics in drug discovery and development speed up the discovery of new drug candidate molecules but also predicting success rates for introduction into the market. In the smart manufacturing era, the real-time continuous feedback with real-time quality control returns products of higher quality with adherence to regulatory standards (Ma et al., 2024). This will allow bringing to patients, faster than ever before, safer and more effective medicines. The digital twin, being the digital replica of a physical process, system, or product, may predict and control the manufacturing process in the virtual world before executing it in reality (Hassani et al., 2022). This way, the risk is reduced while efficiency is enhanced. The adoption of these technologies is an area of interest to everyone, but empirical research on factors driving the usage and discontinuance by the customer can help in their continued adoption.

The technologies like AI, ML and even Blockchain are intruding into the different domains of pharmaceutical operations. This is through the way they are doing things, from the discovery of drugs to patient diagnosis today, with insights from large sets of data at a rate much faster than humanly possible (Wang et al., 2021). The blockchain technology proffers promises for augmented security, integrity, and transparency within the pharmaceutical supply chain to ascertain that drugs are authentic and free from counterfeiting or tampering. The road to full integration of Industry 4.0 technologies in the Indian pharmaceutical sector, therefore, is winding and full of pits, but the potential paybacks in efficiency, cost savings, and improvement in patient results are mammoth. These will open room for more research, definitely, and redesign the pharmaceutical industry landscape (Al-Khatib, 2023; Dhiman & Madan, 2024). Some important factors responsible for the slower adoption of recent technology in the pharma industry include integration challenges with existing systems, limited awareness of benefits, resistance to change, data security concerns, inadequate infrastructure, and trust-related issues such as skepticism toward technological accuracy, reliability, and decision-making autonomy. These factors collectively hinder progress by creating both technical and psychological barriers to implementation (Singh and Dev 2021; Benn & Shaw, 2021).

This takes us into these theories of technology adoption almost like a foray into why we go ahead and buy that new smartphone or try that flashy new app in the first place. At their center, these theories are essentially concerned with the "why" and "how" questions of our technology adoption. These are the stories behind why some of us are first in line for the latest tech gadget, while some of us are waiting to hear if it's worth the hype. They include psychology, sociology, and economy to untangle factors that can influence us, such as perceived usefulness of the technology, or how easy it is to use, or simply because everybody else is using it. It's about piecing together the puzzle of human behavior in the digital age. Many researchers in the past have made use of technology adoption theories to study the adoption of emerging technologies such as digital library, telemedicine, big data in healthcare using prominent models such as UTAUT, task technology fit, etc. (Pillai & Sivathanu, 2020; Standing & Standing, 2008). However, the selection method of these models is not specified in the studies.

This research paper aims at finding out a best fit theory out of multiple options available to study the adoption of i4.0 technologies in Indian pharmaceutical sector. Here, the author aims to evaluate multiple options to find the best technology adoption model for Industry 4.0 adoption using six MCDM methods: PIPRECIA, MARCOS, TOPSIS, EDAS, ELECTRE, and CODOS. Some of these methods such as MARCOS, VIKOR, AHP, etc., have been utilized in the past literature for the selection of a technology adoption model. In this research, we aim to apply all six above-mentioned MCDM methods and compare the results obtained. The remainder of the paper is structured as: the introduction gives an overview of Industry 4.0 and its adoption. The literature review identifies research gaps and justifies the selection of the MCDM methods and the shortlisted theories (TTF, TAM, TOE, IDT, and TAM 2). The methodology section explains the application and evaluation process of each MCDM method, detailing the criteria and data used. Finally, we compare the results from these methods to determine the most suitable theory for technology adoption in Industry 4.0 (Özdağoğlu et al., 2024).

Through the course of this study, the following objectives will be completed:

RQ1: To identify the technology adoption theories that are the most suitable to study the behavioral intentions of people to adopt emerging technologies in the pharmaceutical sector.

RQ2: Formulation of criteria based on which the selection and assessment of these models are to be done using different multiple criteria decision-making methods.

RQ3: To analyze and compare the results obtained from multiple MCDM techniques and state the best fit model obtained from all the methods.

9.2 Literature Review

The methodology to review the papers applies a systematic way to extract insights from the literature. We performed our search for related articles, research papers, and industry reports from the following databases and platforms, with relevant keywords using SCOPUS, Web of Science, Google Scholar, Research Gate, and IEEE Xplore. A systematic review based on the following rigorous screening process: a time frame, abstract relevance, and paper title culminating in a collection of studies contributing to Industry 4.0, technology adoption, and MCDM methodologies.

This study used a set of keywords that best captured technology adoption in industry 4.0. Assisted by the following, we assembled relevant words to fit our subject: "Technology Adoption", "Industry 4.0", "Multi Criteria Decision-Making", "Technology Adoption Theories", and "Attributes and Criteria Important for Adoption of Technology". The identified areas of importance are guided by the following key terminologies to ensure there is an effective alignment of the search efforts for the following study.

9.2.1 MCDM Approaches

This study employs Multi-Criteria Decision Making (MCDM) methods to select the most suitable technology adoption model. To support this, we reviewed literature where MCDM techniques were utilized to choose among various alternatives. The literature indicates that MCDM methods, such as Evaluation based on Distance from Average Solution (EDAS), Technique for Order of Preference by Similarity to Ideal Solution (TOPSIS), and Measurement Alternatives and Ranking according to Compromise (MARCOS), have been effectively applied in various fields. These methods assist in systematically evaluating multiple criteria to make informed decisions (Chakraborty et al., 2024). By integrating quantitative and qualitative factors, MCDM techniques provide a comprehensive framework for decision-making, ensuring a balanced and robust selection process. Selection of methods that align with the study's specific context, considering both the advantages and limitations of previous methods, is required to ensure a comprehensive analysis tailored to the complexities of Pharma 4.0 technology adoption. In this study we have chosen six different MCDM approaches to analyze and compare the results in order to find out the best fit model.

9.2.2 *Technology Adoption Theories*

The Theories/Methodologies as their name suggests are the pillars that help to understand the factors responsible for adoption and constructive change. Industries use theories and methodologies to obtain knowledge about the technology they are about to launch and also check the compatibility of the newly launched technology (Magsamen-Conrad et al., 2019). However, it has been observed in the previous literature that the selection procedure of technology adoption models is not clearly shown while studying the adoption. Shehawy et al. (2024) studied the factors responsible for the adoption of robot-assisted retail services with the help of Technology Acceptance Model (TAM) along with the education levels and social and cultural norms of customers as mediator/moderator. The author has made commendable effort in studying the adoption of robot assistance in retail sector. However, these results can be altered with the usage of a different adoption model. In a similar study, (Teneiji et al., 2024) conducted a literature review to find out the most suitable technology adoption models to study the adoption of big-data in healthcare. The authors quoted that empirical research is lacking in this area where everyone is interested. As a result of extensive literature review, they identified seven models to be suitable for studying the adoption of big data in healthcare. However, empirical studies are still lacking in the selection of adoption models to be used. In this study, the author has aimed to bridge this gap. Table 9.1 presents a critical review of the application of these models in the adoption of different technologies done in past literature. A few of the technology adoption theories and their applications are discussed below.

9.2.2.1 Innovation Diffusion Theory (IDT)

IDT introduced by E.M. Rogers in 1962 explains how and why new ideas and practices are adopted over time. It categorizes adopters into five groups from Innovators to Laggards. The theory highlights four key elements: Innovations, Communication, Time, and Social Systems. The theory underscores that for an innovation to be successful, it must be accepted and disseminated within a social system (Aggarwal & Chanda, 2017).

9.2.2.2 Task Technology Fit (TTF)

Task Technology Fit (TTF) theory examines the relationship between technology, tasks, and individual abilities. It posits that optimal performance is achieved when there is a strong alignment between these components. TTF has been applied in domains such as knowledge work, team performance, and education, showing that better task-technology fit leads to more efficient task completion (Fuller & Dennis, 2009). However, the theory has limitations, including complex models that are difficult to test empirically, weak predictive power, and limited applicability in different

Table 9.1 Applications of technology adoption models in adoption of technologies in different sectors

Reference	Area of Study	Technology Adopted	Research Objective	Theoretical Framework	Key Findings
Mabad et al., 2021	Construction firms	RFID	Investigate factors influencing adoption of RFID	TOE and DOI	Identified barriers: Cost, lack of expertise. Facilitators: Organizational culture, management support, relative advantage.
Gangwar et al., 2015	Information technology	Cloud computing	Examine adoption patterns of cloud computing in SMEs	TAM and TOE	Barriers: Security concerns, lack of trust. Facilitators: Cost savings, scalability
Noor et al., 2024	Healthcare	Internet of things (IoT)	Explore factors influencing adoption of IoT	UTAUT and TAM3	Barriers: Privacy concerns, interoperability issues. Facilitators: Improved patient care, cost savings
Wu & Yun, 2024	Financial services	Artificial intelligence (AI)	Investigate adoption of AI	TAM	Barriers: Regulatory constraints, resistance to change. Facilitators: Improved decision-making, cost reduction.
Baral et al., 2023	Retail	Blockchain	Assess factors influencing adoption of blockchain technology	TOE	Barriers: Lack of standards, complexity. Facilitators: Improved transparency, reduced costs.
Pinho et al., 2020	Education	Educational technology	Investigate adoption of educational technology in K-12 schools	IDT	Barriers: Lack of training, resistance to change. Facilitators: Personalized learning, student engagement.

(continued)

Table 9.1 (continued)

Reference	Area of Study	Technology Adopted	Research Objective	Theoretical Framework	Key Findings
Zhou et al., 2010	Banking	Mobile banking	To propose a mobile banking user adoption model	TTF and UTAUT	Performance expectancy, task technology fit, social influence, and facilitating conditions significantly affect user adoption; task technology fit significantly affects performance expectancy.
Kamble et al., 2018	Supply chain	Blockchain	To understand user perceptions on the adoption of Blockchain technology in supply chains	TAM, TRI, TPB	The constructs of TRI have a minimal influence on perceived ease of use and perceived usefulness. However, perceived usefulness, attitude, and perceived behavioral control significantly affect behavioral intention, while the subjective norm has a limited impact.

contexts. Despite these challenges, TTF remains valuable for understanding how well technology supports specific tasks and individual capabilities, thereby enhancing overall performance (Lee et al., 2007).

9.2.2.3 Technology Acceptance Model (TAM)

The Technology Acceptance Model (TAM), developed by Fred Davis in 1986, identifies two primary factors influencing an individual's intention to adopt technology: perceived usefulness and perceived ease of use. Perceived usefulness is the belief that technology enhances performance, while perceived ease of use refers to the simplicity of using the technology. TAM suggests that these factors shape attitudes toward technology, which in turn determine the actual usage. In educational settings, for example, mobile devices are seen as useful for accessing academic resources and facilitating learning, while their ease of use encourages widespread adoption (Yuen et al., 2020). TAM's simplicity and focus on user perceptions make it a widely applied model for studying technology adoption (Lee et al., 2006).

9.2.2.4 Technology Organization Environment (TOE)

TOE framework explains how technology adoption is influenced by technological, organizational, and environmental factors. Technological factors include the technology's functionality, complexity, compatibility, and learning curve. Organizational factors encompass the internal context, such as company size, structure, and resources. Environmental factors involve external influences like market trends, regulatory requirements, and cultural aspects. TOE provides a holistic view of technology adoption, allowing for comprehensive analysis across diverse contexts. Its flexibility makes it applicable to various technologies and organizational settings (Bradford et al., 2014; Yeh et al., 2014). However, its broad scope can be a drawback, making it challenging to apply specifically. Despite this, TOE remains a valuable tool for understanding the multifaceted nature of technology adoption.

9.2.3 Criteria

Criteria are standards or principles by which something is judged or decided. They are the specific, measurable elements utilized to evaluate the performance, quality, or suitability of a person, process, or a product. The following criteria are taken for study and theory ranking.

- **Technological Aspect:** The criterion measures the extent to which the model accounts for technology in the model to be used in the research of technological advancements. When adopted in carrying out the research of technological advancements (TA), the relevance and usefulness of the model in current practice should bear consideration of technological issues (Langer et al., 2018; Navaz et al., 2021).
- **Suitability:** This dimension examines how well the model fits the specific needs and circumstances of its intended users. It considers the relevance and applicability of the model in addressing the unique requirements and challenges faced by the target audience. Suitability is influenced by the alignment of the model's features and capabilities with the practical demands of its users (Bottani & Rizzi, 2008; Lin et al., 2007).
- **Comprehensiveness:** The model's ability to synthesize a wide range of factors and generate a comprehensive analysis. A comprehensive model makes use of many dimensions and variables to give an all-around look at the subject matter (Toshniwal et al., 2023). The overall intention is to assure that all relevant features are brought to light in the evaluation process.
- **Robustness:** Robustness relates to the model's capability to withstand adverse conditions and tough testing. In other words, a model is strong in a case when it shows both sufficient and dependable results for most of the wide range of possible scenarios. In this kind of perspective, the models in question are going

to be valued based on their reliability and flexibility in order for them to be appreciated (Awasthi et al., 2011; Ayodele et al., 2018; Wang et al., 2004).

- **Integrity Aspect:** This dimension ensures that the model upholds principles of honesty, accuracy, and consistency. Models with a strong focus on integrity provide trustworthy and reliable assessments because they adhere to ethical standards and maintain the quality of data and processes. Recognizing and incorporating integrity factors are essential for ensuring that the model's outputs are dependable and credible, thereby fostering trust and confidence among users.
- **Complexity:** The complexity of a model is determined by the extent to which its complexity is controlled. Though comprehensiveness is required for a deep analysis, the model has to be kept user-friendly too. This criterion equally levels the balance between the need for a very detailed evaluation and for practicality and accessibility of the model, ensuring it is informative but at the same time manageable (Gecys et al., 2024; Wissuwa et al., 2022).
- **Framework:** This dimension ensures that the structure, guidelines, and methodologies underpinning the model are thoroughly integrated. Models incorporating framework dynamics offer a more structured and coherent assessment as they acknowledge that a well-defined framework, when in place, significantly influences the model's effectiveness and reliability (Miltgen et al., 2013). More realistic and applicable assessment since they recognize that human factors, when present, influence the outcome.

9.3 Methodology

9.3.1 PIPRECIA

Pivot Pairwise Relative Criteria Importance Analysis (PIPRECIA) is a decision-making methodology dealing with the study of alternative ranking and selection indices based on preference indices established by analyzing the pairwise comparisons between the best of the best (Smarandache et al., 2018). The algorithm of the PIPRECIA method is described below:

Step 1: Determine the set of criteria which will be used for evaluation.

Step 2: Set the relative significance s_j of each criterion, except the first, as follows:

$$s_j = \begin{cases} > 1 & if\ C_j > C_{j-1} \\ 1 & if\ C_j = C_{j-1} \\ < 1 & if\ C_j < C_{j-1} \end{cases} \tag{9.1}$$

Step 3: Calculate the value of coefficient k_j as follows:

$$k_j = \begin{cases} 1 & if\ j = 1 \\ 2 - s_j & if\ j > 1 \end{cases} \tag{9.2}$$

Step 4: Calculate the recalculated weight q_j as follows:

$$q_j = \begin{cases} 1 & j = 1 \\ \frac{q_{j-1}}{k_j} & j > 1 \end{cases} \tag{9.3}$$

Step 5: Determine the relative weights of the evaluation criteria W_j as follows:

$$W_j = \frac{q_j}{\sum_{k=1}^{n} q_k} \tag{9.4}$$

Where: k denotes the number of the criteria.

9.3.2 *Marcos*

MARCOS finds the best compromise solution from the preference of the stakeholders, considering the distance of each alternative to the best fit solution (Koohathongsumrit & Chankham, 2023). The algorithm of Marcos method is described below:

Step 1: Initial matrix is constructed according to the following formula:

$$X = \begin{bmatrix} x_{11} & \dots & x_{1n} \\ x_{21} & \vdots & x_{2n} \\ x_{m*l} & \dots & x_{m*n} \end{bmatrix} \tag{9.5}$$

Where, m is the number of options, n is the number of criteria, and x_{mn} is the value of the n criterion in m.

Step 2: Construct an expanded matrix by adding an ideal alternative (AI) and the anti-ideal alternative (AAI).

$$X = \begin{matrix} AAI \\ A_1 \\ AI \end{matrix} \begin{bmatrix} x_{aa1} & \dots & x_{aan} \\ x_{11} & \vdots & x_{1n} \\ x_{ai1} & \dots & x_{ain} \end{bmatrix} \tag{9.6}$$

In which: $AAI = \min(x_{ij}); i = 1, 2, \ldots, m; j = 1, 2, \ldots, n$ if j is the larger the better.

$AAI = \min(x_{ij}); i = 1, 2, \ldots, m; j = 1, 2, \ldots, n,$ if j is the smaller the better.

$AI = \max(x_{ij}); i = 1, 2, \ldots, m; j = 1, 2, \ldots, n,$ if j is the larger the better.

Step 3: Normalize the expanded initial matrix.

$$n_{ij} = \frac{x_{AI}}{x_{ij}} \quad ij\ j \text{ is the smaller the better} \tag{9.7}$$

$$n_{ij} = \frac{x_{ij}}{x_{AI}} \quad ij\ j\ is\ the\ larger\ the\ better \tag{9.8}$$

Step 4: Building a normalized matrix multiplying the weights of the criteria.

$$v_{ij} = n_{ij} * w_j \tag{9.9}$$

where w_j is the weight of the criterion j.

Step 5: Calculating coefficients K_i^+ and K_i^- according to the formula.

$$\mathrm{K_i^-} = \frac{\mathrm{S_i}}{\mathrm{S_{AAI}}} \tag{9.10}$$

$$K_i^+ = \frac{S_i}{S_{AI}} \tag{9.11}$$

In which: S_i, S_{AAI} and S_{AI} are the sums of the values of v_{ij}, x_{aai}, and x_{ai}, respectively, where $i = 1, 2,.., m$.

Step 6: Calculate the functions $f(K_i^+)$ and $f(K_i^-)$ according to the formula.

$$f\left(K_i^-\right) = \frac{K_i^+}{K_i^+ + K_i^i} \tag{9.12}$$

$$f\left(K_i^+\right) = \frac{K_i^-}{K_i^+ + K_i^i} \tag{9.13}$$

Step 7: Calculating the function $f\ (Ki)$:

$$f(K_i) = \frac{K_i^+ + K_i^-}{1 + \frac{1-f(K_i^+)}{f(K_i^+)} + \frac{1-f(K_i^-)}{f(K_i^-)}} \tag{9.14}$$

Alternatives are ranked on the basis of $f\ (Ki)$ higher the better.

9.3.3 ELECTRE

ELECTRE focuses on the pair-wise comparison of alternatives, and the poorest qualities from these comparisons are eliminated, i.e., those not satisfying a set of minimum criteria (Zhong & Yao, 2017). The Steps of the ELECTRE method are described below:

Step 1: Normalize the Decision Matrix:

$$X = \begin{bmatrix} x_{11} & \dots & x_{1*m} \\ \vdots & \ddots & \vdots \\ x_{n1} & \dots & x_{m*n} \end{bmatrix}_{n*m} \tag{9.15}$$

Step 2: Assign weights to the Normalized Matrix (V):

$$v_{ij} = w_j \times r_{ij} \tag{9.16}$$

Step 3: Determine the (C_{kl} (Concordance) and D_{kl} (Discordance): $l \neq k$) sets for each pair of alternatives.

v11 < v21; v12 < v22; v13 ≥ v23; v14 ≥ v24; v15 ≥ v25; v16 ≥ v26.

Generally, the concordance and discordance sets are:

$$C_{kl} = \{j | v_{kj} \geq v_{lj}\} \tag{9.17}$$

$$D_{kl} = \{j | v\_kj < v\_lj \} = J - C\_kl \tag{9.18}$$

Step 4: Constructing the Concordance Matrix, the concordance, and discordance sets identified earlier are utilized. The concordance index is then determined by summing the weights linked to the elements within the concordance set.

$$C = \begin{bmatrix} - & c_{12} & \dots & c_{1n} \\ c_{21} & \vdots & \dots & c_{2m} \\ c_{m1} & \dots & c_{m(m-1)} & - \end{bmatrix} \tag{9.19}$$

Step 5: Constructing the Discordance Matrix emphasizes the extent to which one alternative is inferior to another, based on pairs of alternatives. To quantify this, the discordance index is computed as below:

$$d_{kl} = \frac{\max_{j \in D_{kl}} | v_{kj} - v_{lj} |}{\max_{j \in J} | v_{kj} - v_{lj} |} \tag{9.20}$$

$$D = \begin{bmatrix} - & d_{12} & \dots & d_{1n} \\ d_{21} & - & \dots & d_{2m} \\ d_{m1} & \vdots & d_{m(m-1)} & - \end{bmatrix} \tag{9.21}$$

Step 6: Determining the Concordance Index:

$$\overline{c} = \sum_{k=1}^{m} \sum_{l=1}^{m} \frac{c_{kl}}{m(m-1)} \tag{9.22}$$

Step 7: Determining the Discordance Index:

$$\overline{d} = \sum_{k=1}^{m}\sum_{l=1}^{m} \frac{d_{kl}}{m(m-1)} \tag{9.23}$$

Step 8: Aggregate Dominance Matrix:

$$e_{kl} = f_{kl} \times g_{kl} \tag{9.24}$$

So, the elements of the aggregate dominance matrix can have just zero or one value for k $\neq$ 1.

Step 9: Eliminating the Less Favorable Alternatives.

If $e_{kl} = 1$; for both concordance and discordance criteria A_k are preferred overA_i.

9.3.4 Codas

CODAS method evaluates the compromises in such a way as their Euclidean distance from a negative ideal solution, seeking to find the most different or distinct choice (Ghorabaee et al., 2016). The algorithm of the CODOS method is described below:

Step 1: The decision-making matrix () for CODOS method is constructed as shown below:

$$X = \left[x_{ij}\right]_{n*m} = \begin{bmatrix} x_{11}\ x_{12} \cdots & x_{1m} \\ x_{21}\ x_{22}\ \ \vdots & x_{2m} \\ x_{n1}\ x_{n2} \cdots & x_{nm} \end{bmatrix} \tag{9.25}$$

Where, x_{ij} $(x_{ij} \geq 0)$ denotes the performance value of $_{th}$ alternative on $_{th}$ criterion (∈ {1, 2, …, } and ∈ {1,2, …, }).

Step 2: Formulating normalized matrix:

$$n_{ij} = \begin{cases} \frac{x_{ij}}{\max_i x_{ij}}, \mathit{for\ benefit\ criteria} \\ \frac{\min_i x_{ij}}{x_{ij}},\ \ \mathit{for\ cost\ criteria} \end{cases} \tag{9.26}$$

Step 3: Weighted normalized matrix is formulated.

$$r_{ij} = w_j n_{ij} \tag{9.27}$$

Where $(0 < wj < 1)$ denotes the weights of j_{th} criterion, and $\sum w_j = 1$ j=1.

Step 4: Negative-ideal solution is determined as follows:

$$ns_j = \min_i r_{ij} \tag{9.28}$$

Step 5: Calculate the Euclidean and Taxicab distances of alternatives.

$$E_i = \sqrt{\sum_{j=1}^{m} \left(r_{ij} - ns_j\right)^2} \tag{9.29}$$

$$T_i = \sum_{j=1}^{m} \mid r_{ij} - ns_j \mid \tag{9.30}$$

Step 6: Construct the relative assessment matrix, shown as follows:

$$Ra = \lceil h_{ik} \rceil_{n*m} \tag{9.31}$$

$$h_{ik} = (E_i - E_k) + (\varphi(E_i - E_k) * (T_i - T_k)) \tag{9.32}$$

$$\varphi(x) = \begin{Bmatrix} 0 & if\ |x| \geq \tau \\ 1 & if\ |x| < \tau \end{Bmatrix} \tag{9.33}$$

Here, the value of threshold parameter τ is considered 0.02 to check the difference between Euclidean distances of two alternatives.

Step 7: Assessment score of each alternative is calculated as below:

$$H_i = \sum_{k=1}^{m} H_{ik} \tag{9.34}$$

Step 8: Rank the alternatives based on the descending order of their assessment scores ($\mathrm{H_i}$). The alternative with the highest $\mathrm{H_i}$ value represents the optimal choice among the available options.

9.3.5 EDAS

The EDAS method calculates the average solution for criteria and evaluates alternative compromises as their relative distance from this average, balancing between the extremes (Ghorabaee et al., 2017). The algorithm of EDAS method is discussed below.

Step 1: Evaluation matrix is constructed.

$$R = \left[\delta_{ij}^{r}\right]_{m*n} = \begin{matrix} A_1 \\ A_2 \\ A_m \end{matrix} \begin{bmatrix} \delta_{11}^{r} & \delta_{12}^{r} & \ldots \delta_{1n}^{r} \\ \delta_{21}^{r} & \delta_{22}^{r} & \ldots \delta^{r}{}_{2n} \\ & & . \\ & & . \\ & & . \\ \delta_{m1}^{r} & \delta_{m2}^{r} & \ldots \delta_{mm}^{r} \end{bmatrix} \tag{9.35}$$

Where, δ_{ij} denotes the Performance value of ith alternative on jth criteria.

Step 2: Determining average solution for each criteria:

$$AV = \left[AV_j\right]_{1\times m} \tag{9.36}$$

Where,

$$AV_j = \frac{\sum_{i=1}^{n} \delta_{ij}}{n} \tag{9.37}$$

Step 3: According to the results of AV, we can compute the positive and negative distance from average:

$$PDA_{ij} = \left\lceil PDA_{ij}\right\rceil_{m*n} = \frac{\max\left(0, \left(\delta_{ij}' - AV_j\right)\right)}{AV_j} \tag{9.38}$$

$$NDA_{ij} = \left\lceil NDA_{ij}\right\rceil_{m*n} = \frac{\max\left(0, \left(AV_j - \delta_{ij}'\right)\right)}{AV_j} \tag{9.39}$$

For cost criteria:

$$PDA_{ij} = \left\lceil PDA_{ij}\right\rceil_{m*n} = \frac{\max\left(0, \left(AV_j - \delta_{ij}'\right)\right)}{AV_j} \tag{9.40}$$

$$NDA_{ij} = \left\lceil NDA_{ij}\right\rceil_{m*n} = \frac{\max\left(0, \left(\delta_{ij}' - AV_j\right)\right)}{AV_j} \tag{9.41}$$

Step 4: Calculate the values of SP_i and SN_i.

$$SP_i = \sum_{i=1}^{n} w_j PDA_{ij}, NP_i = \sum_{i=1}^{n} w_j NDA_{ij} \tag{9.42}$$

Step 5: The results of step 4 can be normalized as:

$$NSP_i = \frac{SP_i}{\max_i(SP_i)} \tag{9.43}$$

$$NSN_i = 1 - \frac{SN_i}{\max_i(SN_i)} \tag{9.44}$$

Step 6: Compute the values of appraisal score.

$$AS_i = \frac{1}{2}(NSP_1 + NSN_i) \tag{9.45}$$

Where, $0 \leq AS\_i \leq 1$.

Step 7: Alternatives rankings are done on the basis of decreasing values of appraisal score.

9.3.6 TOPSIS

TOPSIS is a decision-making method that evaluates alternatives based on their proximity to an ideal solution and a nadir (worst) solution. This approach allows for the ranking of each alternative, facilitating a straightforward ranking system (Wu & Liu, 2011).

Step 1: Formulate a decision matrix and determine criteria weights.

Step 2: Compute the normalized interval decision matrix. The normalized values n_{ij} are calculated as:

$$n_{ij} = \frac{x_{ij}}{\sqrt{\sum_{i=1}^{m}\left(\left(x_{ij}\right)^2 + \left(x_{ij}\right)^2\right)}}, for\ i = 1 \ldots m; j = 1 \ldots n \tag{9.46}$$

Step 3: Find the weighted normalized interval decision matrix. The weighted normalized values v_{ij}^{+} *and* v_{ij}^{-} are calculated as:

$$v_{ij} = w_j n_{ij\ for\ i=1\ldots m, j=1\ldots n} \tag{9.47}$$

$$\overline{v}_{ij} = w_j \overline{\mathrm{n}}_{\mathrm{ij}\ \mathrm{for\ i=1\ldots m, j=1\ldots n}} \tag{9.48}$$

Where, w_j is the weight of the j_{th} criteria.

Step 4: Determine the positive ideal and negative ideal solutions.

$$A^{+} = \left(v_1^{+},\ v_2^{+}, \ldots v_n^{+}\right) = \left(\left(\max \overline{v}_{ij} | j \in I\right), \left(\min v_{-ij} | j \in J\right)\right) \tag{9.49}$$

$$A^{-} = \left(v_1^{-},\ v_2^{-}, \ldots v_n^{-}\right) = \left(\left(\min_{-ij} v \mid j \in I\right), \left(\max \overline{v}_{ij} \mid j \in J\right)\right) \tag{9.50}$$

Where "I" is associated with benefit criteria and "J" with cost criteria.

Step 5: Separation measures are then computed from the positive ideal and negative ideal solution as:

$$d_i^{+} = \sqrt{\sum_{j=1}^{n}\left(\underset{-ij}{v} -- v_j^{+}\right)^2 + \sum_{j=1}^{n}\left(\overline{v}_{ij} -- v_j^{+}\right)^2},\ i = 1, 2, ..m \tag{9.51}$$

Step 6: Relative closeness to the positive ideal solution is defined as:

$$R_i = \frac{\mathrm{d}_i^{-}}{d_i^{-} + d_i^{+}},\ i = 1, 2, ..m \tag{9.52}$$

Where, $0 \leq \mathrm{R_i} \leq 1$.

Step 7: Select the alternative closest to 1 or Rank on the basis of preference order.

9.4 Results

9.4.1 Expert Ratings

In the present changing and increasingly complex business world, decision-makers, mainly at the higher level, often come across multi-dimensional problems, where the consideration of multiple criteria and alternatives had to be done carefully. This complexity has led to various tools and techniques in decision-making, including multiple criteria decision methods (MCDM), an effective framework for assessing and ranking the available alternatives based on the set-out criteria. We have chosen some MCDM methods as mentioned above.

To assess the alternatives based on the criteria outlined in Sect. 2.3, a survey form was issued to the experts which were chosen from industry and academia. Ideally the number of experts should depend upon the different areas discussed in the survey questionnaire, assuming that one person is an expert mostly in one area. We have used this method to identify the number of experts for our study. One of our experts was a director in an institute with a strong research background, Expert 2 was a professor with about 28 years of experience, and the third expert was from pharmaceutical industry, working at the position of general manager with over 22 years of experience. Chosen experts were very experienced professionals and had deep knowledge of areas like Industry 4.0, technology adoption models, and human behavioral studies. Experts were asked to fill the responses in the separate Google Sheets and forms shared with them. Upon collection of ratings from the experts, these were compiled and analyzed with the help of MCDM methods. The analysis's findings are shown in the section below.

Following are the five alternatives:

1. IDT (Innovation Diffusion Theory).
2. TTF (Task Technology Fit).
3. TAM (Technology Acceptance Model).
4. TOE (Technology Organization Environment).
5. TAM2 (Extended Technology Acceptance Model).

Criteria used to rank the above-mentioned alternatives are:

1. Technological aspect.
2. Suitability.
3. Comprehensiveness.
4. Framework.
5. Integrity.
6. Robustness.
7. Complexity.

9.4.1.1 Ratings by Experts

A survey questionnaire was circulated with the experts. They provided ratings across several criteria: technological aspect, suitability, comprehensiveness, framework, integrity, robustness, and complexity. All these criteria were explained to the experts before the start of the questionnaire. Ratings were collected on a 9-point linguistic scale coded from IL-insignificantly little to C-completely agree. A 9-point scale provides a wide range for the experts to rate the relationship between the criteria and the attributes and also helps identifying the results after analysis clearly. The criteria chosen for analysis were also explained in the survey questionnaire shared with the experts so as to maintain the consistency of understanding. Ratings obtained from expert 1 are presented in Table 9.2.

9.4.2 Calculation of Criteria Weights Using PIPRECIA Method

With the help of the methodology presented in Section 3.1, these are the final results for the PIPRECIA method for obtaining the criteria ranks. Table 9.3 shows the weights for each criteria that will be further used during the normalization step in further calculations.

Table 9.2 Ratings are given by expert 1

Decision Matrix 1	Technological aspect	Suitability	Comprehensiveness	Framework	Integrity	Robustness	Complexity
IDT	6	7	4	4	9	5	4
TTF	9	7	8	6	8	7	3
TAM	7	5	5	4	6	4	7
TAM 2	8	7	4	8	7	7	3
TOE	7	8	7	7	6	7	4

Table 9.3 Criteria weights from PIPRECIA method

S.No.	criteria	W_j^1	W_j^2	W_j^3	W_j^*	W_j
C1	Technological aspect	0.19	0.193	0.187	0.19	0.191
C2	Suitability	0.147	0.193	0.162	0.166	0.167
C3	Comprehensiveness	0.147	0.154	0.162	0.154	0.155
C4	Framework	0.117	0.119	0.125	0.12	0.121
C5	Integrity	0.147	0.132	0.125	0.134	0.135
C6	Robustness	0.147	0.12	0.113	0.125	0.126
C7	Complexity	0.105	0.089	0.126	0.1054	0.106

9.4.3 Ranking of Alternatives Using MCDM

Using the formulas presented in Chap. 3 the results for alternative rankings were obtained using MCDM methods like MARCOS, TOPSIS, CODOS, ELECTRE, and EDAS. The alternative rankings obtained using these methodologies are presented in the following sub-sections.

9.4.3.1 Matrix after Geometric Mean

After evaluation and expert responses, the average of all results was taken using geometric mean. Although there are several methods of computing the average of ratings collected from the experts but geometric mean provides an advantage over basic average techniques as the results obtained are not biased towards one set of ratings as it allows for a more balanced average when data points vary significantly. The geometric mean of ratings given by experts will be used in all the MCDM approaches in this research as presented in Table 9.4.

9.4.3.2 MARCOS Method

By using Eqs. 9.5 to 9.14, we can get our final results with the MARCOS method. These results are shown in Table 9.5.

After the calculations of MARCOS methodology, we finally get the value of utility function $f(k_i)$, and on the basis of these values, we finally compute the final ranks of Alternatives. Table 9.5 shows the ranks obtained after MARCOS method calculation.

Table 9.4 Matrix after geometric mean

Decision Matrix 1	Technological aspect	Suitability	Comprehensiveness	Framework	Integrity	Robustness	Complexity
IDT	5.64	4.82	4.30	5.19	4.48	4.30	4.57
TTF	8.32	7	7.65	6.60	6.07	6.31	3.30
TAM	5.94	3.10	3.10	3.91	6.31	4	5.19
TAM 2	6.95	4.37	3.17	5.03	6.25	4.37	4.76
TOE	7.31	6.21	6.25	6.64	6	6.25	4.30

Table 9.5 MARCOS calculations

Ai	Si	Ki-	Ki+	f(K-)	f(K+)	f(Ki)	Rank
Innovation diffusion theory (IDT)	0.68	1.17	0.68	0.36	0.63	0.56	4
Task technology fit (TTF)	0.99	1.71	0.99	0.36	0.63	0.81	1
Technical adoption model (TAM)	0.62	1.07	0.62	0.36	0.63	0.51	5
Extended technical adoption model (TAM2)	0.71	1.23	0.71	0.36	0.63	0.58	3
Technology organization environment (TOE)	0.89	1.54	0.89	0.36	0.63	0.74	2

9.4.3.3 TOPSIS Method

By using Eqs. 9.46–9.52, the rankings using the TOPSIS method were obtained. Table 9.6 shows the TOPSIS method calculation. Section 3.6 presents the complete methodology of the TOPSIS method.

The task technology fit theory is ranked first with this method followed by technology model.

9.4.3.4 EDAS Method

Using Eqs. 9.36–9.45, the results for EDAS methodology were calculated. Table 9.7 presents the EDAS method results.

9.4.3.5 ELECTRE Method

By using Eqs. 9.15–9.24, we got our final results for this MCDM method. We have a few terminologies in this model which are discussed in detail in Sect. 3.3 (Eqs. 9.15–9.24) for understanding of those terminologies. Table 9.8 shows the concordance interval matrix results.

Table 9.9 shows the Discordance interval matrix results. Section 3 can be referred to for further explanation of Discordance interval matrix.

Table 9.10 represents the net superior value and net inferior value of the ELECTRE Methodology.

According to EDAS methodology, the ranks obtained are: Task technology fit model has the highest net superior value and the least net inferior value. Hence, it is ranked 1 followed by technology organisation environment model. The net superior value for TAM is the least, and the net inferior value for this model is the highest. Hence, it is ranked last.

Table 9.6 TOPSIS calculation

Theory	Technological aspect	Suitability	Comprehensiveness	Framework	Integrity	Robustness	Complexity	S_i+	S_i-	PI	Rank
IDT	0.06	0.06	0.05	0.04	0.04	0.04	0.04	0.01	0.007	0.29	4
TTF	0.10	0.09	0.10	0.06	0.06	0.06	0.03	6.36	0.02	0.99	1
TAM	0.07	0.04	0.04	0.03	0.06	0.04	0.05	0.02	2.38	0.0008	5
TAM2	0.08	0.06	0.04	0.04	0.06	0.04	0.04	0.021	0.005	0.19	3
TOE	0.09	0.08	0.08	0.06	0.06	0.06	0.04	0.01	0.01	0.56	2

Table 9.7 Final Calculation EDAS

MODELS	Spi	Sni	NSPi	NSNi	Asi	Rank
Innovation diffusion theory (IDT)	0	0.12	0	0.46	0.23	4
Task technology fit (TTF)	0.27	0	1	1	1	1
Technical adoption model (TAM)	0.01	0.22	0.040	7.67	0.02	5
Extended technical adoption model (TAM2)	0.01	0.11	0.04	0.50	0.27	3
Technology organization environment (TOE)	0.15	0	0.55	1	0.77	2

Table 9.8 Concordance interval matrix

Theory	Innovation diffusion theory (IDT)	Task technology fit (TTF)	Technical adoption model (TAM)	Extended Technical Adoption Model (TAM2)	Technology organization environment (TOE)	SUM
Innovation diffusion theory (IDT)	0	0.1	0.56	0.44	0.1	1.2
Task technology fit (TTF)	0.88	0	0.75	0.75	0.76	3.16
Technical adoption model (TAM)	0.42	0.29	0	0.23	0.23	1.14
Extended technical adoption model (TAM2)	0.55	0.23	0.75	0	0.29	1.84
Technology organization environment (TOE)	0.88	0.23	0.75	0.63	0	2.51
SUM	2.76	0.82	0.28	2.06	1.4	9.88

9.4.3.6 CODAS Method

By using eqs. 9.24 to 9.34, we calculated the final results and conclusions for this MCDM method. We have a few terminologies in this method; which are presented in detail in Chap. 3. Table 9.11 represents the relative assessment matrix of CODAS methodology, followed by final rankings obtained with the help of Hi values obtained depicted in Table 9.12.

The Hi value obtained for TTF model is the highest and IDT model is having the least Hi value. The same can be observed in the rankings of these alternatives.

Table 9.9 Discordance Interval Matrix

Theory	Innovation diffusion theory (IDT)	Task technology fit (TTF)	Technical adoption model (TAM)	Extended Technical Adoption Model (TAM2)	Technology organization environment (TOE)	SUM
Innovation diffusion theory (IDT)	0	1	0.77	1	1	3.77
Task technology fit (TTF)	0.3	0	0.33	0.25	0.57	1.46
Technical adoption model (TAM)	1	1	0	1	1	4
Extended technical adoption model (TAM2)	0.82	1	0.25	0	1	3.07
Technology organization environment (TOE)	0.11	1	0.21	0.11	0	1.43
SUM	2.23	3	0.79	1.37	2.57	13.76

Table 9.10 Electre method's net superior value.

THEORY	NET SUPERIOR VALUE	RANK	NET INFERIOR VALUE	RANK
Innovation diffusion theory (IDT)	−1.546	4	1.54	4
Task technology fit (TTF)	2.346	1	−1.53	1
Technical adoption model (TAM)	−1.684	5	3.2	5
Extended technical adoption model (TAM2)	−0.221	3	1.7	3
Technology organization environment (TOE)	1.105	2	−1.13	2

The Hi value for technical adoption model is higher in this case as compared with innovation diffusion theory. Hence, IDT model is ranked at the last in this model.

Table 9.11 CODAS Methods

THEORY	Innovation diffusion theory (IDT)	Task technology fit (TTF)	Technical adoption model (TAM)	Extended Technical Adoption Model (TAM2)	Technology organization environment (TOE)
IDT	0	−0.09	−0.01	−0.03	−0.06
TTF	0.09	0	0.07	0.05	0.02
TAM	0.01	−0.07	0	−0.02	−0.04
TAM2	0.03	−0.05	0.02	0	−0.02
TOE	0.06	−0.02	0.04	0.02	0

Table 9.12 CODAS Method's Hi value

Model	Hi	RANK
Innovation diffusion theory (IDT)	−0.2	5
Task technology fit (TTF)	0.25	1
Technical adoption model (TAM)	−0.13	4
Extended technical adoption model (TAM2)	−0.01	3
Technology organization environment (TOE)	0.1	2

9.5 Discussion

In a general sense, the research was directed to make the following challenges regarding the choice of appropriate technology adoption theories for the pharmaceutical industry in this era of rapidly growing technologies of Industry 4.0, such as AI, IoT, and blockchain. There arises a pressing need for an effective method of selection, as the implications are very high, relating to privacy, security, and technology familiarity, especially in a field where organizational and patient trust have very deep roots. This study proposes a structured approach, with the help of MCDM techniques, to be applied for the analysis of technology adoption models of different studies. Table 9.13 depicts aggregate ranks of the alternatives.

The comparison of results obtained from the MCDM methods used is depicted in graphical form in Fig. 9.1. This can be clearly seen that with all the methods used, the

Table 9.13 Final ranking

Adoption Theory	Rank
Task technology fit (TTF)	1
Technology organization environment (TOE)	2
Extended technical adoption model (TAM2)	3
Innovation diffusion theory (IDT)	4
Technical adoption model (TAM)	5

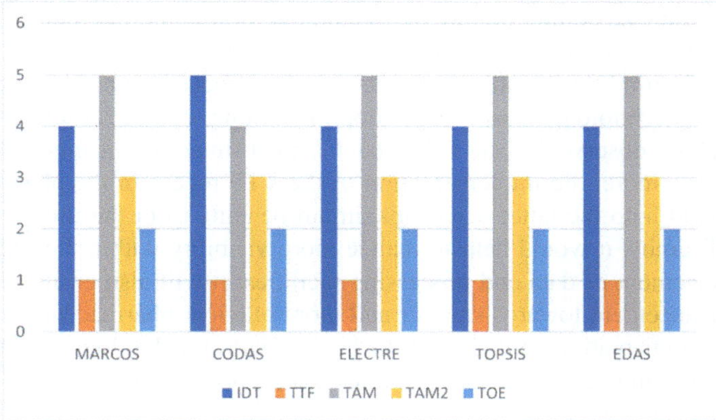

Fig. 9.1 Comparison of rankings obtained by different methods

task technology fit model is ranked first. The results obtained from CODAS method are slightly different from other approaches.

Following is the highlight of some of the MCDM methods that are found suitable for our analysis through rigorous literature review: MARCOS, PIPRECIA, EDAS, ELECTRE, TOPSIS, and CODAS. This was subsequently used for establishing the criteria such as Technological Aspect, Robustness, Comprehensiveness, Suitability, framework, Integrity, and Complexity to evaluate different technology adoption theories. Against these established criteria, all these theories were evaluated by a panel of three experts. Therefore, the collected expert rankings were processed by the selected MCDM methods. All the methods in this study showed that the synthesis of these assessments indicated that TTF scored the highest, meaning it's the best model suitable for this study. This model is especially useful for Industry 4.0 adoption in the Indian pharmaceutical sector since it stresses the alignment of technology with specific activities, resulting in improved performance outcomes. Unlike other technology adoption models, TTF focuses on the technology's practical fit and usability in the operational context, making it better suited to increasing productivity and efficiency in this highly regulated and task-specific business.

9.6 Conclusion and Implications

This study highlights how it is of vital importance to associate technological capabilities with current activities in the pharmaceutical industry to maximize operational efficiencies and handle concerns of critical security and privacy. The innovative approach of the study using MCDM techniques to make an objective assessment among models that differ widely in their philosophy, purpose, and complexity surely adds great value to the literature, as it brings a structured methodology into technology theory selection that could be applied and adopted for use in other sectors facing the same challenges. All the models ranked TTF and TOE model at the highest as our survey was focused on including a model which is focusing on the psychological as well as the technological aspects of adoption. Along with the criteria defined for this research we observe that the TTF model is most suited for the targeted adoption study. What is more, the implementation of the TTF model in the pharmaceutical industry could help the latter derive maximum benefits from the use of i4.0 technologies. Thereby, it would help to realize more visibility within the industry and better management of data and processing facilities. It will also ensure a balanced form of advancement towards smarter and more efficient pharmaceutical practices by securing human alignment, so that the human part of technology adoption is not sidelined. The findings of this study indicate that the Task Technology Fit (TTF) model is the most effective framework for facilitating technology adoption in the pharmaceutical industry. These results can guide future researchers in employing the TTF model when investigating technology adoption within the pharmaceutical sector. Additionally, this research offers a comprehensive approach for selecting alternatives based on specific criteria. The detailed explanation of various MCDM methods provided in this study will enhance researchers' understanding of these methodologies.

References

Aggarwal, R., & Chanda, U. (2017). Optimal duration of advertising campaigns for successive technology generations using innovation diffusion theory. *International Journal of Operational Research, 28*, 415. https://doi.org/10.1504/ijor.2017.081913

Al-Khatib, A. W. (2023). The impact of industrial internet of things on sustainable performance: The indirect effect of supply chain visibility. *Business Process Management Journal, 29*, 1607–1629. https://doi.org/10.1108/bpmj-03-2023-0198

Awasthi, A., Chauhan, S. S., & Omrani, H. (2011). Application of fuzzy TOPSIS in evaluating sustainable transportation systems. *Expert Systems with Applications, 38*, 12270–12280. https://doi.org/10.1016/j.eswa.2011.04.005

Ayodele, T. R., Ogunjuyigbe, A. S. O., Odigie, O., & Munda, J. L. (2018). A multi-criteria GIS based model for wind farm site selection using interval type-2 fuzzy analytic hierarchy process: The case study of Nigeria. *Applied Energy, 228*, 1853–1869. https://doi.org/10.1016/j.apenergy.2018.07.051

Baral, M. M., Chittipaka, V., Pal, S. K., Mukherjee, S., & Shyam, H. (2023). Investigating the factors of blockchain technology influencing food retail supply chain management: A study using TOE framework. *Statistics in Transition, 24*(5), 129–146. https://doi.org/10.59170/stattrans-2023-067

Benn, R., & Shaw, A. (2021). Examining the barriers to accepting big health data from a health marketeer's perspective. *Health Marketing Quarterly, 40*, 1–18. https://doi.org/10.1080/07359683.2021.1994115

Bottani, E., & Rizzi, A. (2008). Economical assessment of the impact of RFID technology and EPC system on the fast-moving consumer goods supply chain. *International Journal of Production Economics, 112*, 548–569. https://doi.org/10.1016/j.ijpe.2007.05.007

Bradford, M., Earp, J. B., & Grabski, S. (2014). Centralized end-to-end identity and access management and ERP systems: A multi-case analysis using the technology organization environment framework. *International Journal of Accounting Information Systems, 15*, 149–165. https://doi.org/10.1016/j.accinf.2014.01.003

Chakraborty, S., Raut, R. D., Rofin, T. M., & Chakraborty, S. (2024). On solving a healthcare supplier selection problem using MCDM methods in intuitionistic fuzzy environment. *Opsearch*. https://doi.org/10.1007/s12597-023-00733-1

Dhiman, A., & Madan, P. (2024). Revolutionizing Pharma: Prioritizing industry 4.0 implementation challenges in the Indian pharmaceutical landscape through analytical hierarchy process analysis. *Journal of Pharmaceutical Innovation, 19*. https://doi.org/10.1007/s12247-024-09849-3

Fuller, R. M., & Dennis, A. R. (2009). Does fit matter? The impact of task-technology fit and appropriation on team performance in repeated tasks. *Information Systems Research, 20*, 2–17. https://doi.org/10.1287/isre.1070.0167

Ghorabaee, M. K., Zavadskas, E. K., Turskis, Z., & Antucheviciene, J. (2016). A new combinative distance-based assessment (codas) method for multi-criteria decision-making. *Economic Computation and Economic Cybernetics Studies and Research, 50*, 25–44.

Ghorabaee, M. K., Amiri, M., Zavadskas, E. K., et al. (2017). A new multi-criteria model based on interval type-2 fuzzy sets and EDAS method for supplier evaluation and order allocation with environmental considerations. *Computers & Industrial Engineering, 112*, 156–174. https://doi.org/10.1016/j.cie.2017.08.017

Hassani, H., Huang, X., & MacFeely, S. (2022). Impactful digital twin in the healthcare revolution. *Big Data and Cognitive Computing, 6*, 83. https://doi.org/10.3390/bdcc6030083

Koohathongsumrit, N., & Chankham, W. (2023). Route selection in multimodal supply chains: A fuzzy risk assessment model-BWM-MARCOS framework. *Applied Soft Computing, 137*, 110167. https://doi.org/10.1016/j.asoc.2023.110167

Lee, C.-C., Cheng, H. K., & Cheng, H.-H. (2007). An empirical study of mobile commerce in insurance industry: Task–technology fit and individual differences. *Decision Support Systems, 43*, 95–110. https://doi.org/10.1016/j.dss.2005.05.008

Lee, H., Fiore, A. M., & Kim, J. (2006). The role of the technology acceptance model in explaining effects of image interactivity technology on consumer responses. *International Journal of Retail & Distribution Management, 34*, 621–644. https://doi.org/10.1108/09590550610675949

Ma, S., Huang, Y., Cai, W., et al. (2024). Integrated sustainable benchmark based on edge-cloud cooperation and big data analytics for energy-intensive manufacturing industries. *Journal of Manufacturing Systems, 74*, 1037–1056. https://doi.org/10.1016/j.jmsy.2024.05.010

Mabad, T., Ali, O., Ally, M., Wamba, S. F., & Chan, K. C. (2021). Making investment decisions on RFID technology: An evaluation of key adoption factors in construction firms. *IEEE Access, 9*, 36937–36954. https://doi.org/10.1109/access.2021.3063301

Magsamen-Conrad, K., Wang, F., Tetteh, D., & Lee, Y.-I. (2019). Using technology adoption theory and a lifespan approach to develop a theoretical framework for eHealth literacy: Extending UTAUT. *Health Communication, 35*, 1435–1446. https://doi.org/10.1080/10410236.2019.1641395

Miltgen, C. L., Popovic, A., & Oliveira, T. (2013). Determinants of end-user acceptance of biometrics: Integrating the "big 3" of technology acceptance with privacy context. *Decision Support Systems, 56*, 103–114. https://doi.org/10.1016/j.dss.2013.05.010

Noor, B. D., Katheeth, Z. D., & Noor, A. D. (2024). Internet of things in public healthcare organizations: The mediating role of attitude. *IAES International Journal of Artificial Intelligence, 13*(1), 57. https://doi.org/10.11591/ijai.v13.i1.pp57-65

Özdağoğlu, A., Acar, E., Güner, M., & Bakadur, A. Ç. (2024). Applications of MCDM methods for the assessment of sustainable development: A case study of fashion textile group. *Management of Environmental Quality an International Journal, 35*, 1028–1047. https://doi.org/10.1108/meq-05-2023-0147

Pamucar, D., Ecer, F., & Deveci, M. (2021, September). Assessment of alternative fuel vehicles for sustainable road transportation of United States using integrated fuzzy FUCOM and neutrosophic fuzzy MARCOS methodology. *Science of the Total Environment, 788*, 147763. https://doi.org/10.1016/j.scitotenv.2021.147763

Gangwar, H., Date, H., & Ramaswamy, R. (2015 Feb 9). Understanding determinants of cloud computing adoption using an integrated TAM-TOE model. *Journal of enterprise information management., 28*(1), 107–130.
Gecys, T., Tupenaite, L., Kanapeckiene, L., & Naimaviciene, J. (2024). Multi-criteria assessment of timber-based structural Systems for a Grocery Store. *Buildings, 14*, 1335. https://doi.org/10.3390/buildings14051335
Kamble, S., Gunasekaran, A., & Arha, H. (2018). Understanding the Blockchain technology adoption in supply chains-Indian context. *International Journal of Production Research, 57*(7), 2009–2033. https://doi.org/10.1080/00207543.2018.1518610
Langer, K., Decker, T., Roosen, J., & Menrad, K. (2018). Factors influencing citizens' acceptance and non-acceptance of wind energy in Germany. *Journal of Cleaner Production, 175*, 133–144. https://doi.org/10.1016/j.jclepro.2017.11.221
Lin, H.-Y., Hsu, P.-Y., & Sheen, G.-J. (2007). A fuzzy-based decision-making procedure for data warehouse system selection. *Expert Systems with Applications, 32*, 939–953. https://doi.org/10.1016/j.eswa.2006.01.031
Navaz, A. N., Serhani, M. A., Kassabi, H. T. E., et al. (2021). Trends, technologies, and key challenges in smart and connected healthcare. *IEEE Access, 9*, 74044–74067. https://doi.org/10.1109/access.2021.3079217
Pinho, C., Franco, M., & Mendes, L. (2020). Application of innovation diffusion theory to the E-learning process: Higher education context. *Education and Information Technologies, 26*, 421–440. https://doi.org/10.1007/s10639-020-10269-2
Pillai, R., & Sivathanu, B. (2020). Adoption of AI-based chatbots for hospitality and tourism. *International Journal of Contemporary Hospitality Management, 32*(10), 3199–3226. https://doi.org/10.1108/ijchm-04-2020-0259
Sahi, G. K., Gupta, M. C., & Cheng, T. C. E. (2020). The effects of strategic orientation on operational ambidexterity: A study of indian SMEs in the industry 4.0 era. *International Journal of Production Economics, 220*, 107395. https://doi.org/10.1016/j.ijpe.2019.05.014
Shehawy, Y. M., Khan, S. M. F. A., Khalufi, N. A. M., & Abdullah, R. S. (2024). Customer adoption of robot: Synergizing customer acceptance of robot-assisted retail technologies. *Journal of Retailing and Consumer Services, 82*, 104062. https://doi.org/10.1016/j.jretconser.2024.104062
Standing, S., & Standing, C. (2008). Mobile technology and healthcare: The adoption issues and systemic problems. *International Journal of Electronic Healthcare, 4*(3/4), 221. https://doi.org/10.1504/ijeh.2008.022661
Smarandache, F., Stanujkic, D., Zavadskas, E. K., et al. (2018). The use of the pivot pairwise relative criteria importance assessment method for determining the weights of criteria. *Zenodo (CERN European Organization for Nuclear Research)*. https://doi.org/10.5281/zenodo.1411312
Vanita, S., Vedant, D. (2021). Telemedicine adoption in India identifying factors affecting intention to use. *International Journal of Healthcare Information Systems and Informatics, 16*. https://doi.org/10.4018/ijhisi.20211001oa37
Teneiji, A. S. A., Salim, T. Y. A., & Riaz, Z. (2024). Factors impacting the adoption of big data in healthcare: A systematic literature review. *International Journal of Medical Informatics, 187*, 105460. https://doi.org/10.1016/j.ijmedinf.2024.105460
Toshniwal, V. P., Jain, R., Soni, G., et al. (2023). Technology adoption theories towards environmentally sustainable pharma 4.0: A rational selection approach. *Management of Environmental Quality an International Journal, 35*, 684–711. https://doi.org/10.1108/meq-08-2023-0248
Wang, G., Huang, S. H., & Dismukes, J. P. (2004). Product-driven supply chain selection using integrated multi-criteria decision-making methodology. *International Journal of Production Economics, 91*, 1–15. https://doi.org/10.1016/s0925-5273(03)00221-4
Wang, Z., He, D., & Hou, Y. (2021). Data-driven adaptive quality control under uncertain conditions for a cyber-pharmaceutical-development system. *IEEE Transactions on Industrial Informatics, 17*, 3165–3175. https://doi.org/10.1109/tii.2020.3004132

Wissuwa, F., Durach, C. F., & Choi, T. Y. (2022). Selecting resilient suppliers: Supplier complexity and buyer disruption. *International Journal of Production Economics, 253*, 108601. https://doi.org/10.1016/j.ijpe.2022.108601

Wu, M., & Liu, Z. (2011). The supplier selection application based on two methods: VIKOR algorithm with entropy method and fuzzy TOPSIS with vague sets method. *International Journal of Management Science and Engineering Management, 6*, 109–115. https://doi.org/10.1080/17509653.2011.10671152

Wu, X., & Yun, X. (2024). Navigating firm competitive performance through artificial intelligence: Moderation of ethical compliance. *International Journal of Information Systems and Change Management, 14*, 70–84. https://doi.org/10.1504/ijiscm.2024.138083

Yeh, C.-H., Lee, G.-G., & Pai, J.-C. (2014). Using a technology-organization-environment framework to investigate the factors influencing e-business information technology capabilities. *Information Development, 31*, 435–450. https://doi.org/10.1177/0266666913516027

Yuen, K. F., Cai, L., Qi, G., & Wang, X. (2020). Factors influencing autonomous vehicle adoption: An application of the technology acceptance model and innovation diffusion theory. *Technology Analysis and Strategic Management, 33*, 505–519. https://doi.org/10.1080/09537325.2020.1826423

Zhang, G., Yang, Y., & Yang, G. (2022). Smart supply chain management in industry 4.0: The review, research agenda and strategies in North America. *Annals of Operations Research, 322*, 1075–1117. https://doi.org/10.1007/s10479-022-04689-1

Zhong, L., & Yao, L. (2017). An ELECTRE I-based multi-criteria group decision making method with interval type-2 fuzzy numbers and its application to supplier selection. *Applied Soft Computing, 57*, 556–576. https://doi.org/10.1016/j.asoc.2017.04.001

Zhou, T., Lu, Y., & Wang, B. (2010 Jul 1). Integrating TTF and UTAUT to explain mobile banking user adoption. *Computers in Human Behavior, 26*(4), 760–767.

Chapter 10
An Integrated Data Analytic Approach for Achieving Operational Excellence in Supply Chain

Prasun Das and Satyaki Basu Sarbadhikary

Abstract Supply chains are quiet complex structures consisting of suppliers, manufacturers, distributors, retailers, and consumers themselves. Accordingly, this raises many issues like delays in production, logistical bottlenecks, thus causing overstock or stockouts. In order to ensure that it functions efficiently and adapt to changes in demand, supply disruptions, and other uncertainties, our study utilizes a data analytics-based approach to achieve operational excellence in a simulation environment that spans over 1-year time horizon. The proposed approach involves predicting demands using the XGBoost technique, managing inventory dynamically under stochastic demand and lead times by calculating safety stocks, reorder points, and predicting lead times through linear regression. The effectiveness of these strategies is evaluated by visualizing key performance metrics such as inventory turnover, service level, and the order fulfillment rate for each product considered in simulation process. Through this study, we aim to enhance decision-making processes in real-life supply chain management, for ensuring that enterprises maintain high service levels and meet customer demands effectively in a rapidly evolving dynamic market environment. The study also highlights on some potential research extensions as well.

Keywords Demand forecast · Stochastic lead time · Lead time demand · Inventory turnover · Service level · Order fulfilment rate · Dynamic inventory management

P. Das (✉)
SQC & OR Division, Indian Statistical Institute, Kolkata, India
e-mail: prasun@isical.ac.in

S. B. Sarbadhikary
NUS, Singapore

I. Mukherjee et al. (eds.), *Decision Sciences for Quality and Productivity Improvement*,
https://doi.org/10.1007/978-981-95-7545-9_10

10.1 Introduction

Modern industries often require complex supply chain management for sustaining an equilibrium between demand and supply, in order to enhance overall efficiency. The advent of the fourth industrial revolution along with the convergence of disruptive technologies like artificial intelligence (AI) and robotics, has increasingly blurred the traditional differences between human and machine roles. Over the past decade, this shift has rapidly transformed the area of supply chain management, reflecting a new era in industrial operations (Arrieta et al., 2019). In recent years, the concept of sustainable supply chain (SSC) has got global attention because of its inclusion of sustainability throughout its processes. Innovations in artificial intelligence (AI) have revolutionized these networks, providing new solutions to longstanding challenges faced by supply chain (SC) systems (Naz et al., 2022).

In the present demanding environment where systems are growing more complex, the need for efficient supply chains is very much essential. This study aims to optimize inventory management, reduce costs and increase service delivery in order to achieve operational excellence within a supply chain. This is done by using data-driven methodologies in conjunction with advanced machine learning techniques. Supply chains are quiet complex structures consisting of manufacturers, distributors, retailers, and the consumers themselves. Every component here has a role to play, ensuring that the products are available when and where they are needed and in quantities as per the demand. However, this complexity brings many possible issues into the scenario: from delays in production to logistical bottlenecks that will cause overstock or stockouts. These inefficiencies increase operational costs but, at the same time, degrade customer experience and service quality, which further increases the necessity for a robust and flexible supply chain.

Our approach involves the use of simulated data in modeling these uncertainties and variations embedded within supply chain's demand and lead times. By creating a synthetic dataset that mimics real-world conditions, we can test and validate our supervised machine learning models in a controlled environment. It includes the daily demand for certain products over a year, as well as corresponding lead times, taking into consideration the day-to-day fluctuations and uncertainties characteristic of supply chains. In the realm of supervised machine learning, algorithms are trained using a dataset where each entry is labelled, referred to as the training set. After training, these algorithms can then be applied to new, unseen datasets to classify data or predict outcomes based on learned patterns. Popular techniques in supervised learning encompass a variety of models such as decision trees (DT), linear regression (LR), support vector machines (SVM), k-nearest neighbors (KNN), random forests (RF), and neural networks (NN) (Bhattacharya et al., 2024). One of the key challenges in supply chains of industries is accurate demand forecasting. In certain industries, like that of healthcare, the demand for medicines can be highly variable and influenced by many factors; these may include seasonal illnesses, pandemics, and demographic changes. Normal ways of forecasting often have trouble with changes, causing wrong demand predictions that lead to running out of stock or having too much. Having too much stock ties up money and raises storage fees, while running out of items can cause important delays, especially in healthcare. To fix these problems, we use smart machine learning methods like boosting and regression for better demand forecasts. These forecasts also include lead time predictions, looking at things like production plans, shipping delays, and legal approvals.

A main part of this project is changing how we order, which updates order amounts and timing using real-time data and predictive analysis. Unlike old fixed-interval or fixed-amount methods, dynamic ordering lets supply chains—especially in healthcare—react quickly to sudden increases in demand or supply problems. This flexibility is essential to reduce having excess stock while lowering the chances of running out.

Our method also adds strategies for inventory optimization to find the best order amounts and reorder points, balancing holding costs, ordering costs, and service level goals. By combining these strategies with predictive models, we manage inventory effectively, cutting waste and boosting reliability.

To check how well it works, we look at supply chain metrics like inventory turnover, service levels, and order fulfillment rates. Tracking these metrics over time shows how our approach reaches operational success. With ongoing checking and updating, we make sure our methods help create a smooth-running, strong, and flexible supply chain.

The remainder of the sections is organized as follows. Section 10.2 provides an extensive literature review and gap analysis on the relevant research domain in respect of this study. Section 10.3 highlights the objective and plan of work for the study to attain operational excellence in the supply chain. Section 10.4 explains the preliminaries and associated methodologies undertaken in this study. Section 10.5 provides details of the data generation procedure adopted to go for analysis of the data. The detailed steps of data analytics carried out in this study are explained in Sect. 10.6. Section 10.7 involves the illustration of the results and findings achieved. Section 10.8 presents the particulars of implementation scheme, Sect. 10.9 includes a case study, and Sect. 10.10 includes challenges and mitigation strategies. Section 10.11 discusses about adoption of AI/ML in SMEs, and finally Sect. 10.12 concludes with future research directions.

10.2 Related Works

Artificial Intelligence (AI) is reshaping the healthcare supply chain, particularly through machine learning (ML) to enhance operational excellence. It puts emphasis on the SCOR model for supply chain excellence, outlining essential processes and performance measures, including PLAN, SOURCE, MAKE, DELIVER, and RETURN (Peter Bolstroff Robert Rosenbaum, 2007), which are crucial for streamlining and cost-effective distribution in healthcare supply chains. In Henningson (2009), operational excellence and key performance indicators (KPIs) in supply chain management put stress on the alignment of performance measurements with organizational goals. These KPIs can be adapted to healthcare to enhance patient care and facility operations. The integration of Artificial Intelligence (AI) and Machine Learning (ML) into supply chain management (SCM) has been extensively explored in recent literature, revealing its transformative potential to enhance operational excellence. The inclusion of AI and ML in supply chain management (SCM) helps with the increasing complexity, distribution, and clarity of modern supply chains by allowing systems that can learn, recognize situations, and make autonomous decisions. This greatly improves many aspects of SCM (Petri Helo & Yuqiuge Hao, 2022). In managing inventory, ML models such as XGBoost help in predicting demand, which cuts down on excess stock and shortages, especially aiding small to medium enterprises (SMEs) in becoming more efficient (Soumit Roy & Mainak Mitra, 2021). In the healthcare sector, ML classifiers like Random Forest and KNN improve processes like inspection, transportation, and resource allocation, leading to better cost efficiency (Soumit Roy & Mainak Mitra, 2021). Reinforcement learning techniques show promise in areas like inventory and budget planning, choosing suppliers, and promoting sustainability (Rolf et al., 2023). Genetic Algorithms (GAs) work to reduce total supply chain costs by actively managing stock levels, keeping things balanced and cost-effective (Toorajipour et al., 2021).

AI-based systems help with demand forecasting, optimizing inventory, and enhancing supply chain visibility. However, there are issues such as data quality, costs of integration, and the requirement for specialized skills, which are especially challenging for SMEs (Chaudhary et al., 2023; Javaregowda et al., 2020). Ongoing adjustment of models is vital to match the changing supply chain situation, which requires teamwork between data scientists and supply chain experts (Rolf et al., 2023). In healthcare, AI and ML boost operational efficiency but also bring up worries regarding data privacy and security (Soumit Roy & Mainak Mitra, 2021). Choosing the right algorithms is essential; reinforcement learning fits well in changing settings, while GAs are better at optimizing static inventory situations (Toorajipour et al., 2021). Decision support systems (DSS) that integrate AI and ML offer real-time analytics for enhancing the inventory management process and thus help in reducing the costs and inefficiencies resulting from erroneous demand forecasting as stated in Doborjginidze et al. (2021), Praveen and Hatim 2019). This calls for the need to develop efficient techniques to manage the large amount of supply chain data that has been growing at an ever-increasing rate, while conventional approaches are failing to meet the current SCM challenges (Tirkolaee & Sadeghi, 2021). As artificial intelligence (AI) gains prominence in various industries, its influence in academic discussions has also broadened. This expanded presence is evident across numerous disciplines, including business research, where the examination of AI has evolved to encompass a more holistic view (Toorajipour et al., 2021). Table 10.1 presents the gap analysis of all the articles discussed here with respect to some important drivers, including the scope of our work.

Table 10.1 Literature gap analysis

Paper Serial. Number (Reference)	(a) Demand Forecasting	(b) Inventory Optimization	(c) Lead Time Prediction	Combined (a), (b), (c) for achieving OPEX	Scalability and Computational Efficiency	Real-Time Data Integration and Processing	Robustness to Uncertainty and Variability
Bhattacharya et al. (2024)	Yes	Yes	No	No	No	No	No
Peter Bolstroff Robert Rosenbaum (2007)	Yes	Yes	No	No	No	No	No
Henningson (2009)	Yes	Yes	Yes	No	No	No	No
Petri Helo and Yuqiuge Hao (2022)	Yes	Yes	No	No	Partially	No	No
Soumit Roy and Mainak Mitra (2021)	Yes	Yes	Yes	No	No	No	No
Rolf et al. (2023)	Yes	Yes	No	No	No	No	No
Glock and A comment (xxxx)	Yes	Yes	No	No	No	No	No
Chaudhary et al. (2023)	Yes	Yes	Yes	No	No	No	No
Toorajipour et al. (2021)	Yes	Yes	No	No	No	No	No
Doborjginidze et al. (2021)	Yes	Yes	No	No	No	No	No

(continued)

Table 10.1 (continued)

Paper Serial. Number (Reference)	(a) Demand Forecasting	(b) Inventory Optimization	(c) Lead Time Prediction	Combined (a), (b), (c) for achieving OPEX	Scalability and Computational Efficiency	Real-Time Data Integration and Processing	Robustness to Uncertainty and Variability
Javaregowda et al. (2020)	Yes	No	No	No	No	No	No
Praveen and Hatim (2019)	Yes	Yes	No	No	No	No	No
Tirkolaee and Sadeghi (2021)	Yes	Yes	No	No	No	No	No
Toorajipour et al. (2021)	Yes	Yes	No	No	No	No	No
Our work	Yes	Yes	Yes	Yes	Yes	Yes	Yes

10.3 Objective and Plan of Work

A supply chain (SC) represents an intricate network that integrates human effort, machinery, various activities, resources, and technology to produce and distribute a product to consumers. This network spans the entire process, from sourcing raw materials or intermediate products from suppliers to the manufacturing stages, and ultimately to the distribution of the final service or product to consumers (Bassiouni et al., 2023).

Enterprises order given quantities of components (order sizes) and the orders are made a number of periods before the due dates taking into account (Hnaien et al., 2016). In recent years, the integrated production inventory problem involving a single vendor and a single buyer has garnered increasing attention. This surge in interest is largely driven by an intensified emphasis on optimizing supply chain management (Ben-Dayaa & Hariga, 2004). Businesses are recognizing the advantages of managing inventories more effectively throughout the supply chain by enhancing coordination and fostering greater cooperation, which benefits all stakeholders involved. This study presents a comprehensive approach towards achieving operational excellence in a simulated supply chain data using data analytics, machine learning by means of:

- predicting demands by using XGBoost technique;
- implementing dynamic inventory management for variable demand and variable lead time by using safety stocks (*SS*) and Reorder Point (*ROP*);
- performing lead time prediction using linear regression technique; and
- visualizing supply chain performance metrics such as inventory turnover, service level, and order fulfillment rate for each product.

10.4 Preliminaries and Methodologies

In this section, we explain some basic components of inventory management, which are used in this work under stochastic environment. The means of achieving operational excellence is also explained here along with usage and significance of some supply chain metrics to ensure the excellence about inventory management operations throughout the supply chain.

10.4.1 Safety Stock

Safety stock (*SS*) is additional inventory kept to protect against uncertainties in demand and lead time. It acts as a buffer to prevent stockouts caused by variations in these factors. Safety stock is often calculated using the desired service level (the probability of not running out of stock during lead time) and the variability of demand

and lead time. The formula for safety stock considering variable demand and lead time is:

$$SS = z \times \sqrt{(\sigma_D^2 \times \underline{L}) + (\underline{D}^2 \times \sigma_L^2)} \tag{10.1}$$

where:

- z is the z-score corresponding to the desired service level.
- σ_D is the standard deviation of demand.
- σ_L is the standard deviation of lead time.
- $\underline{D}$ is the average demand.
- $\underline{L}$ is the average lead time.

10.4.2 Reorder Point

One of the major concepts in inventory management is the Reorder Point (ROP) that sets the exact time when a new order has to be made so that the inventory is replenished before it reaches the zero level. This ensures that there is no stockout and the company can still meet the demand of the customers. The ROP helps in determining the right time to place an order so that the cost of holding excess inventory is not high while at the same time ensuring that the business does not run out of stock. Lead time demand (LTD) and safety stock (SS) are used to determine the reorder point (ROP). LTD is the total demand for a product during the lead time which is the time taken between placing an order and receiving it. The ROP defines the inventory level that triggers a purchase order for more stock before it depletes to zero. The ROP is calculated as the addition of LTD and SS.

$$ROP = (\underline{D} \times \underline{L}) + z \times \sqrt{(\sigma_D^2 \times L) + (\underline{D}^2 \times \sigma_L^2)} \tag{10.2}$$

10.4.3 Order Quantity

The order quantity (Q) is dynamically determined to ensure optimal levels of inventory. Based on the difference between the safety stock and the current inventory level, the order quantity is derived. If a product has inventory lower than its safety stock, then there is a potential risk of stockout. At these instances, a restocking order is placed on the stock. Otherwise, no purchase of that item is made, and order quantity is zero if the current inventory is higher than safety stock.

Since the safety stock acts as a cushion against lead time and demand variability to ensure a high service level perceived by the customers, when the value of inventory decreases to safety stock level, the order quantity (Q) is determined to bring the inventory to safety stock level plus expected demand over the lead time. More specifically, the order quantity is the demand during the lead time period plus the difference between safety stock and current inventory. By having enough stock on hand to meet customer demand until the next replenishment arrives, this strategy minimizes the risk of stockouts and maintains a smooth supply chain operation.

10.4.4 Operational Excellence

Optimizing inventory management and supply chain operations involves combining precise lead time prediction, accurate demand forecasting, and ideal inventory ordering. This guarantees the effective operation of the supply chain, reducing expenses and optimizing service quality (Toorajipour et al., 2021). Supply chain connection dynamics are changing dramatically in the setting of global economic integration. It appears that businesses can only successfully grow and thrive nowadays if they constantly modify their plans to take into account changes in the market. Therefore, it is essential for modern enterprises to have a smooth, effective, and economical flow of information, finances, logistics, and human resources.

10.4.4.1 Demand Forecasting

Accurate demand forecasting is crucial for predicting future demand. By using advanced models like XGBoost, we can improve the accuracy of these forecasts. These models take into account historical demand data and can capture complex patterns and trends. Mathematically, *if*D_t represents the demand at time t, then the forecast $\widehat{D_t}$ is given by:

$$\widehat{D_t} = f(D_{t-1}, D_{t-2}, \ldots, D_{t-n})$$

Here, f represents the forecasting model, which plays a pivotal role in reducing demand uncertainty—a critical factor for achieving operational excellence. For this study, XGBoost was chosen due to its robust gradient boosting framework that constructs sequential decision trees, correcting prior errors and enhancing predictive accuracy. XGBoost is particularly well-suited for demand forecasting as it can handle complex data relationships as it is capable of learning even the non-linear relationships between features. This means that it has L1 and L2 regularization, which helps in reducing the tendency of the model to overfit especially in cases where there are different demand patterns. In addition, XGBoost has capabilities for adaptive pruning of the decision tree, manages missing values effectively, and is capable of parallel processing to handle large data sets especially those with high dimensionality. It was robust and fast and thus suitable for providing efficient and precise forecasts for various products.

Working procedure of XGBoost works in demand forecasting:

The model aims to predict future demand $\widehat{D_t}$ based on past values $D_{t-1}, D_{t-2}, \ldots, D_{t-n}$. The model combines M decision trees, each represented by f_m, to minimize the objective function that includes both the prediction loss and a regularization term. The prediction for $\widehat{D_t}$ at time t can be expressed as:

$$\widehat{D_t} = \sum_{m=1}^{M} f_m(D_{t-1}, D_{t-2}, \ldots, D_{t-n})$$

The objective function to be minimized is:

$$\text{Obj} = \sum_{i=1}^{n} L\big(y_i, \widehat{y_i}\big) + \sum_{m=1}^{M} \Omega(f_m)$$

where $L\big(y_i, \widehat{y_i}\big)$ is the loss function, typically mean squared error, measuring the difference between the actual demand y_i and the predicted demand $\widehat{y_i}$ and $\Omega(f_m)$ is the regularization term, defined as:

$$\Omega(f_m) = \gamma T + \frac{1}{2}\lambda |w|^2$$

In this term, T is the number of leaves in the tree, w represents the weights of the leaf nodes, γ is the parameter controlling tree complexity, and λ is the $L2$ regularization parameter that penalizes larger weights.

The gradient boosting process involves sequentially adding trees that correct residual errors from the previous step. At each iteration (m), residuals are calculated by taking the gradient of the loss with respect to the predictions from the prior step:

$$r_i^{(m)} = -\frac{\partial L\left(y_i, \widehat{y_i^{(m-1)}}\right)}{\partial \widehat{y_i^{(m-1)}}}$$

Each new tree f_m is then fit to these residuals. The updated prediction after adding this tree is:

$$\widehat{y_i^{(m)}} = \widehat{y_i^{(m-1)}} + \eta f_m(x_i)$$

where η is the learning rate that scales the contribution of each tree to control the model's incremental adjustment. The final forecast is the sum of all trees, providing a cumulative model that captures the relationship between past and future demand in a way that minimizes overall error and balances model complexity through regularization.

10.4.4.2 Lead Time Prediction

Lead time prediction helps in planning the ordering process more accurately. By using models like linear regression, we predict the lead time based on various factors such as current inventory levels, supplier performance, and historical data. Let LT_t be the lead time at time t, and the predicted lead time $\widehat{LT_t}$ is given by:

$$\widehat{LT_t} = g(X_t)$$

where, g is the prediction model and X_t represents the input features. Precise lead time prediction ensures that orders are placed at the right time, minimizing the risk of stockouts or overstocking.

10.4.4.3 Inventory Management

In this simulation, inventory management is executed through a systematic process that considers the initial inventory levels, generated daily demands, and lead times for each product. Each day, the current inventory for each product is updated by subtracting the total demand for that day from the initial inventory of that day. If the current inventory drops below the calculated safety stock level, a procurement order is triggered. The calculation of the safety stock is cushion against lead time and demand fluctuations, guaranteeing a high degree of service. The anticipated demand over the lead time plus the safety supply determines the reorder point, which indicates when to restock. No purchase is required and the order quantity is zero if the current inventory is more than the safety stock. The order quantity is determined to raise the inventory to the safety stock level plus the overall demand for that time frame if the inventory drops below the safety stock. Sufficient inventory levels are maintained with the aid of this dynamic ordering system.

10.4.5 Supply Chain Metrics

10.4.5.1 Inventory Turnover

Inventory turnover ratio is the number of times that inventory is turned over or sold and used within a given period. It provides an indication on the efficiency of the company in replacing its inventory.

$$\text{Calculation: Inventory Turnover} = \frac{\text{Total Demand}}{\text{Average Inventory}}$$

Average Inventory is calculated as the mean of the beginning and ending inventory over a specific period. A high inventory turnover ratio indicates efficient restocking, reducing holding costs and the risk of obsolescence. In contrast, a low turnover ratio suggests inefficiencies like overstocking or slow-moving products.

10.4.5.2 Service Level

Service level measures how well a supply chain meets customer demand while keeping stockouts at an acceptable level. It's a key indicator of the supply chain's reliability and ability to respond effectively to demand.

$$\text{Calculation: Service Level} = \frac{\text{Number of Units Filled}}{\text{Total Demand}}$$

- Number of Units Filled: This represents the quantity of inventory that was available and used to meet the demand.
- Total Demand: This is the total quantity of inventory required to meet all customer needs during the period.

A strong service level ensures the supply chain meets most or all customer demand, minimizing disruptions in delivery. This is particularly crucial in sectors like healthcare, where delays in essential supplies can impact patient care. For example, hospitals with high service levels can provide timely treatments, directly boosting patient satisfaction and outcomes.

10.4.5.3 Order Fulfillment Rate

Order fulfillment rate quantifies how well and efficiently the supply chain completes orders precisely and on schedule. It shows how well the supply chain can fulfill delivery obligations.

$$\text{Calculation: Order Fulfillment Rate} = \frac{\text{Orders Fulfilled On Time}}{\text{Total Orders}}$$

- Orders Fulfilled On Time: This represents the number of orders that were delivered within the expected timeframe.
- Total Orders: This is the total number of orders placed during the period.

A high order fulfillment rate ensures a reliable supply chain, timely resource availability, and uninterrupted customer service. It minimizes delays, reduces stockout risks, and fosters trust and satisfaction among customers and service providers.

10.4.5.4 Importance of Metrics in Supply Chains

One of the characteristics of efficient supply chains involving fresh product items, such as food and medicines, is that there should be high inventory turns. Safety and satisfaction are achieved through timely replenishment in reducing spoiled products. For manufacturing JIT (just-in-time), effective maintenance of high service levels prevents unwanted delays in production, losses not obtained.

Timely order fulfillment leads to improved customer satisfaction, competitiveness, and operational efficiency. Good inventory control minimizes waste and holding costs, frees up funds for innovation and customer service, and improves sustainability for time-sensitive industries. Reliable supply chains ensure the availability of resources, minimize downtime, and allow businesses to scale without sacrificing quality. Trust in supply chains in volatile markets promotes stability, client loyalty, competitive pricing, and resilience during disruptions.

10.5 Data Generation Process

We modeled a realistic inventory management scenario for five distinct products over a 365-day period by generating data for initial inventory levels, lead times, and daily demand. This structured approach ensures the model reflects the variability and uncertainty inherent in supply chain operations.

Initial inventory levels for each product were generated using a normal distribution with a mean (μ) of 270 units and a standard deviation (σ) of 10 units. To avoid infeasible negative values, any generated inventory levels below 1 were set to 1. This method ensures reasonable and normally distributed starting inventory levels, providing a robust foundation for the simulation.

Lead times, representing the time required for restocking, were calculated using a normal distribution with a mean (L) of 5 days and a standard deviation (σ) of 1 day. This captures the natural variability in supply chain activities and adds a realistic dimension to the model.

Similar to the initial inventory generation, any lead time values less than 1 are adjusted to 1 to ensure validity. This step results in a realistic lead time for each product of the simulation period. Daily demand values for each product are generated using a Poisson distribution with a mean (λ) of 10 units. The Poisson distribution is chosen because it effectively models the random nature of demand over time, which is a common characteristic in many real-world scenarios. For each day, demand values are generated over the respective lead time period to justify the *lead time during demand* under stochastic environment. The mean and standard deviation of these sampled demand values are then calculated for each lead time period to provide a comprehensive view of the demand distribution during lead time for each product.

By following this data generation process, we ensure that our simulation accurately reflects the complexities and uncertainties of a real-world inventory management scenario. This synthesized data serves as the foundation for further analysis and optimization of the inventory management process.

10.6 Phases of Data Analytics

Our plan of work involves several key phases, each with specific objectives and steps designed to thoroughly investigate and optimize supply chain dynamics (ref. Fig. 10.1).

10.6.1 Initial Inventory Generation

The first step involves setting initial inventory levels for each product. We generate these initial inventory levels using a normal distribution. The mean value (μ) is 270 units, and the standard deviation (σ) is set at 10 units so that the values can represent the initial inventory quantities as being normally distributed. Any values generated as being less than 1 are corrected to 1 in order to ensure practicality for actual inventory management. The correct initial inventory values for all five products are kept in an array, thus building our simulation.

10.6.2 Lead Time and Demand Generation

Simulating daily lead times and demand figures for every product is the next stage. A normal distribution with a mean (μ_L) of 5 days and a standard deviation (σ_L) of 1 day is used to create lead times every day. Any numbers below 1 are set to 1 to guarantee that all lead times are legitimate.

Fig. 10.1 Flowchart for data analytics steps

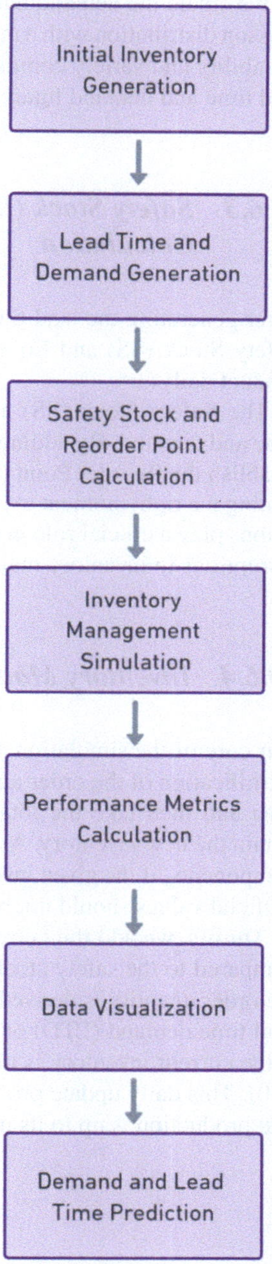

We create the demand numbers for each day during the lead time period using a Poisson distribution with a mean (λ) of 10. This method accurately depicts the unpredictability and variety commonly found in actual demand situations. Each product's lead time and demand figures are kept in arrays for later processing.

10.6.3 Safety Stock (SS) and Reorder Point (ROP) Calculation

After generating the lead time and demand data, we use Eq. (10.1) to calculate the Safety Stock (SS) and Eq. (10.2) to figure out the Reorder Point (ROP) for each product daily.

The Safety Stock (SS) acts as a buffer, protecting against fluctuations in lead time and demand. By adding the estimated lead time demand to the safety stock, we establish the Reorder Point (ROP). This ensures we have a reliable system for determining the right moment to place new orders and helps avoid stockouts. These calculations play a crucial role in maintaining a steady supply of products and preventing disruptions in inventory management.

10.6.4 Inventory Management Simulation

Our core of the simulation addresses updating stock inventory on a daily basis and identification of the order quantities (Q). First, we take the total inventory at a given time and then take the total demand for the entire day, and then we are able to obtain the new inventory. As for the presence of non-zero coefficients of self-service components, if the given inventory value turns negative, we take it as zero so that the artificial values should not be negative.

Thirdly, we add the current inventory to the new reorder point (*Rp*), so that it is compared to the safety stock (SS). If the ending inventory is less than the SS, then the order quantity is derived from either the formula Q = SS – current inventory + lead time demand (LTD) or the order quantity is equal to ROP – current inventory. If the current inventory is more than or equal to the SS then no reorder is made (Q = 0). This daily update process creates a good stock management control to ensure that production is up to its mark.

10.6.5 Performance Metrics Calculation

In order to assess our inventory management system's efficacy and efficiency, we compute order fulfillment rate, service level, and inventory turnover are the three main performance indicators.

Inventory turnover calculates the frequency of sales and replacements over time. Foreachproduct,inventoryturnoveriscomputedinsidethealgorithm'scontext. Average inventory is the mean inventory level during the same time period, whereas total demand is the sum of all demands over the course of 365 days. A greater inventory turnover rate, which denotes frequent product replacement and sales, is indicative of effective inventory management. The current inventory and the total demand for the day are compared to determine the service level for each day.

If the current inventory is greater than or equal to the demand, it is counted as a day with sufficient inventory. The *Service Level* is the ratio of these days to the total number of days (365). *Order Fulfillment Rate* is determined by counting the number of days where no additional order (Q) is needed because the current inventory is sufficient to meet demand. It is then divided by the total number of days (365).

10.6.6 Data Visualization

For better understanding and analysis, we visualize the performance metrics. We create bar charts for Inventory Turnover, Order Fulfillment Rate, and Service Level for each product using *matplotlib* library in Python.

10.6.7 Demand and Lead Time Prediction

To improve the accuracy of demand and lead time predictions, we employ machine learning models. We use XGBoost for demand prediction, training the model on 80% of the demand data and testing it on the remaining 20%. The performance of the model is evaluated using mean squared error (MSE). For lead time prediction, we use linear regression, similarly trained and tested on 80% and 20% of the lead time data, respectively. The predictions and their respective MSE values provide a robust evaluation of the model's performance, enhancing the accuracy of our demand and lead time forecasts.

10.7 Results and Findings

The table below (ref. Table 10.2) shows the performance of the three metrics for evaluating operational excellence for our work.

In general, high inventory turnover and service levels must be complemented by high fulfillment rates to ensure operational excellence. Products with lower fulfillment rates, despite high other metrics, may need to re-evaluate their inventory types, quantities, or management strategies to better align with actual market demand and order processing capabilities. As observed in Table 10.2, Products 2 and 5 maintain high service levels, suggesting they often have stock available to meet demand, yet especially for Product 5, this doesn't translate into successful fulfillment, pointing to possible issues in logistics, order processing, or inventory management specifics (like SKU mismatches). While all products demonstrate high inventory turnover, indicating efficient use of inventory, the order fulfillment rates highlight significant operational challenges. High turnover rates might be leading to frequent stockouts or may indicate that sales exceed the replenishment capabilities, as evident from the evaluated metrics for some products. The performance of individual products out of this study is elaborated next.

10.7.1 Inventory Turnover

- Product 1: reflects an inventory turnover of 777.34, indicating extremely high turnover, suggesting either very efficient inventory management or potentially insufficient inventory leading to stockouts.
- Product 2: shows a slightly lower turnover of 761.99, still very high, indicating that inventory management is efficient, but slightly less so compared to Product 1.
- Product 3: with a turnover of 750.34, this product shows lower efficiency in inventory management compared to Products 1 and 2.
- Product 4: exhibits the highest turnover among the listed products at 798.15, possibly indicating the most efficient inventory management or, like Product 1, a risk of running into stockouts due to high sales volumes.

Table 10.2 Performance of the three metrics

Product	Inventory Turnover	Service Level	Order Fulfillment Rate
1	777.34	90%	62%
2	761.99	95%	82%
3	750.34	92%	49%
4	798.15	89%	68%
5	765.82	93%	24%

- Product 5: shows an inventory turnover of 765.82, which falls in the higher range among the products listed, suggesting that its inventory is being sold and replenished very frequently. Overall, it has a pretty efficient inventory management but slightly lesser compared to product 1 and product 4.

10.7.2 Service Level

- Product 1: 90% service level suggests fairly good reliability in stock availability.
- Product 2: at 95%, it shows the best performance in meeting customer demand reliably.
- Product 3: 92% service level, which is robust and indicates good customer satisfaction in terms of availability.
- Product 4: the lowest at 89%, suggesting potential improvement areas in maintaining stock to meet demand.
- Product 5: 93% service level, which is quite high, indicating effective demand fulfillment in terms of stock availability.

10.7.3 Order Fulfillment Rate

- Product 1: a fulfillment rate of 62% indicates challenges in converting available stock into fulfilled customer orders.
- Product 2: at 82%, this shows a better capability to fulfill orders effectively.
- Product 3: only 49% of orders are fulfilled on time, indicating significant issues.
- Product 4: a 68% fulfillment rate suggests some difficulties in meeting customer orders fully on initial request.
- Product 5: with a 24% fulfillment rate, this product has severe issues in order fulfillment, likely due to mismatches between the types and quantities of inventory and the specifics of customer orders.

Figure 10.2 illustrates a comparative performance of the service levels and order fulfillment rates for all the products (P1, P2,..., P5) under consideration.

10.7.4 Demand Forecast Performance

The table below (ref. Table 10.3) shows the performance of demand forecasting based on mean squared error (MSE) of the models for all the five products considered under the study.

The performance of forecasting models for individual products is explained below.

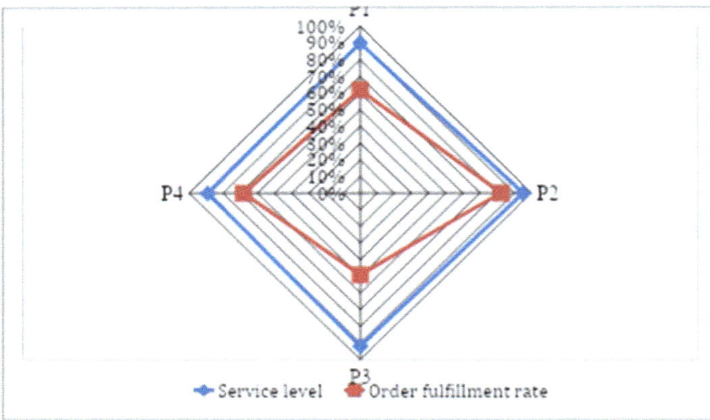

Fig. 10.2 Visualization (radar chart) for products' performance

1. Product 1: This extremely low MSE indicates that the demand forecast model for Product 1 is highly accurate. The predictions are very close to the actual demand values, showing excellent performance.
2. Product 2: The MSE for Product 2 is low, indicating that the demand forecast model performs well with only minor discrepancies between predicted and actual demand values. The model is quite accurate.
3. Product 3: This MSE is relatively higher compared to the other products. It suggests that the demand forecast model for Product 3 is less accurate, with more significant differences between the predicted and actual demand values. There might be more variability or unpredictability in the demand for Product 3.
4. Product 4: The MSE for Product 4 is very low, indicating high accuracy of the demand forecast model. The predictions closely match the actual demand values, demonstrating good model performance.
5. Product 5: The MSE for Product 5 is relatively low, indicating that the demand forecast model performs reasonably well, though not as accurately as for Products 1, 2, and 4 respectively. The model predictions are still quite close to the actual demand values.

To delve deeper, we have compared the demand forecasting performance using the other three ML models, namely, K-Nearest Neighbors (KNN), Decision Tree, and Random Forest, which is shown in Table 10.4.

The comparative analysis of demand forecasting models across five products reveals distinct performance patterns, highlighting each model's strengths and limitations in capturing demand dynamics. Random Forest consistently demonstrates robust performance, achieving the lowest MSE for Products 2, 3, and 4, indicating its strength in generalizing across varied demand patterns. Its ensemble averaging reduces overfitting, making it well-suited for products with complex or fluctuating demand. For Product 5, Random Forest achieves the lowest MSE (0.009984), underscoring its effectiveness in stable demand environments. However, for Product 1,

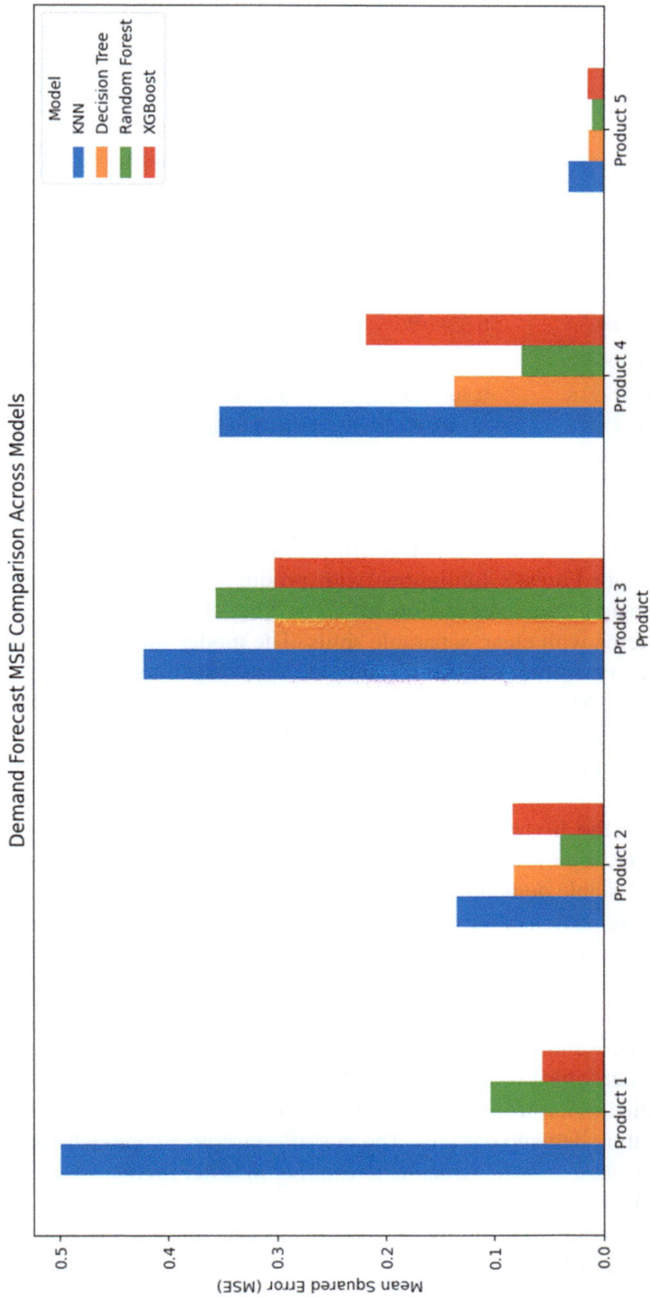

Fig. 10.3 Visualization (bar diagram) for products' forecasting performance

Table 10.3 MSE of demand prediction

Product	MSE
1	1.1082418196777214e-06
2	0.06839838101796102
3	1.3289398776164676
4	0.013766200490340141
5	0.10984137240980277

Table 10.4 MSE comparison for simulated data using multiple ML models

Product	KNN	Decision tree	Random forest	XGBoost
P1	0.498630	0.054795	0.103644	0.055998
P2	0.134795	0.082192	0.039584	0.083232
P3	0.421918	0.301370	0.355627	0.301794
P4	0.352877	0.136986	0.074000	0.217513
P5	0.032329	0.013699	0.009984	0.013925

Decision Tree (MSE = 0.054795) and XGBoost (MSE = 0.055998) perform better, suggesting Random Forest's limitations with products that have clearer decision boundaries. Decision Tree achieves low MSE for Products 1 and 5 proving effective for demand patterns with clear, separable splits. The model struggles with complex demand patterns, performing better for simpler ones due to its simplicity and low computational cost. XGBoost handles non-linearity well and performs well for Products 1, 2, and 3 but shows higher MSE for Product 4 (0.217513), indicating potential overfitting. While effective for complex patterns, XGBoost needs tuning for optimal accuracy.

KNN exhibits the highest MSE overall, indicating limitations with complex demand. However, it performs better for Product 5 (MSE = 0.032329), suggesting utility in simpler, stable demand scenarios.

A detailed visualization of the models' performance is illustrated through adjacent Bar diagrams (Fig. 10.2), which presents a comparative analysis of Mean Squared Error (MSE) for four models—KNN, Decision Tree, Random Forest, and XGBoost, across five products, highlighting differences in forecasting accuracy. The chart clearly shows that Random Forest consistently achieves lower MSEs across most products, particularly for Product 2 and Product 4, where it exhibits superior performance. This indicates its strong generalization capability and robustness in handling complex, fluctuating demand patterns. The model's ensemble approach appears to be well-suited for diverse demand structures, resulting in better predictive accuracy. For Product 1, both Decision Tree and XGBoost closely compete, with MSEs just above 0.05, suggesting that the demand for this product has clearer splits or linear patterns that these models can efficiently capture. However, KNN shows a significantly higher MSE for this product, underscoring its limitations in accurately forecasting more complex demand patterns, as it relies on local averaging, which may not effectively capture demand variability. Product 3 demonstrates a different trend where all models, except KNN, perform similarly, with Decision Tree having a slightly lower MSE than Random Forest and XGBoost. This suggests that the demand pattern for Product 3 has clear decision boundaries, making tree-based models more effective. In the case of Product 5, all models achieve low MSEs, indicating that the demand for this product is likely stable and predictable, allowing even simpler models like KNN to perform reasonably well. However, Random Forest still maintains a slight edge in accuracy, demonstrating its robustness even in more straightforward scenarios.

Overall, Random Forest emerges as the primary choice for diverse and complex patterns, while Decision Tree serves as an efficient alternative for simpler demand. XGBoost, with its tuning potential, suits intricate patterns, while KNN is a viable baseline for stable demand. Operationally, prioritizing Random Forest, with Decision Tree and XGBoost as complementary models, can enhance forecasting accuracy and inventory management. This tailored approach aligns model deployment with demand variability and computational efficiency, ensuring precise, product-specific forecasting strategies.

The scatter plots (ref. Fig. 10.4) present a comparative analysis of actual versus predicted demand across four ML models for five different products. Each subplot represents the correlation between actual and predicted values for a given product and model, with the red dashed line indicating perfect alignment (where predicted demand equals actual demand). The degree to which the green dots cluster around this line illustrates the model's predictive accuracy. The plots we have got, show that Random Forest and XGBoost closely follow the red dashed line, which indicates strong accuracy, especially for Products 2, 4, and 5. This provides evidence that these models capture demand trends well and generalize across products. Decision Tree is also seen to have performed well but shows slight deviations in Products 3 and 4, hinting at occasional overfitting. KNN has a wider spread, particularly for Products 1, 3, and 4, showing lower precision and struggling with complex patterns due to its reliance on local averaging. We can conclude overall from the findings that, Random Forest and XGBoost are the most effective for demand forecasting, handling both simple and complex trends, and supporting better inventory management.

10.7.5 Lead Time Prediction MSE

The extremely low MSE (1.030652175828137e-30), while predicting lead time for all the products together, indicates that the lead time prediction model is highly accurate, with predictions almost identical to the actual lead times. The model performs exceptionally well in predicting lead times.

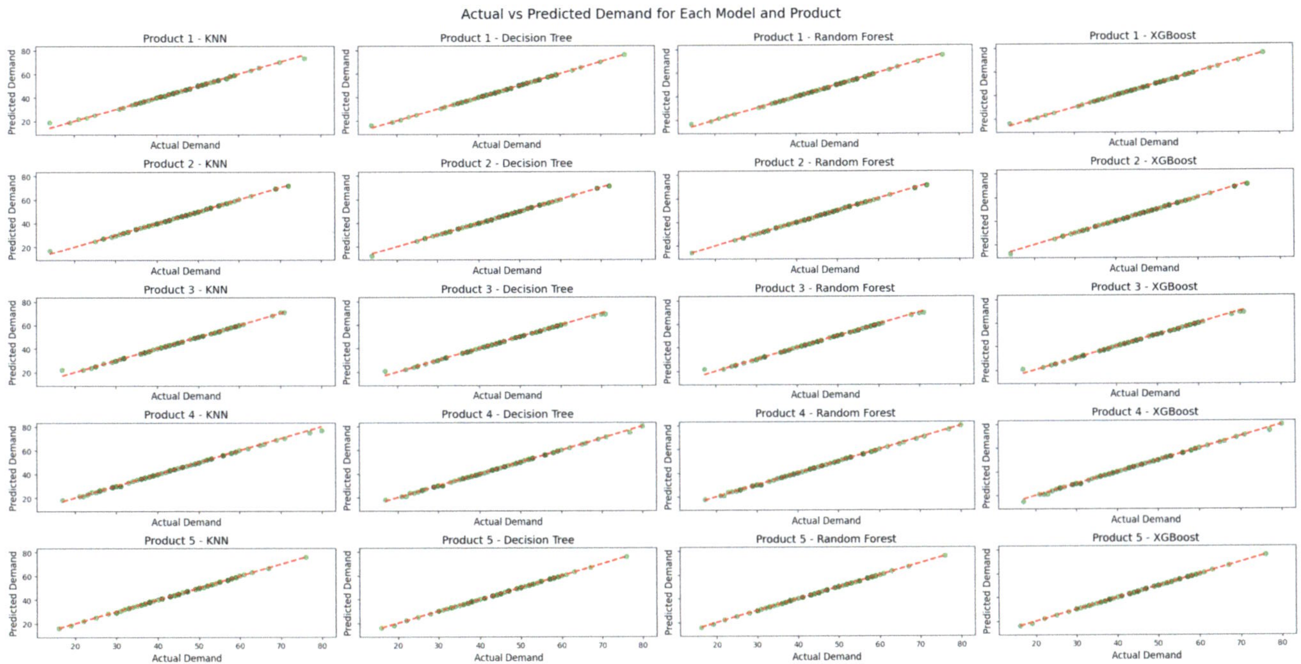

Fig. 10.4 Visualization (scatter plot) for ML models' performance in forecasting

10.8 Implementation Scheme

To implement this supply chain dynamics at organization level, a structured approach should be followed that encompasses data preparation, model development, training, evaluation, and performance monitoring. Here's a step-by-step outline of the implementation:

- Data Collection:
  - Inventory Data: Obtain archival information of products' inventory stock, including initial stock and daily stock.
  - Demand Data: Get a historical view of demand data: daily sales or consumption rates of each product.
  - Lead Time Data: Acquire historical data of lead times for replenishment, and variation of lead times.
- Data Pre-processing:
  - Cleaning: It handles missing or inconsistent data. All records should be completed and accurate.
  - Normalization: Normalize data to ensure consistency, especially if data comes from different sources.
  - Segmentation: Segment data by product to prepare for individual analysis and modeling.
- Parameter Initialization:
  - Initial inventory levels is usually set based on historical data or relevant business rules.
  - Lead Time and Demand Parameters: Calculate mean (μ) and standard deviation (σ) for lead times and demand rates from historical data.
- Modeling and Simulation:
  - Safety Stock Calculation: Use historical demand and lead time variability to calculate safety stock (SS) for each product.
  - Reorder Point Calculation: Determine the reorder point (ROP) for each product using the calculated safety stock and average demand during lead time.
  - Inventory Simulation: Simulate inventory levels, safety stock, and reorder points over a set period (e.g., 365 days).
- Demand Forecasting:
  - Model Selection: Make use of models such as XGBoost for demand forecasting and similar others based on historical demand data.
  - Model Training: Train the forecasting models using a portion of the historical data (e.g., 80% for training, 20% for testing).
  - Model Evaluation: Evaluate model performance using metrics like Mean Squared Error (MSE) to ensure accuracy.

- Lead Time Prediction:
  - Model Selection: Use Linear Regression or other similar models to predict based on historical data.
  - Model Training and Evaluation: Train and evaluate the lead time prediction model using historical data.
- Implementation:
  - Real-Time Data Integration: Integrate real-time inventory and sales data to constantly update models and simulations.
  - Automated Replenishment: Implement systems that reorder based on safety stock levels and reorder points.
  - Monitoring and Adjustment: Continuously monitor inventory levels, demand patterns, and model performance. Adjust parameters and models as needed to maintain optimal inventory levels.
- Performance Metrics Calculation:
  - Inventory Turnover: Calculate inventory turnover to assess how frequently inventory is sold and replaced.
  - Order Fulfillment Rate: Measure the percentage of orders fulfilled without delays.
  - Service Level: Calculate the service level to determine the percentage of time inventory was sufficient to meet demand.
- Visualization and Reporting:
  - Dashboards: Create dashboards to visualize key performance metrics such as inventory turnover, order fulfillment rate, and service level.
  - Alerts: Set up alerts for low inventory levels or other critical metrics to enable proactive management.

10.9 A Real-World Case Study

Below we have illustrated a case study using a dataset that captures daily sales data for a branded footwear retail outlet in Kolkata, focusing on six primary footwear categories: BOYS, GENTS, HAWAI, LADIES, SHOE, and W&W. These categories represent more than 80% of the total footwear sales at the store, making them critical for analyzing store performance and understanding customer preferences. The dataset spans 365 days (one full year), providing granular insights into seasonal trends, weekday versus weekend fluctuations, and monthly variations in demand.

10.9.1 Demand Forecast Performance

The comparative mean squared error (MSE) analysis across products and models is illustrated in Table 10.5.

Decision Tree emerges as a strong performer with the lowest MSEs across multiple products, particularly achieving zero error for the "BOYS" category, suggesting its ability to capture simpler, clearer demand structures effectively. Random Forest closely follows, demonstrating robust consistency across more complex demand categories, such as "GENTS" and "LADIES," where it significantly outperforms other models (MSEs of 0.127551 and 0.460542, respectively). This performance reflects Random Forest's ability to generalize across varying demand levels due to its ensemble approach, which mitigates overfitting. XGBoost performs well in capturing specific demand patterns, especially in "BOYS" and "HAWAI" products, where it achieves low MSEs (0.000607 and 0.015486). However, its elevated MSE for the "LADIES" product (1.908603) suggests potential overfitting or sensitivity to noise, indicating that XGBoost might require further tuning for products with more erratic demand. KNN generally exhibits the highest MSEs, particularly struggling with "LADIES" demand (MSE of 1.379077), indicating its limitations in handling complex, fluctuating demand due to its reliance on local averaging, which may smooth out nuanced demand patterns.

The analysis indicates that Decision Tree is highly effective for products with clear, separable demand structures, while Random Forest provides the most consistent performance across a range of complexities. XGBoost offers potential for high accuracy but requires careful tuning to avoid overfitting. KNN is less suitable for complex demand but may serve as a basic benchmark. These insights suggest that adopting a tailored model selection strategy, prioritizing Decision Tree and Random Forest while applying XGBoost selectively, can optimize forecasting accuracy across diverse product demand profiles.

Table 10.5 MSE comparison using multiple ML models

Product	KNN	Decision tree	Random forest	XGBoost
BOYS	0.013538	0.000000	0.002880	0.000607
GENTS	0.485538	0.276923	0.127551	0.365699
HAWAI	0.017846	0.015385	0.004148	0.015486
LADIES	1.379077	0.753846	0.460542	1.908603
SHOE	0.166769	0.061538	0.040265	0.059302
W&W	0.042462	0.015385	0.004972	0.023909

Table 10.6 Performance Metrics across the products

Product	Inventory turnover	Order fulfillment rate	Service level
BOYS	40.939436	0.984424	0.943925
GENTS	219.980994	0.741433	0.380062
HAWAI	66.734356	0.993769	0.900312
LADIES	319.868993	0.598131	0.193146
SHOE	80.353553	0.965732	0.838006
W&W	89.565778	0.968847	0.819315

10.9.2 Performance Metrics

The analysis below as shown in Table 10.6 reveals distinct performance variations in inventory metrics across product categories, each managed with a safety stock threshold of 50 units.

BOYS, HAWAI, SHOE, and W&W categories demonstrate high Order Fulfillment Rates (ranging from 0.965 to 0.994) and Service Levels (ranging from 0.82 to 0.94), indicating a consistent capacity to meet demand without frequent stockouts. These products also show moderate to high Inventory Turnover ratios, with BOYS at 40.94 and HAWAI at 66.73, suggesting efficient inventory management relative to demand. Conversely, GENTS and LADIES display markedly high Inventory Turnover ratios (219.98 and 319.87, respectively), pointing to rapid stock depletion. However, their Order Fulfillment Rates (0.741 for GENTS and 0.598 for LADIES) and Service Levels (0.38 and 0.19, respectively) fall significantly below other categories, indicating a challenge in maintaining adequate stock levels to meet demand consistently. For GENTS and LADIES, the high turnover coupled with low service levels suggests that demand often exceeds inventory capacity, leading to frequent stockouts despite replenishments. These results highlight potential opportunities for revisiting safety stock or reorder strategies to optimize service consistency for high-turnover products while sustaining efficient inventory levels across all categories.

10.10 Challenges and Mitigation Strategies

There are many obstacles to overcome when implementing AI/ML for operational excellence, which calls for meticulous preparation (Li et al., 2023). Since AI and ML models depend on precise, reliable, and timely data, data availability and quality are fundamental challenges. Data governance frameworks are crucial for standardizing the collecting, cleaning, and validation of data since poor data quality compromises the integrity of decisions. Accessibility and model resilience are enhanced via centralized integration systems, audits, and data augmentation. Another issue is model interpretability; deep neural networks and sophisticated models like XGBoost are frequently "black boxes." Stakeholder trust is increased via explainable AI (XAI) methods and more straightforward beginning models. Operations may be disrupted when AI is integrated with older systems; cross-functional teams and a modular strategy help manage expectations and guarantee compatibility.

The adoption process is further complicated by skill gaps and change management; a data-driven culture and employee buy-in are fostered by upskilling programs and change initiatives that emphasize the benefits of AI/ML and gradual transitions; scalability and maintenance challenges arise because models may underperform when expanded across contexts; retraining, modular architectures, continuous monitoring, and cloud-based solutions ensure flexibility and adaptability to evolving requirements; ethical and regulatory compliance, including addressing bias and privacy concerns, necessitates bias detection algorithms and regular audits; and, finally, cost constraints, especially for smaller enterprises, require phased adoption strategies with ROI-proving pilot projects.

10.11 AI/ML Adoption in SMEs: Cost–Benefit Issue with Sustainability

SMEs may increase productivity, make better decisions, and become more competitive by implementing AI/ML (Samdanis et al., 2023). In order to succeed, cost-effectiveness and sustainability must be balanced, and operations must be in line with CSR objectives. SMEs can begin with high-return trial projects like demand forecasting and inventory optimization (Akkineni et al., 2022), even if adoption requires expenditures in infrastructure, data, and expertise (Song et al., 2023). Scalability and cost-effectiveness are guaranteed by utilizing cloud platforms and open-source frameworks.

A data-driven culture is promoted by filling skill shortages with training and outside knowledge (Geller et al., 2017). While APIs provide continuity, the modular integration of AI with legacy systems reduces interruptions (Dionicio et al., 2023). AI models that incorporate sustainability measures, such as waste reduction and carbon footprint, promote ethical supply chains and satisfy consumer demand for environmentally friendly operations.

SMEs can attain operational excellence and competitiveness by prioritizing cost-effectiveness, talent development, ethical compliance, and sustainability. This will provide them a competitive advantage in environmentally concerned markets.

10.12 Conclusions and Future Research Directions

Supply chain efficiency can be greatly increased by combining lead time prediction, inventory optimization, and demand forecasting into a single system. By simulating scenarios and offering actionable insights, advanced AI-ML models—including generative AI—allow for accurate demand projections, ideal inventory levels, and proactive disruption control. Businesses of all sizes can benefit from scalability, and reliable models continue to function even when supply and demand patterns change.

Subsequent studies should investigate the application of these strategies in adaptive real-time systems for fast supply chain management. In this particular context, stressing on issues such as computing efficiency, scalability, and timeliness yields reliability and cost optimization advantages. Also, embracing IoT and smart devices will enhance the visibility and realism of a business's supply chain, and the foundation for smarter and more elastic supply chains will be established.

Appendix: A

1. Initialize parameters:
–num_products = 5.
–$\mu = 270$, $\sigma = 10$.
–$\mu_L = 5$, $\sigma_L = 1$.
–$\lambda = 10$.
–days = 365.
2. Initialize initial_inventory array with normal distribution (μ, σ).
3. Ensure no negative inventory:
–For each value in initial_inventory:
–If value < 1: set value to 1.
4. Loop through each product:
–For product in range(num_products):
–Draw random numbers for lead time L1 with normal distribution (μ_L, σ_L).
–Ensure no negative lead time in L1.
–Generate demand values D for each lead time in L1 using Poisson distribution (λ).
–Calculate D_{avg1} and D_{sd1} for each iteration.
5. Calculate Safety Stock (SS) and Reorder Point (ROP):
–For each iteration:
–SS = Z_0_05 * sqrt(μ_L * Dsd12 + Davg12 * σL2).
–ROP = μ_L * D_{avg1} + SS.
6. Initialize inventory and order quantities:
–Set initial inventory I0 for each product.
–Initialize lists: I1, Q, demand_sum_list, demand_values_list, ss_list, rop_list, q_list.

7. Daily simulation loop:
–For day in range(days):
–Calculate total_demand as sum of D[day].
–Update current_inventory = I1[-1] - total_demand.
–Ensure current_inventory is not negative.
–If current_inventory < SS1[day]:
–Calculate order_quantity = SS1[day] - current_inventory.
–Append order_quantity to Q.
–Update current_inventory.
–Else:
–Append 0 to Q.
–Append current_inventory, SS1[day], ROP1[day], and Q[–1] to respective lists.
8. Create DataFrames for each product:
–data = {
'Day No.': range(1, days + 1),
'Initial Inventory': I1[:–1],
'Current Inventory': I1[1:],
'Lead Time': L1,
'Demand Values': demand_values_list,
'Sum of Demand': demand_sum_list,
'Safety Stock (SS)': ss_list,
'Reorder Point (ROP)': rop_list,
'Order Quantity (Q)': q_list.
}
–Create DataFramedf from data.
–Append df to product_dataframes.
9. Print the first 5 rows of each DataFrame:
–For df in product_dataframes:
–Print the first 5 rows.
10. Calculate performance metrics:
–Initialize lists: inventory_turnover, order_fulfillment_rate, service_level.
–For product in range(num_products):
–Calculate total_demand, average_inventory, turnover.
–Calculate fulfillment_rate as percentage of days with Q = = 0.
–Calculate service_level as percentage of days with I1 > = sum of demand.
–Append turnover, fulfillment_rate, and service_level to respective lists.
11. Print performance metrics:
–Create metrics_df with performance metrics.
–Print metrics_df.
12. Plot performance metrics:
–Plot bar charts for inventory turnover, order fulfillment rate, and service level.
13. Demand prediction using XGBoost:
–Prepare demand_data and lead_time_data.
–Initialize lists: xgb_models, forecasts, mse_list.
–For i in range(num_products):

–Train XGBoost model on demand_data.
–Generate forecasts and calculate MSE.
–Append model, forecasts, and MSE to respective lists.
14. Lead time prediction using linear regression:
–Train linear regression model on lead_time_data.
–Generate predictions and calculate MSE.
15. Display model performance:
–Print demand forecast MSE for each product.
–Print lead time prediction MSE.

References

Akkineni, A., Koohborfardhaghighi, S., & Singh, S. K. (2022). Centrality of AI quality in MLOPs lifecycle and its impact on the adoption of AI/ML solutions. *International Conference on Intelligent Systems Design and Applications.*

Arrieta, A. B., Rodríguez, N. D., Ser, J., Bennetot, A., Tabik, S., Barbado, A., García, S., Gil-Lopez, S., Molina, D., Benjamins, R., Chatila, R., & Herrera, F. (2019). Explainable Artificial Intelligence (XAI): Concepts, taxonomies, opportunities and challenges toward responsible AI. *Information Fusion, 58*, 82–115.

Bassiouni, M. M., Chakrabortty, R. K., Hussain, O. K., & Rahman, H. F. (2023). Advanced deep learning approaches to predict supply chain risks under COVID-19 restrictions. *Expert Systems with Applications, 211*, 11860.

Ben-Dayaa, M., & Hariga, M. (2004). Integrated single vendor single buyer model with stochastic demand and variable lead time. *Int. J. Production Economics, 92*, 75–80.

Bhattacharya, S., Govindan, K., Dastidar, S. G., & Sharma, P. (2024). Applications of artificial intelligence in closed-loop supply chains - Systematic literature review and future research agenda. *Transportation Research Part E: Logistics and Transportation Review, 184*, 103455.

Chaudhary, V., Bharadwaja, K., Meena, R. S., Acharjee, P. B., Chaudhari, N. C., & Gopinathan, R. (2023). Exploring the use of machine learning in inventory management forincreaded profitability. *A Journal For New Zealand Herpetology, 12*(1), 658–666. ISSN No: 2230–5807.

Dionicio, R. J. A., Serna, Y. P. O., Claudio, B. A. M., & Ruiz, J. A. Z. (2023). Sales processes of the consultants of a company in the bakery industry. *Southern perspective/Perspectiva austral.*

Doborjginidze, G., Petriashvili, L., & Inaishvili, M. (2021). Optimization of inventory management in the supply chain. *Journal of Communication and Computer, 16*, 1–5. https://doi.org/10.17265/1548-7709/2021.01.001

Geller, L., Barzily-Rokni, M., Danino, T., Jonas, O., Shental, N., Nejman, D., & Straussman, R. (2017). Potential role of intratumor bacteria in mediating tumor resistance to the chemotherapeutic drug gemcitabine. *Science, 357*, 1156–1160.

Glock, C.H.: A comment: Integrated single vendor-single buyer model with stochastic demand and variable lead time. *The International Journal of Production Economics, 122*, 790–792.

Heck, H., Sick, B., & Tomforde, S. (2018). Security issues in self-improving system integration – challenges and solution strategies. In *IEEE 3rd international workshops on foundations and applications of self systems.*

Henningson, P. (2009). Operational excellence in supply chain management - using a holistic view and key performance indicators. *Master's thesis*, Faculty of Engineering, Department of Industrial Management and Logistics, Lund University.

Hnaien, F., Dolgui, A., & Wu, D. D. (2016). Single-period inventory model for one-level assembly system with stochastic lead times and demand. *International Journal of Production Research, 54*(1), 186-203. https://doi.org/10.1080/00207543.2015.1066518

Javaregowda, M., Praveen, K. B., Prateek, J., Kumar, P., & Pragathi, G. (2020). Inventory management using machine learning. *International Journal of Engineering Research & Technology (IJERT), 9*(6), 866–869. ISSN: 2278–0181.

Li, P., Williams, R., Gilbert, S., & Anderson, S. (2023). Regulating AI/ML-enabled Medical Devices in the UK. In Proceedings of the first *international symposium on trustworthy autonomous systems* (TAS).

Naz, F., Agrawal, R., Kumar, A., Gunasekaran, A., Majumdar, A., & Luthra, S. (2022). Reviewingthe applications of artificial intelligence in sustainable supply chains: Exploring research propositions for future directions. *Business Strategy and the Environment, 31*(5), 2400–2423. https://doi.org/10.1002/bse.3034

Bolstroff, P., & Rosenbaum, R. (2007). Supply chain excellence a handbook for dramatic improvement using the SCOR model. In *AMACOM-American Management association* (3rd ed.).

Petri Helo & Yuqiuge Hao. (2022). Artificial intelligence in operations management and supply chain management: An exploratory case study. *Production Planning & Control, 33*(16), 1573–1590. https://doi.org/10.1080/09537287.2021.1882690

Praveen, U., Farnaz, G., & Hatim, G. (2019). Inventory management and cost reduction of supply chain processes using AI based time-series forecasting and ANN modeling. In *29th International conference on flexible automation and intelligent manufacturing,(FAIM2019), June 24–28, Limerick, Ireland.*

Rolf, B., Jackson, I., Müller, M., Lang, S., Reggelin, T., & Ivanov, D. (2023). A review on reinforcement learning algorithms and applications in supply chain management. *International Journal of Production Research, 61*(20), 7151–7179. https://doi.org/10.1080/00207543.2022.2140221

Samdanis, K., Abbou, A. N., Song, J., & Taleb, T. (2023). AI/ML service enablers and model maintenance for beyond 5G networks. *IEEE Network, 37*, 162–172.

Song, H., Han, S., & Yu, K. (2023). Blockchain-enabled supply chain operations and financing: The perspective of expectancy theory. *International Journal of Operations & Production Management.*

Soumit Roy & Mainak Mitra. (2021). Enhancing efficiency in healthcare supply chains: Leveraging machine learning for optimized operations. *International Journal for Multidisciplinary Research, 3*(6), 1–8. https://doi.org/10.36948/ijfmr.10323

Tirkolaee, E. B., Sadeghi, S., Mooseloo, F. M., Vandchali, H. R., & Aeini, S. (2021). Application of machine learning in supply chain management: A comprehensive overview. *Mathematical Problems in Engineering, 2*, 1–14, Article ID 1476043. https://doi.org/10.1155/2021/1476043

Toorajipour, R., Sohrabpour, V., Nazarpour, A., Oghazi, P., & Fischl, M. (2021). Artificial intelligence in supply chain management: A systematic overview. *Journal of Business Research, 122*, 502–517.

MIX
Papier aus verantwortungsvollen Quellen
Paper from responsible sources
FSC® C105338

If you have any concerns about our products,
you can contact us on
ProductSafety@springernature.com

In case Publisher is established outside the EU,
the EU authorized representative is:
Springer Nature Customer Service Center GmbH
Europaplatz 3, 69115 Heidelberg, Germany

Printed by Libri Plureos GmbH
in Hamburg, Germany